Dark Siege: A Connecticut Family's Nightmare

"An amazing real life horror thriller. The prose is dynamic, well crafted and clear. A must-have for anyone interested in horror thrillers or paranormal events. I enjoyed it thoroughly."
Serafin Mendez, Ph.D., Professor of Communication,
Central Connecticut State University

"This book is an unexpected treasure. The story is fast-paced and builds up quickly to the epic final battle where survival is uncertain. Highly recommended for everyone interested in the paranormal."
Ajit Kokkat, M.D.

"This real life supernatural thriller had me fighting goosebumps throughout the entire book. McLeod's unique and suspenseful writing style made this a refreshingly fun and scary read."
Didacts and Narpets

"This is a very well-written book. It's very scary. Read it! I especially enjoyed learning about McLeod's belief systems at the end of the book."
Carmen Reed – 'A Haunting In Connecticut.'

"This is one suspenseful read that could be classified in the horror genre, and would be a best seller as such, but this book is based on a true story. The style affords an enthralling and captivating read. More frightening is knowing there are people out there who are scarred for life having lived through this."
Dennis Waller – Top 500 Reviewer on Amazon.com

"Great story telling! I felt like I was there going through everything in the book. I have read numerous books from the guys at *Taps, Ghost Adventures* and the Klinge brothers of *Ghost Lab* fame, but none of them tell a true story or paint a mental picture like McLeod does. The Analysis section was great and shows McLeod's vast knowledge of the paranormal realm. Five stars and two thumbs up!"
John Delgado

"The imagery and character development take McLeod's *Dark Siege: A Connecticut Family's Nightmare* to the next level. This book keeps you on the edge of your seat and keeps you craving for more. The analysis at the end is a brilliant addition that delves into what was really happening in the story and the metaphysical truths about this strange world we share with spirits. Highly Informative and thought provoking."
Leo Freeborg

"*Dark Siege* is the retelling of actual events that occurred to an unsuspecting family. Readers can read it as a horror novel, or if they choose to, they can read the analysis section at the end of the story which delves deeper into the description and rationale behind the events. I picked up this book after hearing McLeod speak at a Paranormal Convention and by the end of the first chapter, I was hooked. I quickly read the entire book, amazed at the horrors, the unbelievable claims, the strange occurrences and life-threatening moments contained within. Though I am a paranormal investigator, I must honestly say that I hope I never see or experience anything like this!"
Reading RN

"This book is a Must-Read! After reading this book, any time I pass by a cemetery, I get chilled to the bone!"
Salvatore Bivona

"I am thankful that people like Jason McLeod make it their life's work to help and educate people who fall prey to these evil spirits. This book was an outstanding read!"
Michelle Kuba

DARK SIEGE:

A Connecticut Family's Nightmare

by

Jason McLeod

ISBN 978-0-9884451-2-3 (ePub)
ISBN 978-0-9884451-1-6 (Kindle)
ISBN 978-0-9884451-5-4 (paperback)

Edited by
Tom Kimball, Ph.D.
www.knowbiz.biz

Cover design by Todd Hebertson

Print layout by eBooks By Barb for booknook.biz

Dedication

I dedicate this book to demonologists and exorcists worldwide who risk their health, their safety, and their very lives to help complete strangers who are desperate for assistance dealing with realms far beyond their understanding, especially the greatest demonologist and the greatest psychic whom I have had the pleasure of calling my friends, my mentors, and in my later years, my colleagues—the late Ed Warren and his gifted wife, Lorraine Warren. Lorraine continues her profound work to this day.

I dedicate this book also to my friends and colleagues who have stood boldly by my side against the darkness. I include the men and women of the cloth who defy the denizens of these realms, specifically, the hierarchy of inhuman, diabolical spirits who seek the ruination of mankind.

There is a world apart from our own, bordering on twilight. Its evil and blind terror could become a part of the lives of the living in an instant, and last forever, despite any attempt to sway its incredible power.

It is unseen and unheard most of the time. It is the mysterious place between the sunlit majesty of the material world that we can see and touch, and the invisible and intangible world of energy and spirit.

Jason McLeod

What you are about to read is a re-creation of the most terrifying case of inhuman, diabolical infestation, oppression and possession I have experienced to date. To protect their privacy, the identities of everyone involved and certain locations have been altered, but their experiences both individually and collectively are completely accurate and authentic.

Contents

Part 4....................................347

Part 1 – Infestation

Chapter 1 – Materializing
in the Mist

THE CRISP OCTOBER WIND howled steadily against a grove of aged maple trees on the western edge of the Union Cemetery in Easton, Connecticut. Thick black clouds began to creep across the sky as dozens of red, yellow, and orange leaves snapped free of their branches and rode the winds in torrential curving arcs toward and throughout the cemetery. The leaves whisked toward the roof of the Easton Baptist Church, and violently skimmed the old crooked weather vane on the steeple. They swooped down suddenly toward the frostbitten earth and the black Mercedes station wagon that was traveling southbound on Stepney Road, along the rusted wrought iron fence lining the perimeter of the cemetery.

Linda McLaughlin, a professional artist, wife of a real estate broker, and mother of three, admired the beautiful leaves as they banked along the tall, statuesque memorials, blew over and through the fence, and landed suddenly onto the windows of the car. Linda smiled, glancing into the rear-view mirror at her blond-haired six-year-old daughter in the back seat. "Oh, do you see how colorful the leaves are, Kelly?"

Kelly sat on the right side of the car. She held a one-eared stuffed bunny against her loose-fitting white sweater. She smiled and pressed her palm on the window and against the slick red leaf stuck there. "Yeah," she giggled. "They're pretty."

Suddenly, a loud thunderclap came out of nowhere and rattled the windows in the car. "Whoa," Kelly whimpered. She slid down in her seat and cringed.

Linda scanned the sky and said, "It looks like we have some pretty awful weather coming."

"Yeah," Kelly sighed, looking out the window, "...pretty awful."

"Maybe we should get the pumpkins another day," Linda said.

"Okay," Kelly replied. She pouted a bit, because she wanted to carve the pumpkins with her big brother, Tyler, but she knew that she'd get completely soaked if they tried to sort through all of them outside Silverman's Farm Stand.

As they continued down the road, Linda thought about scarecrows, witches, candy corn, apple cider, and of course, the one thing on the minds of everyone, what with only a week left until Halloween. "Be very watchful, Kelly. Maybe you'll see a ghost. We wouldn't want one to follow us home, would we?"

Kelly cringed and yanked her hand away from the window. She squeezed her bunny tightly, touched its pink nose, pouted some more, and said, "Stop it, Mommy. That's scary."

Linda chuckled as they drove alongside the cemetery. "Oh, sweetheart, there are no such things as ghosts."

As they drove along, Kelly turned to look out of the right side windows and glared at the many tombstones in the distance that were casting long gray shadows on the ground, and stretching away as far as she could see. She studied the multitude of shapes, from small black grass-covered markers to larger graying stones with obscured, mossy faces. Kelly frowned. All of these things were a mystery to her. She had never known death. She was too young to know how to name what she saw.

Moments later, as the car passed under an overhanging tree, a sudden wall of water rained down and completely covered the windshield. Kelly gasped and closed her eyes. She thought about being at home and curling up in her warm, soft pink comforter. She felt the car slow down and heard the windshield wipers come on at full speed. When the car lurched forward slowly, Kelly opened her eyes. She studied the gravestones and spotted something out of the right side of the windshield, ahead in the distance. She leaned forward, squinted, and strained to make out a faint cloudy shape among the memorials inside the cemetery, but it was too far away for her to see it clearly. Intrigued, Kelly reached to the side window and rubbed the condensation off the glass with her palm, trying hard to see what was there. 'What was standing inside the cemetery in this terrible storm? Had her mother not seen it?' she wondered.

As the car continued, and the shape became closer, she saw that it looked to be a gray smoky mass collapsing in on itself into the shape of a man. Moments later it appeared to solidify completely. It stepped out of a thin, stagnant wall of mist. Kelly's mouth fell open in awe as it walked straight toward them, walked through a grave stone, and then straight through the iron fence. It stopped suddenly on the curb at the edge of the cemetery just as they were about to drive right by him. Kelly inhaled deeply and slid down in her seat, trying to make sense out of what she had just seen, and trying to avoid being seen by the scary man. She closed her eyes tightly and squeezed her stuffed friend with all of her might.

A quick flash of lightning lit up the sky, followed instantly by a loud, reverberating thunderclap. Kelly opened her eyes again and inched up in her seat so that she could peek over the edge of the door and see out of her window. As she did so, the man slowly turned his head in their direction, as if he could see exactly what Kelly was doing. When they passed right beside him, his eyes, two dark holes as black as night, pulsed twice. Kelly gasped and forced her eyes shut again. When she opened them a few seconds later, he had completely vanished. Kelly clutched the armrest and turned toward the back corner of the window. He reappeared suddenly and turned his head slowly toward her as he stepped off the curb and moved into the road. Kelly's breathing became short and labored. The man turned to face the car. Her heart beat faster, as if it would break through her chest. Then, in the dimly-lit road behind her, Kelly watched completely spellbound as the monster, for it certainly had to be a monster, faded away right before her eyes as if he were never even there at all.

Thunder boomed overhead and forked lightning flashed throughout the sky. Kelly unbuckled her seat belt and spun around onto the edge of the seat. She held her stuffed bunny as tightly as ever, as if she would never let it fall. She peered over the top edge of the seat in wonder. Another bright flash of lightning lit the sky in an eerie, jagged bolt. The wind howled and forced the rain against the car in sheets. Suddenly, as if he were immune to the forces of nature itself, the man reappeared again. But this time, he was staring longingly at her. Kelly moaned as he vanished and reappeared again, more quickly this time, and closer still. She thought to herself, 'How could he be closer when they were going so fast?' Loud, violent thunder shook her soul. She trembled with fear. "Mom," she said, faintly. She mouthed the word the second time, too frightened and intrigued to notice that she hadn't made even the slightest audible outcry.

The car slowed and came to a sudden halt. Kelly panicked. She saw that they were at a stop sign. She wanted her mother to keep moving, so she rocked her entire body as if she could nudge the car back into motion with her movements. She couldn't remember when she'd ever been as relieved as she was when the car turned and started moving forward again. The car slowly accelerated and continued northbound along the western edge of the cemetery. Kelly turned around, squinted, and saw the empty road fade away into the rain and mist behind them. 'Maybe we've lost him,' she thought. 'Maybe he's finally gone away.' Her hopes were quickly shattered when she saw that the man was taking a shortcut through the trees, back along the southern tip of the cemetery, at an angle, as if he were intending to close the distance between himself and the car. Kelly lifted her bunny before her face. Mere moments later, she lowered it enough to allow her to see over its missing ear. He appeared and disappeared again as he approached the western edge of the cemetery. Kelly turned sideways, and counted to three, when out of the corner of her eye, a sudden scary shadow loomed over the rear of the car and the monstrous man appeared again in the center of the road behind them. He reached forward, pointed at her, and dissolved in an instant. Then, seconds later, he appeared right up against the rear window. He thrust his hands forward, pressed them against the glass, looked into Kelly's panic-stricken eyes, and snarled at her. Kelly threw her arms up in the air, recoiled, and wailed in terror as her mother jerked the steering wheel, and the man's gray, shadowy hands made that awful screeching sound as they slid down the slick rear window. The car spun around and around on the soaked leaves and wet pavement.

When the car finished spinning and the front tires had struck the curb, it finally shuddered to a halt. Kelly's bunny flew into the front, bounced on the passenger seat, and fell onto the floor. Linda reached back and rubbed her neck. She moaned and looked into the rear-view mirror.

"Kelly, are you all right?" There was no response.

"Kelly!" Linda whipped her head around and peered into the empty back seat.

"Kelly?" She panicked.

Kelly was gone.

Chapter 2 – Bringing Chaos Home

LINDA UNBUCKLED HER seat belt, turned around, and leaned over the seat. When she spotted her daughter's little pink shoes in the corner, she sighed in relief. Then she saw Kelly hunched on the floor, holding the back of her head with both hands and crying silently.

"Are you hurt? Honey, did you hit your head?" Kelly shook her head.

Relieved, Linda asked, "Honey, why in the world were you screaming?"

Kelly sobbed, "He was so scary!"

Linda gasped and asked, "Who was scary?" She looked out of the windows and scanned the surroundings.

"The man I saw in the graveyard. He followed us. He was a ghost, and he followed us, just like you said."

"Oh, Kelly, there are no such things as ghosts!"

Kelly began to cry. "There are too," she insisted.

Linda leaned into the back seat, checked Kelly's head, and looked at her for several moments to make sure that she was unharmed. "Are you sure that you're not hurt?"

Kelly shook her head. Linda hoisted Kelly up and helped her into her seat. "Kelly, it is dark, stormy and dangerous out. Our eyes can play tricks on us in this kind of weather." She fastened the seat belt around her daughter's waist.

"Please don't ever unbuckle your seat belt when the car is moving." She backed away, reached down, turned back around and handed Kelly her bunny. Kelly hugged it instantly. Linda leaned in and touched her palm against

Kelly's face. "And, really, there are no such things as ghosts, honey."

Tears rolled down Kelly's face as the wind howled against the side of the car. "I want to go home. Please let's go home." As the car lurched forward, Kelly slowly turned her head around and looked out of her window. They drove away from the cemetery at last. The man was gone, but she knew, somewhere in the back of her mind, that he was still out there somewhere. Kelly frowned. She turned back and looked at her mother in the mirror and said, "There are ghosts, Mom. Really there are."

When they started down Route 111 in Monroe, Kelly bounced up and down with excitement when they passed her school. Then, as quickly as her brief moment of happiness surfaced, it was instantly shattered when howling winds shot fallen leaves across the lawn and into the road. When the leaves stuck themselves onto the windows of the car, Kelly jolted back, recalling the scary episode when they had passed the cemetery just twenty minutes earlier. Wanting desperately to avoid a repeat of the spooky encounter, she closed her eyes and started to hum a song to herself.

Further up the road, in the deluge, another car swayed into their lane. The bright, high-beam headlights nearly blinded Linda, so she slammed her hand on the horn and pulled over closer to the edge of the road until the other car had passed by safely. Just as they started to accelerate, a bright blue jagged bolt of lightning streaked down from the heavens and cut a nearby tree in two. Linda and Kelly screamed in unison as the flaming tree limbs began to fall into the road. Linda yanked on the steering wheel and slammed her foot down on the gas pedal. Kelly grimaced, aching against the pressure of the seat belt as Linda's quick reflexes allowed her to swerve out of the way just in time as the smoking ruins of the tree fell into the road, its broken pieces littering the pavement behind them. Linda glanced into the mirror and winced at her daughter's discomfort.

Long, stonewall-lined roads, shrouded by mammoth overhanging tree branches, led the way back home. Thunder boomed overhead. When they finally took the left fork off the road, Kelly stared ahead out of the front window. She looked down and hugged her bunny. The man in the cemetery was still fresh in her mind, so she tried to force his image out with just about anything she could think of. She thought about her teacher, and her coloring books.

"We're home!"

They turned down the driveway and saw a set of brake lights inside the garage. The lights went off as they pulled in beside the other car. Kelly smiled when she noticed her sixteen-year-old brother, Tyler, standing behind their father's black BMW. Tyler pulled a brown paper grocery bag out of the trunk, smiled and waved at them as they drove in. He recoiled when thunder resonated just over the house.

Matthew McLaughlin stepped forward smiling and opened Kelly's door. She held her bunny by the arm, hopped out, and hugged her father's legs. Matthew knelt, hoisted her up onto his hip and kissed her gently on the cheek.

"How was your day?" Kelly wrinkled her nose and pouted. Linda walked toward them and wrapped her hand around Matthew's waist. "You look like you could use some dinner," he said. He gently kissed her on the cheek.

"I could use a therapist. Kelly thought she saw a ghost today."

Tyler wiggled his fingers toward Kelly. "Oh, Boo!"

"Tyler, stop it," Linda said.

"A ghost, give me a break," Tyler chuckled.

Linda looked at her husband and leaned into his

protective embrace. "She nearly made me have an accident. The drive home was terrible."

"I know. It's a very bad storm and it's been much colder than usual for late October. They say we may even have snow over the weekend. That is definitely odd. I'm glad we're all home safe."

Matthew looked Kelly straight in the eyes. They touched noses and smiled. "You saw a ghost, did you?" Kelly nodded, and laid her head on his shoulder. Matthew turned toward his son, Tyler. "I think you've been watching too many scary movies with your brother." He winked at his son.

Tyler smirked. His long black bangs hung close to his nose. "Sure, if you say so, Dad."

Matthew grabbed a bag of groceries and went deeper into the garage, and then through the door that led into the kitchen. Kelly, still resting her head on her father's shoulder, twirled the curly hair at the back of his neck with her finger.

Linda slung her pocketbook over her shoulder. She noticed Tyler scanning the cement floor, smirking. She sighed and raised a finger. "I know what you're planning, or plotting, and you knock it off before you even start."

Tyler feigned injury. "Plotting? Planning?"

"You don't need to go frightening your sister any more than she is already. Don't you dare, young man!" She scanned the trunk, ducked inside, and retrieved a can of soup that must have rolled out of the bag on their way home. When she backed out and turned to toss it into Tyler's bag, she noticed that he was gone. When she turned toward the door to the kitchen and back again, Tyler suddenly shot up from behind the car.

"Boo!" he shouted.

Linda clutched her chest. Tyler smiled with satisfaction and let loose with his typical annoying sixteen-year-old cackle. Linda dropped the can inside his bag. He closed the trunk and walked away. Linda leaned back against the car, closed her eyes and listened to the rain fall for several long minutes.

As thunder rumbled overhead, she turned and walked through the door into the kitchen. She stood on the landing and groaned as she witnessed her kitchen in complete and utter chaos. Matthew stooped before a smoking oven, fanning smoke away with his hand. She heard a series of 'thuds' and 'pings' that resonated up from the cellar through the door to the right and saw her eldest child dragging a bag of dog food down the stairs. The dog food shot out of a golf-ball-sized hole in the bag, and each piece hit and ricocheted off the steps and bounced down until they came to rest on the cement floor.

"Sarah," Linda roared, "will you watch what you're doing? You clean that mess up, young lady. And I mean now!" Linda closed her eyes in disbelief and shook her head. It wasn't even their dog they were feeding. It was the neighbor's dog, who always came by for a snack after Sarah had fed him that one time the previous summer. She did enjoy the dog sometimes, she admitted to herself, as did the kids, but sometimes it was just too much trouble, and definitely an inconvenience.

Sarah called up from below, "I'm sorry, Mom."

A few seconds later, the phone rang. "I got it," bellowed Sarah. She stormed up the cellar steps and ran past Linda like some sort of wild giraffe.

Kelly looked at the counter. She pointed and gasped. "Uh, oh." She walked over to the counter. When the phone rang again, it didn't sound right. Both Sarah and Tyler scanned the room in anticipation, looking for the receiver.

"Where is it?" Sarah demanded.

"Heck if I know," Tyler replied.

When they looked over at the counter, they saw Kelly standing on her tip-toes, sticking her hand into the mixing bowl. Linda scowled, stormed over, flung her purse on the counter, and gently tried to pull Kelly's hand out. When Kelly resisted, Linda yanked Kelly's arm out. Kelly held the cordless phone by the antenna. The phone was completely covered in blueberry muffin batter.

"You have got to be kidding me," Linda groaned.

The phone rang again, and of course, sounded nothing like the phone should. Kelly stared up at her mother, her mouth agape. "Mom, I saw it. It fell off the wall and fell right into the bowl."

Linda grabbed the phone and unwound Kelly's fingers. As she did so, blueberry muffin batter ran down her hand, into the sleeve of her coat, and down her arm. Sarah snatched the phone out of her hand. As she did so, she swung it defiantly away from Tyler, who was trying to grab it with both of his hands, and the batter splattered all over her face and coat, the cabinets, the counters, and all over the kitchen windows behind her.

Linda clutched the counter and made a fist with her other hand. She closed her eyes. Her lower lip started quivering, and then it began to tremble. She had reached her limit. The culmination of all of the terrible unexpected events of the day had finally taken its toll. There was only one thing left to do—one way to release all her mounting stress. And so, a horrific scream erupted that deafened everyone in the room, a scream that lasted nearly five long, shrill seconds.

When it was over, Linda moistened her lips and opened her eyes. The rest of the family seemed to have frozen in whatever task they were engaged in. Everyone stared at her in awe: Matthew, blankly as he held the smoking broiling pan; Sarah, as she held the dripping phone away from Tyler as if it were some sacred treasure; and Tyler, who held a dishrag out toward Sarah in an obvious gesture of assistance. Kelly held her hands over her ears and pouted. They all stared at her for five silent seconds.

"Seriously, Mom," Sarah said. She snatched the rag from

Tyler and started to wipe the phone off. Batter dripped all over the floor as she walked to the sink.

Tyler followed after her with a wet rag and said, "Don't worry, I'll get it."

Linda turned toward the sink and began to wash her hands. "Somebody had *better* get it, or someone is *really* going to get it."

Then, when things couldn't possibly get any worse, they all heard the familiar jingle of the neighbors' dog's collar. Kelly turned around and moaned, "Uh, oh."

Tyler suddenly let out with a wild cackle. Linda turned to see the Jacobsons' golden retriever prancing through the garage entrance into the kitchen, soaking wet and tracking mud all over the floor.

"Oh, brother," Sarah said.

"All right, that's it, goddamn it!" Linda screamed, pointing at the door.

Kelly charged at the dog and pressed her entire body against him. The dog barked playfully as she forced him to back away into the garage. He was always very gentle with her. Tyler stuck a finger into the dog's collar and led him back out through the garage and outside into the driveway. He slapped the automatic garage door buttons, and when the doors finally closed, Tyler knelt and started to wipe up the mess. "Great," Tyler said.

Kelly looked down at herself. "Uh, oh," she said, worried. Her hands and dress were covered in mud. She turned to face her parents, pouted, and held out her muddy hands. Linda closed her eyes, took a deep breath and exhaled slowly.

Matthew chuckled, kissed Linda on the cheek, took her hands, held them tightly and said, "The mud complements the batter quite nicely. Don't you think?"

Linda gave a curt smile, walked over and knelt before Kelly and said, "Take off your dress, and put it in the washing machine. Then, we'll go upstairs and run you a bath, okay?"

Kelly smiled and nodded. "Okay."

Later, when the McLaughlins were almost finished eating dinner, Tyler cocked a smile, and spun around in his seat toward his little sister. "So, tell me about the *ghost* you saw today, Kelly."

Sarah patiently nibbled on a spare-rib, eyed them both and leaned back in her chair, carefully watching her mother and father for a reaction. Kelly clearly looked upset, like she did not want to talk about it. She looked down into her lap and pouted.

"Don't tease your sister, Tyler," Matthew said.

"I'm not teasing her," Tyler retorted.

"It's not funny, Tyler," Linda continued. "I mean it."

Sarah nodded, laughed to herself, shook her head, took a sip of milk, and observed the typical family drama.

Tyler rolled his eyes in response. "C'mon, Mom, that's a completely valid question to ask! I just want to know what happened to her today, that's all."

Matthew wiped his mouth. "She doesn't need to give you any ammunition to use to scare her further, Tyler." He tossed his napkin onto his plate and stood to collect his silverware. "Well, there are dishes to be washed, pots to be scrubbed and there is homework to be done." Those three dreaded phrases elicited nothing but grunts and groans, and all but Linda stood in unison, collected their plates and silverware, and walked toward the kitchen sink. "There will be no more discussion about ghosts, and that's final." Matthew leaned over and kissed his wife on the cheek and said, "Honey, why don't you get some rest? We'll take care of the clean-up." He looked at his children. "Won't we, kids?"

Sarah laughed. She placed her plate into the sink and

said, "I can't think of anything I'd rather do. Can you, Tyler?"

Tyler looked at her and smiled. "Nope, my life is a life of service. In fact I live to serve. There is most definitely nothing that I'd rather do. No sir." Sarah chuckled, opened the dishwasher door and dropped her silverware into the bin.

Matthew rubbed the back of Linda's neck, and helped her up. Linda smiled. "Thank you."

"I'll help, Daddy," Kelly said eagerly. She held out two glasses toward him.

Matthew bent over, accepting them gladly, and said, "Thank you, sweetheart. It seems that you're the only one who is genuinely interested in helping out." Linda stepped down into the living room, picked up a magazine from the coffee table, and sat down onto the sofa.

Later, when the kids had gone upstairs into their rooms, Matthew turned off the kitchen light, stepped down into the living room, sat down beside his wife, and extended her a box of chocolates. He wrapped his arm around her, kissed her on the cheek and smiled. "Are you okay?"

"Are you referring to Kelly's ghost earlier—the origin of this throbbing headache and terrible day?"

Matthew chuckled and said, "Well..."

Linda continued, "Or are you referring to the total insanity I had to experience upon returning to my own once-peaceful home?"

"Sometimes things can be a bit overwhelming, I admit. But, again, kids will be kids. They aren't all that bad. In fact, I think we happen to be pretty lucky. By the way, what was with that deafening scream earlier?"

She chuckled. "I must admit, it did feel good. Things got a bit overwhelming."

"I'd say so. The last time I heard you scream like that was on that roller coaster at Six Flags."

Linda smiled and closed her magazine. "I'm concerned about Kelly. She's never acted that way before. Something really upset her, Matt." Linda leaned back against her husband's chest. "Do you think that I scream loud? We should put Kelly on top of the car the next time we're stuck in a traffic jam."

Matthew chuckled and said, "A living siren, huh?"

"Yeah, to be sure. Still, she's not the type to make up lies," Linda continued. She reached for a walnut cluster and took a bite. "Still, I don't know. It was pretty strange."

"Tell me more about what happened."

"It was raining like crazy. We were passing Union Cemetery and I guess I joked about being mindful of ghosts, with it being so close to Halloween and all."

Matthew squeezed her arm gently. "That's not the type of thing I would say to a six-year-old girl on a stormy afternoon, passing by a graveyard, honey."

Linda nodded. "I know it now. I see how silly it was, but seriously, Matt. I mean, something really got to her."

"Well, when you put ideas like that in her head, she'll go looking for it." He exhaled deeply. "What else happened?"

"It began to storm suddenly, and then I noticed her being really antsy, but I assumed that she was interested in the leaves and the lightning, and that she was ducking down in her seat due to the thunder. You should have heard that thunder, wow. I was focusing on driving safely, because it got really intense. Then, all of sudden she let loose with this ungodly wail, so, out of reflex, I slammed on the brakes and the car spun out of control. She nearly gave me a heart attack. When I asked her why she screamed, she told me about this man."

Matthew gave her a concerned look and asked, "What man?"

"She said she saw a man in the cemetery."

"What's so strange about that? There probably was a man, but that doesn't mean he was a ghost. He was probably a caretaker or something."

"That's what I tried to rationalize, Matt. But I'm telling you, there was no one in or around that cemetery, no one that I saw anyway."

"Hey, I believe you, Linda. All we have here are the imaginings of little girl on a scary, stormy afternoon, that's all."

Linda curled her feet up on the sofa. "I told her that there were no such things as ghosts, and as we were driving away, she just kept saying "Yes there are!""

"Well, of course, there are no such things as ghosts, so it's over," Matthew said comfortingly.

"Still, I don't like the idea of leaving her this weekend," Linda said.

"She'll be fine. Julie will have her all to herself and spoil her to death. You know that. I'm sure she's already forgotten about it and everything will be just fine by tomorrow evening. You'll see."

They hugged and Matthew turned on the eleven o'clock news.

Later, after Matthew and Linda had dozed off, a high-pitched scream came from the second floor. It was Kelly. Matthew and Linda looked at each other in horror. Matthew leaped from the sofa, and by the time Linda had reached the foyer, Matthew had already started up the stairs. Matthew burst into Kelly's room and fumbled for the light switches. When Linda reached the landing on the second level, Sarah had just opened her door and had started to come out—squinting due to the bright light in the hallway. Kelly sat huddled in the corner of her bed against the wall, holding her comforter against her face, peering over it with wide terror-stricken eyes. She pointed toward the opposite corner of the room by her closet. "It's a ghost, Daddy!"

Matthew spun around, still bewildered, while Linda and Sarah squeezed through the doorway together. A pearl-white phantom shifted and moved along the far wall of the room. It reached out with what seemed to be appendages of some sort.

"What the..." Matthew fumbled for another switch and turned it on. The bright overhead light exposed the ghost in the corner of the room. Then, the ghost began to laugh. But it wasn't just any laugh. This one was easily identifiable.

"All right...damn it!" Linda roared. She stormed over toward the ghost and reached out for it with determined, flailing arms.

Sarah reached out to stop her mother. "Mom, don't!" Her retainer flew out of her mouth and landed on the carpet as she protested.

Matthew and Linda both reached out for the ghost. It tried to dodge away from Linda's grasp, but she was too quick. She caught its head and tugged. The sheet made a spectacular display of flowing whiteness, as it curled over and in on itself, revealing the black-haired sixteen-year-old boy in his underwear falling to his knees, laughing in hysterics.

Linda held the sheet aloft and growled, "Tyler McLaughlin!"

Sarah rolled her eyes in disgust. "What a jerk!"

"You know what? You really don't think, do you? Why would want to frighten your little sister when she has had such a traumatic day?" Linda demanded.

Kelly began to cry. Matthew kissed her, as Sarah ducked back out of the room.

"Stand up," Matthew ordered. "Do you think you're funny?"

"You take advantage of any situation that suits your own end," Linda added.

"Not to mention," Sarah shouted in the distance as they all turned an ear toward the open door, "it is past eleven and your sisters are trying to sleep."

Linda nodded and said, "That's right! Your sisters are trying to sleep!"

"Da ghosts," Tyler spoke with a Bulgarian accent, "dey do not sleep."

"You need some serious help, young man," Linda said.

"You're telling me!" He laughed, ducked under his father's arms, ran out the door into his bedroom across the hall and slammed his door behind him.

Linda hugged Kelly tightly. "Your brother is a typical mean prankster, just like every other sweet little girl's big brother."

Matthew shook his head and said, "He's not getting off that easily." He unbuckled his belt, pulled it off, exited the room and stormed across the hallway.

Kelly looked frightened for her brother and said, "Uh, oh."

Linda put Kelly down on her bed and covered her up. "And you know what?" Linda asked as she leaned over and kissed her on the cheek.

"What, Mom?"

"That's why little girls like you turn out so sweet."

"Why, Mom?" Kelly snuggled under her pink comforter and stared at her mother.

"Because they see how much they don't want to be like their rotten brothers. That's why." Kelly wrinkled her nose and smiled. She sat up and kissed her mother on the cheek.

Matthew burst into Tyler's room, switched on the light and slammed the door, wielding his belt. "You cannot go on frightening your sister like that! I won't have it!"

Tyler smiled, propped a pillow under his arm and leaned on his side. "That's really cool, Dad! Are you going to whip me?" He laughed.

"This is going to stop!"

Tyler maneuvered another pillow behind his head, sat up in bed, and leaned against the wall. "Yeah, but brothers are supposed to tease their sisters. Do you know the kinds of stuff Jimmy Reading and Kyle Foster do to terrorize their sisters? They sneak around...hide in their clos..."

"I don't want to hear it!" Matthew roared. "Why can't you set..."

"Set the example." He slurred his words to simulate retardation and curled his fingers before his face to mimic deformity. He leaned back and folded his hands behind his head and smiled from ear to ear. "That's just not my style, man."

Matthew opened the door and began to walk out. Then, he turned back and imitated his son in a whining voice by saying, "Dad, can I use the car this weekend?"

Tyler's eyes lit up in amusement. He smiled from ear to ear.

Matthew straightened himself and adjusted his tie. "Sorry, Son," his father said, adding his own powerful tone, "That's just not my style..." He went to turn around, stopped, spun back around, looked his son in the eyes and said..."Man!"

Tyler gasped, pointed at his father and said, "Wait!"

Matthew winked and closed the door behind him. He turned left and spotted Linda in their bedroom sitting on the bed. She stared blankly at him with folded arms.

Matthew walked down the hall as quietly as he could and whispered, "Is Kelly okay?"

"She's better. How is our awful son?"

"Oh, he's having some serious thoughts about what he's done and what repercussions his actions may have from now on, I can tell you that. Alluding to taking the car away straightens him up right quick."

Linda reached out for Matthew's hand as he closed the bedroom door.

Later, in the midnight gloom, when the entire family was sleeping soundly, the doorknob to Kelly's room turned ever so slowly. Kelly lay on her side, staring wide-eyed at the door. She moved her long blond bangs away from her eyes as the door creaked open. A faint sliver of light from the hallway shone on the carpet and grew larger as the door opened further. Kelly was suddenly completely paralyzed with fear.

Then, a hand reached inside the room and patted the carpet as if it were searching for something. Kelly looked down in bewilderment at the mysterious hand that had crept into her bedroom. She slowly scanned the floor to see what the strange hand might be searching for. Then she saw Sarah's retainer, and she sighed in relief. The hand touched the edge of the retainer, snatched it, and withdrew silently back into the hallway. Kelly dropped her head into her pillow as the door finally closed. After a few moments, she finally fell into a much-needed deep sleep, where gruesome, ghastly ghosts were a distant memory.

Chapter 3 – Lurking Shadows

MORNING CAME, AND peace had settled over the house. To New Englanders, nothing was more satisfying than watching a light October snowfall from the confines of a warm house. Matthew sat at the kitchen table in a black business suit, sipping his coffee, and staring at the falling snow. Sarah and Tyler had already left for school. Kelly waddled into the kitchen, rubbing her eyes, followed by her mother who hastily snapped Kelly's pink barrettes into place. Matthew spun around in the swivel kitchen chair, smiled at them and said, "Well, little muffin, it's almost time to go to school. Are you ready?"

"Uh, huh," Kelly said.

Linda said, "I'd better button you up, it's cold out there." She knelt and helped her into her jacket. She fastened the buttons, tied the hood around her head and pulled the drawstrings so tight that only her nose poked through.

"Mom," Kelly protested.

Linda giggled. "Oh, I'm sorry, sweetie." She loosened the hood a bit and saw Matthew admiring her handiwork. He took the last sip of coffee and set the mug down on the table. Linda handed Kelly her lunchbox and she turned around toward her father as he stood up and put his coat on. Linda patted her on the behind as she stomped off toward him. "Have a good day, sweetie."

"Thanks, honey, I will," Matthew said.

Linda groaned as she pulled herself up with the help of

a chair and said, "Actually, I was talking to Kelly, but you have a great day too, honey."

"Gee, thanks," Matthew said as he and Kelly made their way down the hallway, into the foyer and out the front door. They stepped onto the front porch, and he closed the door behind them. "C'mon Kelly, you'll miss your bus."

"Bye, Mom!" Kelly said, pressing her nose up against the oval glass pane in the center of the door. Matthew took her hand gently and walked down the slate steps and down the long, brick walkway. Linda admired them through the windows. Kelly skipped along, hand in hand with her father. She looked at the clouds and the snow falling from above and stuck out her tongue, trying to catch that one stray snowflake. She looked back excitedly and said, "I got it, Mom, I got it!" She giggled. She looked up at her father. "Did you see?" He led her away. "Did Mom see?" She saw the lamppost at the end of the driveway switch on and off again three times to signify that she did, indeed, see. She looked back and saw her mother smiling in the oval pane of glass in the front door. They waved at each other.

Just then, the bus rolled up and Kelly climbed on board. Matthew and Kelly waved to Linda inside the house. Matthew leaned over and kissed Kelly on the cheek, then she boarded. The bus rolled away seconds later and Matthew walked back to the house. When he came inside, he kissed his wife.

"You're lucky you didn't leave without doing that," Linda said.

"Wouldn't miss it for the world," Matthew said with a smile.

She handed him his keys and travel mug. "Okay, see you later."

When she got to the kitchen table, she grabbed a blueberry muffin and chuckled when she thought about the batter being splattered all over her and all over the kitchen. She sank into her chair and admired the light snowfall. She became so lost in a daydream that she didn't even notice the gray shadowy form lurking in the corner of the room behind her.

Later in the morning, Linda had finished cleaning up the dishes, started a pot of soup on the stove, and brought a load of clothes hangers down from upstairs. She opened the laundry room doors and reached for the ironing board. Then she saw it. A gray, smoky shadow hovered silently behind and between the washer and dryer. Her jaw dropped. She could not believe it. Then, as if it knew that it had been discovered, it whisked past her with blinding speed. Linda screeched, whirled around and stared as it faded away in the brightly lit kitchen. She jolted her head back and forth trying to focus on whatever it was that she had just seen. Then she scanned the edge of the kitchen, then down into the living room. It had to be a reflection or a shadow or something.

When she saw nothing more, she calmed down and shrugged. After a few seconds she turned around and started to pull out the ironing board. It was stuck on the side of the dryer, and she nearly fell backwards when it finally slid free. She slammed it down onto its edge and felt for the release. When she hit the lever, the ironing board sprung open, and Linda sighed with satisfaction. Household chores were not the most difficult tasks, but she knew that there were days that went completely and utterly wrong.

After several moments, Linda plugged in the iron, opened the dryer, and pulled out a half-dozen of Matthew's shirts. When she returned to the ironing board she started on the first shirt. A sudden jet of steam shot out of the iron and scalded her arm. "Ouch!" Linda backed away and grabbed her wrist. She picked up the iron, raised it to eye level, and noticed that the temperature dial was turned all the way to steam setting. "Who in the heck?" She had always made it a point to turn off the iron. She thought about her mother, who had warned her too many times when she was a young teen about the danger of leaving appliances on and the many ways in which they could accidentally burn down the entire house and, apparently, the entire neighborhood.

Just then she heard the sizzling. She spun around to see the soup in the process of boiling over the edge of the pot onto the stove burner. "Now, come on," Linda said. She hurried over to the stove, thrust an oven mitt over her hand, and slid the pot onto the opposite burner. She moved gingerly, avoiding the splashes as she shifted the pot's weight. When she checked the dial, she noticed that it was turning by itself onto the high position. She stared at the dial in disbelief. She slowly reached out, intending to adjust it, and then retracted her hand, unsure.

A gray shadow came out of the wall behind the stove, moved directly through its center and passed right through her. Linda felt the icy cold grip of death throughout every fiber of her being. She gasped, turned around and leaned back against the stove. She wrapped her arms around her chest and held herself as if she had just been violated. She felt a chill in her core. She carefully examined the kitchen. There was no trace of any shadow. She looked around. Then she spotted the iron, sputtering and shooting out jets of steam. She realized that she hadn't turned it off yet. She stood there, frozen for nearly a minute. "Am I losing my mind?"

Linda walked toward the laundry area, grabbed the iron, yanked the plug from the wall, rotated the dial to the Off position, and set it down on the ironing board. She then stared back at the stove. Her arm was throbbing. She backed away and then approached the kitchen sink carefully. She turned on the faucet and held her arm under cold running water. She sighed in relief and stared out the window. Then the phone rang. She nearly jumped out of her skin. She reached over and answered it.

"Hello?"

"Hello, Linda," said her best friend, Julie Marsh.

Linda placed her palm on her forehead in relief and replied, "Oh, thank God, Julie."

"Say, I wanted to know if you would like to go to the Trumbull Mall with me?"

Linda smiled brightly as if that was the best thing that she'd heard in days. "Julie, I would pay you to get me out of this house for the day. I'm really losing it. What time will you be here?"

"Well, I'm ready to leave now, so as soon as you can be ready, honestly. What on earth is the matter? You sound flustered."

"I'll tell you when I see you, Julie. I'll be ready by the time you get here. Bye."

Linda hung up the phone and stared at the stove. The pot had settled down, and after starting at it for a few moments, she reached over and turned the dial to the Off position. She touched the handles to test them. When she was satisfied that they were cool enough, she lifted the pot and set it inside the sink. She went into the foyer, opened the hall closet opposite the front door, reached in and found her boots. She peeled her jacket off a hanger and put it on. When she'd finished zipping it up, she glanced out the window and saw Julie's minivan pulling into the driveway. She closed the closet door and opened the front door at the same time. She walked out onto the porch and waved at her friend. She closed and locked the door, walked down the walkway, and smiled.

Julie leaned over, opened the passenger door from the inside and said, "Hi there!"

Linda got in, kissed her on the cheek and closed the door. She buckled her seat belt and stared at her friend with a crazed look. "You know, if you'd like to skip the Mall and take me straight to the psychiatrist, it might not be a bad idea."

Julie turned around and backed the minivan up. When she shifted gears, she gave Linda a puzzled look. "Oh now, you don't mean that," Julie giggled. "What's the matter?"

Linda shook her head in disbelief as they turned out of the driveway. "It's just that Kelly really turned the house upside-down yesterday. She thought she saw a ghost when we passed Union Cemetery, and I think that now I am seeing things that are quite simply—impossible."

"Oh," Julie replied. "What kinds of things?"

The car passed silently along under the first light snowfall of the season. Julie turned on her windshield wipers, and she and Linda discussed what had happened since Linda and Kelly had driven by the cemetery the previous afternoon.

Tyler was leaning inside his locker in the crowded halls of Monroe High School when his two best friends, Jimmy and Kyle, rushed up and pretended like they were going to tackle him. Tyler was adjusting his hair in a small mirror that he had affixed on the inside of his locker. He smiled when he saw them.

Jimmy leaned in to take a look in the mirror with him. "Everything look alright, gorgeous? That mirror won't ever make you look as sexy as me, so don't even waste your time admiring your reflection in it, okay?"

Tyler snickered and said, "Yeah, bite me."

All three boys laughed and then straightened up when they saw the Vice Principal walk up and stop in front of them. "Good morning, Mr. Gates," they said in unison.

He gave them a curt nod. "Gentlemen, I trust that you'll behave yourselves this weekend, and that you'll not engage in any wanton campaigns of destruction throughout our fine town." Mr. Gates locked eyes with each of them for several uncomfortable seconds.

Tyler feigned injury, grabbed a book off the shelf inside his locker, closed the locker door and said, "The last few nights before Halloween, or Mischief Night, as some kids call it, is for *bad* kids, Mr. Gates. You should know very well by now that my fine, upstanding friends here and I would never participate in such tomfoolery." Tyler tried to maintain a straight face as Mr. Gates looked down at him over the upper rims of his glasses and grumbled. The guys immediately broke into laughter.

Mr. Gates smiled broadly and replied, "I am glad to hear it, Gentlemen. See that you stay out of said mischief."

When he was out of earshot, as the guys were walking off toward their next class, Kyle wrapped his arms around his friends and stuck his head between them. Kyle said, "I can't wait to egg the crap out of the neighborhood."

"Yup," Tyler said. "So, get this. You won't believe it." He turned around and walked backwards facing his friends. "My little sister thought she saw a ghost yesterday."

"Kelly?" Kyle asked. He giggled and said, "No way!"

"Serious?" Jimmy asked.

"Of course, I'm serious. So, being the nice, example-setting brother that I am, I scared the crap out of her and my entire family last night." He looked down and became lost in thought, and then he looked back up at his friends. "Well okay, maybe not my *entire* family, but definitely Kelly, which of course was the original master plan."

"No way," Kyle said again.

"Serious?" Jimmy asked.

Tyler snorted. "What are you, a bunch of robots? You always come back with the same comments."

"What did you do?" Jimmy asked. "I need details!"

"I snuck inside her closet, put a white sheet over my head, and hid there until she and the rest of my family went to bed. Then I started whispering things at her and watched her get all upset and scared. I moaned and groaned and finally burst out of her closet and scared the crap out of her."

"Serious?" Jimmy said.

"No way," Kyle laughed.

Tyler reached over, grabbed both of their heads, and rubbed really hard to mess up their hair as much as possible.

Jimmy looked at his reflection in the glass window as they walked past the Office. He ran his fingers through his hair. "Yup, I'm still sexier than you, Tyler."

Tyler snorted. "Whatever. Anyway, you should have seen my parents' faces. They were scared too, until they discovered that it was me under the sheet. Talk about pissed." They laughed heartily and exchanged high fives.

When Linda and Julie returned from the Mall and pulled into the driveway, white smoke was billowing from the chimney and rose up unhindered into the serene snowy sky. "Matt must be home early," Linda said with a smile.

Julie stopped and put the van into park. She leaned over and hugged her. "It was just lovely having you for the day. Thank you for joining me."

"Yes, it was all a real treat," Linda added. She opened the door and grabbed her purse. Julie's smile could warm the deepest reaches of the soul, even on a chilly autumn day.

"It certainly wouldn't have been as much fun without you. And, I certainly wouldn't have heard such interesting stories," Julie replied. "I'll be picking Kelly up in the afternoon, correct?"

"Oh, yes. Thank you for remembering. I will have all of her things packed. She's really looking forward to spending time alone with you."

"I'll take good care of that little angel while you two are

gone. Vermont is it? What lovely leaves there must be this time of year? You're so fortunate."

"Yes, it's a gorgeous bed and breakfast. We are there Friday and Saturday night, and we'll be back on Sunday around dinner time."

Julie smiled. "It sounds like a wonderful getaway. I'll see you later, love. Bye-bye."

"Bye, Julie. See you soon." When Linda reached the door, Matthew opened it and welcomed her in a white apron and chef's hat that he must have dug out of the old Halloween costume bin. "Hello there! I thought I'd whip up some din-din before you got home."

"Well, this is a wonderful surprise." Linda began to take her coat off when she heard the sizzling sound from the kitchen. "Oh, gosh, the rice is boiling over!" He rushed away down the hallway.

When Linda put away her coat and boots and walked in, Matthew was wiping up the spill. She thought about the strange events that had occurred earlier in the day, and she became immediately alarmed. "You know, I've had problems with the stove this morning. I wonder if it's going bad." She looked around. "Where are the kids?"

"Tyler took Kelly to pick up Sarah up at riding practice. You know how much Kelly loves to see the horses." I saw their headlights at the edge of the driveway as soon as you were walking in the door." Just then two heavy successive thuds hit the front door. Linda spun around, startled. When Linda and Matthew rounded the corner to see what was the matter, Kelly burst through the front door, giggling and screaming.

A snowball whizzed through the open door and struck the closet, sending a ring of snow in its wake. Tyler charged through the door after his sister. On the opposite side of the house, the rhythmical humming of the electric garage door resonated through the kitchen. Sarah opened the door and entered, shaking her head and said, "Animals!"

Kelly continued down the hall, still screaming. She slid on the floor and fell. Tyler toppled over her and they both slid into the kitchen, unharmed but soaking wet. When they saw their father in the apron and chef's hat glaring down at them, wielding a wooden spoon, they broke into hysterical laughter.

Linda knelt. Kelly rolled over to her and met a wet kiss. "Hi."

"Hi!" Kelly hugged her warmly.

"Where's my kiss?" Tyler whimpered.

"Are you beating your brother up again?" she asked. She leaned over and kissed Tyler on the cheek.

"Thanks, Mom," he said.

"No. Tyler threw snowballs at me, and I ran away." She giggled.

"Go take your wet clothes off and I'll run you a warm bath, okay?"

"Hey! How come Kelly always gets the special treatment?"

Linda giggled and asked, "What do you mean, Tyler?"

"How come you never run a bath for your wonderful son?"

"Because you're a big boy, and you can run a bath for yourself," she said. Kelly smiled brightly and scampered upstairs. "Besides, I can't even remember the last time you took a bath." Linda started to walk down the hall and said, "Oh, I remember now, the last time you took a bath a few years ago, I heard all kinds of strange sounds coming from behind the door, and I don't really want to know what exactly they were."

"Gross," Sarah said.

Linda went up the stairs after her daughter.

Tyler called out after her and said, "What strange sounds?" Tyler took a seat at the kitchen table, looked at his father, studied him, shook his head from side to side and smiled, "Hey, Chef Boyardee!"

Matthew chuckled, glanced over quickly and turned his attention back to slicing mushrooms. "Are you going to let the snow melt all over the floor or are you going to take a rag and wipe it up?" He turned on the faucet and washed the mushrooms.

Tyler kicked his heels out and spun around in the seat. "Ya know, Dad, sometimes I think you don't even love me anymore." He studied his father and waited for a reaction. When none came, he got up, knelt down in front of the sink, opened the cabinet door and snatched a rag. He began wiping up the melting snow as he was asked. He turned around and looked at his father who seemed to be lost in thought. "Dad?"

"Yes, what is it?"

Tyler rolled his eyes and said, "Forget it."

He slid down the foyer on his hands and knees, wiping up the water as he went. When he'd finished, he reached over and opened the foyer closet door and noticed a shadow flit down the hall. "Dad?" When he'd taken off his sneakers and coat and put them in the closet, he stood up and returned to the kitchen. His father didn't look like he had moved at all. "Humph," Tyler said. He opened the laundry area doors, put the rag in the washing machine, closed the lid, walked back into the foyer and ran up the stairs to his room.

About an hour later, Matthew stood in the foyer and rang an old brass bell. "Chow's on!" The thunderous sound of approaching children clearly indicated that his call had been heard.

Sarah walked in first and said, "Seriously, Dad? Chow's on?"

Before he returned from putting away the bell in the garage, the table was full and the kids were loading their plates.

"Wow, this looks delicious, honey." Linda came to the table with a pitcher of milk and began pouring for the kids.

"Tyler, Sarah, what are you two planning to do over the weekend?" Matthew asked.

"Huh?" Tyler replied. "Oh yeah," he said, suddenly smiling from ear to ear.

"Your mother and I are going to Vermont over the weekend to show her paintings to the owner of the Four Seasons Bed & Breakfast. Kelly will stay with Auntie Julie and we'll pick her up on Sunday on our way back home."

Sarah nodded and said, "Well, I have a dinner date with Bill, but I won't be out late, because I have riding practice all day Saturday and Sunday."

"Oh, a date," Tyler said."

Sarah squirmed in her seat. Then she straightened herself and resumed her confidence and said, "Yes, I have a dinner date. That's what adults do on weekend nights. And what are you going to do, hit the Trumbull Mall with your dorky friends?"

Tyler shot a look of pure disdain at his older sister. "It just so happens that yes, Jimmy, Kyle, and I *are* in fact going to the Mall tomorrow night." Then he looked at his mother and father. "And, because you guys and Kelly won't be here, can Jimmy and Kyle spend the night, please?"

Matthew and Linda locked eyes momentarily. They both nodded. "Yes, but no parties. Do I make myself clear?" Matthew asserted.

"And no watching scary movies," Kelly added. She set her glass of milk on the table and smiled at her parents.

Tyler thrust a victorious fist in the air. "Yes!"

Sarah grumbled, "Oh, great! What did I do to deserve this?"

"Bite me, Sarah," Tyler laughed.

"Tyler!" Linda protested.

"I'm sorry, Mom. That was inappropriate."

"Did I hear that right, Matt?" Linda asked. "He apologized?"

"Don't know. That is unlike him. Maybe the aliens got him," Matthew replied.

Sarah scoffed and said, "He definitely is an alien! There's no doubt about it."

Chapter 4 – Hearing Voices
from the Beyond

A LIGHT MISTING of rain fell on that Friday morning as Linda helped Kelly onto her bus. She held an umbrella in one hand and a steaming coffee cup in the other. She winked at Kelly who waved out of the window as the bus rolled off. She began to turn away when a thin, motionless, shadowy form blended with the bus exhaust and stagnant fog that sat heavily upon the road. She felt a fear in her core as if she were being watched. Then, for a split second, she swore that she saw a human face in the mist.

She froze and asked, "Who's there?" She was paralyzed with fear staring at the mysterious wafting mists. She became lost in thought. A few moments later, the sound of the white ceramic coffee cup shattering on the slick blacktop jerked her back to reality. She looked down at the jagged fragments. She must have simply dropped it. A cold breeze swept past her. She paused for several seconds. She knelt, delicately picked up the largest pieces of the cup, and laid them in her palm. She stood and scanned the road in both directions. Then she turned slowly back toward the house and said, "Linda, get a grip on yourself!" She slowly walked down the driveway and went into the garage. Matthew had just finished loading the suitcases and paintings into the car. Linda peered around the corner.

"Are we ready to leave?"

"Well, everything is packed. The weather isn't so great,

but we can't have everything our way." He bit into a powdered sugar doughnut. "Everything's all set with Julie?"

"Yes, Julie promised she'd be here when Kelly's bus drops her off this afternoon." Linda dumped the broken coffee cup fragments into the garbage can. "They're both very much looking forward to spending some quality time together this weekend. We can leave just as soon as you return from work and when Kelly is in Julie's care."

"That's great, honey. We're so lucky to have Julie to count on."

"We sure are. She's such a dear friend," Linda said.

Matthew backed the car out, turned it around, winked at his wife and drove off to the office as Linda headed inside.

Several hours later, Linda looked at the clock, went upstairs into Kelly's room and opened her toy chest. She pulled out some coloring books, crayons, and activity books. Then she reached in and selected some of Kelly's favorite stuffed animals. She set them all down in front of the closet and searched through her dresser drawers for the clothes that her daughter would need over the weekend. When she had everything she needed, she sighed and reached for the closet doorknob. Then she heard them—the voices.

She froze and leaned in toward the door. She couldn't believe her ears. She was hearing a conversation—two men having a conversation—coming from inside the closet. At first she felt that it was completely preposterous that two strange men could possibly be inside her daughter's closet. Then her mother's protective instinct switched on like a light. She lost all fear, all concern. She turned the knob, yanked the double doors open and yelled, "What the hell...?" She stopped suddenly and realized that there was no one inside the closet. She blinked repeatedly. Then she listened carefully, intently. The conversation had ended. She spun around and looked around her daughter's room.

"What in the world is going on?" She waited and listened for several more minutes. When she realized that she was alone and that there were no intruders in the house, she leaned in, grabbed Kelly's pink suitcase, placed the items she had gathered inside, and zipped it up. When she turned around, she saw a gray shadow in the doorway. She looked up at the window and then back at the doorway, and the shadow was gone. She looked back at the closet and saw nothing strange. She heard the horn outside and knew that Julie had arrived and said to herself, "Linda, you are really losing your marbles."

Later, Kelly's bus rolled up and Kelly stepped off. Auntie Julie was leaning against the side of her minivan in the driveway. Her red scarf hung loosely from her coat. She smiled warmly and pulled her hands from the pockets of her coat as Kelly ran up for a hug. "Hi, Aunty Julie," Kelly said.

"Hello, angel," Julie replied.

Linda came out from the garage carrying Kelly's suitcase, and Matthew pulled into the driveway and gave everyone a big smile. Linda put Kelly's things in the back seat of Julie's minivan. Matthew got out, knelt in front of Kelly and kissed her. "You be good."

"I will, Dad." She scampered away toward the van.

Linda opened the door and Kelly climbed in. She fastened Kelly's seat belt and kissed her enough times to force Kelly to turn away and giggle. "We will see you soon, sweetie."

"Bye, Mom."

She walked around to Julie's side and smiled. "We'll be back on Sunday. Here is the number to the Four Seasons. Call if you need anything."

"I sure hope you sell them all," Julie said, as she climbed into the minivan and closed the door. "You really do paint beautiful scenery."

"C'mon, Lin, we have to get going," Matthew said.

"Thank you, Julie. We'll see you soon."

Julie shifted into reverse and said, "Have a safe trip."

They pulled out of the driveway in unison and Kelly waved as they parted ways.

Later in the afternoon, Tyler, Jimmy and Kyle sat in the back seat of the school bus. When the bus was beginning to slow in front of Tyler's house, Jimmy lifted the emergency door release latch on the rear door, setting off the alarm and sending the entire bus into instantaneous uproar. The door swung open defiantly as the bus slammed to a halt. The guys leaped out onto the road and ran down the driveway, howling with a victorious roar. Kyle looked back and saw the driver standing at the back of the bus, shaking an old and withered fist at them.

The guys giggled as they ran across the lawn and hooted and hollered as they barged through the front door of the McLaughlins' house. "Party," Jimmy shouted.

"Where are the munchies?" Kyle added. "I'm starving!"

"We have a mountain of food. My folks have stocked up like the end of the world was coming," Tyler replied as he tossed his shoes and coat into the foyer closet next to his friends' book bags.

When he ran and slid down the hallway in his socks, he found Kyle going through the cabinets in search of food and Jimmy surfing through the channels on the television in the living room. He noticed that Jimmy still had his shoes on. "Jim, if you get mud on the carpet, my old man will have your head. You know the rules."

"Oh, I'm sorry, man." He took off his shoes and took them out into the hall.

"Yeah, you pig," Kyle said, digging into a bag of tortilla chips, leaping down into the living room and plopping onto the sofa. He put his feet upon the coffee table.

Tyler looked at him and recoiled. "Dude, your feet reek!"

Kyle gasped, grabbed his foot, twisted it around to his face and sniffed. "They do not!"

Tyler sat next to Kyle, and Jimmy ran in and threw himself on top of them. They wrestled until all three were out of breath and aching with laughter.

Just then a loud reverberating 'thump' struck the sliding glass door.

"What in the hell was that?" Jimmy asked.

"It sounded like a snowball," Kyle answered.

"Surely, your sister isn't foolish enough to mess with us?" Jimmy said.

Tyler said, "Nah, she's at riding practice."

Kyle laughed and said, "Yeah, with the rest of the horses."

"That's not cool," Jimmy interjected, "I think Sarah's kind of hot. No offense."

"Sick," Tyler replied, "Do not *ever* talk about my sister like that, gross."

Kyle shot finger toward the window and asked, "Who the hell is that?"

Tyler and Jimmy leaped to their feet and joined Kyle at the window. "Who are you talking about?" Tyler asked. Kyle pointed toward the far stone wall lining the property.

"I saw an old dude in a black trench coat walking along the wall."

Tyler asked, "Well, was he on *this* side of the wall or on the *other* side?"

"What difference does it make?" Jimmy asked.

"Because, if he was on *that* side of the wall, I don't give a damn. If he was on *this* side of the wall, he's trespassing and he's toast!" Tyler slid the door open and charged out onto the snowy deck in his socks and screamed, "Hey!" Jimmy took off after him. Kyle hesitated, went to set his bag of chips down, cocked his head, reconsidered and ran after his friends with the bag in hand. Ahead of them, Tyler leaped off the deck into the grass and sprinted toward the wall. The faint mists of his freezing breath trailed behind him. Jimmy slipped and drove his knees into the mud. Kyle giggled and sped past him, pulling his over-sized jeans up by the belt hoops. Jimmy grinned, brushed off his knees and continued the chase. When they caught Tyler, he stood triumphantly on the stone wall. He extended his open arms and caught his breath.

"So, where is the guy?" Tyler asked.

Kyle caught up to him and said, "I don't know, Sherlock! Maybe he got spooked and took off into the woods?"

"Well then, where are his footprints?" Tyler said, scanning the ground all around him. "I don't see any at all."

"Look!" Jimmy shouted, pointing toward the house.

The sliding glass door was sliding shut slowly as they all watched, spellbound.

"Are you shitting me?" Tyler asked.

Kyle began to sprint back toward the house, slipped, flung the bag of chips up in the air and landed square on his back. Bright orange tortilla chips landed all around him, a stark contrast to the beautiful white snowy landscape. Tyler laughed, bent down, grabbed some snow, crushed it in his hands, arched back, and launched a snowball as hard as he could toward the house. When he did, he lost his balance in the snow and fell back. The snowball whizzed past Jimmy's ear, hit the glass door and exploded as Jimmy leaped onto the porch and pulled the door handle.

He looked back at his friends in shock. "It's locked!"

Tyler lay in the snow, letting the light flakes land and melt on his face. Then he and Kyle leaped up, tore across the lawn, jumped up and slid across the slick porch and finally crashed gently into the glass door. Tyler pressed his hands up against the glass and said, "That witch!"

Kyle asked, "Who are you talking about?"

"Sarah! She said she wasn't coming home until after her dinner date." He slapped his thigh. "Ah, man, I wanted to get her good. We had plenty of time to play a prank on her or peg her with some snowballs when she came home. And, it looks like she beat us to the punch. Damn it!" Tyler tried the door. He shot a confused look at his friends when the door slid open with surprising ease. He sneered at Jimmy and whacked Jimmy in the shoulder with the back of his hand. "Are you guys playing games with me?"

"What?" Jimmy protested. He rubbed his sore shoulder. "It was locked, man, honest." He started to go in.

Tyler held out his arm, blocked the way, and gave Jimmy a serious, disappointed look.

"What?" Jimmy asked again.

Tyler pointed at their soiled socks, Jimmy's filthy knees and then to Kyle's entire backside.

"Oh," Jimmy said. All three boys stripped down to their underwear and set the clothes in a messy pile just outside the sliding door.

"Where is she?" Tyler demanded.

The teens sounded the battle cry and ran through the house, checking every closet and every room on both floors. Several minutes later, the three converged in the kitchen. They all heard a distant whisper that seemed uncomfortably near.

"What was that?" Jimmy asked.

Their wordless shrugs made them all feel uneasy. There was no one there. They paused. Tyler opened the door to the basement, pointed downward and smiled. They all stormed down the steps screaming, split up and ran off in different directions. They had found nothing when they converged on each other, and they all looked severely disappointed. They looked at each other and ran back up the steps into the kitchen. Finally, Kyle opened the door to the garage and Jimmy flipped on the light switch. They ran inside, split into two and met on the other side of the car. A dank-smelling, empty, oil-stained void was all that they found, rather than a trembling, fragile teen-aged girl trying to hide behind the station wagon. Tyler pressed the electric door opener and both doors rolled up in their tracks. The guys walked across the cold cement garage floor and stood in a row, shivering and staring out at the barren, snow-frosted blacktop driveway.

"Guys, no one's here," Jimmy replied.

The guys froze in their tracks when they heard the door to the kitchen creak. They gave each other uncertain glances and looked back. They watched it open and close slightly as if it were moving by itself. Then, suddenly and forcefully, it slammed shut echoing throughout the garage. Teenage screams cascaded over one another as the guys fled out into the open driveway. They ran until they reached the lawn, panting, eyes wide with terror, each seeking reassurance from the other. They turned around slowly and looked back at the house.

Tyler rubbed the sides of his head and said, "I told you! My little sister saw a ghost, and now it's obviously here in the house!"

"You didn't say it was in the house before," Jimmy answered.

Tyler replied, "Well, I didn't *know* it before!"

"You made fun of your sister about this and now we're totally freaked out," Kyle added."

"Well, what do you want me to do about it?" Tyler asked.

Jimmy shook his head in disbelief. "This can't be real. I mean, this just can't be happening. Can it? This kind of stuff isn't supposed to be real, man!"

Tyler lifted each bare foot in succession, vainly trying to fight the cold. "Well, now what are we going to do?"

Chapter 5 – Troubling Turbulent Teens

THE FIRST HINT of dusk fell over the house as the three trembling teens huddled at the edge of the driveway and the snow-frosted lawn. Large flakes fell lazily from unseen heights and the biting autumn air began to take its toll. Tyler continually lifted his bare feet, mouthing profanities as his two friends gawked at the thought of a ghost in what now, most assuredly, would be defined as a haunted house.

"This is crazy," Kyle said.

"All I know is I'm freezing my nuts off," Jimmy added. "Who ever heard of snow this early in October?"

Tyler stared at his house, the house he had lived in for over sixteen years, as if it were not his own anymore. He remembered teasing his little sister, nearly frightening her out of her mind, and eliciting the wrath of his entire family in the process. 'Who was the frightened one now? How would their other friends at school react to such cowardly behavior?' he thought. He glanced at the long, barren driveway, wishing he'd see his father driving in. But his father was not here, nor would he be, not until Sunday anyway. 'Here I am, sixteen, a man, okay a young man, a rebel,' he thought, 'afraid and standing outside my own house in the snow, my friends looking to me for answers, and all I can do is hope dear old Daddy comes strolling in to rescue me.'

Tyler growled and started across the driveway toward

the garage. His astonished friends couldn't believe their eyes.

"Tyler," Jimmy warned.

Tyler continued, undaunted.

Kyle nudged Jimmy who stood defiantly in the precise spot he had occupied for the past few minutes. "What's a-matter? Scared?"

"Heck yeah, I'm scared," Jimmy said. "And I'm staying right here!"

When Tyler reached the door to the kitchen he looked back. Kyle approached with a big grin and Jimmy stood defiantly at the edge of the driveway with folded arms.

"This is freaking insane! We're living in the movies, like right now!" Kyle said. Tyler looked over at Kyle. He swallowed hard, turned around and reached a trembling hand out toward the doorknob. The silver ring on his finger that his first girlfriend gave him shone under the lights that suddenly came to life when Kyle hit the switch. The bulb clacked and went out in a bright flash.

"Jesus H. Christ!" Tyler hollered in defiance.

"Shush, not so loud," Kyle whispered.

"Why are you whispering?" Tyler asked.

Jimmy called out to them, "What the hell are we doing?"

They giggled and turned to see Jimmy now standing in the driveway with his folded arms, his hair, shoulders and bare feet all dusted with snow. Kyle shot a finger at Jimmy. He gasped and said, "Oh, my God, behind you!" Jimmy's jaw dropped. He ducked and then sprinted toward the garage, slipping on the slick blacktop and sliding across the garage floor into his friends. Tyler and Kyle laughed so hard they nearly fell to the concrete floor.

Jimmy sneered and punched Kyle in the shoulder and said, "You guys are a bunch of dicks!"

Kyle rubbed his aching shoulder and said, "Shit, man! Take it easy!"

Tyler reached for the door again and raised a brow. He took the cold brass knob, bent his wrist and thrust the door open. It creaked as it swung and hit the brass key rack on the wall and swung back at them slowly. Nothing at all seemed odd about the kitchen.

"Whew," Jimmy said. "The coast is clear."

"Thank God," Kyle replied.

"Don't be so sure," Tyler added.

The guys stepped inside slowly. They peered around the corners and inched their way into the living room.

Tyler said, "Maybe we're just letting our imagination get the better of us." He walked into the living room, opened the sliding door, and knelt to retrieve the dirty clothes they had left outside. He closed the door, walked back into the kitchen and put them into the washing machine. "I'll wash our clothes and get us all some fresh ones from my room." He poured in some detergent, closed the lid and started the washing machine cycle. "I'll be right back. Hang tight and make yourselves at home."

Jimmy walked to the refrigerator and opened the door. "We already do, man." Jimmy said. "We already do." He grabbed three sodas and went into the living room. He called out to Tyler. "Hurry up, will ya? Do you want us to catch a cold, or something?"

Tyler giggled and said, "Bite me, Jimmy."

Several minutes later, Tyler came downstairs in fresh clothes and dropped a pair of jeans, a T-shirt and a pair of socks into his friend's laps. Luckily, they were all the same size. Tyler said, "Hey, you know...I've been thinking about you while I was upstairs changing, Kyle..."

"Sick," Jimmy interrupted. He and Kyle smiled at each other.

"You were thinking of me while you were upstairs changing?" Kyle added. Kyle walked behind Tyler's father's bar and started to change. "Is there something you want to tell me, Tyler?"

Tyler laughed and slapped his thigh. "You're so hilarious, Kyle. I was thinking...that you were the only one who saw the dude on the stone wall out back."

Kyle finished putting on the fresh, warm clothes and asked, "And your point is?"

"Maybe you're full of shit perhaps?"

Kyle rolled his eyes and said, "He was there, man."

Jimmy nodded. "He's just saying that *you* were the only one who saw him."

"We all saw the door close on its own, though," Kyle said as he walked past his friends and entered the kitchen. "And that was just plain creeptastic." Kyle opened a cabinet and grabbed a fresh bag of chips. He came back in, sat down on the sofa, reached into the bag and pulled out a chip.

When Jimmy had finished changing, Tyler picked up a cold soda can and pressed it against the back of Jimmy's neck. Jimmy screamed. "Well, there's no sign of him now," Tyler said as he sat beside Kyle, snatched the chip from Kyle's hand, flung it into his own mouth, and completely devoured it.

"That was not cool," Kyle said. He pointed the remote control at the television and turned it on. Kyle found a Beavis and Butthead cartoon and said, "Yes!"

Jimmy slid off the sofa, sat cross-legged in front of the television and imitated the cartoon characters by saying, "Huh-huh, huh-huh, ghosts are cool."

Kyle and Tyler looked at each other and giggled.

"You were *so* scared, Jim. Admit it." Kyle said.

Tyler folded his arms and mimicked his friend. "I'm... not...going back in that...garage."

Jimmy looked back toward them and said, "Stick it!"

"Jim, you'd better check your drawers," Kyle added.

"And you guys weren't scared? Whatever." He turned away and watched the television show.

Tyler and Kyle giggled until they finally broke into hysterics.

Jimmy rubbed his feet. "I think my toes are frost-bitten!"

"Even that didn't kill the stink on them, I see," Tyler added.

Kyle high-fived Tyler and they both tossed chips into their mouths.

"You can't *see* stink, genius," Jimmy retorted.

Kyle noticed a faint, low-pitched laugh. He turned to find its origin and finally held his arms out, shook them and said, "Shush!" He reached for the remote and hit the mute button. They all waited in anticipation.

"What now?" Jimmy asked.

Then, the laugh came again.

"I hear it!" Tyler said. He clutched a pillow in his lap. He scanned the kitchen from the distance. Jimmy shot his head up and listened intently. They sat in silence. Their own labored breathing were the only audible sounds in the room. Then the laughter came again, low and guttural, and this time from right next to them, right near the sliding glass door.

"Whoa!" Jimmy rolled over backwards and crawled to the steps that led to the kitchen. The other boys leaned forward from the sofa to scan the door in anticipation of some grand event that would solve all of the mysteries of creation.

None came.

Jimmy inched back and sat on the arm of the sofa next to Kyle. He scanned the room. "Who are you?" he demanded.

"Yeah, that's good, Jim. Get it pissed off at you!" Kyle said.

Jimmy swallowed and sank down, sliding off the arm of the sofa and pushing Kyle closer to the center.

"Piss *what* off is the question?" Tyler replied. He folded his feet up under him.

"I'm sure glad this is your house and not mine," Jimmy said, nudging Tyler in the side with his elbow.

Tyler looked hurt and said, "Oh, no, you don't! Don't you even think about ditching me."

The invisible laughter became a more pronounced hissing laughter. Jimmy gasped. "Over there." He pointed toward the kitchen. Tyler arched back and hurled a pillow through the living room and into the kitchen. It landed softly on the linoleum floor and slid away into the distance and struck the white French door that led to his mother's art studio.

"Way to go," Kyle said. "Beat it to death with a goose down pillow."

"Do you have any better ideas?" Tyler replied.

Jimmy sat next to his friends. He dropped his head into his lap. Long moments passed. No strange events happened. No miraculous solutions came from any of the teens either. Then Jimmy sat up, his jaw agape. He mumbled something too faint to be heard.

The other guys quickly turned toward him. Tyler asked "What did you just say?"

Jimmy smiled, half frightened and half intrigued and said, "A Ouija board!" He turned his unsure eyes to meet Tyler's.

Kyle wrapped his arms around his bent knees and said, "Wicked!"

Tyler glanced at Kyle. He then scowled at Jimmy. "Are you crazy?"

Kyle snickered, "That's a totally wicked idea, Jim!"

Jimmy protested, "Why not?"

Tyler stood, slapped himself in the forehead and paced the room and said, "Why not? Why not, he says?" He turned and squinted, "Those things are stupid, and they definitely don't work."

Jimmy sank back down in defeat. "Hey, it was only a suggestion, man."

"It's worth a try," Kyle said. Tyler scowled at his friend.

Jimmy stood up and grabbed Tyler's shoulders. "Do you have any better ideas?"

Tyler slapped Jimmy's hands away, wrapped his arms around Jimmy's waist and tugged him to the floor, quickly maneuvering him into a pin position. Kyle dropped to the floor to imitate a professional wrestling referee, and slapped his hand on the carpet as he counted.

"One," he said as Jimmy tried to kick his legs out.

"Two." He noticed Tyler's face turned bright red as he struggled and strained to keep Jimmy's back firmly flat against the carpet.

"Three!"

Tyler grunted and Kyle laughed as Tyler let go and let Jimmy's legs fell to the floor. Tyler moved away and Kyle raised Tyler's arm in the air. Kyle said, "Ladies and gentlemen, we have a new champion."

Jimmy scrambled to his feet, out of breath and hit Kyle with a pillow. Kyle played along and fell back against the couch and pretended to be knocked out. Tyler moved back and said, "And the defeated loser comes in with a foreign object and strikes down the ref! Oh, my God," he laughed. "Pandemonium has broken loose here at the Coliseum."

Jimmy sat up and sniffed the air. "Do you smell that?"

"What?" Tyler asked.

"Smells like the smell you get before it rains, weird," Kyle added.

Seconds later, a terrible sound of smashing glass startled them. Kyle maneuvered around Mr. McLaughlin's oak bar on his hands and knees. When he peeked around the corner he saw three liquor bottles shattered on their shelves, their contents spilling onto the black rubber mat on the floor and two bottles that were severely cracked.

Tyler walked around the bar and gasped. "Great! My dad's gonna think that I did that and ground me for a month!" Rattling bottles behind the bar sent everyone into a panic. Tyler hopped up onto the slate hearth and backed himself into the brick chimney behind him. There was no place left to retreat to.

Kyle shot his head from side to side, looking for an answer. "What are we going to do?"

The room was dead silent.

Jimmy and Kyle leaned over as far as they could, pressing their cheeks against the glass sliding door to see if anything was still happening behind the bar. A cup of stirrer sticks began to rattle. "Be careful, man! Jimmy warned. The cup spun on its base and spilled over in a rush. Tyler hopped back as the stirrer sticks spilled out all over the floor. He ran out of the room, down the hallway and into the foyer. Jimmy and Kyle trembled in fear next to the front door.

"This is wigging me out," Kyle said.

Tyler set his hands on his hips and frowned. "You said we should go for the Ouija board. Well?"

Kyle nodded and said, "Let's go get one!"

Jimmy checked his watch and nodded. "There's still time."

Tyler inched his way back down the hallway with his back against the wall. He peeked around the corner, snatched the car keys and opened the door to the garage. Jimmy and Kyle rushed down the hallway and through the door. Tyler slammed it shut and he and his friends put on their shoes. Then they quickly climbed into the station wagon. Tyler started the car, backed it out of the garage, maneuvered the car around, raced up the driveway and screamed down the road.

Chapter 6 – Manifesting the Mystifying Oracle

THE TRUMBULL MALL bristled with people of all ages. The guys were all relieved to be out of the house. People, real people you could see and touch, roamed the halls, and they were all glad to be back in normal reality. 'Maybe all of the things that happened were explainable events,' Tyler thought. He still wasn't sure about buying a Ouija board. It seemed like fighting the supernatural with the supernatural —one bunch of intangible bull with another.

Tyler, Kyle and Jimmy wound their way around the food court and down the hall to the Toy & Hobby store. The brightly lit red sign could not have been more alluring. Ever since the guys could remember, this store was like a beacon of light drawing them like moths to flame for games and toys. Tyler and Kyle stopped before a display just inside the store. Jimmy urged them on with a brisk wave of his hand and a growl. The three split up and took separate aisles, hooting and hollering at each other as they progressed.

"Guys!" said Kyle. The other boys converged on him seconds later.

When Tyler saw what Kyle was holding, he punched Kyle in the arm. "Action Figures? Can you be any more childish?"

"No way," Kyle said. He rubbed his arm as he read the back of the package in his hand. "New Star Wars figures, awesome!" He put it back on the rack and followed Jimmy. "I had all the original ones, ya know!"

"We all did, dork." Jimmy said. They rushed away to find the aisle with the board games.

After several minutes of searching, Jimmy shouted from three aisles back. "Tyler, we've found them!" Tyler heard the sounds of a struggle and then horrible choking sounds. He smiled and ran down the aisle, eager to see what tricks his friends were up to. When he rounded the corner, her found Jimmy and Kyle on the floor with their hands around their throats as if they'd been strangled to death. The Ouija board Game lay between them.

Tyler said, "Very funny, guys!" Jimmy and Kyle sat up and laughed. Jimmy flipped the box over to read the directions on the back. Tyler and Kyle slid next to him.

"Well?" Tyler demanded.

"The Mystifying Oracle," Jimmy said.

"Sounds like a bunch of crap to me," Tyler said.

"These things work," Jimmy said.

"How do you know these stupid boards work?" Tyler asked.

"It's just common knowledge, isn't it?"

"Just like the common knowledge that you're an idiot?" Tyler continued.

"Harsh," Jimmy replied.

Intrigued, Kyle asked, "What else does it say?"

"Nothing really," Jimmy replied.

After about a minute of examining the game box, the friends looked up to find a strange, elderly woman wearing a pink shawl looking down at them with a very serious look on her face. Ordinarily, the teens would have instantly made fun of her, but this woman examined them with big blue eyes behind gold-rimmed glasses and seemed to radiate an age-old wisdom and kindness that none of them could contest. She said, "Boys, please, do yourselves a favor, put it back on the shelf, and leave it there."

The guys stared at her, mouths open, spellbound by words that seemed to penetrate their souls. Her smile seemed angelic. The boys looked at each other for several seconds and finally burst into laughter. When they looked back up, the woman was gone. Their smiles vanished as quickly as she had.

Kyle asked, "Really?"

Tyler gasped. He pointed at the shelf and said, "Guys, put it back!"

Jimmy protested, "What? Are you crazy? No way, man!"

Tyler pointed down the aisle. "You heard her! A strange woman appears out of *nowhere*, warns us to do *ourselves* a favor by putting it back, and when we look over a millisecond later, she's *vanished* into thin air? Seriously, an old woman can be gone just like that? I'm not even joking, man. Put the thing back on the shelf."

"No way," Kyle said. He stared at the game in awe. "This thing must really work."

Tyler growled and ran down the aisle to find her. He had to learn more. He checked left and right. When he reached the front of the store, he still saw no sign of her. He slapped the register counter. A red-haired teenage girl with braces smiled at him.

"Did you see an old lady leave here a few seconds ago?" Tyler asked.

The girl stuck a finger under her lower lip. "Umm, I don't think I did, nope."

Tyler sneered and ran out of the store. He whipped his head back and forth, checking both sides of the hallway. He spotted nothing resembling a pink shawl. Then, he clutched the stainless steel banisters and scanned the lower level. He ran down the escalator and tried to spot her. She was gone without trace. "This is stupid. Why am I even looking around this far? What old lady is going to out-run me—if she was even real? Damn!" On his way back up the escalator, Tyler kept scouting the lower level in hopes of finding her waddling down the hall. No such luck. When he met Jimmy and Kyle down the hall, Jimmy revealed a white plastic bag from the toy store.

"Take it back," Tyler demanded.

"Can't," Kyle grinned, clutching the handrail and extending an arm toward the metal bars now closed over the store entrance. The store was barren and unlit.

"I don't believe it!" Tyler said.

Jimmy asked, "What don't you believe?"

"I don't believe that after what that lady said, you guys bought that thing."

"That lady is a kook," Kyle replied.

Jimmy smiled, hunched over and hobbled away from them, imitating the woman and mumbling, "You boys better put that game back...do you hear me?" He laughed. Tyler ran up to Jimmy, snatched the bag from his hands, and sprinted away down the hall. Even though they were all on the track team, he was by far the fastest, and he outran them with ease and turned the corner out of view. When his friends walked around the corner into the adjacent hall, Tyler held the big plastic shopping bag with the box clearly inside it over the edge of the balcony. Jimmy and Kyle gasped. Tyler cracked a smile, and opened his fingers. The guys rushed to the edge of the railing, and watched the bag fall to the water fountain below.

When they looked back at Tyler, he smiled, turned and walked away, swaying his hips. Jimmy and Kyle sighed in relief when they saw the game board sticking out of the back of Tyler's jeans and the strange triangular plastic piece and instruction book in his back pockets. Tyler turned around and let them catch up. When they did, Jimmy and Kyle each wrapped an arm around Tyler's shoulder. They walked down the long, dimly lit hallway and the glass doors in the distance.

Later, Tyler, Kyle and Jimmy burst through the garage door and entered the kitchen carrying a pizza and three video tapes. Jimmy tossed the Ouija board and the strange plastic piece that came with it onto the living room floor. They each grabbed a can of soda, went into the living room and sat down around the Ouija board. Kyle opened the box and Tyler dropped a pile of napkins on the inside of the pizza box lid. They all grabbed a slice of pizza and started eating.

Jimmy opened the instruction booklet and held it in his lap. He took a bite of his pizza and inadvertently dripped olive oil all over the instruction booklet. "Oops." Tyler and Kyle didn't pay him much attention as they both examined the sand-colored board. A sun and moon were the only recognizable symbols. Every letter of the alphabet was printed in two neat rows in black gothic letters, and a row of numbers that began with one and ended with zero lay beneath them. There were two words on each upper edge —'Yes' and 'No,' and two words along the lower edge —'Hello' and 'Goodbye.'

"This is just totally creeptastic," Kyle giggled.

"Okay, take the planchette out, hold it post-side down over the center of the board, and ask your question," Jimmy explained.

"Okay, how many hands?" Tyler asked. "Who does it?"

Jimmy turned toward him. "We all do it!"

"Excuse me, Mr. Expert!"

Kyle tossed the crust of his pizza onto the box lid and said, "Candles, we need candles to make this work, right?"

"Kyle, you can't throw the crust away like that, it's the best part," Jimmy said.

"Have at it, Jim," Kyle said. "Enjoy my saliva."

Jimmy took the crust and tore off a piece with his teeth. Kyle winced and shook his head. "Where are the candles, Tyler?"

"In the drawer beside the dishwasher," he said. "Oh crap, I have to switch the clothes into the dryer." Tyler and

Kyle both got up and walked into the kitchen while Jimmy read the instructions.

When Tyler finished loading the clothes into the dryer, he turned it on and joined his friends. The low steady rumble of the dryer and candlelight casting eerie shadows on the walls lent their own degree of intrigue as the guys waited for Jimmy to finish reading the directions. Tyler sat cross-legged on the floor. Kyle lay on his side, facing them. Jimmy leaned back against the bar, munching on another piece of pizza. Suddenly, a dull scratching sound startled them. Jimmy clutched his heart. They looked around the room.

Jimmy said, "Jesus, it's that damned dog from next door."

The dog barked. Tyler scowled and said, "Yeah, that's Cinnamon, alright. Ever since my sister fed him that *one time*, he always comes over here when there's no food in his doghouse. It's actually kind of funny. Oh man, he came in the other day and got mud everywhere. Okay, that's not so funny. He's a pain in the ass, actually. Cute though. Kelly likes him, a lot. I like to play fetch with him. That's kind of fun. I like dogs. Why don't I have a dog?"

Jimmy and Kyle simply stared at Tyler in awe. Kyle said, "Therapist maybe?"

Jimmy rolled his eyes and looked back down at the instruction booklet. "Okay, here's how it goes. We each have to put our hand on this plan-whatever-it-is, and one of us has to ask a question."

The dog continued to bark in the window, breaking the boys' concentration. "The thing is supposed to move and we have to read the letters as they appear under the clear piece of cheap stupid plastic that it is." He looked up at his friends. "Who is going to write the messages down?"

Tyler replied, "Messages?" He stood and laughed. "We're not going to get any messages, guys." He went down into the basement and came back up with a bowl full of dog food. He walked over and opened the sliding glass door. He set the bowl down and patted Cinnamon on the head. "Here ya go, boy." Cinnamon looked down, ignored the food, poked his head inside and looked at Jimmy. Cinnamon barked, snarled and growled, then barked several more times. "What's wrong?" The dog barked and whined. Tyler pointed toward the food bowl. "There, dummy, eat your food." Cinnamon barked and backed away. Tyler just shook his head and slid the door shut. When Tyler turned around and started to walk back toward his friends, the dog growled and barked again. Tyler lunged toward the door. The dog finally cowered, barked one last time and ran away out of sight.

Kyle smiled, "Finally. That stupid dog was bothering me something fierce. I'll write down the messages."

"All right, boys...here goes," Jimmy said, leaning forward and tossing the planchette onto the board. "Ready?"

Tyler growled and Kyle yawned as all three boys reached out, slowly placing their finger-tips on an edge of the triangular-shaped planchette. Tyler leaned forward and looked inside the clear circular piece in the center.

"Oops, now you've done it," Jimmy said.

"What?" Tyler demanded, wide-eyed.

Jimmy flipped a page in the directions and said, "Once you've looked into the central eye of the planchette, your soul will be cursed forever."

"Shut up," Tyler giggled.

Jimmy giggled and said, "It doesn't say anything like that, dude."

"Are you two done?" Kyle asked.

"Okay, here goes," Jimmy said. "What are we going to ask?"

"Hey, there hasn't been a 'peep' from the ghost since we got back. What if we've imagined this whole thing and we've wasted our money and time with this bunch of B.S.?" Tyler asked.

He and Jimmy scanned the room. "Are you here, scum bag?" Tyler shouted. "Quiet!" He pressed his finger to his lips. Kyle smiled. Tyler didn't move. They all watched their fingers carefully, making sure nobody cheated.

"Are you here, you piece of worthless dung?" Jimmy asked.

They laughed.

The planchette moved.

"Wow!" Kyle shouted. It slid...toward him. "Why is it coming toward me? I didn't ask any questions."

"It's not sliding toward you, it's just moving," Tyler said.

Kyle studied his friend, sneered and said, "You moved it, Tyler!"

Tyler smiled deviously.

"Cut it out, dude! This is serious!" Jimmy demanded.

Tyler smiled and leaned back. "Okay...okay...I did it, I confess. I won't do it anymore, promise." He laughed and took a bite of pizza.

Kyle leaned into the board and asked, "Are there any spirits here?" The planchette moved slowly toward the left and stopped on the 'Yes' in the corner.

"Whoa!" Tyler gasped and let go. Kyle followed suit and the planchette stopped.

When they looked up Jimmy smiled.

The boys grinned.

"Paybacks are a bitch," Jimmy said.

"Well, if we'd stop moving it ourselves maybe we might get some real results," Kyle said.

Long moments passed and the planchette didn't move. "This is bogus!" Tyler said. He stretched and took a swig of his soda. "All that's happening is one of us moves it and everyone else buys into it. It's stupid."

"Well, we know there is something here. Let's try and get some answers, huh?"

"Okay," Tyler said. "I'll do it. It's my house." He reached

for the planchette and shoved his friends' fingers out of the way. He slid the planchette into the center of the board and closed his eyes. "Who are you?"

Slowly, Tyler's hands and the planchette slid to the left. It made a wide circular pattern.

Tyler's eyes shot open and he let go, pulling his hands back and gasping. "Holy crap! It moved, man! I didn't do anything!"

"Uh, huh," Kyle moaned.

"Keep going," Jimmy said, sitting up and watching intently. "What do you want?"

Tyler and his friends nearly leaped out of their skins when the door leading to the garage opened and a black figure appeared out of nowhere. Tyler's sister Sarah stood on the landing in a snow-frosted black coat. She wrinkled her nose. One side of her upper lip was turned up in an expression of intrigue and revulsion. "What the hell are you dorks doing?"

Jimmy sat up and smiled at her. "You have a real live ghost in this house, babes!"

"Well, that's an oxymoron, moron," Kyle said. "It's not alive if it's a ghost, now is it?"

Sarah placed her hand on the black iron railing dividing the kitchen from the living room and looked down to floor level. She leaned over and examined the Ouija board. Then, she looked Jimmy square in the eyes and said, "Don't call me 'babes,' Jimmy Reading, and yeah, I'm so sure."

Jimmy nodded his head and said, "Serious. The ghost your little sister saw followed her home and he's here right now in this very house. *This haunted house.*"

Sarah looked down on them and said, "You guys are N.U.T.S.—nuts."

"C'mon," Kyle said, annoyed. "Let's keep going. There's no convincing the skeptic over there."

Jimmy complied. "Okay, we're asking this question to

the ghost that we all know is here in this house. Who are you?"

Sarah rolled her eyes. The boys waited for the planchette to move, but nothing happened. Sarah fluttered her eyes and backed out into the hall.

After Sarah had left, and after several long uneventful minutes, the guys settled back into the mood to use the Ouija board again. Candles flickered and cast strange shadows on the walls. "Maybe we all have to be touching it or something," Kyle said. "Like, let's hold hands or something."

"Oh, so now you want to hold my hand, Kyle?" Tyler giggled.

Jimmy cracked a smile. "We need our hands, you idiots. God, you guys are so ridiculous. Just kiss each other and get it over with."

"Silence, fool," Tyler said, smashing Jimmy over the head with a pillow. Jimmy gulped and then reached his hands out. He closed his eyes and concentrated on the planchette. He tried to feel any movements, no matter how subtle. "Shush, guys, it worked before. Let's try again." Tyler reached out and touched it as well. Jimmy waited until everyone was quiet. "Why are you here?"

The planchette moved slightly. Tyler's eyes fluttered. He wanted so desperately to open them but refrained, unsure if it would upset the flow.

"Kyle, write this down. I can't see, but it is working, it is happening, guys. Holy moley, it's moving and I'm not doing anything."

"F," Kyle called out, excitedly.

"This thing is really moving, man," Tyler continued. "Wow!"

"O. R," Kyle said, kneeling now, scribbling the letters on a note pad as they came to view in the center of the planchette.

Jimmy called out, "K."

"E." It slid up to the letter and back down again. "L." The planchette swirled in a full circle and passed the letter 'L' a second time.

"Are you getting this, Kyle?"

"Yeah," Kyle shouted. "Y." Kyle stared up at his friends and gasped.

Jimmy whispered, "FORKELLY."

Tyler's eyes lit up like fire and he shouted, "For Kelly?"

"Oh, no," Jimmy whispered. "This is not good."

"Why?" What did Kelly do? Why my little sister? Why are you here for a little girl?"

"Kelly said that she saw the ghost at Union Cemetery, right?" Jimmy asked.

Tyler nodded. He was stunned. "Are you afraid of us?"

The planchette moved again, much more forcefully than before, toward the right corner or the board and over to the word 'No'.

"Well, that settles that," Jimmy said.

"No, it doesn't," Tyler said. He pointed at the board. "Look, it is moving again!"

"O," Kyle said. "T. H."

"E.R.S.C.O.M.I.N.O.E." Jimmy leaned over the board in confusion.

"Others come in?" Kyle asked. He scanned the ceiling. "Others coming now?"

"What the hell does that mean? Others are here too?" He stood up and shook his hands in the air and screamed, "You sick, spineless invisible prick! Show yourself to us if you're such a tough guy! What's up with you? Oh, you can lock the doors and toss around bottles. What a big bad-ass you are!"

"Coward," Jimmy added.

Tyler sneered. He walked around in circles, shoving his fist into the air, making mock punches. "I think I've made my point. He's a big puss."

Suddenly, Jimmy's Coke flipped over on its side and

started to spill all over the pizza box and on the Ouija board. Tyler knelt, and wiped up the soda with some napkins. "Show yourselves!"

Sarah stormed down the hall and into the living room and said, "Will you guys please keep it down?"

Tyler smashed his left hand against the inside of his cocked elbow and thrust his arm into the air. "Show yourself," he demanded.

Jimmy shot a concerned gaze at him. "Um...dude." He flipped through the instruction booklet. "It doesn't say it in the booklet here, but I have a bad feeling that you're not supposed to say that."

Tyler hissed, "Screw it. I'm tired of waiting around for answers and all this crap."

Sarah stood there with her hands on her hips, bewildered. "You're losing it!"

Tyler looked up at big sister and said, "Sarah, we used this thing and it worked. It said it's after Kelly!"

"Bullshit! If you say anything to Mom, Dad, or Kelly about this, they'll flip and you know it. This is a bunch of horse manure, and you know that too!"

Kyle said, "You should know all about horse manure, right, Sarah?" He giggled.

"I'm sick of your snide comments, Kyle Foster, so please keep them to yourself, or I will seriously kick your ass, clear?"

Tyler laughed.

"He's not kidding, Sarah," Jimmy said. "We all saw it."

"Look," Tyler continued. He wiggled his finger and beckoned Sarah. She huffed and came over to them. Tyler grabbed her hand and pulled her behind the bar, so she could see the broken bottles and spilled liquor all over the shelf and on the rubber mat.

She gasped and said, "Oh, you guys are gonna get it." She laughed.

"*We* didn't do it," Jimmy shouted.

"Did the *ghost* do it, Jimmy?" Sarah asked. "Like I'm supposed to believe *that*?"

"Yes, the ghost did it," Kyle groaned.

"You guys should have your heads examined," Sarah said. She laughed.

"It's the truth, Sarah," Tyler said.

"I'm not going to get suckered into your B.S. story!" She looked at the floor, licked her lips and knelt down. "But I will have some of this delicious pizza. Thank you very much." She took a slice, took a bite, sneered, and walked away.

Kyle put his hands on top of his head and said, "Guys, we're so screwed."

Tyler put one hand on his hip and rubbed his forehead with the other, exactly as his father did when he was perplexed. He said, "Let's just get out of here and go up to my room." Tyler kicked the Ouija board. It slid across the room and struck the sliding glass door. The guys stood, put all of their garbage into the pizza box, closed it and put it on the kitchen table. Tyler pointed at the living room and the board in the corner. "This isn't over until I say it's over!" He switched off the lights, passed down the unlit foyer and followed Jimmy and Kyle up the stairs.

Chapter 7 – Laughing and Ringing Bells

WHEN TYLER REACHED the second floor, Kyle had already entered his room and Jimmy stood outside Sarah's bedroom with his ear pressed up against her door, grinning ear to ear. Tyler smirked and came up to him, knowing exactly what his friend was thinking. They looked at each other, raised their fists, nodded and then pounded her door. They ran down the hall, giggling. They heard the distant call, "Freaks!" They ducked into Tyler's room and slammed the door behind them.

"Hey," Jimmy called. "It's Friday night and I seem to remember a cracked, but not completely shattered, bottle of Jack Daniels downstairs that will have to be discarded anyway, so why should that sweet succulent nectar go to waste?"

Tyler cocked a smile and said, "I see your point very clearly, my friend."

"Nice," Kyle added.

Jimmy nodded and opened the door. Then he hesitated. "I'm...not going down there alone!"

Kyle laughed.

Tyler agreed. "I sure wouldn't."

"Well then, are you coming with me?"

"Nope," Tyler said.

Jimmy turned toward Kyle.

"Don't look at me," Kyle said.

"I'll go with you, man," Tyler finally said.

"Good!" Jimmy left the room and led the way.

Kyle sat on the floor in front of the television and leaned back against the bed. He waited, tapped his fingers on the carpet, then stopped and listened for anything his friends downstairs might say or do or for anything unusual to happen.

Tyler followed Jimmy into the foyer and they inched their way down the dark hallway. Then Tyler pushed Jimmy forward into the kitchen. Jimmy turned around to protest and found Tyler tearing back down the hall toward the stairs. Jimmy took a deep breath, looking across the moonlit linoleum floor and into the blackness of the living room. He tiptoed across the floor, switched on the light and ran behind the bar. He found the cracked bottle on the second shelf, grabbed a bar towel, rolled the bottle into it and raced away. Then he cursed, stopped, wheeled around, and ran back to the refrigerator. He opened it, grabbed a soda can, kicked the door closed, ran into the foyer and climbed the stairs.

Just when he reached Tyler's bedroom, the door slammed shut in front of him and he nearly smashed the already fragile bottle in his hands when he collided with the door. He tried to turn the doorknob but it was locked. "God, you guys are a bunch of dicks. I could have cut the shit out of my hands." He heard giggling from behind the door. Tyler opened it shortly thereafter with a broad smile. Kyle sat against the bed with his arms folded against his chest and his head tilted back laughing. Tyler reached for the half-empty bottle.

Jimmy moved the precious wares away. "Uh, uh! I got it, and you left me. It's all mine!"

"Your mama," Tyler said. "It's my dad's bottle!"

Jimmy unwrapped the towel to expose the neck of the bottle and said, "Ah, Jack Daniel's!" He produced a Coke from behind him and said, "And a Coca-Cola chaser. It just doesn't get any better than this." Jimmy took the end of the bottle in his mouth, tossed his head back and took a gulp. Then, his eyes bugged out. He gasped for breath, coughed, and spat out about a third of the whiskey that he'd tried to force down. He wiped his face and mouth and quickly drank the soda.

Kyle laughed and said, "Amateur." Kyle took a swig, coughed and wiped his mouth. Whiskey seeped through his fingers as he took the soda that Jimmy handed him. Finally, Tyler came over, mouth agape, like a kitten in search of the nipple. Kyle lowered the bottle to his lips. Tyler's eyes fluttered as the whiskey soaked his face.

"Yeah, yeah...go, boy," Jimmy said. Jimmy patted Tyler's face with the bar towel and they all laughed harder than any of them could remember. Tyler, still on his knees, wiped his sticky face clean and pulled his wet T-shirt off.

Kyle spoke in a German accent, "Oh, the little girly-man shows off his scrawny body."

Jimmy laughed. "Yeah, man, when are you going to grow some hair?"

Tyler rolled the towel and whipped Jimmy in the arm. "I'm only sixteen!"

"Yeah, and like you have any body hair, Jimmy," Kyle added.

Jimmy replied, "Oh yeah?" He tore off his shirt and threw it on the chair in the corner. He looked down at his chest, scanned momentarily and pointed proudly at a single black hair growing around the edge of his nipple. Both Tyler and Kyle inched in closer, eager to see if Jimmy had truly ascended to manhood before they had. They squinted and finally found the tiny hair that Jimmy had pointed to.

Tyler said, "Whatever. Hair is so Neanderthal. All it would mean if I didn't develop chest hair and the two of you did is that I am simply more genetically advanced than either of you two apes. We don't need hair because we're not roaming the great open plains scavenging for food."

"Yeah, like your sister," Kyle said. "Sarah, the Great Ape of the Amazon."

Tyler chuckled.

"Easy, man, that's so uncool," Jimmy said.

"We are civilized. We wear clothing," Tyler continued. "I'd be perfectly happy if I didn't turn into some freaking gorilla. It's disgusting!"

Suddenly, Tyler felt tingles on the top of his head and had the distinct impression that he was being watched. He stopped laughing and stared out the window facing the front lawn. He turned toward his friends. They lost all of the color in their faces. Tyler parted the curtains and opened the window. He carefully stuck his head out. Outside, in the darkness of night, the snow had stopped and crisp winds sent fallen leaves swiftly across the lawn. He leaned out a bit further and checked the front door and the sides of the house. The wind blew his hair to the side, and his long black bangs whipped against his eyes, causing them to water. Suddenly, the brass lamppost went dark. Then on the first floor the lights in the living room blinked on and off. Tyler shot back inside the room and turned to face his friends with a look of sheer dread.

Jimmy asked, "What is it?"

"It's still here. It's in the living room. The lights just came on downstairs."

Kyle opened the door to check and see if Sarah was in her room. He heard her singing across the hall. He shook his head from side to side, signaling that it was definitely not Sarah.

"I don't want to go down there," Tyler said. "I don't want to deal with this shit anymore." He felt frightened, vulnerable. Tyler stood with his back against the window. He was trembling. Kyle did the only thing that he could think to do. He fumbled with the first VHS tape, put it into the machine, and turned it on. Tyler glanced at the television and rolled his eyes. "How can we just sit down and pretend that nothing is wrong?"

"What else can we do?" Jimmy replied, comfortingly.

Tyler knew that his friends had nothing at stake here. Yes, they were a team, friends since the fourth grade, but Jimmy and Kyle could go to their 'normal' homes any time that they wished. This was his problem, not theirs. He sat down and sulked.

Jimmy patted Tyler's shoulder as if he could sense his thoughts. "Hey, we're all in this together, man! I won't abandon you and only come back only when this thing is over and everything is back to normal. That's what friends are for. We will beat this!"

Tyler smiled and said, "You don't know how much that means to me, Jim." Kyle said nothing and busily worked the remote.

Jimmy turned toward him, annoyed. "Are you getting this, dude?"

Kyle glanced at them and turned back to the television. "I heard you. Did you hear me say any differently?" Tyler smiled and threw a pillow at him.

Kyle forwarded through the previews and tossed the remote to the floor. "Are you going to close the window, or are we going to freeze to death? Let's watch the movie."

"We need to draw straws to see who gets the bed and who gets to sleep on the nice cozy floor," Jimmy said.

Tyler nodded. He got up, knelt before his desk, opened a drawer and pulled out the three toothpicks that they usually used when they needed to draw straws. He held them in his palm. "Kyle, you go first, because you won the last time. You know the drill."

Kyle reached for one, then changed his mind and went for another. He stuck his tongue out of the corner of his mouth and finally pulled one out. It was the shortest of them all. He had instantly won. He chuckled. "I did it again." He smiled deviously.

Jimmy said, "Are you serious?" He examined the toothpicks. "He's got to be cheating, somehow. That's the third time he's won in a row. How the hell is he doing that? I can't keep getting stuck on the floor, guys. My back is a freaking wreck in the morning." Jimmy wrestled Kyle to the ground. "You freaking cheater!"

Tyler slid the window shut. "I think Kyle is just about the luckiest guy I know."

The guys did their best to ignore the living room light that had turned itself off and on earlier. They finished the last remnants of the whiskey, and they were well into the second movie, when they finally drifted off to sleep.

Somewhere between the haze and silent lucidity of sleep, Tyler's dreams were shattered by an odd reverberating noise. It happened again, and it became clearer, but it was still not easily identifiable. After the third time Tyler came completely out of his dreams and identified the sound as the untimely clang of the front doorbell.

Jimmy moaned, turned over and asked, "Who the hell is here this late?"

"Party," Kyle replied.

Tyler said, "*This early* is what you meant. It's 3:02."

The doorbell rang again.

Tyler shuffled out of his blankets and went to the window. He opened it and looked down at the front porch. No one was there.

"Who is it?" Jimmy asked.

Tyler leaned back in and said, "There's no one out there!"

He closed the window and turned toward his friends.

The bell rang again.

"What the hell?" Tyler asked.

Jimmy joined him at the window. Kyle ducked inside his blankets to fight the cold air coming in.

"Let me see," Jimmy demanded. He studied the porch

landing below and the bushes along-side it. There definitely was no one there, but the bell was ringing.

Sarah yanked open Tyler's door and stormed inside in her nightgown. "Who the hell is coming over at three in the morning?"

Kyle pulled his head out of the covers and smiled. "It's the bogeyman!"

She went over to Tyler and Jimmy at the window and pushed them away so she could see. She leaned outside and scanned the front yard. "Who's out there?"

"Sarah, there was never anyone there," Tyler tried to explain.

"This is too weird," Jimmy added. Sarah started to walk out. Jimmy said "Nice nighty, Sarah." Sarah scoffed, left her brother's room, went back into her room and slammed the door behind her.

Kyle called out from underneath his blankets, "Can you close the..."

"Yeah, I know! Close the damn window!" Tyler answered.

Jimmy lay down on his blankets and wrapped himself up. "Maybe there was someone there, Tyler. Did you tell anyone we were partying?"

"Are you kidding?" Tyler answered.

The doorbell rang again. Kyle flung the blankets away from his face and all three of them looked at each other is disbelief. They all got up.

When Tyler opened his door, Sarah met him in the hall, and they stormed down the stairs together. Jimmy and Kyle followed.

The bell rang a seventh time.

The slate foyer floor was a shock to their bare feet when they stepped off the carpeted stairs. Sarah peeked out the window set into the door. The doorbell rang an eighth time. It seemed like an eternity as her slender hand slowly grasped the brass doorknob. In the dim foyer, an ominous, lingering silence swept over them. Sarah swung open the oak door and a sudden biting wind shot inside. Their hair flew straight backwards in the powerful gust. An empty cement landing and steps that led down into deeper darkness were all that greeted them. The full moon hung heavily in the distance.

Sarah stepped out onto the landing.

"Uh, Sarah," Jimmy warned.

She glanced back, annoyed. "What?"

"Don't go out there," Tyler pleaded.

She ignored her brother and checked for fresh footprints in the snow, sure signs of high-school party-goers hiding in the bushes. There were no tracks. There was no sign that anyone had set foot on the landing. Then the laughter came from nowhere—faint, long, terrible laughter. Sarah turned around, her face devoid of all color. Jimmy nodded, satisfied that Tyler's sister had finally been given some evidence of the ghost's existence. Sarah pressed her palm against her forehead, clutched her temples and paused. "What the hell was that? Where did that laugh just come from?"

"That's what we're trying to tell you, Sarah," Tyler said.

"What exactly are you trying to tell me?" Sarah asked.

"Exactly...what we've been telling you all along, woman," Kyle replied.

"There's a ghost in here! Kelly was right!" Tyler said.

They all stared into the early morning darkness. Tyler closed the door and leaned back against it. He looked his sister in the eyes and folded his arms over his chest. "You heard it. Don't you believe your own ears?"

Sarah shook her head. "If you expect me to believe you, you are out of your mind. Nothing can convince me that this has anything to do with phantoms. For all I know you hid a tape recorder somewhere."

Kyle walked away down the hall and entered the kitchen.

Jimmy dropped his arm in frustration. "Come on! Did we make the doorbell ring?"

"No way," Kyle said.

Tyler looked over and asked, "What now, Kyle?"

Kyle said, "Um...guys...you should see this!"

Tyler and Jimmy hurried over into the kitchen. Kyle was leaning over the railing into the living room. He pointed at the carpet.

Jimmy said, "Holy shit!"

Tyler called to Sarah. "Come here and look at this, Miss Skeptical."

Sarah walked into the kitchen briskly and asked, "What?"

Tyler pointed to the Ouija board on the floor. It was no longer next to the sliding glass door where he had left it, but it was in the exact spot that they had used it earlier.

Sarah gasped, and covered her mouth. The small plastic piece in the center was rotating *by itself.* Sarah screamed a more horrific scream than her mother had produced two days earlier. They all leaned over the railing for a closer look. The planchette spun on the lower center of the board over the word 'Hello.' When Tyler started to back away, the planchette rose up in the air. It hovered there for three seconds and then dropped onto the word 'Goodbye.'

"Holy crap," Jimmy shouted.

The planchette wobbled, flew across the room, struck the brick fireplace and exploded into pieces. Sarah screamed again and ran upstairs. Kyle followed her. Tyler stormed into the living room, picked up the board and the planchette pieces, and climbed the steps into the kitchen. He looked at Jimmy with determination. "Open it!" He leaned his head over to the right. "The door to the garage. Open it!" Startled, Jimmy opened the door and switched on the light. Tyler marched across the garage and pulled the lid off the metal garbage can. He tossed the board and the planchette inside and banged the lid on with excess force. The sound echoed throughout the garage. He came back inside, switched off the light and slammed the door. "I'm done with it, all of it!"

Jimmy shook his head in disbelief. "Well, what if it's not done with *us*?"

When Tyler and Jimmy entered Tyler's room, Kyle was spreading blankets on the floor. Sarah was lying in the bed trembling. Kyle complained, "She kicked me out of the bed that I won the right to sleep in."

"Well," Jimmy said as he walked over to the bed, "I'll just slide in next to Sarah and..."

"You wish," Sarah shouted, as she hit Jimmy so hard with a pillow it nearly knocked him over.

Jimmy lay down on the floor, looked at Kyle and they smiled at each other.

"Nice try, Jim," Kyle whispered.

"It was pathetic actually," Tyler replied.

They all lay there staring at the ceiling, hoping that nothing else would happen. When things seemed peaceful, they had no choice but to finally surrender to sleep.

Chapter 8 – Getting Ready for Mischief Night

THEY ALL AWOKE in the stillness of morning to a terrible smell so bad that they all had to bury their faces inside their blankets. Kyle looked around the room and asked, "Who farted?"

"Wasn't me," Jimmy replied.

"Whoever smelt it, dealt it," Kyle answered.

Sarah said, "You guys are so gross!" She sat up in bed, covered her nose and mouth and said, "Phew."

Tyler got up and opened the window. The bright sunlight lit up the room and a fresh breeze blew inside. The smell immediately became strong and overpowering, like a month's worth of rotten fruit. Sarah ran out of the room, holding her hand over her mouth. She slammed her door behind her. A moment later she screamed. Tyler and Jimmy rushed into her room. Sarah turned around, holding her nightgown over her chest. "What are you doing? Get out of my room!"

Jimmy replied, "You screamed."

"I screamed because I'm going to be late for riding practice," she said. "Now get out!"

Jimmy tried to calm her. He walked closer, holding his hands out and said, "Seriously, if you need me to stay with you, I can..."

Sarah stomped her foot, pointed at the door and said, "Out!"

Jimmy closed her door went back into Tyler's room. Tyler laughed at his friend's ridiculously obvious advances. Kyle stood at the window with his head outside. "This reeks!" Kyle said.

Jimmy still couldn't believe the smell and asked, "What *is* that?"

"I don't know," Tyler replied. "Leave the window open and let it air out while we go get some breakfast."

The house seemed unusually peaceful, considering what had happened a few hours earlier. The guys toasted some bagels, smeared them with cream cheese, poured themselves some milk, and had breakfast in front of the television. Sarah rushed downstairs in her riding gear, grabbed an apple and left without saying a word.

About an hour later, the guys got a football and left for Wolfe Park for the day. Once outside in the crisp air, they found new energy and enjoyed the drive to the park. A Saturday afternoon, with plenty of rest, no school, and five or so hours to spend playing football was all that they could have asked for. They met their other fiends from school and completely forgot about the house and all of their supernatural troubles.

When the game was over, they drove to the Merritt Canteen for dinner. It had been the best place for burgers, hot dogs, shakes, onion rings and fries since 1942. All the local teens made a habit of gathering there to unwind, kick back, and seriously stuff their faces.

The boys stood in line for about ten minutes, while Tyler took the time to read some of the ads on the nearby bulletin board. Tyler pointed to one in particular. "Hey guys, get this! 'Spookeytown Haunted House', and it's only six bucks to get in. That's a laugh, isn't it?"

Kyle came up to take a look. "Man, we could make some serious coin."

"Yeah, if only anyone would believe us," Tyler snorted. He folded the flyer and stuck it into his pocket.

"What'll it be, guys?" came the powerful voice of the huge, muscular man behind the counter.

"Umm, three cheeseburgers with lettuce, tomato, salt, pepper, ketchup, and onions, three dogs with the works, three large fries, and three Cokes," Kyle said.

The cashier repeated the order to the staff behind him in the same jargon they were used to hearing. He hit the register keys with blazing speed and excessive power. "Twenty bucks, guys." Tyler locked eyes with Jimmy. No matter how many times they'd observed the routine, it always amazed them. They could never quite get used to how massive the man's biceps were, nor could they understand how the register wasn't broken by now with all of the usual excessive pounding. The guys each handed their share to the cashier, and they waited patiently for their food amidst a long line of loyal customers.

When they got their food, the boys sat in one of the booths and enjoyed their meal. They always thought that it was cool that the restaurant had small, wooden, two-pronged forks to use with the fries, kind of like it's cool to use chopsticks at Chinese food restaurants. It was something different, something unique, and part of their neck of the woods that made home feel like—home.

Jimmy took a bite of his hot dog. "Hey, let me see that flyer."

Tyler handed it to him and they studied it together as they nibbled on their fries. "Well, now we know that 'haunted houses' don't necessarily need to look so creepy, right?"

"Yeah, you can say that again," Jimmy replied.

"Speaking of Halloween," Kyle said. "What are we going to do?"

"Screw Halloween, that's for kids. Tonight we are going to go and cause some mischief, and I'm really looking forward to it," Jimmy smiled. "We should go snag some eggs and toilet paper before they run out."

"No one's going to run out of toilet paper and eggs, Jimmy," Kyle said.

"What about Michele Dierdork? We definitely need to peg her house," Tyler suggested.

"Without question," Jimmy said as he and Kyle high-fived each other.

A middle-aged woman who must have overheard them spun around and gave them a stern, displeased look. Jimmy and Kyle looked at each other, and lowered their heads until she turned away. When they were finished eating, they drove across into the adjacent parking lot and walked into the grocery store. They bought six dozen eggs, a twelve-pack of toilet paper, chocolate syrup, three cans of whipped cream, and three bars of white bar soap. When they got to the counter, the cashier waved his manager over. He gave the guys a disappointed look. "Planning to have some fun this evening, fellas? If anything happens to *my property*, I know who I'm going to go find." He chuckled. The guys all made fun of him and mimicked his laughter. "Seriously, though, we sure did have some fun back in the day," he continued. "Don't make too much of a mess, okay? It's unsightly."

"Did they even have Mischief Night or Halloween back in the Stone Age, when you were a kid?" Kyle giggled.

The manager pointed toward the exit doors and scowled. "You're lucky I don't call the cops!"

The guys hurried toward the doors. "Bite me," Tyler roared.

"Yeah," Kyle added. "Which car is yours exactly? We can practice on it!"

"They'll be looking for you," the manager promised.

They ran into the parking lot, got in the car, and sped away. Kyle looked back at the two silhouettes standing in the windows watching them.

When they arrived back at the house the lights were on, and Sarah's boyfriend's car was in the driveway, so at least someone was home, and hopefully there wasn't any trouble going on inside. Tyler hit the remote and the garage door rolled up. He honked the horn twice. When they pulled into the garage, Tyler leaned back and looked at his friend. "Jim, I really wouldn't say anything inappropriate to Sarah while Bill is here. He is freaking huge, and I think he'd pound you into oblivion if you tried."

Kyle laughed.

Jimmy scowled and asked, "Inappropriate?"

Kyle coughed. "Yeah, like you're always saying cheesy things to get into Sarah's pants kind of inappropriate?"

"Kyle, Jesus." Tyler protested.

"What?"

"Don't talk about my sister's pants or anyone trying to 'get into them,' especially Jimmy. That's just as inappropriate." He locked the car doors preventing anyone for getting out.

They waited in the car in uncomfortable silence for several seconds before Jimmy said, "Well, why are we waiting here? Let's go."

"We have to wait here in the car for five minutes before going inside," Tyler said.

"What? Why?" Jimmy asked.

"It's a pact that Sarah and I have. When one of us could be getting it on, and the other comes home, we promised to signal we were home and give the other five minutes to finish up whatever it is we are doing—if anything."

Kyle laughed. "And in your case, you aren't really doing anything, right, Tyler?" Jimmy burst out into laughter and messed Tyler's hair.

They sat in the car for five more minutes. Jimmy kept rapping his fingers against the center console and peering out the windows. When he finally couldn't contain himself any longer, he spoke, "Do you think they're doing the nasty?"

"Jimmy, come on! Jesus," Tyler roared.

"Well, what else would they be doing?" Kyle asked.

Tyler didn't really want to even think about what his sister was doing. For some reason it's okay to think about what a guy is doing with his girlfriend, but not what a girl is doing with her boyfriend—especially one's own sister, gross. "Okay, let's put the supplies here in the garage. Sarah has no clue we are going out for Mischief Night, and I don't want to deal with her or Bill scolding me for being a menace to society."

They got out of the car, set the bags down in the corner, and walked into the kitchen. Their jaws dropped. Sarah and Bill were dressed in olive green clothes and were applying black face paint on each other. The kitchen table was loaded with eggs.

Kyle said, "No way!"

Jimmy laughed and ran out into the garage to get the grocery bags. "When in Rome, do as the Romans do!" He opened the bag and put all of the supplies onto the table.

Sarah asked, "Chocolate syrup?" She smiled and picked up the bottle. "Nice! I didn't even think of that. Way to go!"

"Sarah McLaughlin, I am shocked," Tyler said. "You ought to be ashamed of yourself. Now give me some of that face paint." He grinned from ear to ear.

"Hey, it's my last year of high school, and from then on it is all business, so why not have some fun, right?" Sarah laughed.

"And you, Bill? You're in college now, so what's your excuse for this despicable behavior?" Tyler asked.

Bill turned around and smiled brightly. "College is simply four more years of wild debauchery taken to the next level, boys."

Jimmy gave him a sly look. "Or...in your case, you mean —five or six years, right, Bill?"

Bill grabbed Jimmy by the collar, jacked him up, and slammed him against the door. "Watch it, punk!" His eyes looked like they'd explode out of his skull, and his teeth were clenched and dribbling saliva.

Kyle and Tyler laughed.

"Easy, man, take it easy," Jimmy pleaded.

Bill let him go. He grunted as Jimmy collapsed on the floor.

"Okay, so are you tools going to go get changed into some dark clothes or not? I'm not going to get caught because of you amateurs. That's for damned sure," Sarah said.

Tyler smiled and motioned for his friends to follow him upstairs. When they got into his room, Tyler opened his closet and started throwing black, dark blue and dark green shirts, sweats, and socks at his friends. "What am I, the wardrobe consultant? This is getting ridiculous. And I told you to watch it with Bill, Jimmy."

Jimmy shrugged as he put on a green sweatshirt. "I can take him."

Kyle laughed. "Yeah, right, that's funny."

"Everybody falls to their knees when they kicked in the nuts, no matter how much muscle they have," Jimmy replied. "He'll get his, next time, trust me."

"Oh, man, that's dirty pool," Tyler laughed. They finished changing and scrambled down the stairs. They went out into the garage and loaded all of the supplies into Bill's car. When everyone was inside, Bill turned the key and the engine just moaned and whined.

"Oh, great," Jimmy said from the back seat. "Nice car, Bill. What year is this *crate*, anyway?"

Kyle and Tyler just looked at his friend in shock. Tyler mouthed the words "shut up" to Jimmy.

Bill turned around and asked, "Jimmy, how old are you?"

"Are you going to ask me and then tell me that if I keep

it up, I'm not going to live to see my next birthday," Jimmy asked.

Bill got out, and slammed his door. Jimmy knew he was going to get it, so he just closed his eyes and waited. "Like that's supposed to be funny?" Jimmy continued, undaunted. Bill tore open Jimmy's door, grabbed him by the collar and hauled him out of the car. His friends just shook their heads in pity.

"You just don't know when to shut your mouth, do you?"

Jimmy smiled. It was all he could do. Bill turned Jimmy sideways, pressed his fist against Jimmy's shoulder, arched back, and nailed him as hard as he could. Everyone heard it. Jimmy groaned deeply and climbed into the back seat. Bill got in front and turned the key. Remarkably, it started. He looked back at Jimmy and they locked eyes for several seconds. He backed the car around and headed out of the driveway. They turned out onto his road and kept going deeper into Monroe.

After a few miles, Tyler asked, "So, where are we going?"

"The old folks home, for starters. It's freaking hilarious watching those crusty, crippled bastards get all bent out of shape when their windows get plastered with eggs," Bill said.

"Nice," Kyle said. "But they can't bend so well, so can they really get 'bent out of shape?'"

Chapter 9 – Smelling and Flying Mischief

"HAR, HAR, HAR," Bill said. "Dork!"

"Oh, so Kyle doesn't get a charlie horse for that snide little comment, huh?" Jimmy asked. "Gee, why am I so lucky?"

"Because you just ask for it," Bill replied.

They pulled off onto the edge of the road and into a small unused, overgrown dirt driveway. Bill pulled in further and turned off the car. "Everyone out and assemble their gear. If anything goes wrong, you meet back here at the car. If you get caught, you're working solo, ya get me?" Everyone nodded and agreed.

After several minutes of assembling their gear they hiked through the woods quietly and came to the perimeter of the Shady Grove Retirement Home. They wrote profanities all over the cars parked out front with their soap, whipped cream, and chocolate syrup. Then they littered the place with the toilet paper and launched about two dozen eggs at the windows of the home itself. When some poor elderly man opened the door, Bill commanded, "Nail that old codger!"

Before he knew it, the man got pegged with about three direct hits and was splattered with close to a dozen more eggs as they exploded all over the door and against the door frame. He hollered at them, "You rotten kids!" The voice was weak and feeble. "You're going to burn in hell!" He cursed as he hid behind the door. "Bastards!"

Everyone laughed in hysterics as they bolted back toward the woods and back to the car. They got in and recounted the events that just took place with roars of laughter. Bill backed out, turned around and screamed down the back-country roads toward the house. When they neared the house, Bill turned into the driveway and turned off his lights just as the police car came roaring over the hill with its lights flashing and siren wailing. Everyone ducked down in their seats to avoid being seen.

"That was so great," Jimmy laughed.

"Awesome," Tyler added.

"Hell, yeah," Kyle laughed. "What's next?"

"Michelle Dierdorff's house," Jimmy replied.

Sarah looked back at her brother and his friends.

"Oh, you guys really have it in for her, don't you?" Sarah smiled. "I wonder what the real reason is. Did she refuse a kiss? Maybe Jimmy tried too hard to get into her pants, so she refused?" She turned back around to see out of the front window.

"Oh, nice," Kyle said, giggling.

"That's funny, Sarah," Jimmy replied. "You're a real laugh."

Bill started the car and turned on the lights. "Okay, tell me where to go."

"I don't recall the name of the road, but it's just past the school, dude," Tyler said.

"Got it," Bill said. Bill was careful enough to watch his speed during their quick drive.

About a mile past the school, Tyler said, "Here, turn here! They turned sharply down the road and slowed to a crawl when they saw that the trees were already heavily laced with toilet paper. "Man, someone already really did a serious job here," Tyler said, admiring the handiwork.

"Pull over here, Tyler urged," smacking Bill on the

shoulder excitedly. Bill cut the wheel and they pulled over. They all got out quickly and followed Tyler through the trees, then stopped short of the Dierdorff's lawn. All of the lights in the house were off. Tyler reached into the bag and grabbed a can of whipped cream and began shaking it. "Oh, man! This is going to be so much fun." He crouched low and tried to stay within the shadows of the trees as best he could until he reached bushes on the right side of the steps. He crept up onto the porch, took out his soap, and started writing on the glass door.

He never saw the window above the bathroom slide open slowly and silently, nor did he see Michelle and her brother tilt the plastic bucket overhead. It was too late. Tyler had fallen into the trap. He had been lured in by his resentment of the girl who never acknowledged him. His friends watched from a distance as the wave of ice-cold water struck Tyler in the head, neck, and shoulders and totally drenched him. He squealed when it hit him and ran down his neck into his sweatshirt. Then, he heard Michelle and her brother howling with laughter from above. It made him furious. He gritted his teeth, turned and started to skulk away across the lawn. Then, he whirled back around toward the house. He had to get back at them somehow.

He tore out a can of whipped cream and started to come back toward the house, and then they hit him in the chest with the garden hose that they must have brought up through the back of the house and aimed out the front to repel other hostile pranksters. It was numbing cold, and it soaked him completely. They aimed up and hit him in the face. Tyler recoiled and shot his hands up to deflect the freezing-cold water. When he turned to run away, they soaked his back and his butt and shouted at him, "Loser... run...loser..." Tyler made a mad dash for the woods and his friends huddled safely therein.

His friends were roaring with laughter. Tyler could say nothing. He was utterly defeated and completely soaked and humiliated. His shivered in the cold, but his blood was boiling. "Let's just get outta here!" Tyler was soaked. They all piled into the car and headed home. Tyler sulked and shivered in silence until Kyle just had to say something.

"Dude," Kyle said, "that was awesome."

Tyler sneered at his friend, then smiled slightly and said, "Yeah, it was pretty good, I'll give them that." He stared out the window, planning and plotting his revenge all the way home.

When they neared the McLaughlin house, they saw two teens hop the stone wall lining the front of the property and run across the lawn. "Some bastards are hitting your house. Let's get em!"

Sarah said, "Kill the lights!" Bill switched the lights off, cut the engine and let the car glide to a halt on the grass. They watched the kids climb the steps up onto the front porch and converse with each other. One started spraying the front door with whipped cream.

Tyler roared, "Oh, those pricks! Who are they?" They watched as one boy directed the other to the porch by pointing at the brown paper bag set there. The other fished something out of his pocket and knelt beside it. They saw a brief, faint flicker of light. Then it went out. They saw it again and realized that it was the flame from a cigarette lighter. The one boy set his can of whipped cream down and started to unravel some toilet paper while the other set the bag on fire. Suddenly, the roll of toilet paper appeared to be violently and powerfully batted away from the one boys' hand. It flew back onto the lawn and rolled down across the sidewalk. The bewildered boy called out. Both boys flew back as if they were suddenly struck in the chest by a linebacker. They wailed in horror.

Kyle whispered, "What the hell is going on?" They looked at each other in confusion. The guys who were attacking the house started running their hands through their hair, as if they were being attacked by a swarm of bees. They screamed and rolled around on the ground. Then, when it appeared to have stopped, they shot their heads up, got to their hands and knees, stood, and sprinted away across the lawn and into the neighbors' yard, leaving their wares behind.

"What the hell was that all about?" Bill asked.

"Must've been the ghosts," Jimmy said.

Bill looked over and asked, "Huh?"

Tyler closed his eyes while clutching the wall and said, "Tell me you've told him, Sarah," Tyler said. He opened his eyes and shot her a look of pure disdain.

"Told me what?" Bill pleaded.

"We think our house is haunted," Sarah said.

Bill asked, "Seriously?"

Tyler shivered in the cold. "Oh, so now you admit it, Sarah?"

"You all think your house is haunted?"

"Explain what those two poor sods just went through then, Einstein," Jimmy replied.

Bill shot his head toward Jimmy, glared at him, clenched his fists, arched back, took a deep breath and roared. Jimmy smiled, leaped over the wall and ran toward the house, giggling. Bill ran after him, but Jimmy was far too fast. They ran across the lawn and around the back of the house. Kyle and Tyler climbed over the wall. Sarah got into Bill's car and started it.

When she drove down into the driveway, Jimmy was making a second circuit around the house, panting, as Bill tried to catch him. Kyle and Tyler launched several snowballs at both of them, but none of them came close. Bill slowed and came to a stop by the front porch. Jimmy began walking cautiously back toward them. Bill was catching his breath until he finally said, "Let's take a look at this haunted house, shall we?"

Sarah covered her nose. They all recoiled. The unmistakable smell of burning dog crap coming from the smoking brown paper bag on the porch was permeating their nostrils. "That is so nasty," Sarah said.

Kyle thrust his arms into the snow, scooped some up, and dumped it on the bag, extinguishing it immediately.

"Good thinking, Kyle," Sarah said.

"What can I say," Kyle replied. "I'm a genius."

"Kyle E. Foster," Tyler laughed. "Super genius."

"Lord," Sarah groaned. "It was good, but let's not exaggerate, Kyle."

Tyler stepped up onto the porch and peered into the window. He turned the doorknob and swung the door open. He reached in and turned on the lights. "It doesn't look like there are any problems. Guys, let's go get changed." Tyler ran upstairs to change out of his soaked clothes, and Jimmy and Kyle scampered up the steps behind him. They quickly changed out of their camouflage and into their own clothes they'd left in his room.

Sarah and Bill walked into the hallway and turned on the kitchen and living room lights. She noticed a vile smell, and gasped when she saw a large yellow pool of water on the living room carpet. "Oh, gross!"

Bill stepped down into the living room and knelt before the puddle. He leaned down and sniffed. "It smells like dog piss!" He and Sarah heard the thuds on the stairs as the guys made their way back down. They came right in to find out what was the matter.

"Oh, man, that smells awful," Kyle said. He put his hand before his face and mouth.

"Did Cinnamon get inside somehow and piss on the carpet?" Tyler asked. He opened the garage door, went to the cupboards, and grabbed some towels. He unfolded them, set them down, and started to walk on them to soak up the mess. "Man, they're soaked! Look at how much is being absorbed into the towels, that's nuts!"

"Did your neighbors' dog do this?" Bill asked.

"Ghosts, dude," Jimmy said. "Tyler, here let me get you

a garbage bag to put those towels into." He went over to the sink and bent down. That's when he noticed the black flies coming up and out of the drain—two at a time, then a group of seven or eight. They rose up, swirled around each other and went back down. "Guys," Jimmy warned. "You'd better get over here quick!"

Sarah rolled her eyes. "What now?"

Jimmy opened the cabinet door below the sink and recoiled. The others leaned in to take a look. Thick black ooze leaked from the pipes under the sink and collected into a pool of slime that was expanding until it was dangerously close to leaking over the edge of the cabinet. "Jeez, what the freaking hell is this goop?" Jimmy asked. He sat back and pushed himself away from the cabinet. Bill crouched down and stuck his finger out. Jimmy grabbed it, and shot him an astonished, crazed look. "Are you crazy? We don't know what that stuff is!"

Bill yanked his hand back and nodded at Jimmy. "Yeah, well that was probably not a good idea, thanks for the save." He reached up into the drawer and pulled out a butter knife. He extended his hand and dabbed the slime with the knife. A piercing whine came from the cabinet, as if he had just stuck a pig. They all leaped back in shock. Bill touched it again. It was syrupy, like molasses. Then, the knife stuck to it. Bill winced. He tried to pry the knife off, but it would not budge. "What the...?"

Suddenly, the pipes under the sink started to vibrate and shake violently. The sound of a thousand black flies trapped in the pipes erupted so loud that it became maddening. Everyone covered their ears. Bill got up and gazed in horror at the sink and the drain. The flies started to come up in groups of ten to twenty. Bill thrust his hand out for the drain plug and that's when the endless column of filthy black flies rose up from the sink drain and spread out into the house like a swirling black cloud. Bill tried to push the drain plug into place. Flies flew into his mouth and crawled into his nose. He spat them out, and exhaled as hard as he could through his nose in one final effort to close the drain off. Sarah screamed. Kyle ran out into the foyer and out the front door, wailing in horror. Tyler checked under the sink. The pipes were shaking so violently they were sure to burst any second.

"I'm using all of my strength to keep this drain sealed, oh, my God," Bill wailed.

Tyler closed the cabinet doors, leaned back against them and held them shut as best he could. He closed his eyes and said, "The pipes are going to blow. Watch out!" Bill grabbed Tyler by the shirt collar and dragged him across the linoleum floor with one hand. Tyler got to his feet in the hallway and stopped to take a look into the bathroom. He checked the sink drain. For a split second there was nothing. Suddenly, the black horde blasted out of the sink and struck the ceiling. Flies cascaded over the other and completely filled the room. Tyler yanked the door closed, ran out the front door and stood in the yard with the others.

"I can't believe it," Bill said.

"Welcome to Spookeytown," Jimmy said.

"I'm telling you, we can make a fortune steering people through this 'real haunted house,'" Kyle added.

"What are we going to do?" Sarah asked.

"Well, we are not staying here, I can tell you that, Bill said. "You and I can go back to my place." He took Sarah's hand and led her down the walkway toward his car. He turned back. "And guys, I don't suggest staying here, either."

"No shit, really? Ya think?" Jimmy agreed.

Tyler just looked at his friend and couldn't even muster words.

Bill clenched his fists and then calmed himself. "I'm going to give you a pass this time for the save earlier, but Jimmy, I swear to God, you had better watch your mouth."

Jimmy looked deflated, empty and completely drained. Tyler wrapped his arm around Jimmy's shoulder. Kyle came in and joined them in the huddle, though this was definitely not going to be a pre-track meet pep talk, he was sure. "This is getting really bad," Kyle said.

"I don't know what we can do," Tyler said. He walked over toward the house to take a look. He expected to hear the buzzing of a billion black flies inside, but he didn't. "I don't hear anything." He leaned inside. "There's nothing." He disappeared through the doorway.

Bill honked the horn as he and Sarah drove up and stopped adjacent the walkway. Bill stuck his head out of the window. "What is it?" Jimmy waved Bill over.

Bill gave him an odd look.

Just then, the garage door opened behind them and Tyler ran out to the car and up to the window. He scared Bill when he slapped his palms on the door. "I don't know if I should be relieved or more frightened but...they're gone!"

"What do you mean, they're gone?" Sarah said.

"I mean, the flies are all gone. Like all gone, totally."

Bill turned off his car, opened his door and got out. Tyler nodded and gave him a crazy look. He waved he and Sarah inside. Jimmy and Kyle walked into the kitchen from the hallway. Bill walked inside. He put his hands on his hips and turned around several times. Sarah went and looked under the sink. "Nothing, just like they all just vanished."

Kyle asked, "Dude, what the hell?"

"The pee is gone, too," Tyler said. He held the towels up for everyone to see. They're completely dry. He sniffed them. "There's no smell either, just my Dad's car wax." He knelt down and patted the carpet and shook his head.

Bill sat down in one of the white kitchen chairs. He rubbed his eyes with his palms. "Okay, I need to be filled in here, and I mean from the beginning." He looked up at Sarah with a huge frown. "I can't believe you didn't tell me about this when we were here earlier, Sarah. Jesus!"

Sarah knelt and held Bill's knees. "I wanted you to experience it for yourself, so you wouldn't go looking for things to happen. That way, I'd know that we weren't all crazy."

Jimmy stood there with folded arms, looking down at Sarah. He studied the angles of her face, and his eyes traced her body from her perfect lips, her exposed neck, the beautiful round breasts, her slender hips and thin legs, right down to her ankles. Then he studied her fingers resting on Bill's knees. He imagined what those delicate hands would feel like on him. He didn't know it, but Sarah turned, looked up and saw him studying her. Jimmy licked his lips, closed his eyes and smiled. Then Tyler karate-chopped Jimmy in the chest. "Dude, can you be any more obvious?" Jimmy clutched his chest and did his best to hide the pain.

Over the next hour, Sarah, Tyler, Jimmy and Kyle did their best to explain what had happened from the initial story about Kelly seeing the ghostly man at Union Cemetery, right up until the unbelievable situation with the flies. Bill just sat back in awe pretty much the entire time. He looked over at Sarah often, and his expression varied from intrigue, to disgust, to remorse, to pity, to bewilderment, and back to pity again.

When it was all over, and no one had anything left to say, he finally sat up and spoke. "Well, what in the freaking hell are you planning on doing about this?"

"Heck if we know," Tyler replied.

Bill shot his eyes open, flew out of his chair, ran over to the sink, knelt and opened the cabinets. "The goop," he said. "We can take a sample to my friend's lab, and find out what it is. He noticed the butter knife securely affixed to the hardened, dried pool of slime. "Get me a hammer and chisel, or a...a screwdriver or something."

Tyler ran into the garage, returned, and handed Bill the tools. "Here ya go."

Bill wedged the screwdriver under the edge of the thick tar-like pool of slime and the cabinet. He arched back and struck the edge of the screwdriver. The slime buckled. He struck it again, and a piece broke and ricocheted off the inside of the cabinet. He tossed the tools to the linoleum floor and looked up at Tyler with satisfaction. "Give me a plastic bag and a paper towel.."

Sarah tore off a sheet of paper towel and handed it to him. Tyler fished out a small baggie and held it open. Bill picked up the slime with the paper towel and placed it into the baggie. Tyler folded it in on itself. Bill snatched it from Tyler's hand and stood. "Our first piece of evidence," he said.

He started to put the baggie into his pocket when they all heard the tell-tale sound of buzzing flies. He felt them writhing in the baggie and held it up, astonished. There was no broken piece of hardened ooze in there any longer, but about a dozen black buzzing flies. Sarah screamed. Horrified, Bill dropped the baggie onto the floor and stomped on it with his size thirteen boot. When he pulled his boot off, the flies were gone without trace and all that remained was a pool of black water. Then, they watched spellbound as the water completely evaporated before their eyes until there was not a single drop left in the bag. "You have got to be kidding me."

"Wicked," Kyle said. "This is all just totally freaking wicked!"

"Just when it couldn't get any weirder," Sarah said.

Bill looked under the kitchen sink again and all that remained of the black pool of ooze were dead fly carcasses. "Look!" The others knelt and saw the impossible display before them. They carcasses were lying in a perfect ring where the borders or edges of the pool of slime used to be.

"It's weirder," Jimmy said.

Tyler got out the vacuum cleaner and set it up in the kitchen. Sarah and Bill went upstairs, and Jimmy and Kyle sat down in the kitchen chairs. Tyler slid the long tubular attachment into place and hit the power switch. He reached in and began sucking up the dead flies. They all cringed when they heard the dead fly carcasses being sucked through the hose.

Then the power started to fluctuate. He looked down at the vacuum cleaner and then at his friends. It slowed, as if it were losing power. Jimmy and Kyle walked over and dropped to their knees on the kitchen floor. The suction power was reduced to practically nothing. It couldn't even suck up the last fly. Jimmy turned the vacuum over and examined it. Suddenly it ground to a halt and went completely dead. "I'm getting really sick and tired of this bullshit, let me tell you, guys," Tyler said. He wound the cord up and stuck the vacuum in next to the clothes dryer. "Let's just get the hell out of here."

"That's the best idea I've heard in a long while," Kyle said.

"You won't get any complaints out of me. Let's blow this joint," Jimmy agreed.

Tyler walked over to the edge of the stairs, climbed them, peeked around the corner, called out and said, "Sarah, Bill, I'm going to stay with the guys tonight at one of their houses. I can't take this shit anymore."

Sarah emerged from her room with an overnight bag. "We have the same plan. Why remain here when we can go stay in a perfectly normal house? Let's meet up here around six tomorrow night. I have riding practice from one to five. I'll pick up dinner on my way home, and then Mom and Dad should be back with Kelly shortly afterward."

"Okay, cool. See you tomorrow." He shouted upstairs. "See ya, Bill."

Chapter 10 – Feeling All Alone

THE GUYS SPENT the night at Kyle's house playing board games, and were sprawled out all over the den when they finally woke up close to noon. Jimmy had a plastic battleship sticking into his cheek when he stirred and lifted his head. It fell down and clattered onto the game board when he rolled over, winced, and said, "Oh, man, my aching back." He moaned.

"Yeah, I hear you," Tyler added.

"Is anyone here?" Jimmy asked.

"My parents know better than to try and wake three lazy teenagers after a late Saturday night. They're probably at church," Kyle said.

"I'm not lazy," Jimmy argued.

"You're lazier than lazy," Kyle replied.

Tyler sat up and stretched his back. "Let's get something to eat, I'm starving."

The guys got up, drove off down Route 111 and pulled into Bill's Drive In. It was another local burger restaurant that the guys frequented on a regular basis, and it was definitely a great place to rendezvous with friends.

After lunch, they went to the movie theater. When they had finished their movie, they walked into the bathroom. They each took a stall, locked the doors, and sat up on the tanks with their feet on the toilet seats until the next crowd was let in. The ticket taker was notoriously wary of kids trying to catch a free movie when the one that they had paid for had ended. He never figured out that the 'smart kids' hid in the bathroom with their feet on the toilet seats, so it would appear that no one from the previous group was hanging around. When the time was right, and the next crowd streamed inside, they flushed the toilets, washed their hands, and walked right into a different theater with the rest of them, and the ticket taker was none the wiser.

Once inside, they lost themselves in another two-hour adventure where ghosts and creepy crawling things were but a distant memory. When the second movie was drawing to a close, however, Tyler knew that soon he'd have to return home and face the cold, hard reality that his life had been entirely and completely turned upside down.

After the movie, they didn't really talk at all on the ride back to Kyle's house. When they pulled into Kyle's driveway, they exchanged unsure glances.

Tyler said, "Well, I'll see you later, Kyle."

"Yeah, man. Call me if anything weird happens, okay?" Kyle replied.

"You know I will, man."

Not much was said during the drive to Jimmy's house either. When they pulled into Jimmy's driveway, Tyler grasped the steering wheel and his head quickly sank.

"You'll be all right. Your parents will be home soon," Jimmy reassured him.

"Yeah, I know. I guess you're right. Umm...will you call me every once in a while? J-just to make sure everything is okay?"

"Sure, bud," Jimmy said.

"Thanks, Jim. I hope your shoulder is okay. I told you Bill is not someone to toy around with. He's a good guy but I think he gets his violent streak from his old man. He was a drill sergeant or something. For your own sake, just tone it down with Sarah, will ya, jeez? Actually, do it for my sake too, because I really don't want to see it."

Tyler knew that his friend never liked it when he told

him to cool his jets with regard to Sarah, and that he certainly didn't like it when Bill was mentioned at all.

Jimmy said, "I know, I know. It's just that..."

Tyler interrupted him. "Jim, it's obvious, I get it."

He shifted into reverse, then put the car right back into park and shook his head from side to side. "I just can't even think about it."

"Think about what?" Jimmy asked.

Tyler looked his friend squarely in the eyes and said, "I can't think of going home alone. Do you know what I mean?"

Jimmy exhaled heavily. "Yeah well, why don't you call me as soon as you're home, okay?"

Tyler sighed. "Okay. I will. It's all I can do, really."

Jimmy waved as Tyler spun the car around and drove away alone.

The snow drifted down lazily that afternoon, but in no significant amounts as Tyler made his way back home. He didn't feel any urgency to rush right home either. He let his mind wander, as sometimes happens when people drive a long way and don't remember the time in-between—when they let it wander and then regain their focus, or how they had traveled several miles without remembering it at all, and how they didn't have an accident when they certainly should have.

He thought about the mysterious man that Kyle said he saw walking along the edge of the yard the other day, and then about the invisible force moving objects and speaking to them from some unknown world where darkness reigns. Then he thought about Kelly. He examined the station wagon controls. He remembered that this was the car his mom and sister were in when Kelly said that she first saw the ghost. 'Did the car have anything to do with it, he wondered?'

In no urgent need to go home, Tyler decided to pull into

the neighborhood McDonald's for a chocolate shake. He walked inside and stood in line.

It was refreshing to be in the company of so many real, normal people. Well, normal for McDonald's standards anyway. He checked out the cute blond girl who took his order. 'Does she like me?', he wondered. 'Would she like me if she knew what I was going through?'

What if the activity in his house never ended? What if, because it never ended, he would never have a girlfriend again? He thanked her for the shake and sat down in the corner.

He drank about half of his shake while he studied the people eating all around him and at the laughing, smiling children in the playground who were climbing over and inside the giant replicas of the McDonald's characters, just as he used to do as a young boy. He studied them as they played. He watched a young couple giggling and smiling at each other, nibbling on the opposite end of a French fry until they had eaten it all and their lips had finally touched. They smiled at each other warmly, and Tyler smirked and rolled his eyes. He thought about how easy they all had it— oblivious to the unseen realm that had collided with his own. Tyler shook his head. His life had always been pretty much perfect—until now.

After a few minutes of feeling sorry for himself, he got up and walked out to the car. He got in, started the engine, turned on the radio, and took a sip of his shake. He drove away feeling sad and lonely. 'Why don't I have a girlfriend to be there for me, like Sarah had Bill and like his parents had each other?' he wondered.

Then, he thought about poor Kelly. Their parents were all the loving tenderness that she could ask for. Tyler didn't feel loved nearly half as much as Kelly was lately, but she was the baby of the family, and that's just the way it usually goes, from what he has heard and experienced anyway.

Part 2 – Oppression

Chapter 11 – Bringing Back the Board

WHEN HE BANKED onto his road, he took special notice of the surroundings. Had anything changed recently? 'Was there anything to this haunting that affected not only his house, but others as well?' Maybe someone had noticed something and had found some kind of help. Or, at least, they knew where to get it if they needed it. Tyler approached the driveway and stopped just short of it. He peered through the windshield to see the entire empty house, trying vainly to find something to explain what was happening.

The house seemed cold and uninviting. But how else would a 'haunted house' feel? He eased the car into the driveway. He pulled in nose-first toward the garage and sat there motionless for several long minutes. "Better to be facing out," he said. He swallowed hard, put the car into Reverse and glanced toward the back window, his ice blue eyes scanning the situation behind him. He put the car into Park, turned off the engine, and sat there quietly, listening for anything peculiar. He felt it better to leave the car outside, in case he needed to escape and the garage door wouldn't open. 'What if the ghost could lock the garage door, as he had earlier in the living room?' Tyler imagined all kinds of ways he could be tormented by unseen spirits if he were locked inside of his house. 'Which of those things could or would actually happen?' He hoped he'd never find out.

Tyler went around to the back sliding door, put his hand up over his eyes, and peered into the immense glass window to make sure everything was all right. He slid open the door and stuck his head in. When everything looked normal, he slid the door closed and stood there silently, listening for any disturbances. His nostrils flared. There were no strange scents. He slid off his sneakers and set them neatly against the door, then second guessed himself and looked back down at them. 'Shouldn't I keep my shoes on, in case I need to run out of the house?' He decided that soiled carpets and his father's wrath were a certainty. The ghost's antics were not. He exhaled strongly and shook his head. 'How can this be happening?' he wondered.

Tyler walked up into the kitchen and inspected the drain in the sink. He knelt and picked up the empty plastic bag still lying on the floor. He held it up to the light and studied it for a minute. He pressed the bag in his hand between his thumb and index finger and squeezed several times. There was not a single trace of anything inside the bag. "This is so weird," he said. Then he just threw it into the trash can next to the counter. He bent down and picked up the hammer and screwdriver and walked toward the door that led to the garage. He tested to see if the doorknob would turn. It did. He opened it quickly and shot his head inside. Then he laughed at himself for thinking that he could actually startle whatever it was that could have been waiting for him on the other side. He put the tools back into their drawers, walked back into the kitchen and slammed the door shut. The sound resonated through the kitchen. The house had never seemed so disturbingly quiet.

He walked briskly into the foyer to the closet. The cold slate floor sent a chill up his spine. He took his trembling hand out of his pocket. A cold rush of air cascaded over his face as he flung the closet door open. He sighed in relief when he realized that the breeze was simply created by the swiftly swinging door rather than any supernatural attack or dark phantom whisking by. Tyler exhaled loudly and hung his coat. He closed the door and pressed his hand against it to ensure that it was properly shut. He turned to look out the front windows.

The snow was still falling. He went into the kitchen, wet a rag at the sink and walked down into the living room. He picked up the rubber floor mat and carried it from behind the bar with him into the garage, and dumped the broken shards of glass into the garbage can. He scanned the entire garage and noticed nothing peculiar, so he wiped the mat with the dishrag and made sure that even the tiniest fragments were completely gone. He walked back inside, closed the door and spent close to an hour cleaning up the bar area—doing his best to make it look like nothing out of the ordinary had happened.

When he was finished, he put the dishrag in the washing machine and grabbed the cordless phone. His fingers went to work on the keypad. It rang and rang until finally he heard the familiar voice. "Hello?" Jimmy's voice answered.

"Hey, everything's cool. There's no sign of anything weird."

"God, I'm glad. Call me if anything happens, I have a butt-load of homework."

"Okay, later."

He dialed Kyle who picked up immediately. "Hello?"

"Hey, Kyle," Tyler said.

"Are you okay, man?" Kyle asked.

"Yeah, it just sucks to be alone here, ya know?" Tyler replied.

"Heck ya, I do. Hang in there, man," Kyle said.

"I don't really have any other choice, bud."

"Yeah, well, call me if anything happens."

"Okay, later," Tyler replied. He held the phone in his

hand as if it were his only link to the normal world. Still gripping the phone, he went into the living room and turned on the television. He found the last half hour of a Lethal Weapon movie and became engrossed enough to detach himself from the obviously awful situation that he was in.

When the movie ended, he rapped his fingers against his thigh and listened. He dialed the phone.

"Hello?"

"Jim, it's me, Tyler."

"Really?" He laughed. "I couldn't tell. How's everything going?"

"Okay. Hey, I just wanted to check in again and tell you I'm still all right."

Jimmy exhaled heavily, paused and said, "Cool. I hope it's all over, ya know?"

"Yeah, you and me both," Tyler replied. "Do you think that the fact that the goop and the flies disappeared means that the ghosts left or something?"

"I don't know," Jimmy replied. "Hang on a sec, my mom is calling me from downstairs." There was a brief pause in the conversation. Tyler listened intently, waiting, and then his friend came back on. "Hey, sorry but I have to go. My mom is calling me for dinner."

"Yeah, my parents should be here soon. Thank God, too. I never thought I'd be so happy to see them come home." He laughed.

"Yeah, I know what you mean." Jimmy laughed. "See ya."

"Bye." Tyler hung up, and put the phone down on the coffee table. He leaned his head back against the wall and closed his eyes. Then the phone rang, but it sounded strange, like it was losing power. His eyes shot open. It rang again. He tilted his head forward and studied it. Something was wrong. It seemed like the whole room before him was stretching back away from him. He reached out for it. It rang again. When he grabbed the phone, he hit the answer button, brought it to his ear, and asked, "Hello?"

There was no response.

"Hello?" All that he heard was a strange static.

"That's not very funny, guys." Tyler waited to hear something, anything that he could identify. When none came, he hung up and held the phone in his lap. It rang again. Tyler growled, "Hello?"

Nothing.

Tyler flung the phone down onto the floor, leaned his head back and closed his eyes in frustration. Moments later, the wall behind him started to vibrate. He leaped off the couch, crouched, snatched the phone and ran into the kitchen. He opened the door to the garage, and ran right into Sarah just as she was about to open the door herself. She gasped and dropped a red and white bag. Tyler shot his hands out and caught the bag before it hit the floor.

Sarah asked, "Tyler, what are you doing?"

"It's hot."

"It's Won Ton Soup, genius. I got us Chinese food. I told you that I was picking up dinner, remember?"

"I remember."

Sarah walked past him into the kitchen and asked, "Has anything strange happened while I was gone?"

Tyler cocked a smile and asked, "Like what, noisome stenches, things moving by themselves, swarms of flies, or piss on the carpet? Those kinds of strange things?"

Sarah chuckled, set the bags down on the counter and said, "That's actually very funny." She handed her coat to Tyler who scoffed and took it to the foyer closet. He stopped short in front of the closet doors. 'What if something was in there this time?'

Sarah called to him from the kitchen. "I've been

thinking about everything that happened last night and I don't think we should tell Mom, Dad, or especially Kelly."

"I cleaned and straightened up the mess behind the bar. What are we going to say about the booze bottles if Mom or Dad notices?" Tyler asked.

"You're either going to have to make up some really big bullshit story or you'll have to own up to that one. In either case, that's no reason to tell them about the freaky things that have been happening lately. There is no evidence at all, and you know Dad. He won't believe us." Sarah took two plates out from the cabinets. "Hell, I'm still not even sure if I believe it. I mean I saw it with my own two eyes, there is no denying that, but it doesn't really help explain anything, does it?"

"Well, I believe it has to do with ghosts," Tyler admitted, "but I don't know how I'm going to explain the booze bottles."

"Maybe Dad won't even notice," Sarah said. "They never drink. That whole bar is for decoration and for when Mom and Dad have company, we both know that. And when do we ever have company, honestly? He may not notice for a long time, if ever."

They both sat down at the table and started eating. Tyler took a few sips of soup and looked at his sister very seriously. She looked up at him, afraid to hear what he had to say. "What is it?" she asked.

"Sarah, you didn't believe us when we told you, and maybe you forgot, but when we asked the board, or ghost why it was here, it spelled out Kelly's name."

"What? You were serious?" Sarah asked. "Really?" She held her hands over her mouth. "Oh, my God!"

"What are we going to do?" Tyler asked.

"What can we do? I have no clue."

Then, the phone rang. She saw Tyler cringe. "I'll get it," Sarah said. "Hello?" She sighed. "Yes, hang on." She handed it to Tyler.

"Hello?"

He recognized the voice. It was Jimmy screaming at him, "You douche!"

Tyler asked, "Huh? What's the matter?"

"Why did you do it?" he demanded.

Tyler put his egg roll down on the plate and yanked out a piece of pork stuck between his teeth. "What the hell are you talking about, Jim?"

"You put it there, didn't you? I asked Kyle already, and he said he didn't do it. So, why did you do it?"

"Jim, what are you talking about?"

"The Ouija board! I found it in my book bag! Why did you put it in my book bag?"

"Jim, I put it in the garbage. You saw me do it."

"And then you put it in my book bag when I wasn't looking!"

Tyler stood up, stormed into the garage and switched on the light. "I didn't put it in your book bag, Jim, honest." Sarah, who immediately took a serious interest in the conversation, followed Tyler and came up beside him. Tyler pulled off the garbage can lid. "I told you..." he said, then paused. "You've got to be kidding me! Jim, it's not here!"

"No shit, it's not there! It's in my book bag! Are you feeling so sorry for yourself that you wanted to turn my house into a freak house too?"

Tyler asked, "A freak house?" He was crushed. Now, one of his best friends had turned against him. "I didn't put it there, Jim! Honest."

"Well, who did?" Jimmy went dead silent.

Tyler waited for a response. "Hello?"

More silence.

Jimmy sounded very frightened, "Do...do you think the ghost put it there?"

"It had to be," Tyler answered.

"Well, Jesus Christ!"

Tyler held his head in his hand and thought for a few

uncomfortable moments. "Hey...well, don't use it!" Tyler suddenly fell into the deepest depths of despair.

Jimmy's sudden reply startled him, "Of course I'm not going to use it!"

A loud 'clack' caused Tyler to duck and spin around. The garage door began to rise and the car headlights forced Tyler and Sarah to shield their eyes. Tyler waited as Sarah waved and walked back into the house. "I have to go. My parents are home. Bring the board to school and we'll figure out what to do with it then. Call me later." He clicked off the power button and wedged the phone into his back pocket.

He smiled broadly as Kelly jumped out of the car. Kelly said, "I have to pee-pee!" Tyler giggled at his sister as she ran past him into the kitchen. Tyler opened his mother's door, leaned in and kissed her on the cheek.

"Well, a kiss. Thank you, Tyler." She got out of the car. "Did you and Sarah have dinner?"

"Yeah, Sarah brought Chinese."

"Well, that was nice of her."

"Yes, it was."

Matthew got out and opened the trunk. "Did everything go all right, Tyler? How was your weekend?"

Tyler paused. "Yes, sure, Dad. Everything was absolutely unbelievable."

His father gave him a strange glance and said, "Hmmm, can you help me with these paintings, please?" He beckoned him over with his finger.

Tyler walked over to the trunk, looked inside and gave his father a puzzled look. He walked around and opened the rear side door, checked the back seat, came back out and asked, "What paintings?"

"Exactly," his father said, smiling. He folded his arms and pointed at his mother who clapped her hands and hopped up and down, excitedly. "I sold them all, isn't that fantastic?" She was giddy.

Tyler smiled. "That's awesome, Mom, congratulations." He took a suitcase that his father handed to him, went into the kitchen, and set it on the washing machine and dryer. He huffed. "What do you have in that thing, rocks?"

Matthew closed the door and went into the foyer to put away their coats. Tyler was far too obvious with the concerned glance he shot in his father's direction as Matthew walked away into the hallway. Linda placed her hand on Tyler's shoulder. "Honey, are you okay? You seem distracted."

Tyler clutched the front of his head. "Yeah, I just have a headache, it's bothering me, that's all."

"Well, why don't you go lie down and get some rest? I'm sure you've had a very busy weekend." Tyler went into the living room and sat down on the sofa. Sarah threw away the takeout bags and washed the dishes.

Minutes later, Mathew, Kelly and Sarah came down into the living room. Linda followed with five cups of steaming hot cocoa. Kelly lay down on the floor with her coloring books and crayons and began coloring. Linda handed everyone their cup, sat down and took a sip. She smiled. "Now, that's good." She rubbed the back of Tyler's neck and he closed his eyes in satisfaction. "The bed-and-breakfast was gorgeous. The owner was so excited, he asked me to help him hang the paintings."

"Mom, that's fantastic," Sarah said as she sat on the hearth.

"It sure is," Matthew added. "That pretty much cleans us out, too." He nudged his wife with his elbow. "You'd better start painting some more. Maybe I can quit my job if this keeps up," he chuckled. "There are plenty of bed-and-breakfasts to decorate."

Linda scoffed and said, "Don't count on it, honey. There are plenty of starving artists out there."

"You are certainly not starving, darling," Matthew countered.

Tyler set his cocoa down and lay down across from Kelly. She giggled as Tyler watched her color. "Are you going to be an artist like Mom?" Kelly giggled.

Tyler's interest in Kelly wasn't missed by his parents. They looked at each other and smiled, but they wisely said nothing.

After a short while, Matthew stood up and said, "Well, I've been sitting in the car for hours and I need to go work out the kinks in the Jacuzzi."

"That sounds like a wonderful idea," Linda said. They went upstairs together.

Kelly spent the next hour drawing and coloring. Tyler and Sarah kept her company. It was more like a 'watch,' Tyler knew, but he would watch her as long as it took until he was confident that she was in no danger. Sarah read her magazines with one eye on Kelly also.

Later, Matthew came down in his robe and poured out the remains of his cocoa. He stopped halfway across the kitchen. "Whew! Did either of you take out the garbage? It stinks to high heaven." He looked into the living room. "Son?"

"Huh?" Tyler turned to face him.

"Can you please take the garbage out? It reeks."

He felt paralyzed. "Sure, Dad, I'll take care of it." Sarah returned his gaze with a look of utter concern.

"Thanks," he said. He stopped on the landing and reached his hand out. "Come on, Kelly, time for bed." Kelly grunted and put her crayon down. She rolled over and ran to her father.

As Kelly and Matthew headed upstairs, Tyler took the garbage bag out of the tall white garbage can in the kitchen. He sniffed and didn't notice any bad smells. He looked inside and saw nothing but the Chinese food cartons inside. He walked toward the door. Sarah opened it for him and stood there with her hands on her hips. Out in the garage, Tyler took off the garbage can lid and froze. He stood there paralyzed with the garbage bag in one hand and the lid in the other. He moaned, "Not again!"

"What is it?" Sarah asked.

Tyler set the bag on the floor, turned to face her, and tilted the can toward her, so that she could see. "The Ouija board is back." Sarah gasped. Tyler put the garbage bag on top of it and sealed the lid on tight. "I've got to call Jimmy!" He ran past Sarah, searching the kitchen for the phone. He ran into the living room searching for it. He wheeled around toward his sister. "Sarah, where is the phone?"

She rolled her eyes and waved him toward her. "Come here." He came closer. She held out her index finger, pointed it toward the ground, spun her hand around in circles and said, "Turn around, Tyler."

"What for?" he asked, obviously upset and in no mood for games.

She became very stern and frustrated. "Do it!"

Tyler turned around and asked, "What for?"

He felt the tug at his pocket and then he remembered he'd forced it in his pocket when his parents startled him as they drove in earlier. "Oh, yeah," he said. He snatched it from Sarah's hand and dialed. Sarah laughed.

Jimmy answered, "Hello?"

"Jimmy!"

"Yeah?"

"The Ouija board is back in my garbage can!"

"Huh? Are you serious? Are you sure?"

"Yes, I'm sure," he insisted.

"Hang on, let me check my bag."

Tyler paced the room. He couldn't believe this was happening. Jimmy's frightened voice answered. "Dude, it's gone!"

"Gone from your house, but now it's back in mine."

"I'll call Kyle," Jimmy said. "I'll get back to you."

The dial tone was long and terrible. Tyler huffed and puffed. He held his forehead and rubbed the back of his neck. Sarah reached out and squeezed her brother's shoulders. They stood alone in the kitchen. He hung up the phone very slowly and dragged his feet down the hallway. Tyler looked and felt totally defeated and asked, "What are we going to do?"

"Just let the garbage men take it away in the morning, that's all we can do," Sarah replied.

With renewed strength and conviction, Tyler stormed into the garage, slipped on his shoes, hit the garage door opener, grabbed the garbage can and hauled it off up the driveway to the curb. Sarah followed slowly and stopped at the edge of the garage and watched her brother.

Tyler scanned the road and visualized the garbage truck coming by in the morning and taking the Ouija board away forever. He looked up at the night sky. He stared at the stars. 'Surely there had to be some help from somewhere that could overpower the spirits in the house and rid them of this nightmare,' he thought. He felt alone. He felt afraid.

He walked to the garage and Sarah hugged him and said, "Let's check on Kelly." When they got upstairs, they peeked inside Kelly's room. The light must have frightened her, because she sat up in her bed and said, "Don't scare me, Tyler."

Tyler's heart sank. He decided at that moment that he would never tease or try to frighten his little sister ever again. "I'm not going to scare you, Kelly. I'm just making sure you're all right."

Sarah and Tyler stood in the doorway for a minute or so, staring at their little sister until Kelly finally felt comfortable enough to lie back down. When she smiled, Tyler said, "Good night, Kelly." He closed the door quietly.

Monday mornings at the McLaughlin household had a history of being hectic and hurried. And that was comforting to Tyler for the first time in his life. After finishing his morning shower, he came out of the bathroom with a bath towel wrapped around his waist. Sarah whisked by him and raced into the bathroom.

"Did anything abnormal happen to you last night?" Tyler asked.

"No, thank God. If this ghost has any wits, he's long gone by now. Nothing messes with Dad, living or dead," she said. They heard a faint hissing sound.

Tyler cocked an ear and listened intently.

Kelly ran out of her room, holding her stuffed bunny under her arm. Sarah peered around the corner from the bathroom and watched her until she disappeared downstairs. When she went into her room, she looked out the window and noticed the big green garbage truck rolling by. She exhaled in relief. "Tyler."

Tyler answered, "Yeah?" He stood in the doorway to see his sister pointing out the window. He walked into her room and gazed out the window. "Man, I sure hope that's the last time we will ever see that damned thing."

Chapter 12 – Braving the Depths

KYLE AND JIMMY were leaning against the brick wall outside the gym, where all the kids go to smoke, when Tyler rounded the corner. None of them smoked, however. They knew the risks. They weren't stupid. In fact, they made a point to give an earful to anyone they saw smoking.

"Hey, guys," Tyler said.

"How's Spook Central?" Jimmy inquired.

"Oh, that's very funny."

"Sorry, man. We were just talking about how weird you are anyway, and that this probably happened because of that very same weirdness," Kyle said. Tyler sneered, and Kyle and Jimmy backed away.

"Look out! He's possessed!" Jimmy warned.

Tyler giggled and said, "The garbage truck came this morning and took that evil freaking board away—finally."

The pre-class bell rang. Jimmy threw his arm around Tyler's shoulder, and they headed for the doors. The halls were crowded. By the time they reached their lockers, all three conveniently located within ten yards of each other, the class bell was already ringing. Tyler opened his locker, reached deep inside and pulled out his history book. They all leaped backwards when the Ouija board rolled out of the locker and produced a solid 'clap' when it hit the tiled floor.

"Oh, my God," Tyler screamed. Kyle and Jimmy rushed over and gazed down at it in horror.

"What the hell?" Jimmy asked.

"Jesus, this is bad!" Jimmy turned around full-circle. He

pointed at the floor. "You...you didn't put that there, did you?"

Tyler shook his head and said, "Definitely not! Sarah and I saw the garbage truck take it away this morning."

"Yeah, well, obviously *it* knew that the board would be taken away too," Kyle said.

"What are you saying, Kyle? That the board knew it would be taken away?" Tyler asked.

"No, I'm saying that the ghost knew, so it put it in your locker," Kyle said. "Think about it. It obviously wants us to use it again."

Jimmy asked, "Why would you think that, Kyle?"

"Because when Tyler put it in the garbage can and refused to use it again, the ghost moved it to Jimmy's house, hoping that he'd use it there."

"Oh, that actually makes sense," Tyler said. "He's right."

"Exactly," Kyle said, nodding.

The class bell rang. Wild classmates walked past them in herds. "I don't want to hear any more," Jimmy said.

"Well," Kyle replied, "maybe it doesn't care what we want. Maybe it won't go away until it says what it wants to say."

"We have to use it again," Tyler said. He knelt down, picked up the board and began unzipping Jimmy's bag.

"Oh, that's just great!" Jimmy said. "If that's what it wants us to do, it's not a good idea at all!"

"And Jimmy is the one who is supposed to ask the questions," Tyler continued.

"Huh?" Jimmy asked. "Why am I the one who is supposed to ask the questions?"

"It showed up at your house. You're the one it wants to talk to," Kyle said.

Jimmy laughed, more out of surprise than anything else. He pointed at Tyler. "It's in your locker now! You're the one who's supposed to be doing the talking!"

"Guys, we're going to be late!" Kyle said.

"Yeah," Tyler added. "We'll be more screwed if we're late than if we don't show up at all." Kyle nodded.

Tyler slammed his locker and turned toward the stairs. "Let's go!"

Jimmy asked, "Where to?"

"To the abandoned wrestling room, dummy!" Tyler said. "We have to be in a quiet place to use this damn thing."

As much as they wanted to refuse, Kyle and Jimmy moaned and followed Tyler downstairs into the basement and the secret passage into the older part of the school, which was sealed off after the flooding and cave-ins during the Blizzard of '78.

Tyler peeled a piece of old rubber matting away from an antiquated, rusted door hidden behind it. He reached through a small section of glass conveniently broken years earlier by other students and unlocked the door from the inside.

A long creaking sound echoed throughout the stair well as the door opened. Kyle and Jimmy coughed loudly to conceal the noise of the metal door as best they could. They all passed through, closed the door, and the rubber matting folded back into place on its own as it had done for the small number of students who knew of this secret hiding place.

Dank, musty smells, sudden blackness, and shadows cast by peeling paint, hanging ceiling fixtures and wiring lent a sense of gloom to the abandoned halls. A sudden flicker of light penetrated the darkness and was joined by two others. The boys' faces radiated with eerie luminescence. Here, walking through the darkness, unable to see one foot away from the feeble light of each of their cigarette lighters, each of them felt vulnerable and afraid.

'What are we doing?' Tyler thought. 'After the Ouija board suddenly appeared, then disappeared in my house, and then reappeared in my locker, why are we thinking of using it again? Why are we doing it in absolute darkness and in a place where no one would ever think to look for us if something bad happened to us?'

Kyle kept to himself, though Tyler knew that he was imagining fates worse than those that the likes of Stephen King and Clive Barker combined could concoct.

Tyler could still smell the sweat and musk cologne of the old football players and wrestlers who had earned the school a reputation for athletic excellence. Lockers, abandoned after the school board condemned this level of the school, had been left unopened for decades, and the students who used this part of the school never risked making the noise that forcing them open would generate. They passed silently down the hallway. When they reached the downward gradient in the floor, they knew that they were almost there.

They stopped before a gaping hole in the floor. It nearly consumed the entire ramp that sloped down into the gymnasium. Naturally, it had been covered over, but in recent years, the students had reopened it. The hole was the perfect place to toss things...things they didn't want to get caught with...especially, if they were ever discovered by the teachers while they were doing things they knew they shouldn't be doing.

Jimmy went first, inching his way along the narrow ledge while hugging the wall. He started to slip and grabbed at the rough brick. "Jesus!"

Out of the darkness came Kyle's voice. "Watch it, man! Don't fall!"

Seconds seemed like minutes. He heard Jimmy's sneakers clap when he leaped onto the floor beyond the hole. A sudden flame appeared across the hole. Jimmy had made it. Kyle's lighter flickered in the darkness. Tyler waited in the void. He heard Kyle's panting. "Let's go," Kyle said. "It's your turn."

The light became brighter, and when Tyler could see the ledge, he leaned back against the wall in a sweat. The jagged hole in the floor stretched almost five feet across. No one knew just how far down it went. Some say it was a sinkhole just waiting to get larger.

Tyler thought about that freshman boy who fell to his death when the hole opened up beneath him. That was one terrible day, because school was being let out early due to the approaching storm. The fire department spent three days trying to find his body. They finally gave up and sealed off access to the hole.

"Tyler, come on. We don't have all day," Jimmy said. Tyler didn't look down. He slid across the ledge, slowly. At last, he made it to the other side.

After the town leveled the school in the summer of 1979, they built the new one on top of what was left of the first floor, now sunken into the ground. Tyler thought of that boy again. His face on the placard in the office hung in his mind. He knew that none of them ever crossed that pit without thinking of the kid that fell into the abyss.

The fact that Tyler knew—and felt that neither of his friends appreciated—was that they were somewhere that few people in the new school had ever been. They were in 'the place' where it happened. 'Was that boy's ghost here too, hovering somewhere in these dark halls, or was he somewhere down below in that bottomless pit?'

"Tyler!" Kyle yelped. Tyler snapped back to reality and quickly said goodbye to the boy below, wherever he may be, and inched his way across to the others.

Tyler and Jimmy were waiting in the old wrestling room. It was the only room they found that still had power. The halogen lamps whined, and Tyler sat down beside his friends. He set the Ouija board down, and then threw his hands into the air. "We don't have the reader-thing."

"Use a coin," Kyle said with confidence. "It'll slide over the letters just as easy as a cheap plastic ring." He fished into his pocket and slid a quarter onto the board.

"Who's going to use it, then?" Jimmy asked. "We can't

all put our hands on it like we could on the planchette. The quarter is too small."

Tyler placed his index fingers on the quarter. "I'll do it!" He closed his eyes. There was a long silence as Tyler cleared his mind and concentrated. "Are any spirits with us now?" Tyler asked. No one moved. Tyler repeated the question. Jimmy and Kyle watched intently, wishing that no response would come. If there were no response, there would be no more concern. "Tell us if you are here. Give us some sign," Tyler begged.

The quarter began moving, sliding erratically. The quarter slid over to the word 'Hello.' It was so clear and so instantaneous—it was if someone actually said it. Tyler cleared his throat and asked, "Who are you?" The quarter slid along in circles.

"B.," Kyle said.

"R. O.," Jimmy added.

"C. K.," Kyle said.

Tyler snorted and asked, "Brock?"

The quarter slid over to the word 'Yes' in the corner of the board. "Where are you?" Tyler continued.

"H.E.L.L." The boys froze. The hair on the back of their necks stood straight up.

"Great," Kyle said. "He's from hell! Can it get any more creeptastically classic than that?"

"Well...why are you a ghost?" Jimmy asked. The quarter slid over the letters until it spelled the word 'NOTGOST.'

"Guys," Kyle said. "What does that mean?"

"I don't know, Kyle," Tyler replied. He looked down at the board and then into the air and asked, "How did you die?"

"B.U.S."

Kyle chuckled. "You got killed by a bus? Way to go, loser." Kyle leaned back and giggled. "Freaking guy got killed by a bus!"

"Brock, are you here for Kelly?" Tyler asked. The quarter slid to the word 'No.'

"Whew!" Jimmy felt relieved.

Tyler straightened up. "Well, then." He glanced at his friends. "Who are you here for, now?"

"A.L.L."

The boys leapt to their feet. "Oh, shit!" Jimmy said. "That explains why it was in my bag and then in your locker. This bastard wants a piece of everybody."

Kyle knelt down and grabbed the board. "He's gonna push us down the hole!"

The quarter slid over to the word 'Yes.'

"Let's get outta here," Jimmy said.

"He's gonna push us down the hole," Kyle said again. They all heard a laughter that sent chills up their spines. Then they felt a sudden rush of chilling air sweep past them.

"Whose stupid idea was this, anyway?" Kyle asked. "Now we're trapped. He's gonna kill us!" The quarter kept making circles around the word 'Yes.' Kyle snatched the Ouija board and the quarter bounced and clinked along the floor. It rolled down the gymnasium. Kyle ran through the doors and threw the Ouija board down into the bottomless hole in the floor.

"What did you do that for?" Jimmy asked.

The quarter struck the far wall and toppled over. Tyler, Kyle, and Jimmy stood by the hole and gazed down into the void—down deep, where bugs crawl, and worms silently slither in suffocating darkness.

"A diversion," Kyle said, determined. He inched his way along the wall and made it to the other side. "C'mon, you guys. Let's go."

Jimmy looked terrified. He slid against the wall face first, clutching the creases in the wall as if he had steel claws that were able to penetrate the cement blocks for support.

Tyler rushed up beside him. "Hurry, Jim!" He wiped the sweat off his palms and onto his jeans. Jimmy leaped toward Kyle on the far side. Tyler shuffled across the narrow five-inch-wide ledge as quickly as possible. A cold wind swept past him and startled him. Then, he lost his balance. His friends stood there in shock, wide-eyed in terror. They reached for him, but it was too late. Tyler lunged forward and slapped his palms against the cold tile floor beyond the hole, but his legs dropped inside.

"Tyler!" Kyle leaped forward, grabbed his wrist, and tugged as hard as he could.

Kyle had him. Then, part of the edge under their arms gave way. Tyler dropped and dug his fingers into the crevices between the cement blocks, where the aged mortar and paint had crumbled away. He whimpered. He would fall into bottomless blackness and endless sludge where ugly things and the reeking bones of the dead teenager lay, crushed into nothing. And there, at the bottom, in the blackest pitch, the ghost of a man named Brock and whatever else was waiting for him would tear at his flesh for all eternity.

"Hang on, Tyler!" Jimmy whipped his belt over toward him. He held the other end securely in his fists. Tyler snatched the belt with both hands and dug his foot into a crack in the wall. The wind swept by again until it seemed as if it were forming into a whirling cyclone. Tyler moaned in exhaustion as he inched higher. Kyle caught Tyler's shirt and tugged. Then, he grabbed the belt loops in Tyler's jeans and hauled him back toward them. Tyler collapsed on the cold tile floor, holding his bleeding forearm.

"I thought I was gonna die!"

They sat on the floor looking at each other, panting. "Let's get outta here," Jimmy roared. They rushed down the unlit hallway, yanked the door open, pushed the padding away, walked out, closed the door, reached in, locked it and dashed up the stairs. The padding on the outside gently folded back over the door. The boys dashed up the stairs to join the other teens who were rushing off to their next class.

"You saved my life! I don't even know what could have happened to me if I fell into that hole."

"We are never going down there again," Kyle said. "It is way too dangerous, spirits or not."

Jimmy looked at Tyler's arm. "Dude, you'd better go to the nurse."

"Okay," Tyler nodded. "Meet up at lunch."

They hurried off in separate directions under the ominous clanging of the class bell.

Chapter 13 – Calling Names

WITH HER STEAMING coffee cup in one hand and the cordless phone in the other, Linda McLaughlin entered her art studio off to the side of the kitchen. She set down her things, closed the glass French door, and smiled in anticipation of three hours of uninterrupted painting. She slid a new canvas onto the easel and sat down on her antique shaker-built stool that she'd found at an estate sale in Westport. After several minutes of mixing her oils, she finally dabbed her brush into the paint. Just as she made her first stroke, she thought she heard someone call out her name. She spun around on her stool and checked the four corners of her studio. She heard her name again, though this time it was more pronounced.

"Linda." The aged, female voice seemed distant, though frighteningly nearby.

"Who's there?" She glanced at the security panel to see if Julie might have stopped by, but she saw nothing at all that was out of place or unusual.

"Linda." The voice came from behind her.

"Who are you? What do you want?" She spun around, jumped off her stool and backed into the corner of the room. Then she felt the slightest pressure against her arm. The tingling felt like an insect crawling along the length of her forearm. She quickly pushed up her sleeve, fully expecting to find an ant or even worse—a spider. She checked her arm and found nothing.

A faint hissing laughter came from nowhere, and then

she felt three short, spine-tingling breaths like someone were blowing into her ear. She squeezed her paintbrush tightly, held it in the air like a dagger and demanded, "Who's there?"

The rays of sunlight that found their way past the curtain and into the room were suddenly and completely snuffed out like a dark cloud had settled over the house. A chilling breeze swept in and completely surrounded her. She shivered in fear and then lunged toward the door. It was warmer there, as if she'd passed out of an air-conditioned space into one that was room temperature.

"Linda."

She screamed and fumbled with the door. The handle wouldn't turn. She said, "Jesus help me!" She banged on the door and pleaded, "Help me!" She shook the door handle violently, twisting and turning, banging on the frame with her palm. "Help me!" The glass panes in the door began to fog up. She could see her own panting breath forming a fine mist. She turned quickly, and stood with her back against the door, so she could face the unseen terror that would not stop calling her name.

"Linda."

Then, through the mist that hung heavily in the air, she saw the phone on the shelf by the door that she had set it on earlier. She had to call Matt. She reached out toward the phone. She felt the cold air on her fingertips as if she had entered a freezing sphere. It was like being instantly frostbitten.

"Linda."

Her heart pounded as she jerked her hand back. Then she lunged for the phone. As she grabbed it, she heard her name coming from above.

"Linda."

She felt as though her heart would explode through her ribs. She focused on the illuminated keypad, barely distinguishable in the thickening mist. She pressed the speed dial. At the precise moment that it began to ring, the door opened on its own. Linda stumbled into the kitchen, holding the phone firmly against her ear. She spun around, closed the door and pressed all of her weight against it.

Behind her in the misty room she heard her name being called again. When she looked back, she saw a hand pressed against the glass. She backed away in terror. "What do you want? Get out of my house!"

"Matthew McLaughlin's Office. Hello."

She moved deeper into the kitchen. "Yes, Matthew McLaughlin, please."

"Hold, please."

Linda looked at the door to the studio, where she usually checked all of her worries and concerns. She felt sudden refuge in the calm sound of her husband's voice. "Linda, what's the matter?"

"Matt! There's someone in the house!"

"What?"

"I couldn't see her, but I heard her voice. I mean, she wasn't there. There's something in the house."

"Linda, you're not making any sense. Are you all right? Who is in the house? Tell me what's going on."

"I think Kelly was right. I think she did see a ghost, and I think it followed us home. There's a ghost in our house." She explained what happened, and when she finished, there was a long pause.

"Linda Tanner!" It was her maiden name and the one that Matthew used only when he was clearly upset with her.

"Matt!" Linda pleaded. "Please come home!"

"I can't just leave work when I want to, Linda! I have three closings today. Just don't go back into the studio until I get home to check it out, okay? Have Julie come over to stay with you. I'll be home right after work. And call me if anything else happens. I have a meeting now. I have to go. Okay? Linda?"

She pulled the receiver away from her face and stared at it in disbelief. She was alone. Something terrible was happening in the house, and no one—not even her own husband—was coming to help her. "I can't stay here." She clicked off the phone. "I can't, and I won't."

Chapter 14 – Meeting Challenges

LINDA GRABBED HER coat and scarf and ran out the front door. She was thankful that Tyler had left the car parked outside. She slid the key into the ignition and started the car before her door was even closed. She looked around, and when satisfied that nothing seemed to have followed her, she hit the gas pedal, checking her rear view mirror as she sped away. Light snowflakes fell with enough force that she switched on her wipers and headlights. She clutched the steering wheel tightly and when she realized just how tightly, she finally loosened up. She fumbled with the radio. Unable to find a station, she opened the center console for a cassette and slid it in.

She drove and drove, going through the thoughts in her mind and all of the terrible, bizarre events that she had just experienced. When she came out of her daze, she realized that she'd driven all the way into Westport. She pulled over when she saw a pay phone. She got out and dialed. No one answered, but she cursed when she got the answering machine. When the tone came, she practically screamed, "Julie, this is Linda, please pick up!"

Just then, Julie did pick up and replied, "Hello, Linda? I'm here."

"Thank God! Can you meet me for lunch? It's very important."

"Certainly. What's the matter?"

"I have to tell you in person. I'm near Bertucci's Restaurant in Westport. I'll go there, have a cup of coffee and wait for you."

"All right. I know where that is. I'll get my coat and come right away."

Linda got into her car and waited at the traffic light. She exhaled and closed her eyes. A car horn startled her. The light had turned green, and she'd held up a few cars behind her. She waved at the car behind her apologetically.

She drove down the road, pulled into the parking lot, and found an open space relatively close to the main entrance. She slammed the door and hurried over to the restaurant entrance.

The hostess greeted Linda with a smile as she passed through the front doors. "Good afternoon. Are you dining alone or are you expecting company?" she asked.

"Two, please. I'll need a table for two."

"Right this way, please," the hostess answered.

It was warm and delicious-smelling inside as Linda followed the hostess. The young lady smiled and extended a hand. "Will this suffice?"

Linda smiled and took a seat. "It's perfect, thank you. I'd love some coffee, please."

"I'll tell your waiter." She smiled and walked away briskly to greet the next customers.

Linda sat alone in the booth for close to thirty minutes. She stared longingly out the window. She was so lost in her daydream that when she looked down she saw her cup of coffee sitting there and didn't even notice who had delivered it. She tapped her nails against the table. She looked around to see if she could find the server, but there was no sign. She looked at her watch. It had been over forty-five minutes since she had spoken to Julie. She had an uncomfortable feeling in the pit of her stomach. She was growing more and more worried. She grasped the coffee mug tightly to warm her unusually cold hands. Then, she raised the cup and pressed it against her cheek. When she looked out of the window, she saw Julie's blue and red hat as she was walking into the restaurant.

Relieved, she sat up straight, set down her mug, and adjusted her silverware so that it was neatly arranged. Julie walked up and smiled. Her glasses had drops of water on them. She pulled her hat off and whisked away the snow that was rapidly melting.

"I got here as quickly as I could. Have we ever had this much snow in October?" She took off her beige trench coat and slid in across from Linda. "Now what on earth is the matter?"

"What on Earth, indeed?"

Julie looked puzzled. She folded her coat neatly and then remembered her scarf. "This has something to do with the ghostly experience that dear Kelly had, doesn't it?"

Linda nodded and asked, "Julie, you take me for a reasonable, sane woman, don't you?"

Her friend chuckled. "Yes, of course I do." She watched Linda take a sip of coffee as the waiter approached—a handsome young man in his early twenties with a bright smile.

Julie smiled, "Coffee, please, with cream, and a refill for my friend, here." The waiter nodded and silently walked away.

Linda gazed deep into Julie's eyes for several long moments. She saw that Julie was becoming uncomfortable. "There *is* a ghost in my house, Julie. There is no doubt in my mind. The things that have gone on have been simply terrible."

Julie sat back. In fact, she sat back as far as she could. She winced, looked away, paused and cocked her head. She said nothing. She pulled off her glasses and cleaned them with her napkin. After a minute, she slid them back onto her face and blinked several times without speaking a word and finally said, "Honey..."

Linda raised her hand. "Yes, I know what you're thinking. This is Halloween, but I am quite serious, and I am very frightened."

Julie reached out to hold Linda's hands. Linda placed them inside of her friend's hands who cupped them warmly. "You're sure?"

"Kelly saw him the other day, and as I said earlier, I didn't believe her, Julie. I scolded her because I was ignorant, and so help me...it scared me as much as it scared her that first day. But I don't know who to turn to for comfort. I can't fight something I can't see or touch, but it can certainly touch me!"

"Oh, Linda, I don't know what to say, other than I will help as best I can, you know that." She made an odd expression and asked, "Wait, it...*touched* you?"

"Yes, it touched me. It is too awful to describe. It focused around Kelly first, but now it seems to be after me. I can handle it being after me, but not my little girl. Not my little Kelly. I'm afraid to alarm the kids. I called Matt after I was attacked this morning. Even he doesn't believe me."

The waiter handed the coffee mug to Julie. "What can I get you for lunch, ladies?"

"We still need a few minutes, please," Linda said. The waiter nodded and backed away.

Julie inched closer to Linda and whispered. "Well, you know Matt. He is so serious. I'd never expect him to believe ghost stories."

"You know I don't believe that they're just stories, Julie. But you're right. He won't accept it until there is hard evidence. But how can there be hard evidence when there is nothing material to see?"

"What are you going to do?"

"I'm going to take you to the bookstore after lunch, so we can go find some answers," Linda said.

"Oh, that's a splendid idea. I'm sure they have some good books, probably still on display or on sale or something."

Linda smiled. Sales never concerned her. She'd come from money and married a wealthy man. But in this case, all of the money in the world wouldn't help her. "Can we go together after lunch, then?"

Julie smiled and patted her hand. "Let's order, and then I want to hear this story from the beginning. Then, we will go find some books together, of course."

Bright lights and the scents of rich chocolate and brewing coffee are quite welcome when one comes in from gray, gloomy outdoors. Such was the case as Linda and Julie passed through the mahogany doors of Barnes and Noble Booksellers after lunch. Patrons sat in oversized chairs, sipping mochas and lattes, perusing the latest magazine or best-seller, or roaming through the store for something that jumped out at them. Linda walked up to the central kiosk where an elderly gentleman stood proudly amidst a stack of new releases. He nodded to them and said, "Good afternoon, ladies. How can I help you?"

Linda set her purse on the counter. "Hello, sir. We're looking for books on ghosts." The man pointed toward the Halloween display. Linda scowled. "Non-fiction, please!"

The man raised a brow and pointed down the aisle. "Three rows back and two over, in the New Age section."

"Thank you!" Linda took Julie by the hand as they walked away. "Ghosts have been rumored for centuries, so what's so 'New Age' about that?" Julie giggled.

Linda rounded the corner and walked into a wall of some of the latest books on real haunting phenomena and on the world's most famous ghosts and ghost hunters.

"Oh my, there certainly a lot of them, aren't there?" Julie said, scanning the shelves.

Linda immediately pulled two books off the shelf and said, "I'm going to have a look at these. You pick out some that you think are appropriate."

Julie pressed her glasses further up onto her nose. She leaned over and squinted. "Oh, my..."

Over the next two hours, they studied several books on ghosts and the supernatural. Finally, Linda stood up. "I'm going to buy these three." She looked down at her friend who was reading a book intently. She looked completely mesmerized. "Julie, did you hear what I said?" She didn't flinch. "Julie," she giggled. Linda looked around her to see if anyone was close by that would be disturbed with what she planned to do next. She made sure to raise her voice and said, "Earth to Julie Marsh!" Julie nearly leaped out of her chair. She clutched her chest. Linda buckled over laughing. "I'm...I'm sorry," she said. "Oh, Julie, I needed this laugh." She calmed down and leaned in over toward her friend. "I'm going to buy these three." She displayed them for her to see. "Have you found anything good? I'll buy those, too, and let you go over them at your leisure."

"Oh, now, I don't know, Linda. This one is very interesting, to be sure."

"May I?" she asked, reaching for it. She examined the front cover, and then flipped it over and read the back cover. "Yes, let's get this one, too. Anything else?"

When they got to the counter, a young girl greeted them and began ringing them up. "Oh, this is a good one," she said. "It's really scary!"

"May we have two bags, please?" Linda separated the books into two stacks. Once she had placed them into separate bags, she handed one to Julie and smiled.

Linda fumbled with her wallet and handed her American Express card to the cashier. She studied her friend. "Let's see if we can come up with anything useful. We can compare notes tomorrow at lunch."

"Okay," Julie said.

Crisp winds hindered their passage to the cars, but at least they were parked side by side. Linda hated to leave Julie's company, but she knew that Julie had best get home because she hated driving in the dark. Linda came over and gave Julie a hug. "Thank you, and thank you for believing me."

"I'm your friend," Julie said. "We'll get to the bottom of this."

They waved at each other as they got into their cars and parted ways.

When Linda pulled in, she saw Matt's BMW in the garage. He must have just gotten home. She stepped out of her car with a bag as Matthew opened the door to greet her. She rushed over and hugged him. "Oh, Matt, it was terrible."

"Honey," he replied gently. "What's going on? I've walked through the entire house, and I have seen nothing at all out of the ordinary."

She took him by the hand. "Come on. I'll show you."

Linda put her bag down on the kitchen table, led Matthew toward her studio and opened the door. Matthew gave her an unsure look and walked inside. Linda peeked around the corner and followed him. The temperature was normal. The air was clear. And there were no voices. When she finished her explanation, Matthew led her out of the room. She knew that he was convinced that nothing was wrong that couldn't be explained by natural causes. Linda pressed her hands to her face and began to cry.

He held her. "Linda, please. Everything's all right." She sobbed and went over the events in her mind again.

"I heard my name, Matt!"

"Linda, come on," Matthew pleaded.

"I heard my name, several times."

"Linda, everything in here is normal. There are no cold drafts. There is no whispering, or laughing going on. Now, please, you're going to scare the kids." He went back into the kitchen.

Linda came up from behind, grabbed his arm, and

forced him to turn and face her. She scowled. "I...was scared," she said. "I am scared right now." They locked eyes. "Look," she said, opening her bag and dumping the books onto the counter. "Julie and I went to the bookstore today."

Matthew walked closer and turned the books over. He scoffed and said, "*The Demonologist*? *The Devil in Connecticut*? *The Unquiet Dead*? Linda, what the hell is this? Are you serious?"

Linda read the back cover aloud, "A chilling story of demonic infestation." She looked at him and shook her head. "What the hell, indeed?"

"Demonic infestation? Jesus, Linda! What's happened to you?"

The garage door began to rumble open. "The kids are home." He pointed at Linda, became quite serious and said, "Put those away, right now!" He looked up at the ceiling, put his hands on his hips, and paced the room. "Demonic infestation...you have got to be kidding me."

Linda put the books in the bag and hung it on the hook behind the door as Tyler and Sarah came in carrying pumpkins. Kelly smiled warmly. "Look, we got punkins." She held out a small gourd and said, "I got a baby punkin." She giggled. "Can we make jacker-lanterns?"

Linda was in no mood for pumpkin carving. "Oh, gosh, they make such a mess."

Kelly said, "Please?"

"Okay, you can carve them in the garage. Tyler, lay down some newspaper." Tyler and Sarah huffed and walked back out into the garage and set them down on the counter top. They came back in and closed the door.

Tyler went to take off his sweatshirt and took special care around his arm to protect his wound. Linda saw the bloody gash on her son's forearm and asked, "Tyler, what did you do to your arm, honey?"

"I dove to catch a football, that's all. It's no big deal,"

Tyler said. He looked at the kitchen and didn't see anything cooking. "What's for dinner?"

"That's Tyler. He's all right," Matthew said.

Tyler laughed and said, "Yeah." Then the doorbell rang. He froze.

Matthew pulled his wallet from his pants and walked down the hallway into the foyer. The unmistakable smell of fresh melted cheese pizza wafted through the hallway and when he returned with two boxes from Pizza Hut, it created smiles all around.

Chapter 15 – Laying Siege

AFTER DINNER, MATTHEW and Sarah were enjoying a game of chess in the living room while Tyler and Kelly carved the pumpkins in the garage to avoid making any mess inside the house. Linda couldn't gather the nerve to enter her studio and paint, despite her frustrated desire to continue with her piece. She sat at the kitchen table pretending to read a magazine while she secretly thumbed through some of the pages of the books that she'd purchased.

That was when the banging started with one soft 'boom.' At first, it was subtle, indistinct, like someone had dropped something onto the floor. Then it happened again. Linda scanned the ceiling. She was afraid to move. The third unexpected boom sent chills up her spine. Matthew looked up in shock. Sarah sat there with her mouth agape.

The banging gradually became louder and more pronounced. Tyler rushed into the kitchen panting and asked, "What is that?" Matthew stood. Three huge, successive booms sounded like someone with a sledge hammer was trying to break through the garage wall. Matthew quickly opened the door. Kelly stood there frozen in place. Tyler looked in and the banging continued. More booms came from the foyer. Linda peered down the dark, unlit hallway. Suddenly, a 'wa-boom' shook the banister, forcing everyone to jump back and look at each other. The walls showed no sign of physical manipulation, but the incredible noises made it sound like they were being battered.

Kelly crouched in the corner of the garage, crying, and holding her ears. Tyler ran in and grabbed her hand. It sounded like a construction site as they rushed into the living room. The entire family huddled together in the center. They held each other, jerking their heads in random directions as the banging seemed to shift origins and come from different parts of the house. Violent scratching made it seem like the walls were being ripped apart by meat hooks.

"What the hell is going on?" Matthew demanded. Sarah, Kelly and Linda held their ears, sobbing. Tyler and Matthew wrapped their arms around them.

"I told you. I told you," Linda warned.

Tyler stared at his mother in disbelief. "What, Mom? Told him what?"

Matthew roared, "All right! Everybody get out!" He grabbed Kelly and stormed down the foyer, followed by his trembling family. He opened the front door and they all quickly filed out.

They turned around together and stared in awe at the house. They heard the faint booming noises coming from inside. Suddenly, the banging stopped and the front door slammed shut before their terror-stricken eyes. There was no visible damage that was distinguishable from the outside.

The dark, starlit sky shone down on the fragile family as they vainly tried to gather strength from one other. Matthew checked every member of his family. He looked into their eyes and hugged them tightly. Then, he turned toward the house, gritted his teeth and started toward it.

A powerful booming sound forced him to leap back. He looked at his son in awe, then back at the house. He inched closer toward the door. His hands trembled. He looked at Tyler who bravely followed him, although he did so very slowly. Matthew reached for the doorknob and went to turn it. He screamed and yanked his hand back. "Ah, what in blazes?"

"Matt?" Linda screeched. "What's wrong?"

"The doorknob is red hot. I burned my hand!"

"Huh?" Tyler asked. He opened his father's hand and said, "Holy crap! This is insane!"

Matthew came back to the group that huddled together in the cold. Linda looked at his hand and gasped. It was blistering before her eyes. Remembering Kyle's brilliant save earlier, Sarah reached down and dumped a handful of snow in her father's open hand. He moaned in relief and said, "Good thinking, Sarah, that's my girl." Sarah and Tyler smiled at each other. Matthew pointed toward the driveway and waved the girls off. "Wait in the car!" Linda held Sarah and Kelly back.

Matthew and Tyler went back toward the door. Matthew took off his tie and wound it around his good hand. He reached for the knob and briefly touched it. He recoiled quickly out of reflex. He reached back to touch it and yanked it back instantly and did so again and a fourth time until he was sure it was cool enough to grasp it. He turned the knob and shoved the door open. It swung in slowly and hit the door stopper. Then it swung back and slammed shut instantly with such force that the oval glass pane in the center cracked. Matthew leaped back off the steps, knocking Tyler over in the process. Tyler landed in the grass, and his shoulder dug into the snow.

Matthew reached out for him and said, "Son, I'm sorry!"

Tyler lay in the snow looking up at his father. "Watch it, Dad, jeez!" He reached out and helped Tyler up, who shook the snow and slush off his jeans and shirt. He rubbed his shoulder. "They don't want us to go inside," Tyler said.

Matthew asked, "You think it could be several of them? But what exactly are they? This is not possible. C'mon." Matthew grabbed his son's shirt and tugged him toward the car. Matthew got into the driver's seat and Tyler got into the back with Sarah and Kelly. Kelly had her face buried in the cleft of Sarah's elbow and Sarah hugged her tightly.

Matthew started the engine, backed the car up, turned on the high beam headlights and just stared at the house in awe. He clicked the garage door opener and the door opened. He drove closer toward the garage and waited. Then he pulled in closer and opened the window. "I don't hear anything now." He opened the car door.

"Matt," Linda warned.

Sarah said, "Dad, don't go in there. Let's get out of here!"

"Get out of our own house? And go where, exactly?" Matthew got out and pressed his hand against the wall between the living room and the garage. He withdrew his hands and shook them.

"Hot?" Tyler asked.

"No," he replied. He examined his hand and looked at it, frustrated and perplexed. He shook it rapidly. "It's ice cold!"

Tyler got out of the car and tested the wall himself and said, "This is so wild!"

Matthew walked inside and opened the door to the basement. He flicked on the light switch and gave the girls an unsure glance. Linda called out to him from inside the car and said, "I don't think that's a good idea, Matt!" She shook her head from side to side. Matthew disappeared downstairs. The others waited for him, unsure and frightened for his safety.

After ten minutes of checking the walls, foundation, and supports in the basement, he walked up and looked at his family with a blank, expressionless stare. Tyler faced him with his arms crossed across his chest. "I can't explain it," Matthew said. Linda stormed into the kitchen and the others followed quickly. She took the book she had been reading from the table and shoved it into Matthew's hands.

"It can't be explained." Then she grabbed the bag off the hook on the door and dumped the other two books onto the kitchen table. "There might be an answer in these."

"Holy shit!" Tyler shouted. "*The Devil in Connecticut*?"

"Tyler," his father protested, "watch your language, please!"

Tyler scoffed and shouted, "I think we can safely say that foul language isn't the worst of our problems right now, don't you agree, Dad?" Christ on a cracker!" His eyes were practically bulging out of his head.

"Yes, we are in some *holy shit* right this very moment," Linda warned.

"You two and your language, please!" Kelly began to cry.

Matthew took Kelly and held her. "Everyone calm down, please. There's been a lot of talk about ghosts around here. Strange things have been happening to your mother."

Tyler gasped. He looked at Sarah who shook her head in disbelief and simply closed her eyes to shut out the obvious.

"I don't know what to say, because nothing like this has ever happened to me before. I can't explain them, but I want you to know something. And, never doubt this. I am your father, and I will find out what's happening here, and I will let nothing harm you or this house."

Tyler sat down and sank into one of the kitchen chairs. 'How can I tell them about the Ouija board? What have I done? Was any of this my fault?'

"Tyler," Matthew asked.

Tyler shook away his thoughts and fatigue. "Yes?"

"Go get the bug-out bags out of the basement and put them in the station wagon. Do it quickly and keep your head in the game." He locked eyes with the three girls and said, "Slowly and carefully make your way outside into the car. We are going to Grandma and Grandpa Tanner's."

The drive to Greenwich was uneventful and the family was met with disappointment when the housekeeper told Linda that her parents were in Europe for several weeks. Linda explained that their furnace had broken during the early evening. The housekeeper knew the family very well and welcomed them inside wholeheartedly. Everyone was relieved to be out of the house and into familiar and safe surroundings. Linda was relieved that she didn't have to tell her parents what was really happening. The housekeeper showed everyone to their rooms and made sure everyone was as comfortable as possible.

Throughout the night, fear and foreboding prevented anyone from getting any real sleep. Tyler spent most of his time talking to Jimmy and Kyle on the phone, all three boys nodding off on the other, and waking when one of the others asked whether they were still awake. Matthew and Linda held each other in bed, wishing that they could dismiss the occurrence earlier as a natural shift in the foundation or due to the pipes expanding, but it was plainly obvious that even though the supernatural was the last explanation that Matthew could rationally accept, he could no longer deny it.

Shortly before dawn, Tyler woke up when he heard a faint whispering. It was not in his room, but it was nearby. He sat up in his bed and listened. He swung his head around, searching for the sounds that suddenly came from nowhere. He flung the covers off and got out of bed. After walking around the bedroom and listening intently for the origins of the sounds, he gasped and realized that it was coming from next door. "Kelly!" He crept toward the room where his little sister was supposed to be sleeping. He opened the door slowly and silently, so he could see what was going on.

Kelly stood next to her bed in her pajamas, holding her hand out toward the edge of the bed, as if she were petting something. He heard the same strange whispers inside, but try as he did, he couldn't even come close to deciphering them. Outside the window, he saw nothing but darkness and shadows cast by the scraggly trees alongside the house. Kelly seemed to be deeply enthralled. Tyler gulped and called out into the darkness, "Kelly, who are you talking to?"

She spun around with a crazed smile. "Can you hear him, too?"

Tyler gasped. Then, hardened by the experiences he and his friends had with the ghost and the terrible secret he held within him, Tyler walked inside, knelt down and hugged his sister. "Kelly, are you talking to the ghost? He's not good. Don't talk to him!"

She sneered at him and shrieked in protest. "Let me go, Tyler! Let me go!" She squirmed in his grasp. Tyler, wanting to protect her, wanting so desperately to fight back at the thing interacting with her, felt completely and utterly helpless.

Matthew and Linda burst into the room. "Tyler!" Matthew yanked Tyler and Kelly apart and away from each other.

"Let me go," Kelly squealed.

"Tyler, what are you doing?" Linda pleaded.

"Leave her alone," Matthew demanded. "Are you crazy? Are you scaring her again?"

Tyler protested, "No!"

"Tyler, leave her alone!" Matthew said.

Kelly wedged herself into the corner of her bed against the wall. She looked at her brother and said, "He doesn't like Tyler."

Linda gulped. She and Matthew looked at each other uncomfortably. Linda drew closer and sat on the corner of the bed. "Who doesn't like Tyler?" Linda asked. She was afraid to hear the answer.

"Brock," Kelly answered.

Tyler wheeled around in complete terror. He felt the

beating of his heart pounding through his entire body. He fell against the wall and slid down, clutching the hair on each side of his head. "This can't be happening!"

Linda slid in next to Kelly and wrapped her arms around her. "Who is Brock, honey?" Linda asked. She turned Kelly to face her. She squeezed her face and pressed her hand against her cheek. "Who is he, honey?"

Kelly answered, "He's the man that followed me from the graveyard. He doesn't like Tyler cuz of when he tried to scare me. He says Tyler and his friends did stupid things."

Tyler sat against the wall. "Kelly, I'm not trying to scare you," he pleaded.

"You did try to scare your sister, Tyler, and you succeeded," Matthew said. "You don't remember your ghost prank the other night?"

"I was talking about this morning," he reasoned. "I heard whispering coming from Kelly's room here."

Linda gave Tyler a concerned look and held her daughter. She ran her fingers through Kelly's hair. "Tell me more about Brock, honey."

Kelly sat down on her bed. "He followed us cuz he thought I was a good girl and he could tell that I saw him. He's happy I can see him and can talk to him. Then, the other people came after he did. He wants them all to go away. He wants them to leave us alone so we can all be happy."

Matthew asked, "Other people?"

"Can you hear him, Kelly?" Linda asked. "Is he here now? Is he talking to you?"

"Yeah, he tells me funny things."

"Can you see him?" Tyler asked.

"This is ridiculous," Matthew said.

Linda spun around, scowled at her husband and said, "For God's sake, Matt! Wake up! We aren't all imagining this!"

"I see him," Kelly admitted. "Sometimes he looks silly."

She giggled. "He tries to make me laugh. He said my light looks pretty when I laugh."

"Can you see him now?" Matthew asked.

"Nope, he went away when you came in. But I can still hear him. He says bad words at the other people. I tell him he shouldn't say bad words. They fight a lot. I can hear them too, sometimes. A black kitty comes, too, and sits on my bed."

Matthew sat on the bed and extended his arms. "Come here, honey." Kelly slid over into the protective embrace of her father's arms.

Linda hugged her from behind. "Do they do anything to frighten or hurt you, Kelly?"

"No, they're really nice. They do tricks and make me laugh. But they tell me not to laugh out loud or someone will stop our fun."

"Stop your fun?" Matthew repeated. "That's it!" He pointed at thin air and said, "You stay away from my daughter, do you hear me? Get away! Leave us all alone!" He saw that the sun was beginning to rise. He gathered his family around him. "Okay, let's go downstairs together and have some breakfast. After that, we'll all go home."

The family walked into the kitchen of their own home two hours later. The sunlight that pierced the kitchen windows lifted the feeling of dread that seemed to have been hanging over the house when they had fled the previous night. Tyler went to his room and came right back down with his school books. He ran out the door to catch the school bus. Linda studied him as he hung his head low and moped up the driveway. He sat on the stone wall that lined the street and waited. Matthew came downstairs dressed for work and stood by Linda.

"He's really shaken up," Linda said.

Matthew studied his son through the window. "Reality

is hard enough for a teenager to deal with, let alone the supernatural."

Sarah ran into the foyer and kissed her parents good-bye. "See you later."

"Goodbye, honey," Linda said. Sarah ran outside and joined Tyler out by the wall. Linda grabbed his arm, gently. "So, you do believe that there are supernatural things going on here."

"Fine! I admit there is something supernatural going on here. Are you happy?" Matthew asked. "We should hope for the best though, and wait and see if this passes over. We shouldn't alarm ourselves."

Linda turned away and fastened her robe. She recalled the gray and black shapes she'd seen over the past few days. She took him by the arm.

"I'm alarmed!"

Chapter 16 – Seeking Answers

KELLY STOOD BEFORE fascinated classmates and an astonished teacher. "And then," Kelly told her entire class, "the scary man came over to me and my brother when we were carving our punkins and I asked if he was an angel, and then the house shook."

A little boy wearing a yellow wool sweater gulped and said, "The house shook?"

"Uh, huh," Kelly admitted. "Really, really bad."

The teacher stood up from behind her desk and said, "Okay, that's enough show-and-tell this morning." She cleared her throat and led Kelly back to her seat. The other children gave her uncertain glances. The teacher changed the subject as professionally and as politely as possible, and her learned eyes caught Kelly's disapproving, analytical stare when she did so. "Class, let's all draw a picture of our guardian angels. If you had an angel, what would he or she look like?" All of the children liked that idea and responded excitedly.

Tyler grabbed Jimmy from behind when he spotted him leaving his locker. "Dude, Kelly knows his name!"

"Knows whose name?" Jimmy asked. "It's too early in the morning for guessing games."

"Brock!"

Kyle overheard and rushed up to them. He asked, "How?"

"I don't know how. But she does. Some really freaky stuff happened last night. The whole house sounded like a wrecking crew was taking down the walls all night long."

"That's bad, man," Jimmy said. "What are you going do?"

"What are...we...going to do?" Tyler corrected him. "You guys got me into this mess." He saw Michelle Dierdorff strolling down the hall with her friends. He knew that she probably had no clue that it was him that she had drenched on Mischief Night, so he just turned away and mumbled to himself even though he wanted to give her a few choice words.

Jimmy swatted him and asked, "How?" He grunted. "We didn't get you into anything."

Tyler jabbed his finger into Jimmy's chest. "You wanted us to get the Ouija board. This is our problem. You guys said you wouldn't dog me on this."

"You're right, Tyler," Jimmy said. "But how did Kelly know his name? What else did she say?" Tyler gave them the details of the events that occurred the previous night.

"He doesn't like me," Tyler said.

"No shit, Sherlock!" Kyle said.

"He wants us six feet under like he is," Jimmy added.

"So, what's the plan?" Kyle asked. "What do your parents think?"

Tyler shrugged. "I don't know. My dad's pretty level-headed. My mom's more scared than anybody. Kelly thinks Brock is her friend. She said there are more ghosts in there than just Brock."

"What?" Kyle asked, astonished.

"Yeah, she said there's a black cat, and she hears other voices."

"Can you hear them?" Jimmy asked.

"No, I can't hear squat." The class bell rang.

"Okay, let's meet after school. We'll come up with something then," Jimmy said.

"Deal," Tyler said.

"Yeah, I'll see you guys then," Kyle said as he ran off to class.

In mid-afternoon, Linda was changing the sheets on her bed and wrestling with the blankets and comforter when she felt a tingling sensation go up her leg from her ankle to her inner thigh. She screamed and leaped onto the bed. She pulled up her pant leg and examined it. There was nothing, nothing that could be seen anyway.

Then a faint whispering voice spoke her name, sending chills up her spine. She spun around. The curtains ruffled like the result of a strong breeze, but the windows were closed and locked. She felt icy cold fingers slide along her waist and down into her inner thigh. She howled and backed against the wall and covered herself with her hands. The skin where she felt the touch was wet and clammy. "Leave me alone!"

"Linda," the voice came again.

She ran out the door and stopped at the end of the hall, turning around in time to see the bedroom door slam shut. She heard arguing on the other side. Linda screamed again and ran down the stairs. She twisted her ankle on the landing and hobbled into the kitchen, crying, panting, and reaching for the phone which seemed like it was miles away. As she searched for it, she heard her bedroom door open and slam shut a dozen times over. She frantically dialed her friend.

"Hello?"

"Julie, oh dear God, please come over."

An astonished and rushed response came. "What's happening?"

"Just please come over. Please."

"Okay, I'm on my way, my goodness."

Several minutes later Julie's minivan slid on the ice on

the way into the driveway. She hurriedly parked and rushed up the front steps. She turned the front door handle, but it was unexpectedly locked. She peeked into the window and pressed the doorbell. After there was no response, she pressed it again. When no reply came, she rapped on the glass with her knuckles.

"For Pete's sake," she said.

After a few more seconds she pressed the doorbell four times in rapid succession and peered again into the glass. Julie exhaled heavily. Once she'd started to turn around, determined to find another way in, she heard the deadbolt open. Linda stood in the doorway.

"Linda, what took you so long to answer? You had me worried sick."

Linda put her hand on her hip and replied, "What do you mean? I ran to the door as soon as I heard you ring."

Julie tightened her coat around her neck to fight the cold. "Honey, I've been ringing and knocking for over five minutes."

Linda put her hands to her face and began to sob.

"Honey, what is going on?"

"Oh, Julie, it was awful." Tears ran down her cheeks as she dropped her head into her hands.

Julie pushed open the door and hugged her. "You can tell me, Linda. Nothing could be so bad that you couldn't tell me."

Linda's muted reply came through her hands. "You won't believe me."

"Sure I will," she said, reaching tenderly for Linda's hands. "I've read one and a half of those books, and by God, they scared me senseless. Now, come on. What is it?"

Linda allowed her best friend to pull away her hands. "Okay, come see for yourself." They walked inside and Linda closed the door.

Julie went down the hallway, eyes roaming, nostrils flaring. She expected the worst. "Linda, what is going on?"

She saw nothing. She spun around with uncertain eyes. Linda walked over and pressed her hand against Julie's mouth. She looked at the ceiling and pointed upward. Julie looked up.

"Listen." Julie narrowed her eyes and held her breath. She turned her head from side to side. "Can you hear it?"

"What?"

"You can't hear that?"

"Hear what, dear?" The door above them slammed shut and squeaked as it opened back up.

Linda laughed and jumped up and down, excitedly. "There! Did you hear that?"

"Yes," Julie admitted. "Who's up there?"

Linda snorted. "Nobody...is up there!" That's what I'm trying to show you. Someone has been calling my name, touching me, opening and closing my doors, pounding on my walls, talking to Kelly, earning her trust and friendship, and frightening the rest of us out of our minds!"

"Oh, dear!"

"Yeah, oh dear!" Linda said.

Julie started up the stairs. "Well, let's take a look, shall we?" She gave an uncertain look back at Linda, gulped and continued. Linda's new-found strength faltered and the chill in her bones returned in an instant. She feared for her friend's safety.

"Be careful, Julie."

"Oh, I'm always careful, don't you worry about that."

They walked all the way down the hallway and approached the master bedroom door cautiously. Then Linda pointed. "There, can you hear that?"

"Yes," Julie admitted. The distinct sounds of a multiple-person argument emanated from behind the door. Julie reached for the doorknob.

Linda smacked her hand away. "No!" Startled, they both leaped back. The door swung open by itself and struck the closet behind it with a good amount of force. The voices stopped, and a faint gust of air tossed their hair. The bedroom was empty. Julie backed away. Linda studied her. The door slammed shut a second later. They both screamed and ran down the hall and stairs together. Linda feared that Julie would continue running right out the front door, into her van and out the driveway, never to be seen again. Instead, she fled down the hallway into the kitchen. Linda's injured ankle slowed her pursuit, so when Linda reached the kitchen, her friend seemed to have disappeared.

"Julie?"

"Over here." The faint voice came from behind the bar in the living room.

Linda crept around cautiously and crouched behind the bar with her. "I didn't think you could move so fast."

Julie hung onto the third shelf, turned and rested her head in the crook of her elbow. "Neither did I."

While they attempted to catch their breath, Linda turned toward her friend and asked, "So, what do you think?"

Julie exhaled heavily and turned toward her again. "I think you have a serious problem."

"No fooling!"

The bar rattled and several bottles cracked and splintered before their very eyes. They stood up and ran out from behind the bar. Linda clutched Julie's hand.

Long minutes passed and Julie and Linda stood in the corner of the living room whispering reassurances to each other. When they felt that it was safe to move, they ascended the stairs into the kitchen together. Rather than flee, they gathered their courage and sat at the kitchen table with a note pad and pencil, listening and watching for any sign of strange phenomena. After none came, they read through and took notes from two of the books that Linda had purchased.

Julie turned a page and looked up at her friend. "As I read through the books you gave me yesterday, I couldn't really tell what parts were actual fact and what parts were embellished, but there seem to be real people who are serious investigators who know all about the things that go on in haunted houses."

Linda was deeply engrossed in her own book and when she finished the paragraph she looked over. "Like who?"

"Well, they all seem to have happy endings when professional psychics come in and save the day." She fished through the pile of books between them on the sofa and held up another one. "Look in this one, too."

"That's fantastic! Maybe we can contact someone and maybe they can help us?"

"Yes, I believe that is possible. I remember seeing an ad for a psychic fair being held in Stratford. Apparently, they are packed with such people. I wonder if we could get some information from those flyers and get a hold of someone who might be able to help us."

"No time like the present!" Linda exhaled heavily. Linda led Julie through the foyer and to the closet. When Julie tried to open the closet doors, they wouldn't budge. She yanked on the doorknob again. Linda became lost in thought, staring blankly through the window, tracing her finger along the crack that had appeared the other day. 'What was happening to her home? Would she never be free of the invaders' clutches?'

Julie groaned and could not open the door no matter how hard she tugged.

"So help me, the doors won't open, Linda."

"Here let me try," Linda said. Linda applied as much strength as she believed she would need, but the doors opened so easily that she flew back into Julie who fell against the front door and hit her shoulder. Linda looked back with a wild, crazed expression. "Do you think you're funny playing games with me? What the hell are you trying to do?"

Julie righted herself and rubbed her shoulder. She

looked at her friend with a look of pure disgust. "Linda McLaughlin, I would never try and trick you! The doors would not budge. You must believe me."

Linda began to cry deeply, finding it hard even to breathe. "I'm so sorry, Julie. I would never speak to you that way. God help my family. God help us all. Something evil is going on here, something terrible."

Julie snatched their coats off the hangers. She left the closet door open. "Then we need to get out of here, and we need to do it right now!" She opened the door and they stepped outside into the cool air. It was refreshing and the smell was invigorating. Julie closed the door behind them and urged her friend down the walkway. "Don't look back. Let's be free of this place." They got into Julie's van and wasted no time driving away. When they turned onto the road, they felt as if a heavy weight had lifted from them. Linda reclined her seat and rested her head. Julie patted her leg. "We will not rest until we find a way to contact someone who can help us."

Julie turned on the radio and a song by the band, Journey, called *"Don't Stop Believing"* came on, and they both cracked a smile. "That's encouraging," Linda said.

"Oh, I love Journey. We sure are on a strange journey into the unknown, aren't we?"

"You can say that again! Let's go get Kelly at school and take her out for the rest of the day. I have a gut feeling it's what we need to do," Linda said.

Julie switched on her turn signal and said. "That's a good idea. I think I know exactly where we can take her."

"Surprise me, Julie. You're the captain."

Julie giggled. "Warp Speed, Mr. Chekhov."

Linda turned to face her friend slowly. She cocked a smile. "Julie Marsh, are you a Trekkie?"

Julie tilted her head back with a deep, hearty laugh. "I have a lot of time on my hands, dear. When Carl was still alive, we used to watch *Star Trek* all the time. When we each wanted to watch a program that aired at the same time, he'd tell me that he'd never seen that particular episode, and even though I knew he was full of prunes, I let him get away with it. I do catch an episode from time to time. I pretend that Carl is right there next to me watching. The stories really are engaging. And if truth be told, I think Captain Kirk is just dreamy."

"It really is a strange new world, with what we are dealing with, I mean." Linda chuckled. She took Julie's hand and held it in both of hers. "Thank you for being you, Julie. And thank you for being here for me when I need you most."

"I wouldn't have it any other way. You are a dear friend, and I am very fond of the whole family. You all bring joy to my heart, and...." Before she could finish her sentence an unusually large black dog walked across the road and stopped directly in front of the van, snarling viciously at them both.

"Hang on," Julie screamed as she slammed on the brakes. The van skidded out of control and the dog crouched in the road until the last second. It leaped away onto the side of the road just in time. Julie's van turned sideways and just when it seemed that the van was about to flip over, a gray misty orb floated through the passenger cabin, and the van came back down with a huge thud and shuddered to a halt.

Julie's side-view mirror cracked, broke out, and fell to the pavement. Julie's glasses sat at an uneven angle on her face and Linda panted as she held the side of her seat. Linda looked out of her window and saw the dog behind several bushes and rocks. It licked its nose and disappeared into the forest.

They sat there for several long moments, and when Julie came to her senses she maneuvered the van back onto the proper side of the road. Linda just closed her eyes, and Julie could do nothing but stare at her friend. Things were serious. 'Was this related? Would they ever escape the madness that was sweeping over them?'

When they realized that they were all right, Julie started forward. They sat in silence as they drove very slowly down Route 111. After they had parked in front of Kelly's school, Linda and Julie found their way inside and asked that Kelly be released early for a personal family matter.

Several minutes later, Kelly walked in with her teacher, who was holding her jacket.

"Hi, Mom," she said. She looked up at Julie, smiling, and said, "Hi, Auntie Julie!"

"Is everything okay at home, Mrs. McLaughlin?"

"Yes, everything is fine. Why do you ask?"

"Well...Kelly had some interesting things to tell the class during show-and-tell, and I am understandably concerned."

"Oh, has Kelly been telling the same ghost stories to her classmates that she's been telling us? Halloween can elicit all kinds of odd behavior in little children, don't you agree?"

"I certainly do." She held the door open for them.

"Enjoy the rest of your day," Linda said.

Kelly waved to her teacher.

She walked between her mother and Julie and held their hands as they walked down the hallway and outside.

When they reached the van, Julie knelt and took both of Kelly's hands in hers. She smiled broadly and said, "We have to get something at the library, and after we do that, how about if we all go and get a nice, big Jim Dandy Sundae at Friendly's?"

Kelly's eyes lit up. "Okay!" She excitedly hopped into the car and Linda fastened her seat belt. Finally they drove away, dreaming of washing away their concerns in mounds of ice cream smothered in whipped cream and hot chocolate syrup.

Tyler, Kyle, and Jimmy sat in the town library and hastily jotted down passages from several old ghost story compendiums that they had found. They found poems, spells, ceremonies, and a lengthy history of ghost phenomena from as far back as the Middle Ages. Finally, after close to two hours of searching, Tyler closed his book and asked, "Do we have enough, guys?"

"Heck if I know, man," Jimmy replied.

Kyle stood up and put all four books they'd perused back into the bin and put his book bag on. "Now what do we do?"

"Now, we see if we can get rid of the ghost."

"Think it'll work, Jim?" Kyle asked as they brushed shoulders trying to squeeze through the door at the same time.

They walked outside toward the parking lot. "How would I know? Why do you always ask such stupid questions?"

"Hey!" Kyle snorted. "Look who it is!"

"Fancy meeting you in a place like this," Tyler said.

Linda laughed and said, "How are you, honey? What are you guys doing at the library? Are you trying to make me believe that the three of you are actually studious?"

"Cute, Mom," Tyler said. "We're doing research for a project. What are you all doing here?"

"Oh, we're looking for some things for Halloween," Julie answered. She winked at Linda.

"Cool," Kyle said. He knelt down beside Kelly, hugged her and asked, "What are you going to be for Halloween this year?"

"Nothing scary," Kelly answered. "I know. I'll be a fairy princess."

Linda and Julie giggled. "That's a darling costume idea," Julie said.

"Well, we have to get going, Mom. I'm going to have

dinner with the guys tonight. I'll be home around eight o'clock," Tyler said as they walked away.

"Okay, honey, see you later," Linda said.

When they rounded the corner Julie eyed the bulletin board and found the flyer she'd seen before. "Here it is. Psychic Fair on October 31st. She unfastened the thumbtack that was securing it to the cork bulletin board and took the flyer with her over to the counter. "Let me jot this number down. Surely, they have a list of people who could help us." She bent over the counter, took a short pencil and a piece of scratch paper out of the small bin and hastily jotted down the phone number. She smiled, put the pencil in her purse, looked at her friends and said, "Mission Accomplished. Mr. Scott, three to beam up. Warp speed to the ice cream shop."

Kelly licked her spoon for the last traces of chocolate and ice cream as Linda got up to use the telephone. Julie dipped a napkin into the water inside the plastic glass and wiped the corner of Kelly's mouth. "I hope you don't have a tummy ache after so much ice cream, sweetie-pie."

Linda held her hand out. "May I have that piece of paper, please? It's time that I made a phone call." Julie pulled the paper out of her purse and handed it to her friend.

"I've had lots more ice cream than this, and I didn't ever get a tummy ache, Auntie Julie," Kelly giggled. Linda walked over to the pay phone, slipped her quarters into the slot and dialed. The phone rang four times and then connected.

"Thank God! Hello..."

It was obviously a recorded message. All she could make out was: "...ello...s...chic...fai..." She waited until she thought she heard the tone that signaled her to leave a message. Linda studied Julie in the distance looking on with anticipation. "Hello, my name is Linda McLaughlin. I need to talk to you as soon as possible. We are in real trouble. I need to speak to someone who is psychic who can help me with ghosts. I have a really big problem in my house. Please call me back..." She left her address and home phone number and hung up. She looked at the floor in hopelessness. When she walked back, Kelly looked at her and smiled.

"Who were you calling, Mom?"

"I was calling someone who might be able to help us, honey."

"Help us with what?"

Linda knelt beside Kelly and whispered. "With the ghosts, honey. We found someone who can help us make them all go away."

Kelly's entire appearance changed drastically. She clenched her teeth, whipped her head around, and snarled. Her blue eyes suddenly looked like black pearls. Her face appeared to shift and age in an instant.

"No!" she protested. She pushed her mother away forcefully. "I don't want them to go away!"

Linda gasped. Julie tipped her glass over and the icy water spilled all over Kelly's lap. Kelly growled at Julie, though they knew that it was not Kelly at all. She reached over and clawed at Julie like some sort of wild animal.

Julie screamed, "Oh, my! Kelly!" She grabbed Kelly by her wrists and tried to still her, but the little girl had ten times what should be her normal strength. She batted away Julie's arms, tore her glasses off, and dug her nails into Julie's face.

"Kelly! What are you doing?" Linda grabbed her daughter by the hair and tugged it sharply. Kelly's head snapped back. Then her appearance reverted to normal, as if some spell affecting her had been suddenly lifted.

Kelly sat there silently. Julie and Linda stared at each other in disbelief.

Then Kelly began to sob. She said, "I don't feel good."

Julie dabbed at her scratches with a wet napkin. She tried to fight back tears but she was a very sensitive and kind woman. Linda knelt and handed Julie her glasses.

"Thank you, Linda. I need to use the bathroom. Excuse me." Julie slid out of the booth and walked hurriedly to the restroom, sobbing.

Linda stared at her daughter and felt her forehead to check if she had a temperature. It was normal. Kelly stared at her mother. Linda could tell that her daughter knew that something had happened, but perhaps she wasn't exactly sure what it was.

Minutes later, Julie came back out and put on her coat and scarf. "Well, that was a welcome treat. Don't you think so, Kelly? We sure do love ice cream, don't we?"

"Mmmhmm. That was good."

Linda and Julie exchanged wordless glances. They walked outside, got into Julie's van and drove off toward home.

When they arrived, Julie got out and waved. "Well, I best get home. I've had enough excitement for one day."

"I'll call you later so we can talk, Julie." She mouthed to her the words, 'I'm so sorry.'

"Bye-bye," Kelly said as she waved. "Bye-bye!"

Linda held Kelly by the hand, and they walked toward the front door. She waved to Julie who usually waited for a signal that everything was okay. When they walked inside and closed the door, she saw Julie drive off.

Chapter 17 – Binding Ceremony

TYLER, JIMMY AND Kyle hopped out of the taxi cab just after five o'clock, and stood outside the pitted and rusted black iron fence that stretched along the length of the Union Cemetery. Tyler leaned inside and said to the driver, "So, please be back here in two hours, okay?" The driver took his fare, nodded, and drove away. They stood in a pile of pine needles and soggy leaves and watched the taxi roll away into the mist. "Man, that guy had better come back for us," Tyler said. They were all alone. There was no turning back.

Tyler secured his book-bag strap over his shoulder and tied his shoe. "Okay, boys. This is it. You know what we came here to do." Jimmy and Kyle sighed. Rather than walk all the way around to the fence, Tyler leaped up, grabbed the rusted iron tips, scaled the fence, and leaped over into the cemetery. Jimmy immediately followed. Kyle tore his jeans when he caught his pants pocket on the way over. Tyler gazed at the sky. A fine mist drifted down on them slowly, not enough to soak them, but certainly enough to cause a chill deep under their clothing. Kyle wiped his saturated blond bangs away with a swift flip of his hand. Jimmy tugged his baseball cap into place. Tyler, who was usually much more concerned about his appearance, now wasn't, and only stared at the gravestones, "C'mon, guys," Tyler said as he led the way toward the first row of headstones. Each chose a row and started down it.

Jimmy stopped at a large marble monument. He brushed the over-grown grass out of the way. "Jeez, she didn't live very long. That sucks, big."

Kyle patted Jimmy on the shoulder as he walked past him. "Yeah, that's a huge bummer."

Tyler kept to himself, making his way down his row much more quickly than his friends. His shoes and jeans were soaked as a result of treading through the wet grass. After a while he looked for his friends. Jimmy's red cap stood out in the distance. Kyle bent and leaned, bobbed his head in one direction or the other, then stood, cursed and moped over to the next stone. Tyler knew Kyle didn't like doing this. Hell, none of them did. But he was relieved that his friends were sticking by him and helping to try and find a solution.

Low, rumbling thunder rolled overhead, forcing all three to stop, take their eyes off the stones, look up at the sky and finally to look at each other.

"Great!" Jimmy called out.

"Yeah, how classic," Kyle added.

Tyler just laughed and made his way to a few stones covered with black moss. He saw no name, so he tried to move away the moss with his shoe. It smeared along the stone like old grease. "Oh, gross!" He found a stick on the ground and scraped the moss off the name on the stone that the moss had concealed. Unsatisfied, he moved onto the next one.

The thunderstorm still threatened, and the boys were over an hour into the search into the southern end of the cemetery when they finally found what they were looking for. "Yo! Over here," Jimmy called. "I found it!"

Tyler and Kyle wound their way around and leaped over the stones that separated them from their friend and his discovery. Kyle tripped on an obscured stone and stubbed his toe. "Ah, dammit," he growled. Jimmy stood there proudly with both hands on his hips. When Tyler and

Kyle reached him, they stooped over to study the name on the stone.

"Brock Manning," Tyler said.

"Bingo," Kyle said.

Tyler knelt and unzipped his bag, pulling out a bottle of water, a large crucifix, and an assortment of candles. Jimmy crouched over and pulled four small brass candlesticks from his bag. Tyler assembled the candlesticks and candles together. After considerable effort, he pulled an old army blanket out of the bag and handed it to Jimmy. Tyler pointed at the aluminum camping tent posts. "There's no way the candles will stay lit in this rain," he explained.

They assembled the tent over the grave. Tyler took out several pieces of printer paper out of his pocket. He unfolded them and studied one page in particular. He lay the paper down on the blanket and arranged the candles according the diagram on the paper. Jimmy leaned a wooden crucifix with a pewter crucified Jesus figure attached against the gravestone. "All right," Tyler said. He flipped through the other pages. Kyle shone his flashlight on the pages so Tyler could read them clearly. "Okay...here we go: Binding Ceremony."

Walls of misty rain swept through the cemetery and more thunder followed. The candle flames faltered, but didn't go out. Tyler cleared his throat, raised his head and broadcast his voice as powerfully as possible. "We...we, the spirits of the light and the children of God, in flesh and blood, command the spirit of Brock Manning, now discarnate and lost, to appear with all haste to this site where his bones do lie."

The boys waited in silence. There was no response. They gave each other unsure glances. Jimmy took the paper, and Kyle shone his flashlight on it so Jimmy could read.

"Hear us, oh lost and tortured soul," he shouted. "We of the light, protected by the light, and empowered by the light and will of God, command you to appear here now." The candles flickered and went out. The boys cursed. Then, as Tyler was about to light them, the flames came to life again, brighter and burning higher. Suddenly a whispering wind wailed nearby that sent chills through their souls. Jimmy quickly handed the papers to Kyle, as if he wanted nothing further to do with them.

"Not me! No way," Kyle protested. He passed them on to Tyler, who scowled and snatched them from his friend. Kyle smiled. Tyler cleared his throat again.

"Brock Manning, you are a lost soul. When you died, you ignored the light that came for you, and you ran away from it. That light was the passageway to God. That is where you should have gone. Instead, you chose to remain here on Earth. In doing this, you only hamp...ham-per... hampered..."

Jimmy snatched the page out of Tyler's hand and said, "Give it to me. You're screwing it all up." He studied the page intently and then continued. "In doing this, you failed to complete the proper death passage."

A powerful wind flew under the blanket and threatened to blow it up and away. The boys quickly grabbed the edges. "To prevent you from causing harm and disturbances elsewhere, we bind you here, at this site, to contemplate your own misery. Only the light can free you from this prison. Only you can summon the light to come for you, and when it does you must enter it and leave this world behind."

Kyle gasped as the crucifix shook and fell on its side.

"Great," Tyler said. The crucifix rolled over onto its face and the candles blew out.

Kyle said, "Yeah, how classic!"

"Okay." Jimmy held the page in the center so that all could see it. "Together, we have to say the last line together."

They all chanted in unison: "Brock Manning, by the power of God and Saint Michael, we bind you here now." A powerful wind ripped the blanket free and swept it up and away in a great curving arc toward the trees. The candles extinguished themselves and rolled over. Jimmy's hat blew off and rolled away in the grass, flipping end over end.

"Let's get outta here," Kyle roared. Tyler grabbed his bag, Kyle collected the candlesticks, and Jimmy scampered off after his hat. A shrill, continuous wail cascaded down upon them, and they froze in horror. They stopped in unison and stared at the grave. A faint gray silhouette materialized and floated a couple of inches above the grave. Tyler gazed at it spellbound. Then the tree branches above him groaned. They looked up and saw that the green blanket was caught in the scraggly tree branches above them. When he looked back at the grave site, the image had vanished into tiny tendrils of smoke.

"C'mon, Tyler," Jimmy called as he ran toward the fence. They hurled themselves and their bags over the fence in what seemed to them to be a display of dazzling dexterity and speed. Sheets of rain and biting winds lent their own degrees of misery as they huddled together waiting for the taxi.

Excitement stirred when the taxi's headlights pierced the thick fog as it made its way down Stepney Road. They looked like distant moons as it turned the corner and came up Route 111 and stopped beside them. They rode away wordlessly, staring out the windows at the graves of fallen men and the eternal stone that marked their passing from the sunlit majesty of love and joy to the intangible world of shadow and sorrow.

Tyler was lost in deep thought. He knew, or at least hoped, that whatever it was that caused the ghostly intrusion, whatever force it was that violated his home, it was gone forever. There, bound for all of time, the ghost of Brock Manning would stay...or would he?

The taxi squealed to a halt in front of the guys' favorite pizzeria. Tyler paid the driver, and they all walked inside.

They took stools at the counter and after they ordered, Tyler fished a quarter out of his soaked jeans and said, "I'll see if my Mom can come get us." He got up and walked over to the payphone, inserted his quarter, dialed and leaned against the wall. The phone rang and someone picked up at home, but it was a voice that he did not recognize.

"Yes?"

"Hello?" Tyler asked.

Silence.

"Hell-o-o-o?" Tyler said again.

Crackling.

"Mom?"

A different voice answered. It sounded like a little girl, but certainly not either of his sisters. It sounded hoarse, cold and disinterested. "Who is it?"

"Kelly?"

The voice answered, "Kelly doesn't live here anymore."

Tyler gasped. "What? Who is this?" He heard two distinct voices cackling on the other end of the line. Then the phone went suddenly and completely dead. Tyler ran to the counter and tugged at his friends' shirts. "Let's go!"

Jimmy nearly choked on his pizza as Tyler spun him around on the stool.

Kyle asked, "What's going on?"

"Something's wrong!" Tyler answered.

Jimmy asked, "How wrong?"

Tyler replied, "Wrong, wrong!"

They scooped the remaining pieces of pizza into their napkins, threw enough money for the pizza on the counter and scurried out the door, adjusting their hoods and baseball caps, and took off into the rain. They all knew that something was wrong, but nothing they could have imagined could have prepared them for the suffocating terror that they were about to experience back at the house.

Chapter 18 – Swirling Silverware

WHEN THEY GOT to the edge of the driveway, they saw bright white flashes of light shining through the living room windows, as if explosions were going off inside. The guys stood at the end of the driveway, petrified.

Tyler slapped his friends on the back. "C'mon!"

They burst through the garage door into the kitchen amid powerful banging, screeching and moans that seemed to be inches above them one moment and far away the next. They threw their hands before them to deflect the spoons, knives, and forks that were levitating and rotating in mid-air. They stared at the drawers in disbelief. Silverware rose up from the drawers, swirled around each other, and darted back and forth through the room.

Tyler heard his father call out to him. Tyler swiftly turned toward the voice in the living room. His father knelt over his mother and his sisters, shielding them with his arms. Spoons, forks, and butter knives soared through the air by some invisible force and struck Matthew in the neck and all over his back.

"What the hell is going on?" Tyler demanded. He grabbed a sofa cushion and shielded his father with it.

Linda screamed from under Matthew's protective embrace. "I can't take this anymore!"

Kyle and Jimmy looked at each other, unsure, and ran over to join the huddle. They crouched low and wrapped their arms around the girls.

"It didn't work!" Jimmy said to Kyle.

"No shit!" Kelly's panicked shrieks made Tyler cringe.

"What can we do, Tyler?" Matthew asked.

"I don't know, Dad!"

"You're the monster expert! Do something!" Sarah said.

Tyler deflected a spoon away from his head and shouted, "Like what?"

He saw his trembling, sweating father stand before the others who cowered on the floor.

Matthew shook his fist. "This is...this is my house! I didn't invite you in!" He then looked down at Tyler. "You have to let them in, right?"

Tyler shrugged, thinking that was just a fantasy story. Hell, then what was this? He couldn't imagine anything more real than this. "I don't know, Dad!"

Matthew growled, "I command you to get out!" He stood tall and shouted it again. "I command you...I command you to leave my house!"

Tyler knelt and hugged the girls, then watched, horrified, as his father gasped for breath, curled over, moaned terribly and grabbed at his stomach. His eyes bulged and he threw his hand over his mouth and gagged.

"What's happening?" Linda begged. She curled around him. Then she looked at each of her children and Tyler's friends. "Pray the Our Father!"

Tyler, Kelly, and Sarah wrapped their hands together and the others joined in reciting the prayers. "Our Father, who art in Heaven..."

Loud wailing groans shook the walls. They sounded like the resonant calls of bulls and dogs, not anything human. Sarah howled, batting at something near her shoulder. "Ouch! Something's got me!"

Linda put her arms around her. "What is it, honey?" She cried out as she felt the same cold claw-like hands that had attacked her daughter on her now, tugging at her hair, clubbing her back, and then tearing at her sweater. Her daughter was under attack, and her husband was being debilitated. She pleaded, "What's happening, Matt?"

Tyler grabbed his father's arm. "I want to help you, Dad. How can I help you?"

Matthew gagged again and called out, "The smell! Oh my dear Lord, it smells like the rancid smell of death!" He immediately vomited all over the slate hearth.

Jimmy tried desperately to get everyone's attention. "We've got to get outta here!" He twisted around toward the sliding door and tried to slide it open. Something intangible, yet thick and impassable, not only blocked his path to the door handle, but suddenly, slowly pushed him back. Whatever it was, it was cold and indescribably foul. Part of the mass of blackness gave way when he pushed against it, yet he was unable to penetrate it completely and reach the door handle.

Kyle yelled at his friend, "Open the door!"

"I can't," Jimmy roared. "There's something blocking it."

Kyle rushed in to help, pressing his weight against it.

"Do you feel it?" Jimmy asked.

"Yes, and I can't reach the door," Kyle answered.

The lights flickered on and off several times. Whatever had been affecting Matthew seemed to have subsided, so he recovered and got to his hands and knees. Then the invisible barrier before Jimmy and Kyle faded away. Jimmy fell forward and collapsed on the handle. Kyle slid the door open and fell out over Jimmy. While carrying Kelly, Tyler led his mother out by the hand. He came back in and grabbed his father under the armpits and hauled him outside.

Then, without warning and with blinding speed, the screen door violently slid shut, sealing Sarah inside. They heard the lock 'click' into place. They gazed at her in horror. Sarah panicked, pressed her hands against the screen, and dug her nails into it. Kyle and Tyler tried to pry the door open. Then Matthew reached over, ripped the screen out of its frame and threw it away to the side. He lunged inside and pulled Sarah out with him. Matthew fell onto his back on the deck, and Sarah landed on top of him.

They were both unharmed but completely terrified. The group stood helplessly out on the deck. Kelly hid behind Linda's legs, crying, peeking around them every few seconds. Then, from deep within the house, the telephone rang, sending chilling calls throughout with an eerie summons to come back inside.

"Stay back," Matthew ordered. He held the girls tightly against him. The phone rang and rang, but no one was brave enough to enter the house and answer it. The answering machine came to life and the familiar voice crackled.

"Linda, this is Julie. I called the same number that you'd tried at Friendly's. I got through and spoke with an interesting woman named Yvonne. She said that she'd discuss the situation with a colleague of hers and get right back to us. Linda, are you there? Linda? Oh dear. I'll try later. Bye." They all exhaled in relief.

"Thank God!" Linda said. She turned and faced her family. "Maybe this woman can help us." Tyler and his friends looked at each other with optimism. The banging had stopped.

For nearly fifteen minutes they waited outside, until they felt that the activity had stopped. One by one, they inched themselves inside, peeking around corners and listening carefully for any unseen voices or black moving shadows. The flying silverware suddenly had fallen to the floor as if someone had turned off a switch to the power that was allowing it to levitate. Even though the silverware was lying on the floor motionless, a shrill metallic clattering resonated all around them. As quickly as they entered, it started again. Brief distractions came in the form of faint raps, knockings, and whisperings, as if some dire deeds were being discussed in the invisible world that had invaded their own.

Linda grabbed the phone, fished out the scratch paper

from her pocket and dialed the number on it again. A friendly voice answered, "Hello?"

"Hello, Yvonne?" Linda asked.

"Hello! Is anybody there?" the voice beckoned.

Linda sobbed and asked, "Can you hear me?" The person on the other end hung up.

Matthew lost his smile when Linda squatted down, sat on the floor, dropped her arms in her lap and wept. He slid in close and hugged her tightly. Everyone sat down on the kitchen floor close together, watching and listening to the faint but obvious signs that they would never again be left alone. Tyler shook his head in disbelief. He knew deep down that no one would come and rescue them from this terror. The forces in the house would not allow them to make contact with anyone who could help, ever. They all slid into the deepest recesses of fear and depression.

A few minutes later, Kyle and Jimmy stood up and motioned for Tyler to follow. They opened the sliding door. Tyler closed it slowly behind them. On the deck, out of earshot, he grabbed Jimmy by the arm and growled, "Why didn't it work?"

Jimmy pushed him away. "I don't know!"

"Christ," Tyler said. "Who knows if that hokey stuff in those books we copied is any good, anyway?"

"Well, we sure as hell wasted our time if you felt it was a bunch of crap," Kyle replied.

"Well, we 'sure as hell' didn't have any better ideas," Jimmy countered.

"Maybe that Yvonne woman will call, and maybe she'll know what to do," Kyle said.

"I sure hope so, guys," Tyler said.

The boys re-entered the house and joined the rest of the family who were once again in the living room. They huddled together, exchanging wordless glances and reassuring each other that everything would be all right. The phone rang again. Tyler walked into the kitchen and answered it. "Hello?" He handed the phone to Jimmy, who took it hesitantly. "It's your Mom."

"Hi, Mom," He listened and nodded over and over. "Yeah, okay. Bye." He rolled his eyes. "I have to go. My Mom's coming to get me."

Kyle inched over toward him and asked, "Hey, can I get a ride home, too?"

Jimmy replied, "Yeah, sure."

Kyle turned apologetic eyes on Tyler and his family and said, "Sorry, everyone. It's a school night."

Linda forced a smile. "That's all right, Kyle. We'd love your company, but you have your own life to take care of."

Matthew squeezed the arm of the sofa hard, gritting his teeth. "Something very strange is happening here. I don't know what it is, or why it's here, but it is, and it's trying to cause us harm. I want everyone to know that I will do everything in my power to protect all of us, including you, Jim and Kyle. But, whatever it is, it's not going to rip apart my home that I designed and built. It's not going to happen. I believe in God. I've been faithful to him and I have accepted Jesus Christ as my savior."

Bone-chilling winds swept through the room that instant. The kitchen cabinet doors opened and everything inside them flew out and landed on the kitchen floor with a huge crash. "God!" Linda huddled against her husband's chest, silent tears trickling down her cheeks. Linda and Sarah went in and couldn't even contemplate the clean-up required. "I can't take this anymore. I don't have the strength to clean that up," Linda said.

"We're all exhausted," Sarah moaned.

Matthew stormed into the garage and came back in with a banana box and a plastic shovel. He mumbled to himself and cursed as he dropped the box, roared, and dug the shovel into the pile of debris. He hurled it into the box and started into it again. Then they heard the car horn sound outside. Jimmy and Kyle rushed out, waving a hurried goodbye.

Tyler closed the door behind them and sank down onto the floor, watching his father. He folded his arms around his knees and dropped his head into his lap, utterly defeated. Linda got a pail of water and a rag and began cleaning up the putrid mess on the hearth. Sarah held Kelly and never let her go for close to an hour.

They huddled in prayer that night, bound together, fighting what seemed to be an entire realm of darkness that had shattered their everyday normal world—its forces intent on working vile evil against them. Through rosaries, through reciting private prayers, and making pleas for help from heaven on high, terrible thunderous destruction ravaged their home. And despite their most earnest summons, no help came.

Chapter 19 – Getting Brutally Physical

IN THE MIDDLE of the night past the full midnight moon, as her family slept in the living room, Linda studied her Bible silently. She read the twenty-third psalm, careful not to provoke any attacks by reading it aloud. Even so, an ominous force flailed at her arm. She panicked. It struck again, knocking the Bible completely out of her hand. It tumbled to the hearth, rolled onto the floor, and hit Tyler in the head. He stirred in time to hear the sounds of something ravenously hungry, growling and pinning his mother to the ground. Something had her forearm. It twisted it almost completely around and Linda cried out in agony. He witnessed the puncture wounds as some invisible beast sank its teeth into her arm. Tyler watch aghast as his mother screamed in horror.

Matthew fought to regain his senses. He got to his knees and reached in to help in any way that he could. Then, something swatted him away as if he were nothing but a rag doll. He flew back, struck the far wall, collapsed onto the sofa, and rolled down onto the carpet. Linda screamed again. Matthew lay on the floor and stared at her in horror. She knew that he was paralyzed. He could not help her. Linda flailed her free arm in the air in an attempt to fight the phantom away. Sarah wailed, and she felt the invisible claw take hold of her wrist. Linda was suddenly released. She collapsed to her hands and knees. She gazed in horror at three holes, evenly spaced and a quarter-inch-deep, gouged into her forearm. Thin crimson lines of blood flowed down her forearm and into her palm. Sarah was then violently shoved into the wall and rolled around to the floor. Her head just missed the fireplace hearth. It struck the carpet instead.

Then there came the words she couldn't recognize, like a forgotten ancient language, used in the present by a being as old as creation itself. The multiple voices were deep, powerful, and full of rage. They said, "Azh-non-kian! Ste-chee-eon-gore!" A terrible whine followed, like that of some undead steed. It echoed and reverberated throughout the house and seemed like it would never cease. When Matthew found that he was able to move, he grabbed a bar towel, rushed over to Linda, and dabbed at her wounds.

Then Matthew's hair was tugged up, and whatever had a hold of him jerked and yanked his head wildly from side to side. He was propped up straight, like he was nothing but a marionette on strings. The girls could do nothing but wail in terror and shiver in fear as their father was manipulated and attacked. Tyler crouched between them, his arms around their shoulders. He gasped and called out to the etheric invaders, "Stop it! Stop it!." Helpless tears fell from the corners of his eyes. He cried desperately. The invisible hand curled around his throat and squeezed tightly. Tyler panicked. It lifted him into the air and pinned him against the hearth. Tyler closed his eyes and visualized Jesus and his angels appearing in the room and forcing the demon's hand away. Within seconds, he was released. He fell down and scraped his back on the edge of the hearth. He moaned in pain, curled up in the fetal position and wept.

Sarah leaned over and hugged her brother. Kelly just lay there wide-eyed and full of terror, yet unharmed, as if whatever was inside the house had no intention of harming her—yet.

Matthew held his stomach. "Nobody say anything.

Don't provoke it! We're going to a hotel. We are leaving... now!" They all walked through the sliding door out of the house and got into the cars and drove away from their home, quite possibly for the last time.

After they checked into the Curtis House in Woodbury, they lay together in two queen beds with Kelly on a cot between them. Linda tended to Tyler's scraped-up back and wrapped her own arm in a cloth and an ace bandage. Matthew stood watch over the room. He nodded off now and then, but listened intently for anything that he could hear that could signify trouble. 'How could he stop the evil that had invaded his home? How could they ever return to their house?' When the thoughts of anguish finally became too much for him to contemplate, and when the late morning hour and stillness of night overcame him, he forced his eyes shut and he eventually drifted off to sleep.

The frightened family awoke thoroughly exhausted, as if every ounce of energy they accumulated during their brief sleep had been drawn away by some invisible thief.

Matthew tapped Linda. She stirred and opened her eyes. Kelly was gone. Linda sat up, panicked, looked at Matthew and sighed in relief when she saw that Kelly was lying between them. She wound away her ace bandage to examine her wounds. When she pulled the cotton away, she gasped and said, "They're gone!" She displayed her arm for all to see. "My wounds, they're completely healed!"

Tyler and Sarah woke up. Tyler was lying beside her with his arm around her waist. "Gross," Sarah said as she flung Tyler's arm off her side.

"Don't get excited. I must have snuggled with you as we slept, that's all." Tyler sat up and rubbed the residue from his eyes.

Linda held her arm. The fact that the wounds had vanished during the night nearly frightened her as much as when they actually occurred, but not quite.

Matthew examined them and said, "How strange!" He shook his head in disbelief.

"Oh, Matt, I'm so scared," Linda said.

Tyler pulled back the curtains. Bright sunlight shone through. Peace and warmth filled the room. Matthew looked at his watch. "Jesus, I'm late for work!" He got up and searched for his pants and his wallet and went into the bathroom to shower and get ready. Moments later came the unmistakable cry of Matthew's anger from inside the bathroom. "Jesus Christ! Where is that fifty? God damn it!"

Linda called out to him and asked, "What's wrong?"

Matthew stormed over to the beds. "I have to pay for the goddamned room, and the fifty-dollar bill that I was going to use is not in my wallet. So where is it?" He opened his wallet, displayed it for all to see, turned it upside down and expanded it so anything inside would fall out onto the bed. "No money! No fifty!"

Linda shrugged. "Use a credit card. What's the big deal?" Matthew turned and spotted Tyler's book bag hanging on the doorknob. Linda was shocked. "Oh, now, you don't think it's in there?" Matthew yanked it off the doorknob, put it on the bed, unzipped the front pocket and fished through it.

"Hey!" Tyler protested. "Dad!"

He pulled out a fifty-dollar bill that was neatly folded in thirds, examined it, sneered at his son and said, "You filthy thief!"

Tyler gasped. "What?"

Linda snapped at him, "Matthew McLaughlin! What did you call him?"

Tyler sat up in bed looking at his father in complete shock. "I did not take that money!" he shouted.

Matthew stormed over and slapped Tyler across the

face with the back of his hand. "Jesus Christ!" Tyler
protested. His eyes began to water. Tyler reached out to
defend himself from a second strike, but Matthew grabbed
his son's hand and squeezed. "Ouch!"

"Matthew!" Linda pleaded.

"What the hell is wrong with you?" Tyler pleaded. He
buckled to the pressure around his hand and winced in
pain. "You're hurting me!"

Matthew went to strike him again, but Linda grabbed
his arm and yanked it away with all of her might. Matthew
pushed Linda back, and she fell back onto the bed. His eyes
were on fire. Tyler yelped as Matthew slapped him across
the face for a fourth time. Tyler retreated against the
headboard and covered his mouth. A thin line of blood
tricked down his lip.

"Don't hurt Tyler," Kelly pleaded.

Sarah scanned the room for something to hit her father
with. She pleaded with him, "Dad, stop it!"

"Matthew!" Linda roared.

"Don't you ever steal from me, young man!" He knelt
over his son like a rabid dog, sneering and growling, and
viciously asked, "Do you understand me?"

Tyler cowered and held his cheek. "Dad, I didn't!"

Matthew shouted, "Don't you *lie* to me!"

"What's the matter with you?" Sarah pleaded, grabbing
her father's arm.

Matthew pushed Sarah's hand away and said, "Don't
you start with me, too!"

Linda cradled her son and kissed him on the forehead.
She shot an evil glare at her husband. "What the hell is the
matter with you?"

Tyler pressed his hand against his swelling cheekbone.
He just stared at his father in disbelief. Sarah held Tyler's
hand.

Kelly cried in the center of the bed, "Don't hurt Tyler,
Daddy."

Matthew stared at the bill in his palm like he was suddenly confused and dizzy. He rocked back and forth and finally crushed the bill in his fist. "What have I done? I can't believe I just did that. I'm not right in the head. Linda, I'm scared."

"You're scared?" Tyler barked. "What an asshole!"

"Enough," Linda roared. "What the hell has gotten into you, Matthew?"

Matthew clutched his head and paused. "What has gotten into me? I'm not myself. I almost hit all of you. I'm scared."

Tyler whimpered. He wiped away a spot of blood under his nostril. "Dad, I didn't take that money from you, honest!"

"I don't know what came over me." He offered a hand to his son and Tyler recoiled. "I...I'm sorry, son." Tears welled up in Tyler's eyes and rolled down his cheeks. He got out of bed in his jeans, put on a shirt and grabbed his book bag.

"Where are you going?" Linda demanded.

"To get some air," he said. "I'd like to be anywhere but here!" He slammed the door behind him.

Sarah got dressed and said, "We need to go to school."

Matthew knelt before Linda and held her hand. He bowed in front of her and said, "I'm so very sorry, honey."

"You look terrible," Linda said. "Don't go to work. Something is wrong with you, honey. Please stay with me. I really don't want to be left alone, Matt. I can't take this anymore. I'm going to snap."

Matthew rushed off into the bathroom, turned on the sink and washed his face. He studied himself in the mirror. "What is wrong with me?" he asked. He washed his hands and dried them with a towel. "Honey, I have to make sure my office makes its goal this month. Look, I'll drop Tyler and Sarah off at school. You keep the Benz and take Kelly to Julie's and stay there with her if you don't want to go back to the house. I don't know what else to do. I need to go to work for half the day. Call me if you have any problems, or even just to talk. Okay? I'll inform everyone to make sure your call gets right to me."

Linda said, "I really don't want to be alone anymore, Matt."

"Oh, Linda, I'll try to leave early. Call me and tell me what you decide to do. If I don't go to work, we won't have a house, as haunted as it is." He called out to Sarah. "Are you ready? We need to go!"

"So you admit it?" Linda asked.

"What other explanation can there be?" he asked.

"I'm ready to get the heck out of here," Sarah said. She grabbed her duffel bag.

"Bye. I love you," Matthew said. Linda recoiled as he leaned in to kiss her. He stopped, dropped his head in defeat and then looked her in the eyes and said, "That wasn't me, Linda." He looked at his whimpering daughter and said, "Kelly, you know that was not like me, right?" He leaned in and Kelly let him kiss her on the cheek.

"I know, Dad," Kelly said.

Sarah opened the door and said, "Dad, we'll be late."

Matthew backed away. "I have to go, see you all soon."

Linda closed the door behind him and checked on Kelly. She lay quietly in the center of the bed. Linda lay down beside her and sighed.

When Sarah and Matthew walked outside, Tyler was leaning against the pillar. He glared at his father in utter contempt. His long, wet, black bangs looked like splinters in his ice blue eyes. Matthew reached out to him. Tyler swatted his hand away and said, "Don't!" Matthew huffed and walked past him. He and Sarah followed their father out into the parking lot and got into the back seat of the car. Neither of them would sit in the front seat with their father. About a mile down the road, Matthew looked at his son in the rear-view mirror and pleaded, "Son, that was not like me, you know that."

"I know, Dad," Tyler agreed.

"The things happening in our house," he said. "The things in our house must be influencing me to think, say, and do things that I would never, ever do. I would never hurt you, any of you." He looked at Sarah and Tyler in the mirror, and they both just sat there quietly, staring out of their windows in a daze. No one said another word to one another until they reached the school, at which time Tyler and Sarah just got out, closed their doors and walked toward the main entrance of school.

Chapter 20 – Finding Help

AFTER A FEW peaceful hours of sleep, Kelly awoke to a ray of golden sunlight striking her in the forehead. She smiled. It felt so good. It felt warm and protective. She yawned. She looked over and saw her mother sleeping soundly. She shook her arm and said, "I'm hungry." She didn't move. Kelly shook her arm again, gently and said, "Mom? Mom...I want some breakfast."

Linda couldn't function with so little sleep and so much stress. She closed her eyes and moaned, "Oh, God, Kelly, go back to sleep, please. Let me sleep for ten more minutes, please."

Kelly turned away, climbed off the bed and fished out her doll from the suede suitcase next to the wall. She played with it for about a half hour, lost in her own playful thoughts. When she had enough, she crawled over to her mother's side of the bed. She giggled, tugged at her mother's fingers, and leaned in close to her. She studied the tiny blond hairs on her ear for several seconds. Then she huffed and exhaled into her mother's ear. She traced her index finger along its contours. It must have tickled her, because she moved her head to the side and away from her probing fingers. Finally, she leaned in and whispered, "I want pa-cakes."

An hour later, they met Julie at the Blue Colony Diner for breakfast. Kelly hopped up and down when they entered and saw the Silly Putty eggs in the coin-operated vending machine just inside the entrance. Linda saw Julie sitting at the table waiting for them, waving. Linda and Kelly waved back. Linda fished a quarter out of her purse and inserted it down into the slot. Kelly stuck her tongue out of the corner of her mouth as she turned the crank. She needed both hands to turn it. She turned it and turned it a third time and smiled in satisfaction when she heard the 'click.' She opened the metal chute gate and the egg slid into her eager hand. Kelly ran down the aisle and slid in next to Auntie Julie who leaned over and gave her a big kiss. Kelly giggled and rubbed her face with the back of her hand and said, "That tickles."

The waitress came up, opened her order pad, and asked, "What will it be, ladies?"

Kelly smiled and she looked as if she was going to place her order all by herself, but she refrained and looked at her mother as if asking her permission. She encouraged her and said, "Go ahead, honey, you can place your order like a big girl if that's what you want to do." Linda smiled at her and the waitress.

Kelly found her self-confidence once more and said, "Bananner nut pa-cakes, please." Julie, Linda and the waitress laughed heartily.

"That sounds good to me, too. Make it two orders, please," Linda said.

Julie raised three fingers into the air. "Make it three orders, please. And milk for the little one here and coffee with cream for us both." Kelly cracked the plastic egg in half and dug her finger inside to wedge out the beige-colored putty.

"It's gotten absolutely terrible in our house."

"What's happened?"

"Where do I begin?"

"You start from the beginning, my friend. Every tale has a beginning."

"And every tale has an ending too, and I can't wait for this horror story to be over, let me tell you. But how is it ever going to end, if no one that we've called for help ever calls back?" Linda asked.

Kelly cheerfully played with her Silly Putty at the table, as Linda described the events that had transpired since they last saw each other. Julie kept interjecting with an "Oh, my" or a "Goodness, gracious." When their breakfast arrived, the waitress asked if they'd like a copy of the local newspaper to read. Julie accepted it with a smile and set it down on the table.

After they had finished their pancakes, and the waitress had taken away their plates, Kelly opened the newspaper and pressed her Silly Putty down onto the newsprint. She peeled it back, giggled and held it up.

"Look, Mommy. It's backwards."

Linda smiled. "I see that, honey, isn't that fun?" She glanced down at the newspaper briefly, and then looked back up at Julie. She opened her eyes widely and quickly looked down at the paper again. Kelly was pressing her Silly Putty over the image of a classical haunted house and of a young man in his twenties standing before it. She reached over and said, "Honey, let me see that."

She started to peel off the putty when Kelly nudged her mother in the arm and protested by saying, "Hey, that's mine." Linda's eyes never left the page as she pulled it up and away from her daughter.

Julie studied her. She inquired, eagerly. "Something good, I take it?"

"Is your house haunted?" Linda read aloud. "Are you experiencing strange, unexplained phenomena? Then this lecture is for you."

"Hot diggety dog," Julie laughed.

"Please join Jason McLeod—paranormal researcher and expert investigator—for a two-hour presentation that will you never forget. Mr. McLeod is a seasoned investigator who has worked with some of the most famous and respected paranormal experts in the world." Linda laughed out loud. "Ha! Please R.S.V.P. by calling the number below and to reserve your space." Linda grabbed her purse and rushed over to the pay phone in the corner. She called Matthew.

Kelly slid the newspaper over and stuck her Silly Putty on the image of the investigator. She rolled it back, looked at the backwards copy of his face in the putty and giggled.

"Matthew McLaughlin, please."

"One moment, Mrs. McLaughlin, he's expecting your call."

Mere seconds later, Matthew answered. "Hi, honey! Are you okay?"

"Yes, more than okay, in fact, I'm feeling great right now."

"Well, that's good news. How are things going? I'm really sorry about my despicable behavior this morning. I don't know what came over me."

"Matt, we're at the Diner."

"I'm glad you're having breakfast. I didn't have the time. I'm starving!"

"I found a newspaper ad for a man who is a paranormal investigator."

"Well, that's great news! Call him. See what he says."

Linda smiled and gave Julie the thumbs up sign. "I love you, Matt. I just know he can help us. I'm going to call him right now."

"Linda, I feel terrible," Matthew interjected.

"Well, you should," she continued.

"No, I'm not referring to slapping Tyler. I mean, of course I feel terribly sorry about that." Julie came up and stood beside her to listen to the conversation. Linda tilted the phone so they could both hear. "I don't know what I can do to make up for that. I paged him at school and apologized again. I really feel sick. You were right about me looking bad. My secretary said I look like death warmed over. My stomach is killing me."

"Yes, and we know how he is about his appearance. That is one trait he and his son share for sure." Julie giggled.

"I heard that, Julie! I'm coming home early. I suddenly feel extraordinarily lousy."

"I'll head home as soon as I make this phone call to the investigator."

Julie tapped Linda's hand. "Tell him I'll make him some of my chicken noodle soup. It's just right for a cold."

Linda smiled. "Julie says..."

"I heard her," Matthew said. "That sounds delicious. So, everything is okay then?"

"There haven't been any problems today anyway. But we haven't even been home yet."

"Okay, honey. I'm coming home. See you soon."

"Bye." Linda put the receiver on the hook and paused. She was worried about Matthew.

Julie looked stunned and asked, "Well, aren't you going to call that investigator?" Linda looked around her. Several of the waitresses were looking at her, and a man in a blue hat and yellow sweater was staring at them. Finally, when she stared back at him long enough to inform him that he should mind his own business, he lowered his eyes, took a sip of coffee, rested his chin in his palm, and looked down at his plate.

"Let's wait till we get home," Linda said. "There are too many people around here and they've probably heard too much already."

"That's a wise idea," Julie said as she nodded in approval.

After a quick visit to the grocery store, Linda, Julie and Kelly opened the front door and peered inside cautiously. After they determined that the coast was clear, Linda turned to Kelly. "Come with me. Let's go upstairs and get your father's pajamas and slippers ready for him. He's coming home."

Kelly smiled, handed her Silly Putty to Julie and climbed the stairs with her mother. "I'll get started on the soup," Julie said. She walked into the kitchen, set the bags down on the counter, and started emptying their contents.

Minutes later Linda and Kelly came back down into the kitchen. Linda held the advertisement in her hand. She stared longingly at it, as if she had just found the answer to all of her prayers. She picked up the phone and dialed the number in anticipation. Meanwhile, a steady flow of steam rose from the cast-iron soup pot on the stove. Julie worked a knife into a series of carrots, onions, and potatoes.

"Julie, I really—we really appreciate this. Everyone loves your cooking."

She turned with a ladle in her hand and said, "There's no need to thank me. I enjoy cooking for a family again."

Just then, a man answered the phone on the other end. "Hello, this is Jason, how can I help you?"

"Mr. McLeod?"

"Jason. You can call me Jason. How may I help you?"

"Thank God! I found your newspaper advertisement."

"Are you calling to register for my seminar?"

"No. My name is Linda McLaughlin from Monroe. We have a very serious problem here, and we desperately need your help."

"Please tell me all about it," Jason replied. "I will, of course, help you if I can. Let me get my note pad, and I will be right with you. One moment, please." Linda paced the kitchen in anticipation.

"Okay, I am all set. Please tell me what is happening and from the beginning."

Linda walked into the living room, sat down on the sofa and said, "You have no idea how relieved I am to be speaking with you. We have had a very difficult time getting through to anyone. We've had dead phone lines, crackling, scratching, disconnected numbers, you name it."

Jason interrupted her and said, "That's interesting. Is this the first time that you've been able to get through?"

"Yes," Linda said. "It's been enormously frustrating."

"Okay, please tell me when you first noticed something odd, and what happened the day before."

"My daughter Kelly and I were traveling down Stepney Road along Union Cemetery several days ago. Kelly said that she saw a man walking through the graveyard, appearing and disappearing closer to the car and eventually right up against the car, growling at her. We nearly had an accident because she screamed so loud. The next morning I saw a gray form and watched as the stove dial turned all by itself right before my eyes. Things have gotten worse and worse from whispering voices to banging and booming, burning doorknobs, levitating silverware, and we've even been attacked."

"You've been physically attacked by spirits inside your house?" Jason asked.

"Brutally!" Linda said. "I've been bitten, and my husband has been battered. My son and eldest daughter have been choked and beaten."

"Okay, I have heard enough. This sounds very serious. I need to come and conduct an investigation of your house as soon as possible. I need to get calls out to my team. Rest assured, you are in capable hands. We will not let you down, I promise you."

Linda was exhilarated. "You don't know how much that means to me, Jason. Thank you."

"Oh, I can assure you I can totally empathize with you. I know what it feels like to be unable to find help for so long and then finally get through. Please give me your telephone number and address, and I will be in contact as soon as possible." Unbeknownst to Linda, a strange static disrupted the conversation as she eagerly relayed her contact information. "Hello, Mrs. McLaughlin? Are you there? Can you hear me?"

Linda placed the receiver down upon its base. She clasped her hands together in prayer. "Thank you, sweet Jesus." She stood up and sighed in relief. Then she felt the hand dig into her hair, squeeze tightly and yank her head back forcefully. She screamed. "Jesus, save me from this evil." She felt the hand slip away and she fell to her knees, sobbing.

Kelly came up and rubbed her cheek with her hand. "Ouch, you hurt." Linda wrapped her arms around her daughter.

Chapter 21 – Going for the Kill

THE GARAGE DOOR opened and Matthew came in, gaunt and drained. He dropped his briefcase on the floor, stumbled to the kitchen table, and barely managed to sit down. He practically collapsed into the chair.

Linda turned and gasped. "Matt!"

Julie walked over with a cold washcloth and placed it on his forehead. She looked over to Linda, very concerned. "This may take more than chicken soup."

"Matt, honey, what happened to you? Did this all come on suddenly?" His pale skin frightened her. Matthew leaned back in his chair. Julie pulled off his shoes. Linda took Matthew's arm and directed Julie to help her help him to stand.

"I'm so cold," he moaned.

Linda pointed her arm toward the hallway. "Upstairs, right now, straight into the tub." Linda helped him down the hallway and Julie went back to cooking dinner.

When they got to the second floor, Kelly looked out of her room, smiled and said, "Hi, Daddy!" Matthew didn't even acknowledge her. Linda led him into the bathroom and gave Kelly a concerned look. Kelly leaned inside to have a look and said, "Daddy?"

Linda looked tenderly at her daughter and said, "Your father is very sick, honey. Go help Auntie Julie make him some soup." Linda added more hot water to the tub she and Kelly had prepared for him earlier, and closed the door. She undressed her husband and helped him into the tub. Once inside, he moaned and leaned back against the neck pad. Linda turned on the jets and caressed his cheek. She pulled a bottle of pain reliever out of the medicine cabinet, shook two tablets into her palm, drew a glass of cold water and handed them to him. Matthew couldn't even muster the strength to reach out for them. He merely closed his eyes and let his mouth fall open. She saw that his tongue was coated. Linda reached through his chapped lips and placed the tablets on his tongue and poured some water into his mouth. He swallowed, then lurched forward and coughed. One of the tablets flew out of his mouth, landed in the bath tub water and sank below his legs. Linda fished another tablet out of the bottle as Matthew's awful hacking continued. She dropped it into his mouth and tried again. He swallowed hard and drank the entire glass of water. When he had finished it, he slid down into the water and moaned. His hazy, blurred eyes met hers.

"I'm so sorry for everything."

"Oh, honey," Linda whispered. "Sit tight, I'm going to bring you a bowl of hot soup."

When Linda entered the kitchen, Julie had poured some soup into a bowl and held it out for her. "Here, take this to your husband. This will bring the color back to him, guaranteed."

Kelly reached out with a soup spoon and said, "Here, Mom."

"Thanks, you two." She rushed back upstairs.

Fifty minutes later, when she came back down, Sarah and Tyler sat at the table with Julie and Kelly and they were all ready to eat their soup.

"Why's Dad home so early?" Sarah asked. "Is everything alright?"

Linda sat down and replied, "Your father is very ill. He

sat in the hot tub for close to an hour. I fed him some soup and tucked him into bed."

Julie took her seat and slid her napkin into her lap. "Well, this soup is better than any medicine, I can tell you that." She folded her hands. "Now, shall we pray?"

The others bowed their heads for an instant and then looked back up at each other, each obviously thinking it to be a very bad idea. They folded their hands together anyway. "Blessed Father, we ask that you nourish our bodies and minds..." The silverware in the drawers began to shake violently, sending shrill metal shrieks throughout the room.

"Not again," Sarah said.

Linda shook her head and said, "Perhaps we'd better not."

Julie licked her lips. "Yes, I suppose it would be best if we skip grace. Let's do it in our own way, silently."

Linda took a sip of soup and said, "Mm, this is delicious."

"Yeah, Julie, really good," Tyler added. "Hey, I talked to Jimmy and Kyle today. They said they hoped we weren't mad that they left as quickly as they did last night. They were just freaked out and wanted to get out before Jim's mom saw anything, ya know?"

Linda nodded and sipped her soup wordlessly. She had always been very social and welcomed everyone into her home. She wondered what Mrs. Foster must have thought when the boys ran out of the house and urged her out of the driveway so quickly. They continued with dinner and looked at each other for reassurance. "Julie, Kelly and I found a newspaper ad at the diner today about a local paranormal investigator who conducts lectures," Linda said.

Sarah leaned forward, wiped her mouth and said, "Really? How awesome is that?"

"I spoke with him on the telephone and told him everything. He said that it sounded very serious and that he'd be making calls to his team." Sarah and Tyler smiled at each other.

"Everything will be all right," Kelly said.

Linda smiled and held her hand. "How do you know that, Kelly?"

Tyler perked up, interested to learn what Kelly knew. Kelly swirled her spoon around in her soup. "I don't know. Every story has a happy ending. Right?"

Linda's eyes watered up. She rested her chin in her palm and said, "I hope so, honey. I really do."

Later, after Julie left for home, the kids checked in on their father and then went to bed. Linda slept next to Matthew, frequently awakened by his hoarse grumbling and coughing. The eighth time she woke up she checked the clock. It was three am.

She lay back down and drifted off into a comfortable plane of soft quiet and comfort. As soon as she did, she suddenly felt that unmistakable feeling like she was being watched. Then the temperature plummeted inside the room. She was suddenly violently flipped over onto her stomach and shoved deep into the mattress. She couldn't move. The blankets were torn off the bed and a foul smell swept over her. It was repulsive. It smelled like a dead, rotting skunk. Time seemed to stand still. She could feel her heartbeat throbbing in her ears. Then out of the corner of her eye she saw a black, pulsating form float up to the bed. It was blacker than the deepest midnight darkness. Fear enveloped her, stealing her very breath away. It's cold, evil presence paralyzed her. Then another form, equally as black, moved in quickly, effortlessly, and stood beside Matthew. Paralyzed, Linda could do nothing but watch.

The one vaporous intruder kept her at bay while the other was doing God-knows-what to her husband. Whispering, endless whispering nearly drove her mad. She heard Matthew's exhausted moans, dulled, as if all of the power to resist had been instantly sucked out of him. He inhaled deeply and emitted a long, terrible, endless gasp.

When it was over, Matthew sank deeper into the bed and moaned. Then, a terrible, short-lived hissing laughter resonated throughout the entire room. Linda felt the pressure against her subside. She kicked and screamed and rolled over to Matthew. "Matt, wake up!" she panted. "Wake up!" He groaned—dazed and drained. "What just happened to you? What did they do to you?" Matthew moaned and drifted off to some far-away place where nothing at all could stir him. Linda slid back to her side of the bed and stared at the ceiling, trembling.

Chapter 22 – Spooking the Horse

THE NEXT MORNING Linda woke Matthew up to take the cough medicine and pain relievers that she had hoped would help him. He fell back to sleep almost immediately. Linda went downstairs. Sarah and Tyler had already left for school. Kelly lay on the living room floor playing with her dolls.

Julie knocked on the door and came in with some coffee and two bags from Dunkin Donuts. "How is Matthew?" she asked.

"He's sleeping so soundly that I can't wake him. Oh, Julie. I am about to break."

Julie eased her down into one of the seats at the table and held her hands. "What happened now?" She handed the coffee to her friend and spun around in her chair to address Kelly and said, "I brought Jelly Munchkins for you, honey."

Kelly turned her head around and said, "Yay!" She scampered into the kitchen and reached into the box. She pulled out a Munchkin and bit into it. "Thank you, Auntie Julie," she said. Strawberry jelly oozed down her chin and she giggled through lips covered by powdered sugar. Julie handed her a napkin.

"We were attacked in bed last night!"

"Attacked?"

"The temperature dropped so bad, I was freezing cold. Something flipped me over and pinned me down. The smell was so bad, it nearly made me sick. Something came into the room and stood or hovered next to Matt. Oh, my God, what are they? What do they want, and why won't they just leave us alone?"

"We will soon find out what they are when that investigator gets back to you."

"I wonder why he hasn't called back yet," Linda said.

"Give him another call," Julie urged. Linda exhaled heavily, jumped up and grabbed the phone. She dialed the number on the piece of paper in her pocket and got static on the other end. She tried again. '*The number you have reached is not in service at this time. Please try...*'

"You have got to be kidding me!" Linda turned off the phone and held it to her forehead. She closed her eyes and quieted her mind. She focused on the image of Christ and said aloud, "Please, dear God, help me get through!" They heard a low growl. Julie stared blankly at her, praying silently for divine assistance as she dialed again. "They won't let me make contact. That's the only logical reason."

Julie said, "Now, dear, I'm sure it won't be that long before someone gets back to you. Let's go through more of these books and see if we can find something else that might help us."

Over the next several hours, they poured through the books and devoured the entire box of Munchkins. Linda had gone up to check on Matthew every hour. Every time she tried to wake him he moaned and asked her to let him sleep. Around 4:30, as Linda and Kelly sat around the kitchen table, the phone finally rang. Linda rushed over and answered it. Excitement filled the room.

"Hello?"

"Mrs. McLaughlin?"

"Yes?"

"This is Mary Tannenback, Sarah's riding instructor. I'm afraid Sarah's been in an accident. She's been thrown from her horse. It was the strangest thing I've ever seen."

"What happened? How bad is it? Is Sarah badly injured?"

Julie and Kelly looked at each other with concern.

"She's being taken to Mercy General Hospital. She landed on her arm. We're about to head there now. Can you please come immediately and meet us in the Emergency Room?"

"Yes, of course." Linda hung up and took a deep breath. "Sarah's horse threw her off at riding practice."

"Oh, dear," Julie said. "I'll drive." She patted Kelly on the behind. "Come on, sweetheart. Let's get your coat."

Linda ran upstairs. "Matt! Matt!" She rushed into their room. Matthew sat on the edge of the bed. The front of his pajamas were soaking wet and his feet sat in a pool of urine. He had one slipper on. He looked dazed and confused.

"Oh, honey." Linda went into the bathroom and grabbed a towel. She moved his foot out of the way and laid the towel on the carpet. At least he was conscious. "Honey, Sarah was thrown from her horse. She hurt her arm!" Matthew looked down at her with vacant eyes. She applied pressure into the towel to soak up the urine. "We have to get you dressed so we can go to the hospital." She helped him stand and walked him into the bathroom. She turned on the shower. "The doctor can have a look at you, too. Surely, they can give you something that will make you feel better."

She pulled off his wet clothes, helped him step out of them, and eased him into the shower. She went into his closet and grabbed some fresh clothes for him to wear.

When Linda slid open the glass shower door, Matthew stared at her blankly. He spoke in an almost unintelligible tone that was deeply guttural. His face was gaunt, blank, and completely expressionless. "Hospital."

Linda helped Matthew get dressed and helped him down the stairs. Julie knelt with one of his shoes in her hand. Matthew balanced himself on Linda's shoulder and lifted each foot in succession until both of his shoes were on. Linda snatched a jacket for him to wear and put it over his shoulders. Julie opened the front door and helped him out and into the car. They left immediately for the hospital.

When they walked through the Emergency Room doors, Mrs. Tannenback spotted them immediately and rushed over to them. "I'm terribly sorry, Mrs. McLaughlin. She's down this hall over here." They walked briskly down the hallway. Mrs. Tannenback continued, "The horse acted so strangely."

When they rounded the corner and entered the examination room, they saw Sarah sitting on a stainless steel X-ray table in a gown. A doctor was examining her X-ray film up against the light. He pointed at an area near the wrist with the tip of his pen.

"Well, there *is* a hairline fracture, but it's not very bad." He looked over at Sarah and said, "We'll put your forearm in a brace. You should be all right if you protect it and if you don't re-injure it. You're young. You'll heal quickly. Just don't ride for a while, especially on horses that spook easily." He nodded, gave a brief unsure glance at Matthew, and walked out into the hallway.

"Montero doesn't spook, ever," Sarah replied.

"Oh, sweetheart," Linda said, walking inside.

Sarah said, "Hi, everyone. I'm so sorry for causing more problems. We needed this like a hole in the head."

Linda hugged her and said, "Oh, honey."

Sarah looked at her father and asked, "Dad, are you feeling any better?" He shook his head from left to right twice. Then his eyes rolled up inside his head and he collapsed against the wall, taking a small metal table down with him onto the floor. It made a spectacular clamor.

Chapter 23 – Circling the Wagons

"DAD!" SARAH SCREAMED.

Linda yelled, "Matt!"

The doctor who had just examined Sarah ran right back into the room, looked around, and knelt before Matthew on the floor. He held the sides of Matthew's face, grumbled, reached into his pocket and took out a penlight. He opened Matthew's mouth and shone the light inside. Then, he pulled open Matthew's eyelids and shone it in his eyes. He grunted, adjusted his stethoscope, pressed it against Matthew's heart and lungs and listened intently. A nurse and two orderlies came in to check what all the commotion was about. The doctor called out to them.

"This man is gravely ill." He stood and touched Linda's shoulder. "Are you his wife?"

"Yes," Linda said, still in shock.

The doctor leaned out the doorway and waved. Two strong young men wheeled a gurney inside. They helped Matthew up and sat him gently down on the gurney. Matthew was shivering. They lay him back carefully. A pair of male and female nurses came in seconds later. The female took Linda's hand and led her out.

"Take him into ICU! Page Dr. Kent!"

The doctor signed some papers, and attached the clipboard to the gurney. "We have to take care of this right away. Sit tight, Sarah."

After Sarah was fitted with her arm brace, the nurse led Julie, Kelly, and Sarah into the waiting room upstairs in the

Intensive Care Unit, where they waited for nearly two hours for any information about Matthew's condition. Linda returned to her family, exhausted. Her eyes were swollen and red. She sat beside Kelly and took her onto her lap. She said, "Your father has a severe case of pneumonia. He's been admitted and he isn't leaving here any time soon until he's all better."

"What, Mommy?" Kelly asked. "What's wrong with Daddy?"

She held her and said, "He is very, very sick."

Kelly cried and buried her face in her mother's sweater. "He has to stay here so the doctors can make him better, honey."

"I want Daddy to be all better," Kelly sobbed.

"I've got to stay with him. Julie, would you mind watching the kids for me?"

"Not at all," Julie replied. "They can all stay at my house." She got up and shooed the kids out of their chairs. "Okay, kids, let's go."

"I'm sorry, Mom," Sarah said as she started to walk away.

Linda hugged her. "What are you sorry about?"

"For falling and hurting my arm, like we didn't have enough trouble to deal with?"

"We might be very lucky that you hurt your arm and that your father came with us to the hospital. Pneumonia is very serious, and who knows what could have happened if we didn't get him here. Go on!" Kelly ran up for a hug. "Go with Auntie Julie. I will be home later."

"Okay."

Linda spent the evening in Matthew's room. He remained unconscious the entire time, connected to life support and intravenous medications. The steady humming of heart monitors mesmerized her and lulled her back and forth between sleep and wakefulness. Each time she awoke, she stood and made sure Matthew was covered with his blankets. She conversed briefly with several nurses as they came in and drew blood or switched bags of unknown medicines. They offered no answers, only token signs of their understanding and concern.

Later, another doctor poked his head in around midnight. "Mrs. McLaughlin?" he whispered.

"Yes," she responded.

"Can I speak with you for minute?" He beckoned her with his finger. Linda tiptoed out and adjusted her eyes to the brightly-lit hallway as she closed the door behind her quietly. "How about if we go downstairs for a cup of coffee?" he offered.

"That sounds wonderful, you have no idea," Linda said.

"I think I do," he countered, pointing at his identification badge. "I'm a doctor, see?" Linda forced a smile. He put his hand on her shoulder in an obvious attempt to comfort her. "This way, please." They passed silently down the hall together. The doctor pressed the button on the control panel and the elevator doors opened instantly. "I'm Dr. Thomas Kent. I specialize in infectious diseases and immunological disorders." He pressed a button and the elevator started to descend. "I don't want to alarm you, but I felt that it was better discussing this away from Matthew's room. I believe the patient's mind can hinder or help the healing process."

They stepped out of the elevator and walked into the cafeteria. It wasn't very busy at this time of night. They poured their coffee, grabbed their assorted creamers, sugars, and stirrers and took a seat at one of the nearby tables. They sat in uncomfortable silence for about a minute, and then the doctor said, "Your husband is worse off than we initially suspected that he was. We're trying to identify the cause of his skin disorder, but so far, we've had no success." He studied Linda for a reaction and waited for her response. She seemed unsure. Doctor Kent asked, "Are you with me? I'm referring to the extremely dry and raised patches of skin on his arms, chest, and neck, and the rash which seems to be spreading over his entire body."

Linda rubbed her eyes. "I...I'm not sure...what you're talking about?"

"You didn't see any of this?"

"No, he had nothing wrong with his skin last night when I made him a bath, and I saw nothing this afternoon, just a few hours ago when I helped him into the shower and helped him get dressed to come here to see our daughter." She covered her mouth with her hand and began to cry.

"He's on the best antibiotics available. We're conducting multiple tests."

"When will you know what's wrong with him?"

"We will have an answer to his problem soon, but we have to stabilize him until we know how to treat him. Until then, he is unconscious, and that's a good thing. His body can fight the infection better when he's resting."

"When will he regain consciousness?" she asked.

"It is hard to say. How is his general health?"

"He doesn't ever get sick. He's as healthy as a horse. He hasn't had a cold in close to three years."

"Hmmm, has he been under a great deal of stress lately?"

"I'll say."

"That is always a major contributing factor. Right now, he needs rest and quiet. I'm going to have to insist that he sees no visitors until his condition improves."

Linda sighed and thought, 'What the hell is happening? How could I possibly tell the doctor about the bizarre paranormal activity going inside our home?' She became lost in thought. The last thing she wanted was to be put into a straitjacket. Her husband needed her.

Doctor Kent's voice shook her back to reality. "That doesn't mean you, of course. I'll have the lab results at eight o'clock tomorrow morning. You can stay overnight if you want to, but it will do neither of you any good. You'll only be burning yourself out and possibly weaken your own immune system in the process." He shrugged and stood. "We still don't know what caused this, and we don't want you to weaken yourself so much that you become susceptible to the same agent that could be causing his illness if your own immunity drops."

"Agent?"

"It's speculation only. We don't know yet. I will notify you if any change develops. I'd like you to go home and get some sleep."

"It's not going to be very easy for me to sleep, doctor."

He took a final sip of his coffee, winked, pointed at her and said, "Doctor's orders."

Later, Linda stood before Matthew's bed. He hardly stirred. She wished that he would regain consciousness and tell her that he would be fine, but as the doctor explained, it was much better for his body if he just slept. She just couldn't leave his side, she decided, so she sat down in the chair next to his bed, curled up and drifted off into a much needed, deep sleep.

In the morning a nurse woke Linda up with a gentle tap on the forearm. She stirred. "Would you like some hot coffee, Mrs. McLaughlin?"

Linda sat up and massaged her own neck and shoulders. "Oh, that would be wonderful. Has there been any change in my husband's condition?"

The nurse walked around the bed, attached a fresh IV bag and threw the old one away. She checked her watch. "Dr. Kent should have already checked in. Hopefully he'll have some good news for you." She smiled. "I'll be right back with that coffee."

Linda stood beside Matthew's bed. His stillness concerned her. She rubbed his forehead. It was pale and clammy. "Please wake up, Matt. C'mon, honey."

Dr. Kent knocked, came in and said, "Good morning." The nurse came inside and handed Linda her coffee. Dr.

Kent opened his clipboard. "His lab results are in. Non-reactive, negative, negative—strange! This is very peculiar. His numbers definitely do not reflect an infection of this magnitude, or much of any ailment at all, for that matter." He huffed. "This can't be right."

Linda asked, "Negative? Strange? You're the specialist! What's wrong with him?"

Dr. Kent turned to face her and said, "I understand that you're upset, Mrs. McLaughlin, but please understand, we're doing everything that we can." Linda just shook her head in disbelief. Dr. Kent squeezed her shoulder. "Mrs. McLaughlin, we need to run more tests. You'll burn yourself out if you stay here."

Linda nodded, grabbed her purse and coat from the chair and walked to the door. "I need to get something to eat. You will contact me if there is any change?"

Dr. Kent said, "Absolutely."

"Thank you, doctor." Linda walked out of the room and went down the hall to the elevator. She pressed the down button, braced her hand against door frame, leaned forward and cupped her mouth. Tears rolled down her cheeks.

When she arrived back at the house an hour later and rolled into the driveway, Linda noticed that no one was home. She went inside and found a note on the kitchen table:

> *Dear Linda:*
> *Kelly and I will be back at around 5:00.*
> *Don't worry about dinner. I'll take care of everything.*
> *I hope Matthew is better.*
> *Julie*

She dropped her purse on the table and fished through the mail she'd picked up on her way in. She walked over and poured herself a glass of water. She took a sip and stared out the window into the back yard. 'What should I do?' she wondered. "I need to sleep," she said. She started to walk upstairs and remembered the doctor talking about some kind of possible infectious agent. Rather than risk getting contaminated upstairs, she wheeled around, walked down into the living room, lay down on the sofa and covered herself with a blanket. She fell instantly in a deep, peaceful sleep.

Chapter 24 – Painting Reality

LINDA AWOKE AT three o'clock in the afternoon. The house felt cold and inhospitable. She rolled off the sofa and groaned at the pain in her stiff back. She limped into the kitchen to check the answering machine to see if she might have been so deeply sleeping that she could have missed any calls. There were no messages at all. "Oh, this is damned frustrating." What could she do to get her mind off her worries? She could paint. That's what she used to do. She decided that's what she must do. She went to the sink, filled the teakettle and placed it on the stove.

While she was waiting for the water to come to a boil, she became lost in a daydream. She broke out of it when the kettle began spewing steam and whistling. She poured a cup, inserted a bag of Green Jasmine tea, opened the door to her art studio, and walked inside. She closed the door and tried the handle to make sure it hadn't locked behind her. She also checked for cold spots. She sat down and held the steaming cup beneath her nose and inhaled deeply. She closed her eyes and let the steam saturate her face. She waited. She listened. Everything seemed normal. She opened her eyes, smiled, set her cup down and reached for a new canvas. She thought about the Four Seasons Bed & Breakfast as she mixed her paints. She imagined how her paintings looked throughout that wonderful relaxing inn. She decided that her painting would be a country scene with a farm house, a tractor, and a long sun-lit dirt road.

She dabbed her brush into the paint, and the landscape

went down in no time. Her creativity flowed as easily as she had ever remembered. She smiled brightly. Her hands worked a vivid, crisp world where all was well, where demons, darkness, and despair were very far away things. She painted the rich red barn down to perfect detail. She grinned. She felt a joy she hadn't experienced in quite a while. Her arms moved through the air, covering the white canvas with golden fields of wheat and a serene pond reflecting the sunlight.

Then she paused and shivered. She felt cold. She sensed the unmistakably familiar feeling that she was being watched. The icy invisible fingers curled around her from behind, wound their way around her hand, and suddenly seized control of it. She saw the black shape begin to materialize behind her out of her peripheral vision. When she tried to pull away, its overwhelming strength squeezed her hand tightly. She screamed as it forced her brush down into the red paint that she had used for the barn. It forced her trembling hand up into the air and thrust it against the canvas. She screamed again. As much as she resisted, and as hard as she protested, she painted, rather *it painted* a gaping hole in the center of the wheat field—a hole that looked like it descended into the deepest recesses of Hell.

"Help me! Oh, my God! Let me go!" She tried to pull free, and felt as if her arm would be torn from its socket if it continued for one more minute. Her hand trembled.

She gasped as her hand was being used to write a message on the canvas. *Bitch.* Linda wailed in terror as it wrote the three terrible words that followed: *You will all die.*

"Jesus, help me!" she begged. The canvas shook and she felt the hands pull through her hair and wrap around her head. She expected her head to be tugged back as it was before in the living room earlier, but instead she was thrown forward off her stool and onto the floor. Then through tear-filled eyes she saw a hazy gray ball of light pass through the black form. She heard what sounded like a titanic struggle from some far away plane of existence.

Then, she heard the voice that emanated from thin air say, "Bitch!" A freezing, paralyzing cold enveloped her. Then an intense roar shook the entire room and the pressure on her head suddenly subsided. Linda sobbed, and she lay with her face buried in the carpet, exhausted. She was lost in a daze, where even common everyday sounds seemed muted and strange. She thought she heard something familiar—a ringing sound in the distance. Then she heard a pounding as she inched herself back slowly toward reality. She felt like one of those soldiers in a war movie where a grenade had gone off so close to them that everything buzzed and rang. She was dizzy and totally disoriented. She rolled over and made it to her hands and knees. The ice cold temperatures normalized. The black forms were gone.

She shook her head and identified the ringing sound. She nodded. It was the front doorbell. She crawled forward into and through the rarely used dining room on her hands and knees. The doorbell rang again and then she heard a powerful knocking. She cringed, fearing another attack from behind. She gathered her strength and dragged herself across the slate foyer floor. She saw the silhouettes of several people standing outside on the porch. She reached for the doorknob, twisted the lock, turned the door knob, tugged the door open and flopped to the floor. Three men stood there. Their astonished faces were clear evidence that they were not expecting to find her kneeling on the floor, nearly unconscious. Linda collapsed, thoroughly and completely exhausted.

The tallest, the one she instantly recognized from the newspaper ad and the one she had conversed with over the telephone, set his briefcase down on the front steps and knelt down before her.

"Mrs. McLaughlin?"

Linda moaned.

"I'm Jason McLeod. This is my team of investigators, and we are here to help you."

"Thank God," Linda said. She was curled up in the fetal position, sobbing. Jason helped her up to a sitting position.

"Can you tell me what just happened?"

Chapter 25 – Scoping Out the Premises

THE TWO OTHER men unpacked their cameras and took out several attachments and tripods. Linda just sobbed continually. The men looked at each other with grave looks of concern. She leaned out onto the front steps, groped at their feet, grabbed hold of their shoes, hugged them, held them and wept uncontrollably. "Thank God you came. I was just...attacked!" She looked up at the men with tear-soaked eyes. "Help me! Please, in the name of God, help my family!"

Jason held Linda's hands. He motioned for the other men to go inside. They pushed open the door and entered cautiously. "Can you tell me *where* you were just attacked?"

"It was in my studio, off the kitchen." Jason helped Linda stand up. "I'm an artist. I was painting a new scene when the hands, the freezing cold hands, wrapped around mine and took control of them. They made me paint awful words and terrible things."

One of the men rounded the corner and walked into the dining room, and finally into the art studio. "My God," he called out. Linda nodded, knowingly. He came back around, his face blank, and said, "You have to see this."

Jason held Linda by the shoulders and looked at her intently. "Initially, we wanted to follow our standard procedure and do some preliminary filming of the outside of your house and yard before it gets dark." He looked at his fellow investigator. "But because you were just attacked, please show me where it happened, and please show me this painting of yours that's been defaced. I'd like to get all of the information that I can about that. Then, my men and I would like to go outside, and when we return, we'd like to film the entire interior, and conduct a thorough interview with your family and anyone and everyone involved. Is that okay?"

"Are you kidding? Do anything. Do everything you can. Please!" She grabbed his shirt. "Please help us!" Linda folded her hands in prayer, looked out at the sky and smiled, mouthing praises to unseen heights. She sobbed uncontrollably.

Jason smiled. "That's why we are here. We are here to help you," he said, as he followed the blond, curly-haired investigator into the art studio. "Linda, this is Daniel Clemmons. He's a seasoned investigator and an amazing psychic photographer." He called out to the other man. "Aaron, can you come here for a moment please?" A six-foot tall man came back down into the hallway and smiled. "This is Aaron Harper. He's one of my most experienced men. He uses high-speed and infrared film to photograph activity in homes just like this to get hard evidence. You are in more than capable hands."

"Thank you." For the first time she didn't feel alone and utterly helpless.

"Look at that!" Jason said, looking at her ruined painting. "Get some photos of this please." He asked Linda to come closer.

She stood there in the dining room with her arms folded over her chest. "I'd rather not, thank you."

"Very well," Jason said. "Can you please describe in detail what happened here?"

Linda described the attack down to the smallest detail, right up until the time when she first heard the doorbell. When she was finished Jason switched off his mini tape recorder and stuck it in his pocket. Surprisingly to Linda, it didn't seem like her own problem anymore. But then the thought of Matthew sick in bed, and the cold hands that had gripped her a few minutes earlier, caused the hard uneasy truth to come back suddenly, as if it had slapped her right in the face.

"Mrs. McLaughlin?" Jason said, concerned.

"Linda," she said as she came toward him. "You can call me Linda."

Jason smiled. "Would you make the calls necessary to gather everyone here this evening for the interview?"

"Yes, right away, but my husband is in the hospital," Linda said.

Jason suddenly became very serious. "He's in the hospital? Can I ask what caused him to become hospitalized?"

"He has pneumonia. He was admitted yesterday. I'm very frightened for him, because they don't know what's wrong with him or how to treat him." The investigators gave each other knowing glances. They gathered around her.

"When did he first get sick?" Jason asked. "Was it before or after the haunting phenomena started happening?"

"It happened after what we call 'the worst night.' He came home from work early, because he didn't feel well," Linda said. She went into the kitchen to telephone the kids. The investigators followed her.

"I'd like to ask you some things in relation to his sudden illness, but we need to begin filming before it gets dark." He nodded to his cohorts. "Shall we?" Daniel mounted his camcorder on his shoulder. Aaron followed them outside with his special camera. Jason took his pocket recorder out again, turned it on, and began speaking into it. "This is the preliminary investigation of the McLaughlin residence in Monroe, Connecticut. The time is now 3:45 p.m."

A little over an hour later, while the men were outside filming the exterior of the house and the yard, Linda heard the doorbell ring. Linda hurried down the hall to answer it. When she opened it, she found the investigators standing on the front porch smiling at her. "You don't need to ring the bell. Please, come in and feel free to go whenever you please."

Jason nodded. "Okay, thank you. I'd like to begin setting up for the family interviews. Would your living room be a comfortable place where we can sit and talk for about an hour or so?"

"Yes. My son and daughter will be calling shortly. My neighbor is watching my youngest daughter, and they'll be over around five o'clock."

"Great, thank you. Can you show me where the living room is?"

Linda led them into the house, and Jason and the men set their cameras, tripods, tape recorders, note pads and pens on the coffee table and on the bar. The phone rang several minutes later. Linda got up. "That's either Tyler or Sarah," she said. She picked up the receiver.

"Hello?"

"Yeah, Mom, what is it?" Tyler asked.

"Tell your sister that the investigators are here and want to interview all of us, including Jimmy and Kyle, so they can try and figure out what is happening around here."

Tyler gulped and replied, "Uh, sure, but when?"

"Five. Make sure to tell your sister, too."

"Okay, I will. See you then. Bye."

"Bye."

Jimmy leaned against his locker and shook his head. "What do you mean they want to interview us?"

"Jesus Christ!" Kyle said.

"What's the big deal?" Tyler answered. "They want to find out what's happening in my house and what we know."

"Well, what if *we* caused it?" Kyle protested.

"That's dumb," Tyler said. "You guys owe it to me to come over and tell these guys what has been going on!"

"He's right, Kyle," Jimmy said.

Kyle slapped the wall. "Why is it that I am always the last one to agree on things? One of you starts it, and then realizes that the other is right, and then I look like the jerk, because I have to understand a thing is the way that you two see it. Is that fair? I don't think it is."

"It's politics!" Jimmy replied.

"Anyway," Tyler added, "we have to be there at five o'clock, so let's get going."

Jason was adjusting the camcorder in the middle of the living room, centered on the sofa in preparation for the family interview. He was going through a note pad when Linda called out from the kitchen. "Would any of you like some hot tea?"

"No, thank you," Jason replied.

Aaron threw his camera strap over his shoulder and approached Jason. "I'm all set to start the interior."

Jason called out to Linda, "We're going to start filming the inside of the house. Is that alright?"

"Yes, there is no need to ask permission for anything. Do whatever you need to do. I'll be here, doing my best to stay out of your way. I must say that my energy levels have returned since you three showed up."

"Great," Jason said. "I'm glad to hear it. You had us pretty worried. We can conduct the family interview when we're finished outside and when we have everyone else present."

Just then Julie and Kelly came in from the garage with bags of groceries. Linda walked over to help. "Oh, Julie, Kelly, meet Jason. He's the investigator that we've been so anxiously waiting for."

"Hi," Kelly said with a big bright smile. "You're the man on my Silly Putty," Kelly giggled.

Jason chuckled and asked, "...Silly Putty?"

Linda laughed. "We found your advertisement on a newspaper while we were dining out for breakfast. Kelly was playing with her Silly Putty and captured your image on it." She laughed, looked down at Kelly and said, "Honey, Jason and the other men are here to find out what's going on, so they can help us."

Jason offered to take the bag that Julie held in her arms. "Oh, thank you. Good to meet you...finally." She smiled and led him to the kitchen counter. "What a relief."

Kelly giggled, and peeked at him from behind her mother's legs. Then she asked, "Are you a giant?"

Jason laughed and said, "I'm really tall, but if that makes me a giant in your eyes, then yes, I am most certainly a giant. But you have to remember one thing."

Kelly giggled and asked, "What?"

"I'm one of the *good* giants." He smiled and put the grocery bag on the counter. He peeked out the window. "Okay, we're going to get started. I'm sure you'd like us out of your hair for a bit as you prepare your dinner, right?"

Julie scoffed, "Oh, don't be silly."

"Okay, I will see you ladies in a little while," Jason said as he walked away.

Once all of the investigators were out of earshot, Julie and Linda started unloading the groceries together and began to cook dinner. Julie eventually leaned over and whispered, "I'm curious. What did they say is going on?"

Linda shrugged and said, "They haven't explained anything yet. They're going to do a group interview in about an hour or so."

"Oh," Julie said. She nodded. "Maybe we'll find out then."

"I sure hope so."

"How is Matt?" Julie asked.

"Worsening as time goes by. I haven't heard from the hospital in a while though, so I will call again in a few minutes."

Daniel entered the room with his camera. "Linda, can you please show me where the basement is?"

Kelly smiled, and was all too eager to help. She turned the knob and opened the door for him silently.

Daniel placed his hand on her head and said, "Thanks." He turned on the camera's power, raised it to eye level, started filming, and walked slowly down the basement steps.

Tyler, Kyle, and Jimmy came in the garage door. "We're here," Tyler said.

"Hello, everybody," Jimmy said. He held out his hand, and Kelly rushed over and high-fived him. Jimmy went down into the living room to check out the equipment that the investigators had set up throughout the room.

"Wow, will you look at all this tech," Kyle said.

Tyler followed them and said, "They sure have a lot of cool stuff, huh?"

"They certainly do," Linda said. "The others are walking around, filming the house. They have special cameras, too. Now, go wash up for dinner. It'll be ready soon."

"How's Dad?" Tyler asked. Sarah came in with her arm in a sling.

"I have yet to hear from Doctor Kent." Linda took the phone and went into the dining room.

A few minutes later, Linda walked back into the kitchen with a look of sheer disappointment.

"What is it, dear?" Julie asked.

"He's getting even worse. His skin is drying up and chapping so badly, it's bleeding."

"Gross," Sarah said.

Kelly began crying. "I want Daddy to be okay."

Linda sighed and hugged her daughter. "So do I, honey. So do I." Julie came up and hugged them both.

Aaron began touring the house from room to room and then went upstairs.

The guys watched the other investigators and did their best to stay out of the way. They eventually went outside and threw around a football.

Forty-five minutes later, all three investigators converged in the foyer. Jason called out to Linda. "Linda, we've finished with our initial filming. If you'll excuse us, we'll return after you finish your dinner."

"Don't be silly," Julie called out. She walked around the corner so she could see them in the foyer. "There's enough for all of you."

"Thank you, really, but we have to make some phone calls, and we already have dinner plans. Daniel's wife would have us skinned alive if we canceled."

"Can't you tell me what's going on before you leave?" Linda asked.

Jason extended a firm hand. "Linda, we're only in the beginning stages of our investigation. We're here to collect data, evidence of any activity, if possible, and interview everyone involved since the activity began. I'm sorry, I can't offer you any answers, yet."

Linda became pale. 'What if they can't do anything? What if they're leaving and they're never coming back?'

"I feel for you, and I empathize with all of you. I've seen this dozens of times. I can't explain what is causing the problem yet. We'll examine every bit of tape thoroughly. I've learned from the best, trust me on this. We will be back at eight o'clock to conduct the interviews. We need everyone to be completely honest with us and tell us everything we need to know so we can be effective."

Linda nodded. "I'm sorry, I just wanted..." She sobbed. "My husband's getting much worse."

"What's happening with him?"

"He's sick and no one has any answers..."

Jason interrupted her. "There are no easy answers

where things of this nature are concerned. What are his symptoms?"

"Are you implying that this stuff that is happening in my house is contributing to my husband's illness?"

Tyler and his friends shot sudden concerned glances at each other.

"No, Linda, I'm not implying anything. I do empathize with you, and I also realize the seriousness of the situation. We're going to go over some things. We'll be back at eight. We'll begin our interviews then. Enjoy your dinner, and we will see you shortly." Jason led his team outside.

Julie began serving, and they all sat at the table and started eating. The guys and Sarah exchanged unsure glances during the entire meal.

Chapter 26 – Interviewing the Family and Friends

WHEN THE INVESTIGATORS returned after dinner they gathered in the living room. Linda, Julie, Sarah, and Kelly squeezed onto the couch. Tyler, Jimmy, and Kyle sat on the floor, and Jason sat on the fireplace hearth. Aaron and Daniel manned their own unique cameras. "Okay, I'd like you to answer the following questions to the best of your ability."

A shadow suddenly loomed over the back deck. Jason leaned over to have a look. A tall young man came up to the door in his Letterman jacket, peered into the glass and knocked.

"That's my boyfriend, Bill," Sarah said. She hopped up and let him in. "I invited him over because we've all witnessed things together, and I thought he would be able to contribute."

"Excellent, the more witnesses, the better," Jason said.

Linda asked, "Honey, why didn't you tell me about that?"

"Honestly, Mom. We haven't even had time to talk," Sarah said.

"Hello, Bill. Thank you for coming, honey."

"No problem, Mrs. M. Glad to help."

Jimmy glanced at Tyler. He leaned over and whispered, "Mrs. M.?"

Tyler giggled as Bill took a seat on the floor in front of the sofa before Sarah. He glared at Jimmy with blazing eyes.

"Okay, let's begin. Please state your names, your ages, and your relationship to one another. We'll start with Linda, please."

"I'm Linda McLaughlin. I'm 48 years old. I am the wife of Matthew McLaughlin and the mother of Sarah, Tyler, and Kelly."

"I'm Kelly," she said, smiling from ear to ear. She looked around the room at everyone. "I'm six years old, and I am the sweet princess." Everyone laughed heartily.

"I am Julie Hendrickson. I am 56 years old, and I am a friend of the family."

"Sarah McLaughlin. 18."

Bill raised his hand and said, "I'm Bill Miller. I'm 19, and I'm Sarah's boyfriend."

"I'm Tyler McLaughlin, and I'm 16 years old."

Jimmy fidgeted with the pillow behind him. "I'm Jimmy Reading. I'm 16, and I'm Tyler's friend."

"Kyle Foster, 16, also Tyler's friend."

Jason jotted that information down and said, "Thank you, everyone." He looked at Linda. "Have any of you at any point in your lives ever practiced black magic, sorcery, witchcraft, or voodoo, or has anyone been involved in any satanic or religious cults for any period of time, no matter how brief or how insincere?"

"My God, of course not," Linda said.

"That's a strong conviction, Linda," Jason said. "But that doesn't answer the question for everyone else present in the room."

He followed them one by one with his eyes and got the same blank stares from them all. When he got to Tyler and his friends, he asked, "Guys?"

Jimmy said, "No way, man!"

"Never," Kyle said.

Jason asked, "Tyler?"

Tyler gave him a look of sheer disgust that seemed to have answered the question perfectly, because Jason sat up straight and tapped his pen against the note pad he was writing in.

"Okay, then," Jason said. "Let's switch gears a little, shall we? Linda, what is the age of your home?"

"The house is five years old. We built it."

Jason asked, "Do you know the history behind this property?"

Linda replied, "The history? Oh, yes. It was forest land."

Jason continued, "Have any of you used any occult paraphernalia, such as a Ouija board or a deck of Tarot cards? Has anyone ever performed a séance in this house?"

"Absolutely not," Linda said.

Jason studied each of them very carefully.

"What's a gee-gee board, Mom?" Kelly asked.

"It's a game, sweetie," Linda answered.

"I can assure you, it is most definitely *not* a game," Jason warned.

Aaron studied the teenagers and asked, "Guys?"

"No, never," Tyler answered. He felt a knot develop in his stomach.

Jason asked, "Sarah, Bill?"

"No, sir," Bill said.

Sarah shook her head from side to side and added, "And no one has performed a séance in the house, either."

"Okay, no use of any occult paraphernalia," Jason said. "Do you know if anyone has placed a curse on any of you?"

The boys laughed. Tyler wiggled his fingers at his friends and said, "Oh, a curse."

Jason sighed. "I see that you're not taking this very seriously. Let me share something with you," he said. "Curses are very real. Something as simple as telling someone to 'go to hell' can cause serious psychic harm. I know these questions seem mundane, silly, insulting, or even outrageous, but they are very serious questions. You should take them as such, if we are going to get to the bottom of this and figure out how to help you."

"How do I know if someone told me to 'go to hell', or made a voodoo doll of me and stabbed it with a needle when I wasn't looking?" Tyler laughed.

"That's very amusing, buddy," Aaron said.

"Easy, Aaron," Jason said calmly. "What we meant is, do you know anyone who actively practices black magic or witchcraft or the like, who might have cursed you or who may have cast some spell on you or your family?"

"I think I can speak for all of us," Linda said. "The answer is a solid, definite no."

Sarah rubbed the brace on her arm and said, "You can't speak for all of us, Mom. I understand what he's getting at."

"Thank you, Sarah," Jason said. "It could be someone at school, or in the community, or it could even go back centuries. There are such things as cursed families."

"Look, this all started when Kelly saw the ghost at the cemetery," Linda said.

"Yes, I agree. But the activity you and your family are experiencing is not simply caused by a brief passing-by of a local cemetery," Jason added. "There have to be other causes."

This next question is never easy to ask, but I'm going to ask it anyway. Many medications can cause hallucinations, so I must ask if any of you are taking pharmaceutical or recreational, mind-altering drugs?"

"Oh, my," Julie said.

"I'm not talking just narcotics, folks. I mean any medication that could induce fatigue or hallucinations."

"No. We're all very healthy," Linda replied.

Kyle sat up straight and said, "I have to say one of the things I most admire about my friends here is that none of us have ever even tried cigarettes, and we have never smoked pot, and we don't ever plan to."

Linda smiled. "I believe you, all of you. And it is also

something that I am very proud of. But does that include alcohol?"

"Mom," Tyler replied. "My friends and I are the epitome of well-balanced, well-behaved, *perfect* teens in every way, shape and form."

"Good grief," Sarah replied. "I have seen all three of you drink, so cut the bull."

Tyler obviously couldn't believe his ears. "Way to throw me under the bus, thanks, Sis."

Linda laughed and said, "I'm sorry but that was just priceless." She shook her head.

Jason chuckled and said, "Okay, so negative on the drug use, aside from some dabbling in alcohol, thank you. Onto my next series of questions, please. What religion are you, and do you practice your religion by attending church? How strong is your faith on a scale of one to ten, with ten being the strongest?"

The general reply was Christianity with various degrees of practice and high levels of faith.

"Are all of you baptized?"

"Yes," Linda said, "All of these kids have been baptized, and Kyle was just confirmed."

Kyle smiled proudly, clasped his hands together in prayer and smiled.

Sarah scoffed, and said "Oh, please, Kyle, you're no angel."

Kyle replied, "Am, too!"

"Has any of you at any time since the activity began experienced mood swings or behaved in any manner inconsistent with your normal personalities?"

"Yes," Linda said. Everyone perked up and watched Linda. "My husband, Matthew, has. He went berserk, accused our son of theft, hollered at him, and slapped him. That was completely unacceptable and it was totally out of character."

"When did this happen?" Jason asked.

"It was right after that terrible night. We were kept awake with this pounding and whispering, and that's when we were attacked and when I was bitten!"

The investigators exchanged glances. Jason became quite serious, leaned forward and asked, "Are you telling me that you were bitten by entities in this house?"

"Yes, yes, right here," Linda said, exposing her forearm. "The wounds healed overnight. We've had our hair tugged on. We've been mauled and attacked."

Jason looked at Daniel. "Get a shot of that, will you?" Daniel snapped a still photo of her arm. "At what time do you notice the most intense activity?" Jason asked.

They all looked at each other. "I can't speak for all of us, but one night my friends and I were awakened at about three or four in the morning," Tyler said. "That's what time it was when the doorbell rang over and over that same night. Remember, guys?"

"Yeah," Jimmy added. "It rang about eight times, and there was definitely no one out there."

"Wait, when was this?" Linda asked, leaning in toward them.

"Mom, lots of stuff has happened when you and Dad were away over the weekend that Sarah and I didn't know how to explain to either of you," Tyler said.

"And we didn't want to frighten Kelly," Sarah added.

"Excuse me?" Linda demanded. "You've been experiencing things and haven't told us about them?"

"Okay," Jason continued. "Have there been any odd smells?"

"Dude, what's with what we smelled the next morning? It was a wicked smell," Kyle added.

Linda became agitated and asked, "What are you talking about? What smells? When did this happen?"

"See, this is what we're talking about," Jason said. "All of you have your own little piece to add to the larger story. Have there been any strange temperature changes?"

"Yes, I've had cold spells come over me several times," Linda said.

Tyler scoffed. "*Excuse me*? Have you been withholding information from us?"

"I didn't want to frighten any of you, so I kept it to myself," Linda countered.

"Exactly," Sarah said.

"Kelly said she talked to the ghosts in her bedroom. Tell them about that, Kelly."

"Is that true, Kelly?" Jason asked.

"Uh, huh. They talked to me lots."

Jason asked, "Who did?"

"Brock," Kelly replied.

Jason said, "Brock is a strange name, isn't it?"

"Yeah," He told me he didn't like my brother or my daddy or mommy. He told me that they will try to spoil our fun."

"What else do they say to you?" Jason asked.

"I don't know." She smiled. "They're silly."

"What did they look like?"

"Um...dark and yucky." She sat up straight and smiled. "A kitty comes and sees me, too." She nodded her head in approval.

"When the kitty comes into your room, is it always a kitty or does it look funny?"

"It comes out of a mushy dark cloud," Kelly said.

"I saw black clouds," Linda said. "I've seen black forms in my art studio and in my bedroom. They take every last bit of warmth from the room and scare me so bad I'm unable to move. There were two of them with us in our room the other night."

"Was this before your husband got ill?"

"No, he was sick in bed at the time. This was late at night."

"Do you recall the time?"

"3:30 a.m.," she offered.

Jason nodded. "Have you ever prayed and seen any kind of strange activity as a result?"

"Yes," Julie said. "I began with grace yesterday and the silverware in the drawers started rattling. We decided to stop, for fear of our safety."

"Yes, and the night before that, when we all slept in the living room, I prayed aloud before I got bitten."

Tyler slapped his forehead. "Tell them about the whirling cyclone of silverware and all the opening and closing cabinets."

"More on that one in a minute, please." He looked at Aaron with wide eyes. "Has anyone directly challenged the spirits in the house?"

"What do you mean by 'challenged'?" Linda asked.

"Has anyone verbally confronted or threatened them in any way, shape, or form?"

"Of course," Linda said. "They've invaded our home. Matt told them to get out. He said it was his house."

Jason asked, "He told them to get out of the house?"

"He *commanded* them to get out—that's exactly what happened," Tyler said.

Jason nodded and asked, "And how soon after did he get sick?"

"The next morning," Linda said. "He looked absolutely terrible."

"No, wait a minute," Tyler said. "He grabbed his stomach and curled over, remember? He complained about a real bad smell and puked all over the fireplace."

"Yes, that's right," Linda said. "Tyler's right. He put his hand over his mouth and vomited all over himself soon after. He complained about a rancid death smell."

"Linda, you were the last one attacked, in your studio, right?"

"Yes. I decided to paint, and my hand was taken over. It forced me to ruin my painting, and it wrote curses on my canvas."

Sarah gasped and asked, "Mom! Are you serious?"

"Yes, honey. Then, it hurled me to the floor and pinned me there. I was terrified."

"Mom," Tyler roared. "Come on!"

"Sarah, tell him about your horse accident," Linda said.

Sarah sat up. Her mother nudged her with an elbow. "It was really weird. I was on Montero, that's my horse. We were trotting down the path I always take him down, and he stopped suddenly. He just started neighing and kicking up with his front hooves. He turned sharply as if he saw something, and that's when he whirled around, threw me off and galloped away."

"So, it seemed like Montero was really spooked?" Jason asked.

"Yeah, he sure was. Luckily, my instructor saw the whole thing. She always carries a radio, so she called for a four-wheeler to come and get me."

"Okay, Tyler, Sarah, please tell me about everything that happened when your parents were away for the weekend." Tyler and the others recounted the terrible phenomena, and Linda held her face and wept for nearly the entire time.

Chapter 27 – Recording Events

"OKAY," JASON SAID. "Those are all of the questions that I have for now. We're going to divide ourselves up throughout the house and see if we can't stir things up a bit, and catch some hard evidence on tape. We'd like everyone to take a room and wait, watch, and listen for anything strange to happen."

"Cool," Kyle said.

"Linda, I'd like you to go and turn off all of the lights." He handed her a flashlight. "Just so no one gets hurt moving around, we'd like you to use these flashlights, okay?" He opened a duffel bag full of flashlights and began handing them out to everyone else.

"Whatever you say," Linda agreed. She turned on her flashlight and walked away.

"Bill, I'd like you to sit in the art studio. Are you up for that?"

Bill stood up and practically saluted. "Yes sir!"

"Okay, just sit tight in there, and all you need to do is wait and see if anything out of the ordinary happens. If it does, just call out to us, or come and get us."

"You got it," Bill said. He kissed Sarah on the forehead and walked through the kitchen into the art studio. He opened the door, walked inside, and sat down on Linda's stool.

"Sarah, I'd like you to stay in the living room. Julie, you and Kelly can stay in the kitchen, alright?"

Julie nodded. She took Kelly's hand and said, "Come on,

dear." Kelly took her hand and they walked into the kitchen together. They both sat down and scanned the room carefully.

Jason asked, "Kyle?" Kyle whipped his head around. His eyes were as wide as saucers. "Are you okay?"

"Yeah, I'm just spooked. I'm sorry, but that's the truth."

"If you would like to leave, there is no shame in that."

He looked at his friends, gulped and said, "No, I'm spooked, but not that spooked."

"Okay, would you feel comfortable sitting in the garage?"

"Hmmm..." Kyle replied.

"We can leave the door into the kitchen open. We just want to cover as much of the house as we can to make sure that if any activity happens someone witnesses it."

"Yeah, I'm cool with the garage." He switched on his flashlight and shone it under his chin. He smiled, walked into the garage and sat down on some furniture moving pads.

"Daniel," Jason said.

Daniel replied, "Yes, yes, I know." He chuckled. "Into the basement I go. I always get the basement." He opened the cellar door and started to walk downstairs. He turned around and called out, "Kyle?"

"Yeah," Kyle replied from the garage, his voice echoing throughout.

"Would you like to trade places?"

"I'll pass, thanks," Kyle replied, chuckling.

Daniel winked and said, "No one ever wants to trade with me, either."

Jason and Aaron went upstairs. Tyler and Jimmy followed them slowly and cautiously. Frightened, Kelly climbed out of her own chair and up into Julie's lap. Tyler and Jimmy stood on the landing and watched the investigators from a distance. Tyler looked around him. Jimmy gave Tyler a look of encouragement. The troops had finally arrived, it seemed.

Jason and Aaron went right up upstairs without a bit of hesitation. Tyler and Jimmy, however, cautiously crept up behind them as silently as they could. When Tyler rounded the corner, dark shadowy halls and silent unlit rooms made the house seem like a foreign and disturbing place. It was incredibly quiet—too quiet. This was no longer a place of happy memories and warm comfort like he was used to. Instead, heavy stagnant stillness prevailed.

Aaron peeked out from Kelly's room and waved Tyler inside. "Where did Kelly say she saw the black cat?"

"She said that she saw it sitting on the edge of her bed."

Aaron sat down on the bed and turned on his camera. "Here," he said, handing the camera to Tyler. "Snap a picture of me from the waist up."

Tyler took the camera. He aimed and hit the button. A faint red light pulsed as he took the picture, but there was no bright white flash like he was expecting. "What the..." He looked at the camera, intrigued.

Aaron reached for it. "It's special infrared film for night shots. It works very well. If there was anything there when you took the photograph, it'll show up."

"Cool," Tyler said. He looked back at his friend. "Did you see that, Jim?"

"Yeah, that's pretty intense tech," Jimmy said. "Ghost Camera Mark IV."

"Pretty much," Aaron said. Aaron snapped his fingers. "Guys, we should all stay focused. Tyler, I need you to yank this door open quickly." Tyler opened Kelly's closet door, and Aaron snapped a series of photos inside. Aaron leaned inside and listened. Then they all heard a light scratching sound along the inside walls. They all got a chance to lean in and witness the activity. Suddenly, it sounded as if it was crawling up into the attic. "Did you hear that?"

"Yeah," Tyler said.

Aaron backed out and turned away. "Come on."

"Okay, but where are we going?"

"The attic," Aaron said with determination. He went out into the hallway where Jason stood with a flashlight, recorder, and microphone, all aimed at the ceiling.

Jason said, "I picked up some moans and then something sounded like it crawled along the wall and went up into the attic."

"We got scratching in the closet in Kelly's room, and it sounded like it went into the attic, also," Aaron replied. Tyler and Jimmy locked eyes. Tyler mouthed the words 'holy shit.'

Jason pulled down the cord to the attic door, and the door popped open. He drew down the steps and unfolded them. Freezing air rushed down the attic stairs. Jason locked the ladder into place and placed his hands on the rails. He put the flashlight in his mouth and started upstairs. He stopped midway and scanned the attic with his flashlight. Then he went all the way up. Aaron started up behind him.

"Oh, my God," Jason said.

"What's wrong?"

"Back down, get back down!" Jason said.

Aaron literally skated down the stairs. Jason scrambled down and stopped suddenly, midway down the steps.

"What was it?" Aaron asked.

"Growling so loud you wouldn't believe it," Jason said. He leaped down onto the carpet. "It happened right beside me. An ice-cold patch of air just took all of my breath away, like someone put a soaking-wet, half-frozen washcloth over my mouth." Just then, a black shadowy form flitted down the attic steps and rushed down the hallway. They all saw it and looked at each other in amazement. They ran down the hallway as fast as they could. As they reached the steps, they heard Bill scream from downstairs inside the art studio.

"Holy shit!"

They raced down the stairs into the art studio as fast as their legs would carry them in the darkness. Bill was sitting on the stool. He had lost all of the color in his face, and he was trembling. Jason asked, "What is it, Bill? Did you see something?"

Bill said, "I was sitting here looking into the dining room, and suddenly this cloud of blackness came out of the foyer, turned the corner, and stopped right in front of me. The temperature dropped like forty degrees in an instant. The thing just stood there. It was like a big black cloud, but it was blacker than black. I felt it looking at me. I aimed my flashlight at it, and it came right up to me. I felt like I had stuck my finger in an electrical outlet, ya know that kind of 'zing' you get when you nearly electrocute yourself?"

"Then what?" Jason asked.

"That's when I screamed out. It went right through the wall here outside."

"Okay, I want everyone to relax," Jason said. The weighted thickness of evil lay heavily all over the entire house.

Just then they heard the neighbors' dog barking feverishly outside. The golden retriever growled and snarled, as if it were attacking someone, or like it was being attacked, for that matter.

Tyler said, "That's Cinnamon." He ran through the dining room into the foyer and out the front door. Jason and Aaron followed. The dog's whimpering drew Tyler toward the side of the house. He called out to him, "Here, boy!" He found the dog cowering in the bushes, whimpering. Tyler leaned in and patted him. "Come here, boy. It's okay." The dog crawled out and lay at Tyler's feet.

The infrared camera flash startled him. He didn't even know anyone had followed him. The dog barked again. It turned toward the woods and snarled viciously. Jason pointed and Aaron snapped a series of pictures.

Jimmy rounded the corner, startling them all. He asked, "What's up?

Loud growling erupted immediately, bear-like, deep, and guttural. Everyone covered their heads in fear of being attacked. The dog whirled around as if someone or something had struck its back. Jimmy ducked as if something flew just an inch over his head. "Jesus."

The growl came again, followed by a whine like that of a pig, in one, long steady stream. The dog leaped up and charged at Jimmy. Tyler couldn't believe his eyes. The dog had never attacked anyone. Tyler called out in protest, only the dog didn't pounce on Jimmy, who fell down into the grass to dodge out of the way. He leaped up against the side of the house, reaching out into thin air, swiping his paws against the sides, barking and snarling viciously.

Aaron snapped picture after picture, one angle after another, until Cinnamon stopped.

Jimmy stood up and brushed his pants off as Cinnamon ran toward the neighbor's backyard and hid inside his doghouse. The men followed. Tyler knelt before the doghouse, reached inside, patted him and rubbed his ears. The dog whined. The men stood in a circle and waited patiently for any other signs of activity. None came.

After a few minutes, they started back toward the house. Tyler stared out at the stone wall where Kyle had first seen the shadowy figure, and he got tingles up his spine.

Jason said, "Tyler, come in and take a seat please." They all walked in and Tyler closed the door. They gathered in the living room in a circle. "Under normal circumstances we would try to get evidence by provoking the spirits to reveal themselves. But I think we've seen and heard enough already to be sure that there are spirits in this house." Tyler, Jimmy, and Kyle exchanged wordless glances. Jason continued, "We should have captured some good activity on film." Linda smiled at her kids, like that was some really good news.

Jason continued, "Some doorway had to be opened for spirits of this nature to come in and do what they're doing. They just don't come in on their own unless they are invited." Jimmy tapped Tyler. They locked eyes and the sure look of guilt ran over their faces. Jason and Aaron didn't miss it, either.

"Spirits of what...nature?" Linda asked.

"These are not the good-natured kind. I think we can all agree on that," Jason said. "I'd like to ask everyone to resume their normal day-to-day activities. Just do whatever it is that you normally do at this time of night..."

"Normal?" Tyler asked. "Right, normal. Everything is just peachy." He threw his hands into the air and shook his head. "You have to be..."

"Tyler, behave," Linda warned.

"Things like this are extremely traumatic. We all understand that. Please do what you would normally do at this time at night. All we will do now is watch. I want to see who is the primary object of their attacks. If anything happens, just yell, and we'll be right there with you. Okay?"

Linda huffed. "Okay, let's do what we do, kids."

Julie yawned and called out from her chair in the kitchen, "I'm very sleepy. I need to go home." She stood, and came in and hugged her. "Call me in the morning and fill me in, will you?"

"I will, Julie. Thank you so much for coming over and participating." Linda walked Julie outside to her car and said goodbye.

Sarah came over and hugged her sister. "I'll put Kelly to bed."

"No, Sarah," Kelly said. She rested her head on Sarah's shoulder. "I don't want to go to bed, I'm scared."

Linda overheard the conversation as she came back inside and said, "You have to, honey. Let's find your bunny.

We have to do this so these nice men can make the ghosts go away. I will be right in the next room."

Kelly began to cry. "I don't want to be alone."

Sarah passed her hand through Kelly's hair. "I'll sleep with her, Mom." Kelly looked at her big sister and nodded in approval. Linda spun around for a reaction from the investigators. Jason shook his head from side to side.

Linda smiled, although she felt like a guinea pig in some wild ghostly experiment. "We need to be in our own rooms, doing what we normally do. I need you to be a brave girl and sleep in your own bed, okay, honey?" Kelly nodded and rubbed her eyes.

Jason called down into the basement. "Daniel, you can come up now." He rounded the corner and came up the stairs. "Did you get anything down there?"

"Not a peep," Daniel said. "You know it's not easy sitting tight when there is other activity going on."

"I understand completely," Jason replied. He turned and peeked into the garage. Kyle sat there shivering. "Kyle, did you experience anything?"

"No, not a thing."

"Well, we're done for the night. Thanks for helping out."

"Sure," Kyle said.

Tyler and his friends went up into Tyler's bedroom and started playing a game of Risk. Sarah and Bill went up into Sarah's room and listened to her stereo. Linda tucked Kelly into bed, kissed her goodnight and walked back into her own bedroom and lay down on the bed.

The three investigators roamed through the house for the next hour and a half, checking in on everyone from time to time.

Linda stared at the moon outside her bedroom window. 'What on earth has happened to my home?' she wondered. 'How could such a happy family be so suddenly plunged into the deepest recesses of hell?' She thought about Matt.

'How was he?' 'How did a man who barely ever had a cold in his life become so deathly ill?' She reached over, picked up the phone and dialed. The orange glow from the keypad cast an eerie glow on her white down comforter.

"I.C.U.," the voice answered.

"Yes, I'm calling on the status of Matthew McLaughlin, please. This is his wife."

"Please hold while I check for you." The nurse came back on a minute later. "Okay. The blood tests came back negative."

"Negative! How is that possible?" She felt a subtle vibration under her bed. Then the bed started shaking. Linda's fear about what was starting to happen in her bedroom quickly overcame her concern for her husband. The bed suddenly shook so violently that the legs rose and slammed down on the hardwood floor. She screamed and tried to hang up the phone, but the shaking made her miss each time she tried. The phone finally flew from her hand and fell onto the floor. She wailed in terror. The bed levitated almost two feet off the floor, was held aloft for several long, terrifying seconds, and suddenly slammed back down. It rose and fell more than a dozen times. Linda lay on her back, clutching the fitted sheet for support. Some force tugged them from beneath her. She howled, turned around onto her knees and grabbed the bed posts. She inhaled deeply and screamed at the top of her lungs, "Help me!"

Bill was the first to run inside. He backed against the wall, aghast, hands spread out against the wall, wide-eyed with terror. Tyler, Jimmy, and Kyle ran inside and froze. "Holy shit," Tyler said. Daniel screamed inside the room and leaped onto the bed to force it down. Then, as if suddenly filled with a strong resolve, Bill, Tyler, Jimmy, and Kyle climbed onto the bed to force it down onto the floor with their combined weight. Even with an added six hundred pounds, the bed rose and fell as easily as it did before they had all jumped upon it. Aaron entered and said, "My God. This is no simple demon!" Tyler backed off the bed, grabbed his mother's waist, and hauled her off safely.

Jason entered and shouted, "Everybody out."

They all backed down the hallway. Linda trembled, grasping at Tyler's shirt. She finally pulled him in close and hugged him as if she'd never let him go. "Thank you, Tyler." She sobbed uncontrollably, despite Tyler's efforts to calm her. Everyone walked down into the living room. Tyler and Sarah did their best to comfort their mother on the couch.

The investigators met briefly outside on the back porch. Then, Jason entered. He nodded and Daniel went back upstairs. "It's trying to frighten you," Jason said.

"Trying to frighten me?" Linda replied. "It's been *terrifying* me for days!"

"It's getting desperate because it's intelligent and it knows that it will soon be defeated." Linda laughed. Tyler and Sarah listened intently. "It knows that we possess the means to expel it and the other spirits in this house."

"I just want it to be gone," Linda said.

"I know that. But you must hold out." Jason held her hand. "Do you know what the most frightening thing is?"

"What?" Linda asked. "Well, yes, I do. It's all...frightening."

"The most frightening thing is that you are facing an invisible spirit. Sure, an invisible force shaking the bed is scary. But what if it were a man, someone that you could see doing the shaking? Is that so scary? Or aggravating?"

"It's damned aggravating, but not quite as scary."

"Right." He patted her knee.

Jason looked at Tyler and then back at Linda. "When you picture the invisible force, imagine that it's a clown with a big red nose and oversized blue shoes in a white silk clown suit," Jason continued. "Put some humor into the situation. Imagine that the spirits trying to frighten you are merely clowns."

"Yeah, like that's going to work," Tyler scoffed.

"Are you going to let them succeed?" He looked at Linda.

Linda replied, "Hell, no!"

"All right, hell, no," Jason said. "What about you, Sarah?"

"I guess," Sarah agreed. "I'll try it."

"Trying isn't good enough. You must convince yourself that you can fight it and win. If you can do that and remain fearless, you are helping to disarm them."

Jimmy looked at the clock and nudged Tyler. They looked at each other. Kyle noticed and nodded. "I've got to give the guys a lift home," Tyler said. All three boys stood up.

"I hate to bail on you all, but it's a school night," Jimmy said. He turned toward the investigators and said, "It was nice to meet you guys."

"Goodbye, Mrs. McLaughlin. See ya, everyone," Kyle said.

Tyler led them out through the garage door.

Bill stood up, kissed Sarah and turned toward the investigators. He walked closer and shook Jason's hand. "I have to head out, too. If you need anything, Sarah can get a hold of me." He waved to everyone. Sarah nodded and walked him out through the sliding glass door.

When Tyler and his friends got into the car, Kyle leaned said, "Guys, we need to tell them what we did."

Jimmy barked, "What did we do? How do we know *we* did anything?"

Tyler gripped the steering wheel. "He's right, Jim. We must have let the bad spirits in by using the Ouija board. I need not remind you, Jim, that it was *you* who suggested that we go buy one and use it."

Jimmy scoffed and said, "Wait a minute. Now it's *my* fault?"

"I didn't say this was your fault," Tyler said. "I'm just

reminding you that it was your idea to get that damned Ouija board."

"We were all at fault," Kyle said. "But we need to co-operate with these guys. They're trying to get to the bottom of what's going on, and we need to help them."

"It's not like the ghost-police are going to come and haul us off or something," Tyler said. "I have to tell them. My mother has been brutally attacked, for shit's sake."

Jimmy said, "Well, will ya look at that?" Tyler and Kyle looked out the window. They all saw Sarah and Bill making out and holding each other tightly. Tyler growled, put the car into drive, and they rolled out of the driveway.

Tyler kept scanning the rear-view mirror, catching his friend gawking at his sister and her boyfriend.

An hour later, Tyler walked in the front door of the house and closed it as slowly and as silently as he could. He stepped into the foyer and slid off his shoes. He made his way down the hallway and entered the unlit kitchen. Simply out of habit he reached for the light switch and retracted his hand, remembering that he shouldn't turn on any lights, so he waited to let his eyes grow accustomed to the darkness.

"Hey, Tyler."

Tyler leaped back against the door. "Jesus! You scared the crap outta me!"

"It's me, Jason. I didn't mean to frighten you, I'm sorry. Don't worry. I'm no ghost."

Tyler stepped down into the living room, groping in the darkness for the small wooden banister against the wall. "What are you doing?"

"Waiting, watching. Your mother went to sleep. She's exhausted. She wanted me to tell you that your father's doctor called. His condition is worsening."

"Oh, man." Tyler's eyes adjusted to the darkness, and he

saw Jason sitting on the sofa. Tyler sat on the stairs and held his knees against his chest with his arms. "Will my dad be okay?"

"There's no telling. I understand how hard this must be."

"Hard is an understatement. It seems like the whole world is caving in on me," Tyler said.

"That's called oppression."

Part 3 – Possession

Chapter 28 – Coming Clean

"WHAT'S OPPRESSION?"

"It's a term we use for a series of events that occurs to a person or an entire family after their home has been infested. You see, when a spirit enters a home, it 'infests it.' We use that term because it refers to something that doesn't belong, just like fleas that infest a home don't belong there. If a spirit that is infesting a house controls the thoughts or actions of others, or causes the kinds of disturbances and attacks like you've been experiencing here, all of those things cause everyone involved to feel a sense of hopelessness and dread. We call that oppression. That's what's happening here. We usually don't tell people that. But I think we both can agree that something terrible is happening here."

"Yeah," Tyler agreed. "It's crazy terrible, that's for sure."

"It's trying to shatter your home, wreck your lives and break your will to resist. There are three stages: infestation, oppression, and..."

"What's the third stage?" Tyler asked.

"The third stage is possession."

Tyler gasped. "Like in...*The Exorcist?*"

"Unfortunately, yes. Did you know that it was a true story? It happened to a boy, not a girl, as the movie suggests."

"I thought all that was hocus-pocus," Tyler said, his

voice trembling. "How did that story come about? I mean what caused it?"

"It was an idol from the Middle East. It was charged with negative energy of a very powerful and evil nature. It weakened the boy through oppression, and ultimately the powerful demon associated with it possessed him. The idol represented a specific demon, whose name I don't want to say at all for fear of summoning it."

"You mean just by speaking a name you can summon it to you?"

Jason said, "Absolutely! Names are very powerful. It is the essence with which an entity identifies itself. That's why even we would never ask a spirit to show itself or to identify itself. Only an exorcist or someone who knows exactly how to deal with them does that, and that's only when they really mean business."

"Man, how did you get involved in this stuff?" Tyler asked.

"It was my Destiny."

"Do you really believe in destiny?" Tyler asked.

Jason sat up straight on the sofa. "Most people who choose to get involved in work of this nature do it because they feel 'a calling' to do so, because they feel a strong urge to help people. Ever since I was a little boy I believed in ghosts and the supernatural. I never saw any ghosts or had any psychic visions, but I believed in the phenomenon whole-heartedly. I just instinctively knew which things people said to me or tried to teach me were real and which weren't. I knew that something was amiss and I started looking for answers. I didn't buy into the illusory world-view that was grafted onto society. I started looking for answers, inner knowledge and anomalous outer experiences that clearly showed a reality that others are oblivious to. I read books of all kinds that were available in the town and school libraries and metaphysical bookstores. I went to psychic fairs and met all kinds of amazing people who were simply a treasure trove of information."

"What about Ouija boards?" Tyler gulped. "Do...do they really work?"

Jason's tone became deep and serious. "Yes, they work! What they work, however, is intangible."

"Hey, I'm sixteen. I'm smart compared to most guys my age, but can you please be clearer in your explanation?" Tyler chuckled.

"A Ouija board is like a key. It has the ability, if used correctly, to open a doorway between the spirit world and ours, the third dimension and others—a portal, a gateway, a vortex, whatever you'd like to call it. It's like taking a loud speaker into a great open space and yelling: "Come mess with my life!" Using a Ouija board is very bad news, because most people don't set parameters with regard to whom or *what* exactly they are inviting to come through to communicate with them, so anything and everything— especially things of an evil nature—will respond to that summons, and they can respond very quickly."

Tyler's silence spoke more than a thousand words. Jason turned on his flashlight and shone at Tyler's chest so that he could see him without blinding him. "Did you and your friends use a Ouija board in this house, Tyler?"

Tyler's head sank into his lap. He folded his hands over the back of his neck and nodded. Then he looked up at Jason, shook his head from side to side and said, "We didn't know..."

Jason nodded and quickly stood up. "I knew it." Jason walked up to Tyler and pressed his palm against his shoulder. "Hang on! The others are going to need to hear this."

Tyler folded his arms over his knees and dropped his head into them. He felt utterly defeated and said, "Now I've done it."

Jason rushed down the hall and went upstairs. Two

minutes later, Aaron and Daniel followed Jason back into the living room and turned on the lights. Tyler remained on the steps and shielded his eyes. Daniel assembled his tripod and video camera as Jason and Aaron took their notepads out, sat on the couch and examined Tyler with their penetrating eyes. "Okay, from the top," Jason demanded.

Aaron gave Tyler a disappointed look and added, "We knew someone did something that they didn't confess to. Things like this don't happen unless someone uses a Ouija board."

Jason said, "It's okay to tell us, Tyler. What you've done is done. Now we need to know when you used the Ouija board, where exactly you used it, and what happened during and afterwards. Tell us everything."

For the next hour, Tyler confessed what he and his friends had done with such graphic detail that it stunned everyone, including him. He didn't forget a thing. When they were finished, Daniel jumped up from the fireplace when he saw the repetitious Low Battery light flash on his camera. He adjusted a knob, took the cassette out, and began to label it.

Jason closed his note pad and asked, "Is that all?"

Tyler wiped a tear from his eye. "Isn't that enough?"

"It's quite enough," Aaron said. "Where is the Ouija board now?"

"It's in that pit at school, where no one will ever get to it."

"And that pool of urine appeared in the exact spot where you had initially used the Ouija board, right?"

Tyler pointed at the carpet and replied, "Yes, right there, exactly."

"And that's the only place you used it in this house, right?"

"Correct." Tyler grabbed Jason's shin as Jason started up the stairs into the kitchen. "Are you going to tell my Mom?"

He looked down at Tyler in pity and asked, "Should I?"

"No!"

"It would cause more harm than good?" Jason asked.

Tyler nodded and said, "Exactly."

Jason's look sent the guilty shivers throughout Tyler's entire body. "You're right, it would, because it would infuriate your mother and cause more chaos, mistrust, and internal strife in the house, and we can't afford to make matters worse. The spirits here would like that immensely. I make a habit of never intentionally doing anything that would make the spirits causing a disturbance happy."

"I didn't mean to cause any problems," Tyler said. "I just wanted to help."

"We know that, Tyler," Jason said. "You wanted to protect your little sister from supernatural harm. We understand that completely. It's completely natural and also commendable. It would have been much easier for all of us though, especially your father, if all we had to do was come in and expel an earthbound human spirit. Now, unfortunately, we have our hands full and will require help."

"Wait, you—need help? I just wanted to get to the bottom of what was going on with the ghost in the house, that's all. Besides, buying and using the Ouija board was Jimmy's suggestion anyway."

Aaron's nostrils flared. "You may be surprised to learn that suggestion may be the key word there, and that your friend Jimmy may not really be the one who suggested it in the first place. The spirits probably suggested it to him." Aaron lost all color in his face and pointed toward the kitchen. "Look!" Aaron whispered.

The others wheeled around and gasped. The powerful smell of sulfur overcame them within seconds. A motionless jet-black specter had materialized in the center of the kitchen. Its vaporous, translucent body pulsed against the light of the full moon shining inside through the kitchen windows. It was blacker than the blackest night. They all felt an intense feeling of hatred emanate from it, and the longer it lasted, the more intense and overpowering the sulfur smell became. Aaron snapped a dozen pictures before the thing dissipated into a sooty-black cloud and rose up and away through the ceiling.

Jason sighed in relief. Then he gasped and said, "Your mother is up there!"

"Oh, my God!" Tyler wailed.

Daniel, Aaron, and Jason tore down the foyer.

"Mom!" Tyler screamed, racing after them. The rumblings erupted within seconds. Loud, powerful banging shook the walls. Tyler heard his mother's screams, then her horrible muted gasps as if she were being...strangled. He gathered his courage, dug his fingertips into the carpeted steps, gritted his teeth, and scampered up the stairs. He screamed, "Mom! I'm coming, Mom!" Camera flashes briefly lit the hallway. He made out several figures up ahead. He slapped the wall switch and the hall lights came on. They short-circuited in a bright flash. Jason and Daniel ran out of the bedroom, clutching Linda and dragging her toward the end of hall. Aaron grabbed Kelly. Sarah backed out of her room.

"Get downstairs, now!" Aaron roared. Tyler wheeled around and fled down the steps before the others.

"Open the door," Jason said. Tyler looked at him, unsure.

Aaron yelled, "Do it!" He appeared to be pulling away from some invisible force that seemed to have him by the hair. Tyler reached for the door as Jason and Daniel fought to bring his mother safely downstairs. Daniel's shirtsleeve tore at the seams and split wide, up to his shoulder. An invisible force tugged at him and drew him backwards one foot for every two feet he gained ground.

Tyler yanked on the door handle and panicked. "It's locked!"

Jason grabbed the door handle with both hands and

strained against it. He swung his arm toward the kitchen and said, "The sliding door in the living room. Go!"

Tyler grabbed Sarah's hand and led her into the living room. The others ran after them. Outside, Cinnamon barked frantically. Jason nearly jerked the sliding door off its tracks, and they poured out of the house.

The dog followed them as they ran across the grass, then into the driveway and finally up to the road. A car sped by. The swift wind of its passing blew everyone's hair to the side, and they all thought it was another imminent attack. Sarah knelt down and checked Kelly to make sure that she was all right. Kelly buried her face in Sarah's legs. They stared at the house together in horror.

"Is everyone okay?" Jason asked.

Tyler watched intently. He was happy that Jason was in charge. He knew what to do.

"Nobody is staying in that house tonight." Jason looked at the family. "Can you all stay with Julie tonight?"

Linda nodded. "Yes."

"Fine," Jason said.

He urged Daniel to come with him. They walked down the driveway, hopped into their cars and drove up to the group. "Get in."

The children hesitated. "Mom, what do we do?" Tyler asked.

"Daniel and I will drive you to wherever you need to go, it's no problem at all," Jason said. "It is not safe to go back into that house tonight for any reason whatsoever." Everyone got into the cars and closed their doors without a word. Jason turned into the street. Tyler, Sarah, and Linda looked out the back windows, and all that they could sense from their house was evil—pure, diabolical evil.

When they pulled into Julie's driveway and stopped, they saw a light come on. Julie pulled her curtains aside, opened the window, and stuck her head out. "Who's there, please?" Linda got out of the passenger side, trembling. Her white knuckles clutched the car door. "My Lord!" Julie said. "What happened?"

"Julie, can we stay with you? It's gotten absolutely terrible at our house."

"Of course," Julie said. "I'll be right down to let you in." She ducked back inside and closed the window.

Linda poked her head in the car and looked at her children in the back seat. "Let's go." She studied Jason. "What do we do now?"

"Stay here overnight, and we'll come back in the morning," Jason said. "Don't go back there until I call you, okay?" He was very stern and serious.

"Don't you worry about that," Linda replied. "We're not going anywhere near the house until you say it's okay to do so."

Julie opened the door and rushed out in her nightgown. "What in God's name has happened?"

Linda hugged her. "We can't stay there tonight, it's overwhelming."

Julie pulled Kelly in closer for a hug. "Of course, come inside." She waved to Jason as they drove away, and she led the broken and battered family inside the house.

Kelly, Sarah, and Linda gathered in the kitchen while Tyler went into the bathroom. Julie found her teakettle and went to the sink.

Linda covered her face with her palm. "Julie, if you didn't see it for yourself, I would never expect you to believe..."

Julie cut her off. "I do...believe you, Linda. Let's make no mistake about it. I've been reading absolutely horrific things as I continued to read those books." Julie ran water in her teakettle while Linda began going over the details of what had happened since she left. The kids sat in the living room in shock, resting and waiting for their tea. After a few minutes Julie handed everyone a cup of steaming chamomile tea. "Here, dear ones. This will settle your nerves a bit." They each eagerly took their cup with smiles and did their best to relax.

By the time Linda had finished filling her friend in on the terrible events that had just occurred, Kelly had fallen asleep with her head in Sarah's lap, and Sarah had begun to nod off as well. "Dear me," Julie said. She sipped the last bit of her tea and set her cup down. She offered another to Tyler who just shook his head, smiled and held up his palm. He sank down in the easy chair he was sitting in. "You can all stay here as long as you like. I have plenty of room." She suddenly became very serious and asked, "How is Matthew?"

Linda gasped. They'd been having so many of their own problems, she'd forgotten about her poor sick husband in the hospital with no family there to be with him. "I'll call again."

Julie reached over and handed her the phone.

Linda dialed and talked to one of the nurses.

After several long minutes she put the phone down. Tears welled up in her eyes. "There has been no change. All of his tests came back negative. They don't know what's wrong with him," Linda said, sobbing. Tyler rapped his fist against the wall in anger.

Julie and Linda looked at him. "Honey, do you forgive your father for slapping you? He really needs your love now, not your anger."

"Of course I do, Mom. I know that it wasn't Dad who hit me. Something influenced him to do it. Something put that fifty into my book bag. I'm no thief!"

"Of course you aren't, honey."

"We can't just let him lie there alone," Tyler said.

"I'm going to go see him tomorrow," Linda said. "The men said we can go back to the house in the morning."

"Oh, my," Julie said. She stood and tapped Kelly's arm. She bobbed her head briefly and fell asleep seconds later. "Let's get this little angel to bed." She gently shook her again.

"She can sleep with me. I think we'd both feel safer together," Linda said. Kelly yawned and stretched her arms out. Kelly took Julie's outstretched hand and Julie led her upstairs.

"Tyler can have the sofa and Sarah can sleep in my son's room," Julie said. "He won't mind. He's only home twice a year, anyway. I should really convert it into a sewing room."

Linda held out her hand and Tyler stood up. He hung his head low. Linda kissed Tyler on the cheek and hugged him. "Are you okay?"

"Mom, I'm not okay. Are you? Are any of us okay? Will any of us ever be okay again? On top of all of the crap happening at the house, I'm really exhausted and I'm worried about Dad, you know?"

"Believe me. I know. We'll go visit him tomorrow." She smiled. "Get some sleep, honey. I'm very proud of you for being so strong through all of this. Good night."

Tyler smiled, sat on the sofa and took off his socks. Julie came in and dropped a pile of linens on the armchair and began unfolding them. "That's okay," he said. "I can arrange the linens. You don't have to bother."

"Oh, it's no bother." She leaned in and waved both of her hands at him and said, "Shoo!" Tyler giggled. "Honestly, I miss this kind of thing," Julie said. "It's a lonely life being a widow with no children around the house anymore. I thank the Lord that I have all of you in my life. I'm not going to let some damned banshees ruin all of that, I can tell you. I love all of you dearly."

Tyler smiled. "We love you too, Aunt Julie." Julie finished, kissed Tyler on the forehead and hurried away to tend to the others. Tyler took off his shirt and jeans and climbed under the blankets. He lay there for several moments. Then he reached up behind his head and switched off the light.

Upstairs, Julie hugged Linda as she came into the room. "Tyler is all set."

"Sarah is out like a light too," Linda added. "Thank you so much for letting us spend the night, Julie. I didn't mean to impose."

"Don't be silly. It's a treat to have you all over. But considering the circumstances..."

Linda inhaled deeply and shook her head, "I don't know what we are going to do."

"I'd trust that the professionals will take care of everything for you. Why don't you get some sleep?" Julie turned to walk out of the room and then looked her friend in the eyes. "Knock if you need anything."

"All right, Julie. Thank you again."

Julie walked off down the hall and Linda turned off the light and climbed into bed, being careful not to wake Kelly. She lay back in the darkness, staring at the ceiling, waiting, listening for signs that the spirits might have followed them. She closed her hands together in prayer—silent prayer, where only God would hear her. She soon drifted off into a sound, restful sleep.

In the morning, Tyler woke up suddenly when he heard clanging noises in the kitchen. He shot his eyes open and listened. Then he smelled the unmistakable smell of frying sausage and eggs. He tugged the blankets over his head and yawned. There wasn't one sign of spirit activity all throughout the night. 'Cool,' he thought. 'It has to be the house.' He was starting to have confidence that Jason and the other investigators would figure out that it was the house that was the problem, and everything would soon be all right. He reached down to the floor, groped for his jeans, yanked them under the covers and put them on. Then he got up and began folding the blankets. He walked into the bathroom and washed his face. He saw his mother and sisters pass down the hallway. When they all converged in the kitchen, Julie was pouring glasses of orange juice.

"Good morning," Julie said. "How did everyone sleep?"

"Like the dead," Linda said.

Tyler cackled. "Good one, Mom."

"I have to call the hospital."

Sarah shuffled over to the counter and poured herself a cup of coffee. "That was the best night's sleep I've had in a long time." She leaned back against the counter and rubbed her eyes. "Mom, I'd like to stay with Aunt Julie until everything is normal back home. In fact, I think it's a very bad idea to go back there, ever."

Julie said, "You are all welcome to stay for as long as it takes. Please accept this as an open invitation without limitation. I love all of you like family."

Linda smiled brightly, though she was paying close attention to her phone call. She spoke to someone on the other end. "Well, this is his wife. Could you please have Dr. Kent call me back with an update as soon as he's free?" She hung up the phone. She looked at her son. "Tyler...did anything happen last night?"

"Nope, everything was quiet. I slept fine." He smiled.

Julie took the skillets off the burners and began serving breakfast.

To the displaced family, for a moment, it seemed like everything was like it should have been—a nice, normal morning following a sound, restful sleep, waking up to a bright, sunny day and a delicious breakfast. "This sure is nice, thank you, Julie." Then Linda thought about Matthew. And her look of concern did not go unnoticed.

Tyler sank down in his chair and nodded. "Dad's the only one that isn't well, isn't he?"

"When can we see Daddy?" Kelly asked.

Linda smiled warmly. "We'll go this afternoon, despite what the doctor says." Kelly smiled. They heard a car horn outside, and a few moments later, the doorbell rang.

Julie nibbled on a piece of pastry and waved. "Tyler, would you?" Tyler wiped his mouth with a napkin, set it down, got up and answered the door. Jimmy and Kyle met him with huge smiles on their faces and directed his attention to Jimmy's father's brand new red Volkswagen Cabrio convertible in the driveway.

"Rad," Tyler said. He walked back inside and said, "Mom, Jimmy and Kyle are here for me." He rushed back into the kitchen and grabbed his things. "I have to go." He kissed Julie and his mother on the cheek. "Thanks for breakfast, Julie. See you later, Mom."

Sarah also stood up and grabbed her book bag. She frowned at the sight of her wrinkled clothes. "Give me a lift too, Tyler. I have to get to school somehow."

"Yeah, sure. Let's go." He ran out the front door.

Sarah kissed Julie, her mother, and her sister. "Thanks for letting us stay the night, Julie. You're a lifesaver." Julie giggled. "I haven't had this many kisses in..." she said. "Well, I can't even remember when."

Tyler stuck his head back inside the house and called out to his sister, "Sarah..."

"Okay, okay, jeez." Sarah ran outside and climbed in next to her brother.

Chapter 29 – Washing Away the Filth

TYLER WAS LEANING into the front. He asked, "How'd you guys know where to find me?"

"We went to pick you up at Spook Central, but the dudes at the house told us that you were staying here," Jimmy said.

Tyler and Sarah gave each other a concerned look. "What dudes?" Tyler asked.

"The investigators were walking around the front yard when we pulled in."

Jimmy leaned back and laughed at his friend. He said, "Tyler, you have some serious bed head." He handed him a red Boston Red Sox baseball cap. "We all know how materialistic you are and how sensitive you are about your looks."

"You're the one who's always looking into the mirror, Jim," Tyler said, as he snatched the hat and put it on. "I think it's amusing that you always tell me that I'm the one who's always concerned about my looks when clearly you're the narcissist." He reached into the front seat and switched on the radio.

"It takes one to know one, Tyler," Jimmy replied.

"Sarah rolled her eyes and said, "You guys are unbelievable."

"So, Sarah, this is a much nicer ride than Bill's, isn't it?"

"It sure is, Jimmy. But it isn't yours, is it?" Kyle and

Tyler laughed at their friend who sneered and hit the gas. They raced off to school, the only normalcy of their lives.

Linda, Julie and Kelly sat at the kitchen table finishing breakfast when the doorbell rang. Julie walked down the hall and answered the door. The three investigators were standing on the porch with smiles on their faces. "Hello, gentlemen," Julie said. Then she turned around and called out to her friend. "Linda, it's the investigators."

Linda walked over and met them. She said, "Hello." She felt relieved to see them.

"Hello, Linda. We went back to the house this morning and everything seems okay, but we've got one small problem."

Linda gasped. "What is it?"

Jason laughed. "Well, we don't have a key."

Linda giggled. "We didn't lock the doors when we left so suddenly last night."

"Yes, I know that," Jason nodded. "Well, it appears that the spirits have taken up residence and *they* apparently don't want us to come inside."

Linda chuckled. "I can give you my key and you can head right back over, but I'm not ready to leave yet."

"That's fine. In fact, it'd probably be better if we had the house to ourselves."

"Okay," Linda replied. "It'll give us some time to shower and freshen up."

"We'll see you ladies later," Jason said. The men waved and he led the men outside.

"Julie, can I borrow some clothes, please?"

"Now, what kind of question is that?" Julie answered. "Of course, you can."

Later, when Linda was showered and ready to depart, she noticed Kelly in the den playing with some dolls. Kelly looked over and said, "Mom, I don't want to go back home. I want to go see Dad."

Julie hugged Linda tightly. "I'll take good care of Kelly

and she'll be less stressed out here. I'll cook a nice dinner for all of us. Just call me later and give me an update."

"All right then," Linda said. "That's probably a smart idea. Okay, I'll see you later today. Thanks again, Julie. I'll call you this afternoon."

When Linda drove into her driveway she examined her house with careful scrutiny. The bright sunlit day helped alleviate the seemingly impervious feeling of doom and gloom that sat heavily over the house during the past several days. She couldn't even think of putting up Halloween decorations with all that had happened. She parked the car, hopped out and walked up to the front door. The men had left the door unlocked.

She walked inside and something immediately made her recoil. A foul smell permeated her nostrils. It was dreadful. She heard a clamor coming from the kitchen. When she turned the corner, Daniel was on his knees before a huge pile of rotting, festering food in the center of the kitchen floor. Linda held her nose. "Phew!"

Daniel looked up at her. "It looks like they emptied the entire contents of the refrigerator onto the floor. I'm sorry, but they really cleaned you out." He tried not to laugh, but he couldn't help it.

Jason walked in from the art studio and waved Linda over. She inched closer as Jason opened the refrigerator door. "Take a look at this," he said. Linda gasped. There were about a three dozen empty containers inside, exactly where she had left them, but they were completely devoid of their contents. They were not only empty, but they were crystal clear as if they had been emptied, washed, and replaced inside the refrigerator. "This is a new one for me," Jason said. "It seems as if all of the organic foodstuffs were teleported onto the floor, and all of the containers were left inside, empty and sparkling clean." He closed the refrigerator door, reached under the sink and pulled out some plastic garbage bags.

Aaron finished taking pictures and set his camera down on the counter. "If you tell me where the mop is, I can get it for you."

"Yes, thank you. It's hanging on a wall hook just inside the cellar door," Linda said.

"Okay, I'll get it." Aaron opened the door and reached for the light switch. Then they heard the struggle and he called out. Then they all heard him falling down the steps. Horrendous banging erupted all around them from nowhere and everywhere all at once. It surrounded them on all sides, forcing them all to cower and cover their ears. "Jesus!" Aaron shouted. Linda rushed over to the cellar steps to see what had happened. Aaron lay at the bottom of the stairs, wincing in pain. His arm was bent and twisted around a support post below.

Jason quickly made his way down the stairs and knelt beside him. "Are you all right?" He helped Aaron gently and carefully free his arm.

Aaron moaned and held his wounded arm against his chest. "I don't think it's broken but, man, it sure smarts."

"What happened?" Linda pleaded.

Aaron looked up at Linda who was peering down from the top of the steps. "Something shoved me. I felt two hands at the center of my back, and when I resisted, it completely overwhelmed me and sent me down the stairs with a quick, powerful push."

Linda whimpered. "It won't ever leave us alone, will it? It won't ever stop!"

Jason called upstairs. "Daniel, help me get Aaron upstairs." Daniel made his way down the steps. He and Jason wrapped their arms under Aaron's armpits and hoisted him up. When they got him upstairs into the kitchen, they checked his arm.

"I think I'm okay," Aaron said.

They eased Aaron down into a kitchen chair. "Oh, man," he said, wincing at the pain in his ribs. Linda pressed a bag of ice against his arm. "God, that's cold. But I'll be all right. Please go ahead and continue with the cleanup. I'm not sure what's worse, that awful smell or the pain." He forced out a painful chuckle.

When the food was gone and floor was clean, Jason and Daniel walked through the house. Linda sat alone in the kitchen with Aaron who had dozed off and was sleeping soundly. Then they heard the scratching, like a razor against glass. Aaron's eyes shot open and he nearly leaped from his chair. He jerked his head around and scanned the room. Then, he looked over and saw the golden retriever pawing the sliding door. He barked when Aaron noticed him. "Oh, thank God. I think we have a friend at the door," Aaron called out.

Linda asked, "What did you say?"

Aaron pointed at the door. Linda leaned over and smiled. Cinnamon barked and Linda walked over. She was actually pleased to see the dog. Cinnamon sat up on his hind legs and begged for her attention. Linda opened the door and rubbed his ears. She slid open the door further and walked into the kitchen. "Come on." Cinnamon lunged forward and pranced into the kitchen. He lifted one of his paws onto Aaron's lap and panted when Aaron patted his head. Linda poured a bowl of dog food and set it down on the floor. "I've never taken care of a neighbor's dog like this before. It's definitely odd, but he seems like part of the family, like a stepchild would, I suppose."

Jason said as he and Daniel entered the kitchen, "Everything checks out. There are no problems upstairs. It seems like everything is okay. How's your arm, Aaron?"

"It smarts, but I'll be fine."

"I see we have a visitor."

The phone rang, startling them. Linda rushed over and picked it up. "Hello?"

"Linda, this is Dr. Vincent Decker. I am calling..."

Linda interrupted him. "Oh, thank God. Please tell me you have found what is ailing my husband."

The voice was soft and gentle. "If I'm right, the doctors can do nothing for your husband."

Linda became agitated and said, "Wait. What? What are you telling me? You are one of the doctors, aren't you? There's nothing any of you can do? My God."

"I'm not affiliated with the hospital, but I am aware of your husband's condition and I feel that there is great need for concern."

"We are already greatly concerned. What are you trying to tell me?"

"I work with investigators like Jason when I believe the case involves more than simple earthbound spirits. I am a doctor of parapsychology. The reason I am calling is because I've gone over the videotapes that Jason dropped off, and I believe that you have a very serious situation—a very serious situation, indeed." Linda's fears had been confirmed. Vincent continued, "When would be a good time for my colleague and I to come over to your house? We would like to meet with you as soon as possible."

"Well, yes, of course, it's a very serious situation," Linda said. "You can come at any time and the sooner the better, please."

"We can be there at two o'clock, and we will see you then. Okay? Bye now."

The rush of excitement gave Linda an increase in energy and suddenly it seemed like more help was on its way, and the evil that had been plaguing them would soon be dispelled. "That was Vincent Decker..."

Invisible hands immediately coiled around Linda's throat and squeezed tightly, cutting her off in mid-sentence. They were not icy cold as before, but hot, slimy, and far stronger than any of the ones she'd endured during the previous attacks. Linda squeezed the phone, gasped, and reached for her neck. The phone fell to the floor. She couldn't breathe. Her hands shot out toward the corners of the room, and then back at her throat. The look of surprise on the faces of the investigators startled her almost as much as the fact that she was being strangled.

"Christ!" Daniel rushed over and tried to pull away the invisible attacker. "I feel nothing! Nothing's there!" Jason shot his hand into his pocket and withdrew an amber glass vial. When he held it up and was ready to uncork it, it was as if the invisible force attacking Linda knew exactly what Jason was doing, so it yanked Linda back away from him. It then shook her like she was a rag doll. When her eyes rolled into the back of her head Jason uncorked the vial, rushed over, and swiped it sideways across Linda's body. The holy water shot out in an arc and splashed against her neck, face, and chest.

Jason spoke with determination and authority. "In the name of Jesus Christ, release her now and be gone from this place!" The attack ceased almost immediately and Linda fell to her knees on the linoleum floor, gasping for breath, sobbing uncontrollably. The men converged on her as she knelt, holding her head, weeping. Suddenly, they saw her cringe and inhale so deeply it sounded like an outcry. She grabbed at her back.

"It stabbed me," Linda screamed. The confused men reached toward her although they had no idea what had just happened or how to help her.

Jason sprayed her back with the holy water. "The power of Christ commands you to leave this place now and trouble this family no more!" Linda gasped and tried to catch her breath. Then, as the men knelt to try and help her, she sprang to her feet and ran out of the kitchen and down the hallway. Jason ran after her. "Linda, please. Don't leave our sight, I implore you!"

Linda ran upstairs, went into the bathroom and slammed the bathroom door behind her. She turned on the shower and tore off her clothes. "I want these spirits out of my house!" She spun her head around and screamed frantically. "Get out of my house! Out! God damn you! Get out!" She stepped inside the shower and doused her head. She reached down for some soap and a washcloth and scrubbed her face and neck. She had to wash away the filth. She heard Jason just outside the door. He knocked urgently.

"Linda, please. Please unlock the door. If it attacks you again, I won't be able to help you. Please." He knocked continually. "Linda? Linda!" The unmistakable sound of fingers sliding along a smooth pane of glass made Linda freeze in terror. She knew what it was. She knew instinctively that it was writing something on the mirror for her to see. It was something to torment her. She refused to look at it, so she slid down into the tub and wailed.

"Leave me alone!" she cried, gasping for breath. "Oh, dear Lord, help us!" When the sounds ceased, Linda stood slowly, opened the shower door cautiously and strained to read the words etched into the mirror above the sink. "God damn it," she bellowed. She draped a towel around herself and tugged open the door. Jason gave her an unsure look as she walked out of the bathroom. "In there, on the mirror," she said. "It will never leave. We will never have peace!"

Jason walked inside and looked into the mirror. "No peace." The words were written backwards on the glass, so they appeared the right way when looking at them in the mirror.

Linda stormed down the hall toward her bedroom, screaming. She turned and saw Jason looking at her with pity. That enraged her. She shouted, "I want it out of my house! Do you understand me? Out of my house! Obviously these things are here. Do something about it. You *can*...do something about it, right? Do whatever you have to do, just please put an end to it." She went into her bedroom and closed the door, but she didn't lock it.

Daniel came upstairs wielding his camera. Jason pointed into the bathroom. Jason leaned against the wall with his hands folded behind his waist while he waited for Linda to finish changing. She came back and saw the bright sudden flashes coming from the Daniel's camera inside the bathroom. She turned and leaned into Jason and hugged him, sobbing against his chest because he was so tall. He held her tightly.

For the next few hours, with no further activity to anguish her, Linda was resting soundly in the living room when her world shattered once more. It was the doorbell again. "What now?" Linda got up, peered around the corner, walked over and opened the door. A well-built and very serious-looking man in his fifties stood there in a big, brown coat, holding a large brown leather bag and a metal case. He stood on the doorstep next to a rotund woman in her early forties with shoulder-length curly brown hair. She wore a black shawl and khakis. A beautiful purple amethyst gemstone hung from around her neck on a glittering silver necklace. Her green eyes were beautiful and deeply penetrating.

Vincent smiled at Linda warmly. "Hello, I'm Vincent Decker," he said. He extended his hand toward the woman and said, "This is my colleague, Yvonne Saxon."

Linda gasped and asked, "Yvonne from the Psychic Fairs' Yvonne?"

The woman smiled and studied Linda from head to toe. "Yes, that would be me. I knew that Vincent and I would be working in tandem on a serious matter very soon. I apologize for not calling you personally, but we felt that it would be best to conceal our involvement from the intelligences that are active inside your home until the very last moment."

"Intelligences?"

"Oh, yes, vast intelligences," Yvonne said.

Jason walked briskly down the foyer and held out his hand. "Vincent. Yvonne. I'm so glad you could become involved on such short notice."

Vincent smiled warmly. "We had no choice but to become personally involved. This is very serious. Mrs. McLaughlin, may we come inside?"

Linda opened the door wide. "Certainly, and please call me Linda. May I take your coat, Mr. Decker?"

"Yes, thank you," Vincent said warmly.

Jason urged Vincent and Yvonne into the kitchen. "Linda was attacked immediately after speaking with you on the telephone. Well, actually, she hadn't even said 'goodbye' yet when she was viciously strangled. I had to use holy water to put a stop to it."

"Something has recently happened in the upstairs bathroom, hasn't it? Something involving a mirror," Yvonne said.

Linda was astonished. "Yes. How did you know that?"

"Yvonne giggled and smiled. "It's what I do, honey." She walked around the kitchen and studied the walls and floors.

Vincent shot a very serious look at Aaron, the other investigators and finally to Jason. "Tell me exactly what happened."

Jason went over the complete details of the attack as Linda poured herself a cup of tea, paying very close attention to the conversation. "Okay, then, it's as I expected." He studied the room with narrow eyes.

"Would either of you like some hot tea?" Linda asked.

"Please call me Vincent. I have never been one to turn down a cup of tea, and I won't start now."

"Yes, please," Yvonne replied.

Linda lifted the tea kettle and raised a brow as she looked at Jason, Aaron, and Daniel. They all politely refused.

"Linda, I'd like to walk around the house now, if that would be alright."

"By all means," Linda said. She took a sip of her tea.

Linda knew that she was dealing with something dire and dangerous, but what exactly that would turn out to be, she realized that she didn't really want to find out as much as she thought she did. She handed Vincent and Yvonne their teacups. Vincent took a sip and said, "That's good, thank you."

Vincent looked around at the group and said, "What we're going to do today is observe the kinds of things that have been reported by the other investigators here. Yvonne and I will walk through the house and see what she can pick up."

"Pick up?" Linda asked.

"Yvonne is a light trance medium. She can hear, see and know or 'pick up' things that exist in this 'invisible plane' that most other people cannot. She'll observe and tell me what is happening, and then I will know how to deal with it."

"Well, okay," Linda agreed.

"I think we should start upstairs in Kelly's room where your son first tried to scare her by pretending that he was a ghost," Vincent said.

"Fine, this way." Linda led Vincent and Yvonne upstairs and into Kelly's room. Yvonne stood still and closed her eyes. Vincent opened the closet door and examined it. After several seconds Yvonne opened her eyes and sat on the bed. "It's very bad in here, Vincent."

"What do you feel?" Vincent asked.

"The pressure in here is terrible on the right side of my head."

"Hmmm. Take a look in this closet," Vincent urged.

Yvonne cocked her head, stood, and walked into it. "Oh, yes! There is definitely a presence in here." She leaped back. "Wait a minute!"

"What?" Vincent asked.

"You did not see that shadow!"

"A shadow?" he asked. "Where?"

She pointed at the corner. "Yes, a black shadow just moved through the wall."

"Where did it go?" Vincent asked.

"Upstairs," she said. She looked up. "It looked like it went right up through the ceiling." Vincent walked out into the hall. Jason tugged on the attic door cord.

"It's the same pattern as before. It went into the attic and started growling at me as soon as I went upstairs," Jason said. "Then, it went right down in the art studio and frightened Sarah's boyfriend, Bill."

Chapter 30 – Materializing the Spirits

"VINCENT!" YVONNE CALLED from inside the bedroom.

Daniel rushed in to make sure she was unharmed. Vincent peeked inside.

Yvonne spoke with her eyes closed and her hands folded neatly on her lap. "There is definitely an earthbound spirit here—a man. His energy is all over this room."

"That's as we expected," Vincent said.

"But there's something else," she continued. "He's not alone. There're others here, too. I sense a conflict. He's definitely being manipulated by these other spirits." She opened her eyes. "I'm going to see what I pick up in the rest of the house."

"Go to Linda's bedroom," Jason suggested. He looked into Vincent's eyes. "As we told you in our report, she was attacked there several times."

"Oh, yes. That would definitely be a hot spot and would be the perfect place to get a second reading," Yvonne said. Vincent followed them into the master bedroom. "The pressure in here is much stronger—much more negative in here."

"Are you sure?"

"No doubt about it! It's like a thickness, like the air is thicker and harder to walk through."

Vincent went into the bathroom and came back out. He inhaled deeply and looked all around him. He asked, "Is there a spirit in this house?" Linda stared wide-eyed and was suddenly full of fear.

"Is there a spirit in this house? Give us some sign." A high-pitched hissing laughter resonated from above them. Vincent moved away from the bed and tugged on Yvonne's sleeve. She moved back cautiously. Jason fished in his pocket.

"In the name of Jesus Christ, I command you to reveal yourself!" Vincent said.

Daniel filmed Vincent and Yvonne. Jason popped off the vial's cork, which dropped down and bounced off his shoe and rolled onto the carpet. The laughter turned to a groan and a black misty cloud began to manifest over the bed. It rotated slowly like a churning cyclone that was gathering strength and speed. "In the name of Jesus Christ, I command you to reveal yourself to us!" Vincent said.

Aaron snapped a continual barrage of pictures. The distinct dark red glow of the infrared bulb shot sudden flashes into the room.

Yvonne closed her eyes and focused on the opaque cloud spinning in on itself. It began to expand into a cigar-shaped form. A terrible sulfuric smell filled the room. Then the form slowly sprouted arms and legs simultaneously. They watched them form from the shoulders on down, until the forearms extended into long, thin, spindly fingers. The legs manifested simultaneously right down to its feet standing firmly on the floor.

"Reveal yourself in the name of Christ!" Vincent continued.

Linda gasped when she saw the intruder. She finally was getting a glimpse of the thing that had shaken her in and on the bed previously. She recalled the experience and started to tremble. Jason held her shoulders from behind. The seven-foot-tall black spirit stood defiantly in what appeared to be long black robes, or a continuation of its sooty black form. Its squat, bulbous head, whose features could barely be distinguished, turned suddenly and glared at Linda.

"The hatred," Yvonne said. "It's sickening!"

Two amber eyes flashed and pulsed. The temperature in the room plummeted within seconds. Frost began to form on the windows. Everyone's breath began to freeze and each exhalation became clearly visible.

Vincent thrust his hand out in protest. "The power of Christ commands you!"

The spirit turned toward him. Linda broke free of Jason's arms and ran down the dark hallway screaming. Daniel snapped frame after frame and cursed when he ran out of film. He ran out down the hall after Linda. Within the bedroom, the smell of decaying carcasses overpowered them. Yvonne grabbed her mouth and backed out into the hall. Vincent stood there defiantly and made the sign of the cross with his hand. In a powerful, determined tone he roared, "In the blood of Jesus Christ, I command you to leave this place and return to where you came from!" Wicked wails erupted all around them. Vincent's hand was viciously slashed. He recoiled and backed away.

Jason made the sign of the cross and said, "Archangel Michael, thank you for drawing your sword and for removing these servants of evil from this house!" An intense roar erupted immediately and deafened everyone.

Daniel came back in with a fresh roll of film, loaded it into his camera and snapped photo after photo. A second black form came through the wall. Jason thrust his hand forward and sprayed the form and the wall behind it with holy water. The black spirit seemed to recoil and lose its volume, shrinking down into the size of a softball. Then it diminished into the size of a golf ball. The first spirit lost all of its physical characteristics and vanished without trace. The smell vanished almost immediately.

Vincent walked out and pulled Jason and Daniel out

with him. "I don't presume that they left because you made them leave, right?" Daniel asked.

"No," Vincent said. He shook his head and motioned for Yvonne and the men to follow him. "I can say it definitely didn't do that," he said. "What we are dealing with is much too powerful."

The investigators went downstairs and found Linda sitting on the living room sofa, trembling. Sarah had come home from school and was sitting next to her, holding her hand. Vincent and Jason came in.

"Hi, Sarah, I'm Vincent. It is a pleasure to meet you. Yvonne here is my psychic assistant. We're here to help."

"Hello. My mom was telling me about the two of you. It's nice to meet you too."

Yvonne walked in and smiled. She noticed Sarah's arm brace. She squinted and walked up to her. "May I touch your arm?" Sarah nodded. Yvonne wrapped her hands around Sarah's arm, closed her eyes and held it for several seconds. "Hmmm," she said. She opened her eyes and smiled at Sarah.

Vincent sat down on the slate fireplace hearth. "Linda, let me explain something to you and your daughter. What you just saw upstairs was something that my investigators spend years looking forward to seeing with their own eyes —the materialization of an inhuman, diabolical spirit."

Linda sobbed and held her hands before her face. "Why in the world would anyone look forward to seeing that?"

Sarah didn't pay much attention to Vincent, but kept a watchful, concerned eye on Yvonne who got up and started pacing over the area in which the guys had used the Ouija board. Yvonne walked around and around, with her palms facing down. "There's something here, Vincent." She lifted her hands up and lowered them down as if she were feeling something, palpating something that only she had the remarkable innate senses to feel.

Vincent studied Yvonne for a brief moment and then

returned his attention to Yvonne. He knew that whatever she was discerning, she would explain in a few minutes. "I won't sugar coat my words here," Vincent continued. "I will be honest and upfront with you, even though I know it will upset you—because I now believe that we have very little time left." Linda looked up at him with an expression of pure hopelessness. Sarah gulped and spun her head around to look at him. "There are several spirits in your house. After reviewing all of the film, tape and still photograph footage that the team has collected and the full testimonials from everyone involved and, most importantly, from what we have just witnessed upstairs in your bedroom, we can say without a shred of uncertainty that there is an earth-bound human spirit in this house. That is the spirit that followed you and your daughter home from the cemetery. In trying to communicate with this spirit, in speaking to it, in challenging it, and with a series of other acts, inhuman diabolical spirits have also entered your home and they have quite frankly taken over."

"What other acts?" Linda asked. She wiped her face with a tissue.

"It doesn't matter how they got in here. All that matters now is getting them out," Vincent said.

Yvonne stood silently in the exact spot that the Ouija board was used and where the pool of urine materialized. She closed her eyes and meditated. She said, "The spirit in your home died a sudden tragic death. He was already full of rage and discontent, so I believe that he had a miserable life right up until the point of his death. He was attracted to Kelly when you drove by the cemetery where he must have been lurking."

Linda asked, "Lurking?"

"Haunting," Yvonne added.

"You see," Vincent continued, "when a person dies, they leave their body and material possessions behind. All that they take with them are their emotions and the culmination of the effect that the life that they had just led has had on them. There is always a portal of light that comes when they leave their body because the physical world is through with them. The proper place to go, the natural place to go, *is into that light*, completing the proper death passage and entering into the realm of spirit. The spirit in this house, for whatever reason, chose not go into that light. Instead, he retreated from it. The second that he chose to do that, he became an earth-bound spirit or what we more aptly call a lost soul."

Linda shook her head. "No! This is wrong! I was taught...my whole family was taught that when you die, you sleep. You sleep until Jesus returns, like it says in Revelations. Then Jesus returns, wakes the dead and takes the living second."

"I understand your confusion, Linda," Vincent said. "I don't want to dispute any religious doctrine or shatter your expectations and challenge your conviction that what you believe is true, but after investigating thousands of cases, I can tell you with great certainty that what we are taught in church about life after death is simply not accurate. Regardless of what you and I believe, these spirits are here with us now in your home. That is a fact." Linda wept. Vincent continued. He looked at Sarah who just sat there expressionless, staring off into space—a daydream where none of this were real.

"They want to break up your family by turning you against each other, destroy your will to resist them, and harm you and everyone else involved. Ultimately, they'd like to kill every living thing that they can, because they are angry at God, and because we human beings are the living embodiment of God, his children, so to speak. We are their natural, vulnerable targets. They can't destroy every living thing, but they will start with you here, because this is where they have been allowed to gain entry."

Linda asked, "But how have they gained entry?"

Yvonne opened her eyes. She pointed to the carpet. "This is where the portal was opened. This is where they gained entry into this house. There is a doorway here, right here in this very spot."

Linda covered her mouth and tried to grasp what she had just heard. "A what?"

Sarah cringed. She looked up at the ceiling, inhaled deeply and began to sob uncontrollably. She looked down with bloodshot, tear-filled eyes at the spot where the psychic was pointing.

Vincent walked over and pulled out his holy water. He motioned for Jason to do the same. "In order for inhuman diabolical spirits to gain entrance into our lives or into our homes, they need an invitation. They also need our permission."

"No one gave anyone or anything permission to enter our home," Linda scoffed. Linda felt new strength. She knew that an injustice was done and she knew that she had to fight.

Vincent raised his hand and tried to placate her. "I'm sorry to have to tell you this, but in their attempts to find answers to the bizarre phenomena happening to them in and around this house while you and your husband were away in Vermont, your son, Tyler, and his friends went and purchased a Ouija board..." Linda stood and gasped. "They used the Ouija board in this exact spot to communicate with the human spirit," Vincent continued. Linda wiped her eyes. She looked at Sarah.

"Tyler caused all of this? Tyler?" Tears welled up in her eyes, spilled over and ran down her cheeks. "My own son is to blame for all of this horror?"

Vincent walked closer and said, "No one is to blame here, Linda. There was no intention to invite anything of a negative nature here into this house. But by not stating their intention, by asking for something non-specific in the spirit world to come and speak with them, they sent out a blind invitation to anything and everything that would hear the call."

Jason broke his silence. "Linda, right now, most importantly, it is absolutely essential that there be no internal strife within this family, and especially not inside this home. It is exactly what evil-natured spirits desire most."

Vincent looked up at his lead investigator and nodded. "They feed off the negative energy of fear, hate, anger, resentment, distrust, blame, and so on." Jason swept his hand away to the side of himself, with his palm facing the carpet. "What's done is done. We need you all to remain strong—together. Love is the highest frequency of them all. It repels these spirits almost as effectively as speaking the name of God or Jesus Christ does. It is the intention that we use and hold when we demand that these spirits show themselves and ultimately leave. We have to seal this vortex, because as long as it is active, it is an open door for more spirits to come into this house."

"Then please do so," Linda said.

Linda knew that she had to be strong for her children's sake and for her husband. But which would she defend? How could she be in both places at once? Her husband was lying in the hospital, getting worse day by day and probably inching closer and closer toward death. Her children were at risk every moment they spent in the house. What could she do? This internal longing to be with her husband could not stay the awesome desire to protect her children and herself. "You said that there is a man in my house. Why would he want to destroy us, if he is just a man?" Linda asked.

"He wouldn't, and he doesn't," Yvonne said. "He is an angry soul who, in my opinion, was never loved or appreciated. That type of person is a very dangerous personality—alive or dead. From what I am picking up psychically, I feel with a good deal of certainty that when the inhuman spirits entered this house and began to perpetrate certain evil acts, this man began to fight against them. He had a change of heart, you see. When he saw the inhuman spirits come in, he tried to protect you and especially Kelly. But like any human spirit, alive or dead, he quickly came under attack, because he could not resist the inhuman spirits' power."

"Inhuman spirits, or demons, did not lose their powers during the Fall of Lucifer," Vincent continued. "These demons are fallen angels. They retained all of their preternatural abilities given them at creation. No man, 'alive or dead,' as Yvonne said, can overpower them. This man, this..." he looked at Yvonne for confirmation.

"His name was Brock," Yvonne added.

"This man, Brock," Vincent continued, "has been caught up by the combined power of several demons."

Linda wept. "I knew it! I knew it would be true. Somehow after reading those books, I hoped it wouldn't come down to this. But it has, hasn't it? Oh, dear Lord..."

"Linda," Vincent said, "I didn't tell you this to upset you. I told you this because, as I have said, we have run out of time."

Linda wiped her nose. "No, I'm not upset anymore. I'm ready to do anything it takes to get these...bastards out of my house!"

Vincent gave Linda a very concerned and focused look. "Your husband became ill immediately following the challenge he issued to the spirits the other evening, did he not?"

"Yes, now he's in the hospital, and no one can identify the source of his illness."

Vincent groaned as he got up off his knee. "I need to see him immediately to test my theory."

"The doctor said that he can't have any visitors," Linda warned.

"Just make the call," Vincent said. "Leave the particulars

to me. I've done this before. Vincent winked at his men and motioned for them to walk outside with him onto the back porch to discuss the case. Linda picked up the phone and dialed. Yvonne studied the carpet and held the purple amethyst crystal dangling on the silver chain around her neck.

"Hello, Mrs. McLaughlin?"

"Yes. Doctor Kent, has there been progress with my husband's condition?"

"I wish I could tell you that there has been. We have a bacteriological specialist coming in from the west coast."

"I have a specialist of my own, and I need him to examine my husband immediately."

"What? In what field? Who..."

"He advised me it's within my rights to request that he...that my husband be transferred into a private room immediately for an examination."

"Well, of course, but..."

"Doctor, please just do as I request. You'll understand when he completes his examination."

"I don't oppose outside assistance, Mrs. McLaughlin. I'm a doctor and my job is to heal people. At this point, I don't know how to heal your husband. If you have found someone who can, you'll have my staff's complete cooperation."

"Thank you, Doctor Kent. We'll see you in an hour." She heard him issuing orders to someone beside him. "Goodbye."

Linda held her head low as she placed the phone on the table. Uncertainty consumed her. Then she felt Yvonne's hand on the back of her neck.

Vincent and the other men came inside. "Linda, we have to act quickly. I'm going to ask that you place your complete confidence in me."

"I trust you."

"Shall we go?" Vincent asked. He called over to Jason.

"I'd like Daniel and Aaron to come with us. We need to have someone look at Aaron's arm. I need my most experienced man to stay here and wait for the guys to come home. Jason, you know what to do. I want everyone in the living room. Leave no one alone. Log anything that happens. Understood?"

"Yes, sir," Jason said.

"Let's go," Vincent said.

From that moment on, Linda noticed that Vincent and Yvonne were stern and expressionless, filled with total concentration and intensity. She knew that something big, something awful, was about to take place.

Chapter 31 – Tying Up Loose Ends

THEY MET DR. KENT in the main entrance of the Emergency Room of Mercy General Hospital. He was waiting for them at the front desk. Aaron went off to get his arm and ribs looked at and Daniel stuck close to Vincent and Linda. Dr. Kent came over quickly and shook Linda's hand. "Hello, Linda. How are you?"

"I wish I could say that I was fine, but given the circumstances..."

"I understand." He extended his hand to Vincent. "I'm Doctor Kent, and you are?"

"Dr. Vincent Decker," he answered with a smile.

The doctor stared blankly at him as he walked past him down the hall toward the elevators. "Up this elevator, please." As soon as the elevator doors closed, Doctor Kent turned and faced Vincent. "Where is your practice, Dr. Decker? What is your specialty?"

The doors parted on the fourth floor. "My area of expertise is the realm of the unseen and the intangible."

Doctor Kent looked shocked and coughed.

As they stepped out of the elevator, Linda covered her mouth with her hand to conceal her smile. Doctor Kent whispered into her ear, "Mrs. McLaughlin, what is this all about?"

"There is something wrong with my husband that I believe only Vincent can cure."

Vincent paused outside the room. He opened the door slowly and walked inside. The others filed in behind him.

The dark room reeked of stale dead flesh. The blanket rose and fell slowly with each of Matthew's strained, gurgling breaths. Linda walked up to the bed and gasped. "Oh, honey!"

She walked to the window and tried to open it. "Get some fresh air here, it's suffocating. It's awful." She gritted her teeth and opened the window. A crisp October breeze blew in and ruffled the drapes. When Linda turned to face her husband, the window slid shut forcefully. Linda cringed. Yvonne shook her head from side to side.

"Doctor," Vincent said, studying both the window and Matthew lying in the bed, "I need two flat sheets and four extra pillows please."

"What for?"

"Doctor, please," Linda encouraged.

The doctor shrugged and opened the door. "I need two sheets and four pillows in here, stat!" Curious, concerned nurses and orderlies were gathering around the shift desk. Doctor Kent placed his hands on his hips and looked at Vincent. "How do you propose we help him, Doctor? You *are* a medical doctor, aren't you?" A nurse came in with two folded sheets draped over her arm. Dr. Kent waved her toward Vincent. She gave a him a confused look, turned, and handed them to Vincent.

"It depends on what your definition of medicine is." He threw a sheet to Daniel who smiled and walked around to the opposite side of the bed. Vincent turned to face Dr. Kent. "I'm no medical doctor, but I am a doctor of parapsychology. I am also a demonologist, and I believe that this man is possessed."

"Wait!" Linda demanded. Yvonne held her shoulders from behind and stilled her.

Vincent unfolded a sheet and tied one end around the steel guard on the side of the bed. Daniel followed his lead on the opposite side.

"Ridiculous," Dr. Kent snorted. "What are you doing to

my patient?" Linda shook her head. Why on Earth would Vincent want to tie her husband down? She believed that Vincent knew what he was doing, so she had to act upon it. She turned and pointed her finger at Dr. Kent.

"He may be your patient, but he's my husband!"

Vincent and Daniel wrapped the sheet around Matthew's wrists and secured his arms to the bed. They propped the extra pillows behind his head and on both sides of him against the railings. Vincent asked the doctor, "How long has he been unconscious?"

"Since he collapsed in the Emergency Room two days ago," he replied.

He turned his head around and frowned. "Despite your every attempt to revive him?"

"Yes," the doctor admitted.

"Walk over to the other side of the bed, please, Doctor." Vincent pressed his hand against Matthew's forehead. His skin was devoid of any color, and frigid like ice. He pressed back his scalp and opened his eyes.

The doctor leaned in over Matthew and shone his penlight into his eyes. He turned off his light and stood back up. "As I said, unconscious," Doctor Kent said.

Vincent patted his own chest, then reached around to the back of his neck and unclasped his gold necklace. "Unconscious or unwilling to communicate?"

"Preposterous."

Vincent replied, "Really?" He pulled a gold crucifix out from his navy blue sweater. He dangled it by its chain for all to see.

"What's that for? What are you doing?" Dr. Kent laughed.

Vincent held the crucifix an inch above Matthew's forehead. Linda leaned in and watched intently. "My experience tells me that there is a spirit possessing Matthew's body. It is the sole cause of his sudden, mysterious illness, an illness that will slowly but surely grow worse and more life-threatening despite any attempt that you make to stop it."

Doctor Kent scoffed, "A spirit? Possessing him? What nonsense..."

Large beads of sweat formed under Matthew's hairline and all over his forehead. Doctor Kent leaned closer and obviously could not believe his own eyes. Matthew's body jerked and his eyes suddenly shot open. Linda and the doctor recoiled in shock. Matthew's chapped lips parted, issuing an endless, blood-curdling bellow. Doctor Kent leaped back and nearly fell over the chair in the corner.

Linda howled with terror and disbelief. She held her face with both hands and screamed. Yvonne held Linda firmly by the shoulders as orderlies and nurses rushed inside to find out what was going on.

Doctor Kent snapped at the orderlies. "I'll call you if I need you!" He rushed over, closed the door and leaned against it. The man, or thing, in the bed sat up. It seemed to be hyperventilating. Saliva dripped in one long strand from its chapped and bleeding lips. It never blinked.

Linda said, "God help us!"

Vincent cupped the crucifix in his palm and backed away closer to the doctor. "You see, Doctor. He can't be cured when the negative spirit inside him is trying to kill him. He's possessed."

The vicious growls began and then something, some intelligence that could not possibly be Matthew, spoke. A garbled, disjointed voice came forth. "Take your relics and useless banter and stick them up your stinking, soggy asses!"

Vincent pressed the crucifix against Matthew's forehead. "Oh, that's not very nice!" The thing shook its arms against the restraints and emitted a blood-curdling scream.

"In the name of Jesus Christ, I command you to leave the human body of Matthew McLaughlin and return to the black pits of hell from which you came!" The growls turned to laughter. Linda saw the surprise in Vincent's eyes. Vincent continued, undaunted. "As Michael cast Satan out of Heaven, it is he who is here now that casts you out of the body of Matthew McLaughlin in the name of Jesus Christ!"

"No...No," it screamed. It twisted and contorted, no longer resembling Matthew, or a human being for that matter, but a reptilian thing with scales and thick clumps of wet, matted brown fur. It struggled against the restraints.

"I cast you out!" Vincent roared.

Then the thing inside Matthew gained the strength of several men, inched up as high as it could, and rammed Matthew's head against the pillows that protected his head from the raised metal railing guards of the hospital bed. It was attempting to smash his skull. If they hadn't put the pillows in place before they started the provocation, Matthew could have been seriously injured or even killed.

Doctor Kent tugged open the door and called for the orderlies. "I need help!" An orderly rushed in, approached the bed and froze in terror. Another who rushed in ran right back out, screaming down the hall.

Vincent splashed Matthew's body with holy water. It sank back into the bed and moaned. "In the name of and by the power of Jesus Christ, I command you to leave this body and return to where you came from, now!"

Doctor Kent took a syringe from the orderly and approached the bed. Matthew sat up. Red eyes, bright and, as impossible as it seemed, glowing, seemed to instantly paralyze the doctor. He didn't move.

"Get your stinking needles out of here and stick them in your eyes!" It spat a ball of yellow phlegm into the doctor's face.

He recoiled in disgust and searched for something, anything he could use to wipe away the scum.

Vincent splashed it with holy water again. "In the name of Jesus Christ, the one and only Son of the Living God, I command you to reveal your name and free this man!"

Vincent splashed more holy water on the thing that had invaded and controlled Matthew's body. "Speak it!" He made the sign of the cross.

"Azandrathu," it said in a hoarse, garbled voice.

"Azandrathu, disfavored by God and cast out of Heaven by Michael the Archangel, I command you to leave this man whose body you possess and leave for all time, never to return."

The demon began chanting in some foreign tongue that none of them could recognize.

Vincent poured the remaining holy water out of the vial and into his palm, then threw his hand forward and showered Matthew's body with it.

The demon faded into stillness and Matthew closed his eyes, his breathing becoming short and labored.

Linda shook in fear in the corner of the room and held her head. She looked up at Yvonne who looked at her, obviously deeply concerned.

Silence seemed to stretch on for an eternity until Doctor Kent spoke.

Doctor Kent leaned against the wall. "I...I don't believe it!"

Vincent nodded. "I thought you wouldn't. If I told you who I was and what I believed was happening, would you have let me anywhere near this man?"

"Absolutely not!"

Vincent slapped the doctor's shoulder. "Exactly. Let's go." They walked out and closed the door.

Linda followed quickly. "What now?" she asked.

"We're going to get some help," Vincent said.

"You need help?"

Vincent answered calmly, "We're not exorcists."

"Exorcists?" Dr. Kent and Linda said in unison.

"Linda," Vincent said, "your husband has been invaded, taken over by an inhuman spirit, a demon. When he challenged the spirits in your living room, they accepted. And the demons won by weakening his body, lowering his defenses, and by finally entering and possessing his body. They now have control of it. First, they wanted to simply debilitate your husband and slowly turn his body against itself for as long as possible. Now that they have been discovered, they are desperate."

"How so?"

"They know who Yvonne and I are. They know that we know how to force them to leave. And because they know that they are now on the losing team, they will kill him as a last resort. We have to act quickly!"

"What can an exorcist do that you can't? You seem like you know exactly what to do," Linda said.

"Only someone who is very pious with incredible faith and resolve, and who is trained in the exorcism ritual from the Rituale Romanum can successfully drive out a demon as powerful as this one is," Yvonne replied.

"Yvonne and I are going to go over all of the data we've gathered back at my home office."

Aaron met them all in the hallway.

Vincent asked, "Aaron, is your arm okay?"

"It's bruised, but not broken, thankfully."

"Do you feel up to staying with the family tonight?"

"I'm very tired, Vincent. I have to decline."

"That's okay. Always follow your instincts. Rest up, gather your strength, and call me when you're feeling well again."

Aaron handed him the videotape and turned to leave. "I just need some sleep. I'll be back in the morning." He turned. "Vincent, I'll call you first thing."

"Okay."

Yvonne smiled. "Thanks, Aaron. You've done a great job."

Aaron smiled and waved goodbye.

Vincent became quite serious. He clasped his crucifix

back in place and tucked it under his sweater. "Doctor, do you trust me?"

Doctor Kent folded his arms over his stethoscope. "This is your area of expertise, not mine. In this matter, I have no experience and quite frankly, I don't think I want any. I defer to you."

"Good, that's one obstacle out of the way. We need your complete cooperation."

Dr. Kent nodded and said, "You have it."

"I need him under constant observation and sedation. The demon inside him is trying to kill him. That is now its ultimate goal."

The doctor nodded. "It's doing a damned good job."

"Keep him on life-support and do anything and every-thing it takes to keep him alive. That's your area of expertise. Be ready to move him on a moment's notice. If his condition becomes critical, call me immediately." Vincent handed the doctor his card, then tapped Linda, and they all started down the hall toward the elevator.

Vincent drove the minivan with Yvonne in the passenger seat and Linda and Daniel in the back. They wound their way up and down the narrow hilly Connecticut roads, through a red-painted covered bridge, and onto Route 25. When they drove out of Newtown, Vincent asked, "Is anyone hungry besides me?"

"I for one am starving." Daniel said.

"I really don't have the stomach to eat at all, but I'll join you. I certainly don't want to be alone right now," Linda admitted.

"How about some hot tomato soup, Linda?" Yvonne asked.

"Mm, that does sound good, I have to admit."

"Fine," Vincent said. He pulled into the Blue Colony

Diner a few miles down the road. They got out and went inside.

After they were seated and had ordered, Vincent stretched his arm along the length of the booth they sat in and took a drink of ice water. "Linda, we didn't want to tell you what we suspected until we were absolutely certain. Not until we were sure he was possessed."

Linda folded her hands and asked, "How did you know?"

"The telltale signs," Vincent said. "You see, Yvonne and I have been doing this for many years. After a while you begin to see the same phenomena. What we're dealing with is an incredibly powerful soul mind. The entity possessing your husband is vastly more powerful than you and I. However, it is not more powerful than God. And it's God that we're going to call upon to force the demon out of your husband. As I alluded to earlier, there is a religious cere-mony called the exorcism ritual from the Rituale Romanum. It is very effective where the demonic is concerned."

"An exorcism," Daniel added.

Linda gasped. "Like in the movies?"

"You see, Vincent and I aren't exorcists," Yvonne added. "We wouldn't want anyone to think that we were. We work with a very pious man—a bishop from Boston. He's helped us in situations like this one on dozens of occasions. Only someone very learned and very pious who has prepared himself for days and established a state of grace can be successful at driving out demonic forces. We're going to meet with the bishop personally later in the afternoon. He needed three days to prepare for Matthew's exorcism."

Three days is an eternity," Linda said.

"Don't worry," Vincent said. "I spoke with the bishop several days ago. He's been preparing since we first spoke, and he arrived last night."

Linda's expectations grew. She was so happy she'd found them.

After they had all finished their lunch, Vincent got up. "We've got to get going if we're going to meet the bishop in time. I'll buy lunch." He slid out of the booth and went to the cash register. The others got up and waited for him by the door.

Linda stepped up beside Vincent and said, "Here you are helping me and my family, and now you're paying for my lunch. We've never even discussed what this whole thing is going to cost us."

Vincent chuckled. "We don't charge for our services, Linda." He looked her in the eyes. "People would have a field day with us if we charged money to go in and expel unseen spirits from houses. We do this because we want to help people, not because there is any money in it." He waved her over and pointed out the window. "I drive a Ford, not a Ferrari," he chuckled. The girl at the register handed him the change and he followed Yvonne and the others outside. A crisp fall wind swept past them as they descended the steps to the parking lot. Yvonne pulled her shawl closer around her neck.

Vincent grabbed the railing and closed his eyes. He stood there for a full minute.

Yvonne looked concerned, came up and held his arm. "Headaches again?"

He opened his eyes. "Everything's fine." He stepped down, smiled, walked over and got into the van. They drove through Newtown and made their way back to Monroe.

"So, I'm curious. What are we going to do now?" Linda asked.

"Since we left your house, Jason has been preparing the house for a ritual that we are going to perform later called suffumigation."

"A ritual? Is there anything I need to know, or anything that I can do?"

"No, Linda, there is nothing you can do, or should feel the need to do. It will all be taken care of. It's a cleansing, a baptism, if you will—for your house. Once we are all prepared to begin later this afternoon, I'd like you to go stay with your friend for several hours until we are finished, because it's far too dangerous for you to be in the house when this is going on. What is your friend's name again?"

Linda interrupted him. "Why is it so dangerous?"

"Because this is very serious provocation," Vincent warned.

Yvonne said, "Julie. Her friend's name is Julie. That's where Kelly is staying."

"Oh, yes. Julie," Vincent said.

Vincent continued, "Yvonne is conducting a telephone investigation this afternoon that she can't miss, and I need to meet with the bishop. We will be back late in the afternoon to begin the suffumigation."

When they arrived at the house, they parked in front of the garage.

Daniel reached back inside for his camera bag and got out of the van. "I need to go and get some more infrared film."

"Okay," Vincent said.

Daniel walked toward his car and got in. Vincent opened the back door of the van and removed several boxes. He balanced the boxes on his knee and tapped on the window. "Linda, would you?" He smiled and made a motion with his thumb to remind Linda to open the garage door.

"Oh," she giggled. She hit the remote control on her key chain and the garage door rolled open.

"Thanks," he said.

Jason heard them, opened the kitchen door and walked outside.

Vincent handed the boxes to him. "Jason, you know what to do, right?"

"I do. It'll all be taken care of." Jason walked back inside and set the boxes on the kitchen table.

Vincent came back out with a smile. "You're in good

hands until we return, and then, of course, you're in even better hands," he chuckled. "I'd like you to do something for me while we are gone, Linda. Can you do that?"

"Sure, I'll do anything."

Vincent slapped his palm against his thigh. He looked clearly disappointed. "How can you say 'yes' when I haven't yet told you what it is that I want you to do? For Pete's sake, when are people going to learn to stop saying 'yes' before they even hear the question?"

Linda was aghast. She didn't know what to think.

Yvonne shook her head inside the van. "Oh, Vincent, stop it. She's going to think you're serious."

Vincent laughed. "Linda, as I said earlier, laughter is a powerful weapon against the demonic."

"I'm not laughing. I was worried that I did something horribly wrong. Have I?"

"No, you're missing my point. Never agree to do something unconditionally when you don't know what is being asked of you."

"Okay, then. What is it you'd like me to do?"

"I need you to go through the house and open every door, cabinet, box, drawer, medicine chest, and container everywhere and leave them open. It is imperative that you do not miss any of them."

"Sure, but why?"

"I can't tell you yet, but trust me, okay?" He winked at her and drove away.

Linda stared hopelessly at the van as if she were a football player in a championship game and the coaches had just walked off the field.

Daniel drove up, looked out his window and said, "Everything will be all right, Linda. Jason is inside, he will protect you. I'll meet Vincent back here in a few hours."

Linda stood motionless as the investigator drove off with a wave. She put her hands into her pockets and walked slowly into the garage.

Chapter 32 – Cleansing the House

VINCENT DROVE INTO the McLaughlins' driveway a few minutes before six o'clock. Daniel pulled in just behind him. Vincent carried a large black leather bag to the door. He rang the doorbell and Jason answered. Daniel stood patiently just behind Vincent. When he got to the top of the steps near the front door, Vincent cocked an ear. His investigators seemed puzzled and looked at each other. "Do you hear that?"

"Hear what?" Jason asked. "Did I miss something?"

"No, that's my point," Vincent said. He stepped down and walked briskly toward the woods. The other men followed quickly. "Where are the crickets? Where are the other insects and animals?" Suffocating silence smothered the house and the entire yard. The only sound besides Vincent's voice was their feet shuffling through the grass. "There are none," Vincent said.

Jason nodded. "Silence, no insects, no animals are all signs of demonic infestation."

"Yes, the demonic," Vincent said. He gripped his bag tightly. "Even the insects and animals flee an area where there's demonic infestation."

A startling noise made them turn sharply toward the house. A window slid open and Linda stuck her head out.

Vincent said, "Linda, do you want to give me a heart attack?"

"Oh, I'm sorry," Linda giggled. Then she looked puzzled.

"What are you doing out there? Are you baptizing my yard? That's actually a good idea."

Vincent chuckled. "No, Linda. Not yet. We're just having a look around." He motioned for the men to follow and they went around back and in through the sliding glass door. Linda greeted them. Vincent went into the kitchen and set his bag down on the table. "Okay, Linda, we're going to light some blessed candles and place them throughout the house in the areas that were the most active. We're also going to burn some high-church incense and use it in every room."

"Why?" Linda asked. "What harm are smells to something that doesn't smell?"

"Oh, it goes much further than that," Vincent explained. "Frankincense and myrrh are nauseating to the inhuman spirits infesting your home, just as the smells of rotting carcasses are to humans. It's not only a physical smoke, but also a spiritual smoke. It's like fumigating the house with holiness and it should force them to leave. That's why I asked you to go through the house and open every door, drawer and cabinet that you could find, so there is no place that the smoke won't penetrate."

Suddenly, the front door flew open. Tyler, Jimmy, and Kyle walked in. "Hello?" Tyler called out. "I'm home." They walked into the kitchen.

Vincent continued. "What we're doing here is chanting holy psalms, praying, summoning God and Jesus Christ, and filling your house with the purest blessed incense and candles." The guys paid close attention. "To the demonic," Vincent continued, "invoking God or the name of Jesus Christ makes them insane with wrath because they rebelled against God, and they despise any thought of him or his son. When the smoke fills the house, the demons will flee into its nooks and crannies. We must ensure that all that they run into is holy incense. When they've had enough, and there's no safe place to hide, they'll leave—hopefully. It depends on how powerful the demons are and how long they can withstand the incense."

Kyle said, "No way!" He smiled broadly and asked, "Can we watch?"

"Watch, my ass," Jimmy said, pushing Kyle out of the way. "I want to help."

"I appreciate your courage," Vincent warned. "This could be dangerous business. What we are about to do will ignite the fire within them. And with this provocation, they can lash out at any one of us, if they aren't too weakened by the presence of holy incense and prayer." He looked around at Daniel and urged him over.

"Daniel, go with Linda and take these eager young men back to Julie's house."

"But we want to help!"

Linda felt her fear return. "I understand. Tyler, let's go." She walked away toward the front door. "Guys, I mean it!"

"You got it," Daniel said. "I remember the last time we did this. I'll pass on it this time." He smiled and followed Linda. "Come on, guys."

"Jason, you know what to do," Vincent said.

Jason nodded and pulled out several boxes of blessed white candles, plastic bases, small white ceramic bowls, small bags of self-igniting charcoal discs and several bags of frankincense. He took the boxes, opened them, and folded their covers over.

"I want to stay and help," Tyler protested.

"Tyler, you'd better go. This is not fun and games," Jason cautioned.

"No way," Tyler said. "I'm staying. Besides, you need an extra hand with Aaron taken out and because Daniel is going with Mom."

"We can all help you, Mister Decker," Jimmy said.

Vincent tossed a few packs of matches onto the table. "Linda, I'll call you when we're through. If Tyler and his friends are feeling brave enough to assist, they're right, this is a large house and I could use the help. Time is of the essence."

"Yes!" Tyler raised a victorious fist into the air.

"Absolutely not! Tyler, guys, let's go!" Linda said from the foyer. "You are not staying here! Help or not, he just said it could be dangerous!"

Tyler argued, "Mom, he just said that he could use the help!"

Kyle interjected, "Sir, we can do something that isn't risky, right?"

Tyler nodded. "There's something I can do that won't get me hurt or into harm's way, isn't there?"

Vincent nodded. "Yes, as a matter of fact, there is something you can do."

"See, Mom?" Tyler said.

"You can hold the flashlight as we go through." He looked at Linda and smiled. "The guy with the flashlight never gets hurt."

Linda folded her arms and sighed. "I don't like this one bit."

"Mom, really, can you please just let me be a man, ever?"

Linda thought about how brave her son had been during all of the chaos that had ensued over the past several days and remembered that he was indeed quite resourceful. "You've got a good head on your shoulders, I know that. I know what happened with the Ouija board, and I want you to know that I forgive you."

Tyler gasped. "You know?" She nodded and held back her tears. After a few seconds, he hugged his mother and said, "Thanks, Mom."

Linda kissed him on the forehead and said, "Just please promise me you'll be careful. Please!" She turned and walked away, then looked back. "Tyler? Please?"

"I will be very careful, Mom. I promise. Trust me!"

Jason began pouring some of the incense from the bags

into the small, white ceramic bowls and stacking them inside the box. Kyle inserted the candles into their bases and set them inside the other box when he turned to Tyler. "Well, that went much easier than expected with zero backlash."

Tyler looked at Vincent. "Thanks for letting us help out. We all want to do what we can."

Vincent nodded. "I know you do."

Linda scowled. "Okay. "I hope it goes well," she said. She gave a courteous smile at Daniel, who opened the door and led the way outside.

Jimmy gave the thumbs-up to Tyler and Kyle and said, "Well, that's a huge relief. Your mom knows and she isn't even really that pissed off."

Tyler said, "I wasn't expecting her to find out, but yeah, that is pretty sweet that she's being so levelheaded about it."

"I wonder what your dad's reaction would have been if it were your mother lying in the hospital bed."

"I don't even want to imagine," Tyler replied.

Vincent pulled out a leather-bound Bible. A dull resonating rumble started in the basement and groaned through the house in a long, steady wave. "We are going to place the bowls and candles throughout the house, with attention to the areas where the activity has been especially blatant. Jimmy, you place the dishes. Kyle, you place the candles. And Jason will light them both. Tyler, if the entities in the house shut any of the cabinets, doors or drawers, your job is to immediately open them so that there is no place that the incense won't penetrate."

"Understood," Jason said.

"No problem, Mr. Decker," Jimmy said.

"Kyle, Tyler? Ready?" asked Vincent. They nodded and Vincent waved them on.

Vincent opened his Bible and cleared his throat. He

began reading aloud. "The Lord is my shepherd, I shall not want..."

Jimmy left a bowl on the kitchen table. He then placed one in the center of the kitchen floor in front of the refrigerator and another on top of the washer and dryer. Kyle set the candles in place and Jason lit them.

Vincent's powerful voice resonated through the house as Tyler led the way with the flashlight. "He maketh me lie down in green pastures: he leadeth me beside the still waters..." Tyler led the way into his mother's art studio and waited for the others to do their jobs. "He restoreth my soul..." Then they went into the adjacent and barely-used dining room. They set the items down on the table and continued into the foyer, placing them on the floor in front of the open doors of the hall closet. "He leadeth me in the paths of righteousness for his name's sake..." A dreadful growl began out of nowhere, startling the younger assistants. But it was ineffective against the seasoned demonologist and his lead investigator.

Jason urged them on. "Keep going, and don't let anything disrupt the flow. Stay focused and don't let anything distract you."

Vincent continued, "Yea, though I walk through the valley of the shadow of death, I will fear..."

Then, horrible banging shook the walls so hard that they cracked.

Vincent backed away, and quickly found the strength to continue despite the obvious display of preternatural power. "I will fear no evil: for thou art with me; thy rod and thy staff they comfort me."

The wall cracked some more and photo frames and pieces of dry wall fell to the floor and smashed into pieces.

Tyler's eyes were wide with fear, all the more so when he saw a picture of his father lying amidst shards of broken glass.

Vincent led them back through the kitchen and into the

living room. They repeated the process like a well-oiled machine. They knelt and placed the religious items in the center of the floor. Tyler shone the light down for them. Jimmy and Kyle looked at each other in silent acknowledgement of the fact that they were placing the items on the exact spot where they had used the Ouija board. They looked up at Vincent, who gave them a knowing glance. They gulped. Vincent shouted, "Thou preparest a table before me in the presence of mine enemies..."

Wicked screeches shot out from all corners of the room.

Jason struggled with a match and struck it three, then four times without so much as a spark. Vincent looked back, obviously frustrated at the delay. Jimmy, Kyle, and Tyler cringed in anticipation. Vincent shouted in a commanding tone, "Thou anointest my head with oil..." Jason's match came alive with flickering brightness. Jimmy and Kyle exhaled in relief.

Jason ignited one of the bowls of high-church incense. Immediately, the screeches intensified and turned into thunderous groans.

Tyler went ahead into the garage. "My cup runneth over..."

Booms began, so deafening that Tyler covered his ears and dropped the flashlight.

The door slammed shut, leaving Tyler alone in the garage. Kyle set the candles down on the table and ran for the doorknob. It opened easily, despite his worst fears.

"Surely goodness and mercy shall follow me all the days of my life: and I will dwell in the house of the Lord forever," Vincent said as he continued, undaunted. The aluminum garage doors started to shake and buckle. "Jason, recite the prayers with me."

Both men chanted together. "Our Father, who art in heaven, hallowed be thy name..."

Kyle joined in and the three voices sounded like a chorus of angelic voices from on high.

The doors ceased shaking but deep, appalling curses resonated before them as some unseen protester tried its utmost to silence them with its own vile words.

"Don't listen to it. Don't decipher the words. Stay focused," Jason warned.

Tyler turned on the basement lights and led them downstairs. It was dank and moldy-smelling, even though it was definitely not moldy, Tyler knew. His father was meticulous and immaculate, even with the basement. It felt unusually warm as well.

Vincent continued and said, "Thy kingdom come, thy will be done on Earth..." Vincent stopped and stumbled. Jason turned fearful eyes on him and saw Vincent's legs quivering. "On Earth as it is in heaven." Vincent gritted his teeth.

Jason fished for a vial of holy water out of his pocket, uncorked it and splashed Vincent's legs with the water.

In the confusion, Jimmy and Kyle had set the bowl and candle in the center of the floor and Kyle lit them both.

The violent tugging subsided and Vincent nodded at Jason and his new teenage assistants with approval. A bead of sweat rolled down Vincent's nose as he waved them on. They started up the stairs while Vincent continued. "Give us this day, our daily bread..."

Jason set a bowl of high-church incense in Kelly's room and inside her closet. Then they did the same in Sarah and Tyler's rooms. Tyler smiled as the sizzling, glowing amber granules produced a small rising column of wonderful-smelling smoke. "And forgive us our trespasses..." Vincent continued as they passed into the hallway again. "...As we forgive those who trespass against us."

Tyler walked into Linda's bedroom and set a candle down on her bed. Jason reached in to light it and the bed began to shake violently. Vincent threw holy water and doused the bed with one swipe. The shaking subsided instantly. "And lead us not into temptation, but deliver us from evil..."

Jason set a burning bowl of incense on Matthew's night stand. "For thine is the kingdom, the power and the glory forever!"

Horrendous wailing erupted in the attic, forcing them to look at the ceiling. Vincent waved them onward into the hallway and pointed toward the ceiling. Tyler reacted instantly, drew down the attic steps, and secured the ladder into place. He braced it from behind and Vincent started up the stairs. "Hail, Mary, full of grace, the Lord is with thee..." Vincent said.

Jason followed, reached up and set the bowl on the ledge. They all heard a scraping sound and suddenly, the bowl of incense bounced back and fell down upon them, dumping its contents onto Tyler and the carpet. The burning granules burned into Tyler's hair and skin, but he shook them off quickly and stomped on them so that they were extinguished before they burned the carpet.

Jason came back, reached into the box and handed a new bowl up to Vincent, who stepped up until he could propel his powerful voice into the vast darkness of the attic. "Blessed art thou amongst women. Blessed is the fruit of thy womb: Jesus." He placed the bowl down and slid it away from the ladder opening.

Scratching and awful gouging sounds literally shook the floorboards as if heavy furniture or unearthly claws were being dragged across the length of the attic. "Holy Mary, Mother of God, pray for us sinners, now and at the hour of our death. Amen."

Vincent came down and urged his assistants onward. They worked their way downstairs and finally outside onto the front porch. Jason walked to the car, retrieved a large brass bowl and a large bag of incense from the trunk and then joined the others. Vincent closed the front door and splashed holy water three times across the door frame and onto the door itself. He pointed at the landing and winked at Jimmy and Kyle, who dropped to their knees and set the bowl and candle into place. Vincent put the vial back into his pocket. Jason poured the contents of the bag over the charcoal into the brass bowl, set it ablaze and lowered it into Vincent's outstretched hands. He then knelt and lit the bowl and candle on the landing before the door and placed a glass globe over them to prevent the wind from extinguishing them.

"Alright, we are almost done," Vincent said eagerly. "Everyone recite the Our Father prayer with me and follow."

"Sounds good to me," Tyler said.

Vincent began walking around the house counter-clockwise, with the huge plume of incense smoke wafting behind him. Tyler opened his arms and breathed deeply, basking in the holy ritual and the sanctity of the smoke. "Our Father, who art in Heaven, hallowed be thy name..."

They continued around the side of the house. Jason pointed at the grass, and the boys set their wares into place. Jason pulled out a glass globe from the box he was carrying, placed it over them, and then reached in and lit the granules from above. They did the same on the back porch, and finally repeated the process just outside the garage.

When they finally set the last globe into place Vincent reached into his pocket, removed a white handkerchief and wiped his forehead. "You all did very well. We make a pretty good team, you know that?" he chuckled.

They all walked inside. The house smelled like fresh flowers. A thin smoky haze filled every room. There was nowhere for the demons to go.

They went into the kitchen and stood there for several minutes, listening. They walked into the living room and waited quietly. They watched and listened for any sign of a disturbance. There was nothing. The suffumigation was successful.

Vincent propped his Bible under his arm, picked up the phone and called Linda. "Hello. Julie, may I speak to Linda please?"

Linda answered within seconds. "Hello, Vincent. Is everything alright?"

"Everything is just fine, Linda. It worked. Your house has been blessed and I believe the spirits have fled. When you come home, your house will be a bit smoky, but it will smell quite nice."

"Oh," Linda said, relieved. "I can't thank you enough. Are the kids are okay?"

"The brave young men are just fine. They performed perfectly. In fact, they may have a future in paranormal investigation." He smiled.

"Oh, well, I don't know about that," Linda warned.

The guys laughed and smiled at each other. Vincent told Linda she could come home when she was ready and hung up.

"Jason, I'd like you, Daniel and the guys to stay here and record any signs of activity."

"Sure thing," Jason said.

"No problem, Mr. Decker," Jimmy said. "We can handle it."

Tyler asked, "Are you going somewhere?"

"Yes," Vincent replied. "This was just the first phase. Now, I have to save your father."

Chapter 33 – Expelling the Demon

AN HOUR LATER Linda pushed open the heavy oak door and walked into Matthew's room. She heard nothing but his heavy breathing and the rhythmical pulsing of the many life-support machines surrounding him. The rank smell of rotting flesh and excrement forced her to cover her mouth. She leaned forward, barely making out the silhouette of his body. Then he stirred and turned over in his bed. He expelled a sudden gurgling sound and she backed away.

"Let me die," he said.

Linda went rigid. Courage and determination filled her and she roared, "No, for the love of God! Fight! Don't let this thing destroy you!" She watched in horror as her husband's face twisted and contorted into something different, something evil.

Then she saw Vincent Decker's face lean out of the darkness, illuminated by the light of the full moon that was escaping the edge of the curtain. "It's not going to destroy anybody, Linda." He rested his chin in his palm. "I have something very special planned for the demon possessing Matthew."

The form in the bed turned sharply toward him and growled in some deep, awful tone. "Eh?"

"Oh, yes," Vincent said. "You wait and see." A distant, shrill call from some ungodly place made the hairs on the back of Linda's neck stand erect. "Go home, Linda. Your house is cleared. There is nothing you can do here. The man you love and cherish is not here. His consciousness has been pushed aside. Go and get some rest. You'll need all of your strength in the morning."

"Eternal rest," the thing laughed.

Linda winced when she heard the voice.

Vincent shot his hand toward the bed and the demon wailed in agony. He corked the bottle of holy water and held it firmly in his palm. Then he said again, "Go home, Linda."

"Okay," she said. She left the room, closing the door behind her. The nurses gave her apologetic glances and went about their business. A gruff, hoarse voice chanted in some foreign language behind the door, driving her away and down the hallway in seething anger. She heard Vincent's voice but could not make out what he said to the thing—but it wailed for several long, terrible moments afterwards.

During the evening into the morning, Dr. Kent kept Matthew sedated and unconscious. Each time the demon stirred, Vincent doused it with holy water. They would not allow the spirits inside Matthew to animate and control his body in the least.

The next morning, Linda arrived fresh and rested. When she walked in she saw Vincent standing by the window, looking out at the gray overcast sky and the colorful leaves sweeping across the lawn four stories below.

"It's time," he said.

Doctor Kent waved at a group of three orderlies that were hovering just outside the room. They immediately rolled a gurney inside and started preparing it.

Seconds later, Yvonne walked into the room with a tall gray-haired priest. Vincent turned slowly. "Linda, meet Bishop Phelan, the man I've been mentioning."

Yvonne smiled and said, "He's here to help your husband."

"Indeed I am," Bishop Phelan said. "Hello, Mrs. McLaughlin."

Linda smiled warmly, held Bishop Phelan's hands and started to weep. "I can't thank you enough, Your Excellency." She covered her mouth and began to sob.

Yvonne held her in her learned embrace. "It'll all be over soon. Everything will be alright, you'll see."

Doctor Kent raised a syringe before his eyes, struck it three times with his finger and stuck it into Matthew's arm. He waved, and the orderlies rolled the gurney next to the bed. They quickly and methodically untied Matthew's arms, slid him onto the gurney, and buckled the straps around his shoulders, hips and calves. Then, they secured his wrists to the undercarriage.

Vincent splashed Matthew with holy water. Bishop Phelan made the sign of the cross and whispered one rising phrase in Latin. Dr. Kent unfolded a sheet and laid it over Matthew's face so that no one would be able to see the frightening, disfigured creature beneath it.

They rolled Matthew out of the room, past several dozen curious hospital staff members, down the hall to the freight elevator and finally to the loading dock where there would be no witnesses. They loaded the gurney into a waiting ambulance. Vincent, Bishop Phelan, Doctor Kent, and the three orderlies got into the ambulance on either side of the gurney and the driver closed the doors.

As soon as they started to drive away, the demon came through. It whispered continually through pursed lips so badly chapped that blood and pus ran from them and collected in sudden vile pools on the sheets and blankets.

The bishop prayed continually.

The demon convulsed and strained against the straps. Groans, wails, and curses issued forth that were so blasphemous that the words alone sickened them.

Every time the demon came through, Vincent showered it with holy water and each time, the demon was subdued and sank back down into the blankets and went silent. However, the length of time in which it was subdued seemed to diminish each time. The demon was gaining strength. Time was of the essence.

Yvonne, Linda, Daniel, Tyler, and Sarah rode in Vincent's minivan which led the ambulance down Stepney Road toward the Our Lady of the Rosary Chapel. Linda watched the ambulance from the back window. The stark contrast of the white ambulance moving silently along among the trees and their vibrant autumn colors made the entire situation seem even more surreal. This was the same cemetery that she and Kelly had driven past when Kelly had experienced the ghostly encounter.

Tombstones whisked past her and the pitted, black iron gate along the edge of the cemetery mesmerized her. It was all too familiar. She became lost in a daze for the remainder of the trip. The sudden drop in speed forced Linda to turn her attention back to the front. She admired the white colonial chapel ahead in the distance. It radiated peace. She knew deep in her heart that this was sanctuary.

They traveled along the edge of the adjacent cemetery and stopped directly in front of the chapel. The ambulance pulled in front of the minivan and came to a sudden stop. Linda studied the ambulance from within the minivan.

The ambulance began to vibrate and then violently shake. The doors flew open so fast and wide, they appeared as if they'd break off their hinges. Then they swung inwards by the same fierce, invisible force. Simultaneously, the doctor and the orderlies stuck out their arms and caught the doors before they closed. They roared and applied all of their body weight against them. Vincent shot holy water against the doors and pushed hard against them as well. It took all of their combined strength to move the doors back enough for them to vacate the ambulance safely and quickly.

When the men were out, the doors slammed shut with

such force that both rear windows shattered, leaving Bishop Phelan and that thing possessing Matthew alone together inside. Vincent knew the seriousness of the situation.

Everyone piled out of the minivan to watch Vincent's desperate attempt to shower the rear of the ambulance with holy water. As he climbed onto the rear bumper and threw holy water inside the broken window onto the demon, the fear ran so thick in the air as to be suffocating.

The gurney rocked from side to side inside the ambulance. Bishop Phelan prayed undaunted. The gurney rose into the air and slammed back down eight times. Unshaken, Bishop Phelan's powerful voice echoed inside the ambulance and through the shattered windows. "Archangel Michael, stand with us in your divine power. Free Matthew of this agent of evil. Loose God's wrath on all who dare to defy him!"

Vincent came down off the bumper and splashed the holy water inside the windows and back and forth against the doors. Daniel uncorked his bottle and thrust it vertically against the doors from top to bottom.

Everyone leaped back as the ambulance doors blasted open and struck the back side of the ambulance with such force that two of the six hinges snapped off.

The orderlies rushed in, grabbed the edge of the gurney and pulled it out. Daniel and Vincent ran in and held the doors back in case they started to close again. They brought the gurney and unlocked the wheels as Bishop Phelan silently climbed out of the ambulance, his face never leaving his Bible. He prayed continually, making the sign of the cross over Matthew's forehead.

The demon shot its eyes open and sneered defiantly as three priests came out of the chapel's white doors and stood at the top of the steps. The demon snarled at them. Its nostrils flared and terrifying snorts followed. They all looked up. The demon's eyes emitted a fiery red glow and it roared in defiance. The priests made the sign of the cross in the air before them. It must have bitten into the demon's soul. Then, they watched as it gazed upon the white marble statue of Archangel Michael slaying Satan. It shot its head back and forth, trying to avoid exposure to the radiant holy symbols.

Vincent leaned over, grabbed the back of Matthew's head, yanked it by the hair and forced it to look at the statue. "Do you see that?"

Matthew's face shriveled. The skin rolled in over itself, horribly altering Matthew's face, transforming him into some otherworldly, beastly thing. Linda and her children cringed. After all, this was their father and husband. But it wasn't Matthew. It couldn't be. It was something beyond the scope of reason, from another plane of existence altogether.

Vincent looked defiantly at the beast on the gurney. "This is just the beginning of your torment!" He pointed at the orderlies and said, "Let's go!"

The demon screeched and wailed as the three men hauled the gurney up the twelve wooden steps toward the chapel entrance. Vincent and Yvonne blessed themselves. The three priests each made the sign of the cross on their foreheads. Linda, Daniel, Tyler, Sarah, Doctor Kent, and the orderlies all followed suit. They passed inside and rolled the gurney down the central aisle past the pews toward the altar. The demon roared so violently and screamed so wildly that Linda had to double-check if it was actually Matthew's voice box making the sounds.

Linda studied the patterns of light refracted through the great stained glass windows on the walls. They created a kaleidoscope of brilliant, beautiful colors behind them. This was a place of rest and sanctuary, a place she would bring her children, hold her husband's hand, and listen to solemn sermons. Never in a million years would she ever have imagined that a demon would be hauled into this very chapel inside the body of her beloved husband. Never would she have ever dreamed about participating in an exorcism. She prayed harder than ever during those brief moments of inner reflection. She prayed for her husband's well-being, but ultimately for his beautiful soul. She knew that his alarming violent outbursts were not his fault, but rather the will of that evil thing inside of him. She knew that for her husband's sake, the thing must be expelled once and for all. And time was of the essence.

The three priests met them all at the altar, blessing each and every one with holy water. Bishop Phelan walked out of the antechamber in a white surplice and purple stole. Three altar boys in white robes followed him, carrying golden trays and candles. Vincent came up and held Linda by the shoulders. It shook her back to reality. "This is where I need every ounce of your strength," he said. Linda stared at the man she barely knew, yet intimately trusted with the life of her husband. "This will be the most difficult, most awful thing that you will ever witness." She looked out of the corner of her eyes and saw the priests rolling the gurney forward. "Remember, this is not your husband that we're dealing with. It is a demon, quite possibly a devil. We'll find out which this afternoon. When the spirit screams, it is not Matthew, but a lost and dangerous spirit who is terrified of God and of what it faces now that it is in the Lord's house. Matthew is in no pain. He will feel nothing, despite what the demon does to his body or what we do to the demon, because Matthew's consciousness is not even here. It has been moved aside.

"The only way we'll fail is if you succumb to the demon's ploy. It'll try to convince you that it's really your husband crying out in anguish. It will do this so that you will interrupt the ritual. This must not happen. As hard as it may sound, you must not answer any pleas for assistance. Honestly, I wish that you would wait outside, but I know that is not going to happen, right?"

Linda said, "Not a chance."

"I didn't think so. That goes for you, too, Tyler and Sarah." He looked at both of them and held each of their shoulders. "You must not allow what this thing says to affect you in any way. Understood?"

Tyler and Sarah nodded. "It won't, sir," Tyler said.

Yvonne led Linda to a studded leather chair and they both watched as the preparations continued. Vincent gathered everyone together and addressed them in groups. First, he addressed the orderlies. "I need your courage and your strength. I need you to help restrain the patient." Then, he addressed the others. He shifted his gaze to every person standing there. "What you are about to witness is an exorcism." The orderlies exchanged uneasy glances with each other and with Dr. Kent. The doctor only shrugged at his men and shook his head. "The spirit inside that man over there is a demon, maybe even a devil. It is a fallen angel or archangel. But, whatever the case, it has far more strength than ten men. We are about to attempt to request God's aid in subduing it and forcing it out of Matthew's body with prayer and provocation. It will try to undermine us by dividing us and breaking our concentration. It is very intelligent. It also knows all of your sins."

The men gawked at one another. "Yes, it knows your sins intimately. It can, and will, use them against you to break your concentration, sap your strength, your resolve and most importantly—your faith. We owe it to the man that lies before us to be centered and focused upon protecting his body from harm until it is free of the demon. The only way we can do that is by remaining fearless and by staying on task. Fortunately, the demon cannot know your sins once they are confessed before God. If any of you have any sins that you wish to confess, the priests will hear them now." The men looked at the tall, gray-haired bishop standing beside the altar. He returned their gaze with a curt smile and waved the three priests over to them. The priests extended their arms and led them all out into the ante-chamber, one by one.

Vincent walked to the chapel entrance, took a deep breath of fresh October air and closed the doors. He turned in the dimly lit aisle and sighed. The time had finally come to free Matthew's body and rid the McLaughlin family of the demons that were plaguing them.

Once the confessions were heard, the group filed out of the antechamber and stood by the sidelines. The three priests, called in from Pennsylvania by Bishop Phelan on very short notice, donned white surplices with purple stoles and knelt before the altar. Linda sat in her chair and watched as the men set up their cameras.

It had all come down to this. She stared at the radiant bishop standing over her husband, only she had to remember that the consciousness that the priests were dealing with wasn't her husband at all. The bishop shot his hand forward and showered the demon with holy water from a glistening silver aspergillum. She knew it was much more effective than shooting a vial of holy water at it because it was a blessed, holy relic and it blotted the demon with dozens of droplets at once.

She saw the demon's head turn to the side. It opened its eyes and looked at her. Its eyes penetrated her soul. It mouthed the words that bore into her like a spike. 'Help me!' She went to get out of her chair. Then, the strong hand of her son held her back in place. He shook his head from side to side as a warning and mouthed the word 'No!'

'What if it really is Matthew resuming consciousness and begging me for help? How could I ignore him?' That thought was instantly dispelled as Linda and her children watched the face contort once again. Seething anger shone on its face. The thing turned toward the bishop with clenched teeth. It growled and lurched forward as if it were trying to bite and gnaw at him. Linda knew that it fought to resist. It was at war trying to keep Matthew's body. Just when Linda thought she'd lose her mind, Yvonne took Linda's hand from the armrest and held it. Yvonne's wordless, expressionless stare brought warmth and reassurance.

Bishop Phelan walked over to the others and blessed them. His unyielding stone-cold expression indicated solid determination and focused strength. Linda smiled when she saw two angelic-looking teenage altar boys in white robes walk inside. They went about their duties and placed three gold trays upon the altar. They proceeded to light the racks of candles around the altar and sides of the chapel. A third altar boy stepped down from the altar waving a brass thurible filled with frankincense and myrrh. Its invigorating smoke filled the chapel within moments, as he proceeded to traverse the entire chapel. The demon hacked and choked at its very presence. She knew that it was the equivalent of fumigating insects. She suddenly felt a great deal of satisfaction that there was finally something causing the beast inside Matthew to feel pain and to suffer for the torment that it had inflicted on her entire family. She nodded in approval. She felt new strength. She knew that however long it would take, the exorcism would be successful. She knew that her husband would be free of the demon, but at what price?

Finally, after much preparation and anticipation, Bishop Phelan began and said, "Blessed Father, we are here to pray for our brother Matthew McLaughlin." Wails issued forth with such intensity Linda thought that the great stained glass windows would blow out of their iron framing. The altar boys leaped back in complete terror. One of them dropped the tray that he was holding and fled back into the antechamber. Bishop Phelan continued, undaunted. Matthew's body that lay bound before him twisted and contorted to such monstrous proportions that it bore no resemblance to the man at all, but a hairy, scaly, reptilian-looking thing with a pig snout, yellowed tusks, and what looked to be gills, like some horrid hybrid beast from some strange alien world. Linda watched as Vincent stepped forward with determination. He must have noticed something going wrong because he reached over, showered it with holy water and said, "The power of Christ subdues you."

Then it tore its hand free of the restraints and struck Vincent in the chest with such power that it blasted him back into the railing. It exposed several rows of small, jagged, impossibly sharp yellowed teeth and growled, "I'll watch in delight when your fat ass lands in hell and burns there in torment for all of eternity, Vincent Decker!" Vincent groaned and collapsed.

Bishop Phelan shot his aspergillum out and blotted the demon's face and throat with holy water. The bishop shouted, "Silence, vile spirit! The power of Jesus Christ binds your tongue. It is he who commands you." The demon moaned and wailed, shaking its head back and forth, and finally looked away from them. Yvonne, Doctor Kent, and Tyler rushed to Vincent's side as he lay on the floor. All three orderlies, each weighing over two hundred pounds, jumped on top of the demon and attempted to restrain it again. Yvonne and Tyler helped Vincent back to his feet. Dr. Kent leaned in and examined him.

Vincent shook his head and said, "I'm alright! I'm okay!"

As the orderlies tied the demon down and secured it, blasphemous curses and the calls of dozen distinct animal sounds came in a dire chorus through its clenched teeth.

Bishop Phelan and the priests each showered the demon with holy water and spoke together: "Our Father, who art in Heaven, hallowed be thy name, thy kingdom come, thy will be done, on earth as it is in Heaven..." Suddenly, the beast on the gurney threw the men off like they were rag dolls and levitated two feet straight up into the air. The orderlies were aghast. The demon's eyes rolled back into its head. A horrible, gnawing, biting, scratchy voice emanated from all around them.

Daniel instinctively and immediately rewound the tape machine that he was using to record the exorcism and played what the demon had just said—but he played it backwards. The words made everyone cover their ears in disgust. It said, "Satan, glorious Satan, The Defiler, The Spoiler, The Scourge of hatred and desolation, abandon me not, guard me from..."

The altar boy acting as the thurifer dropped the censer, ran down the hall and into the antechamber, screaming. Bishop Phelan barked in opposition, "How dare you defile the House of God with your blasphemous curses. I cast you out!" He tore off his crucifix and pressed it against the demon's forehead and growled. Its skin sizzled.

The demon began laughing. "I feel your hatred, priest. Perhaps you are not the holy man that you think you are." The battered orderlies came back in with Vincent's help. They grabbed at its flailing arms.

The priests doused it with the aspergillum and said, "Almighty God has all of the power here. And his one and only Son, Jesus Christ, and all of His true power commands you to leave the body of our brother, Matthew McLaughlin! The power of Christ commands you! Archangel Michael commands you!"

The demon closed its eyes. Matthew's body slowly descended. The demon was being subdued.

"Blessed be the Lord."

The demon then shot its eyes open and hissed so loudly that it sounded like ten different voices speaking all at once, "I will never submit!"

The priests chanted, "The power of Christ will force you to submit! It is he that will cast you out! The power of Christ commands you to leave, now!" The Bishop opened his Bible and continued. "I cast you out, spawn of darkness, spirit of lust and dark works! Abandon this man's body or face the wrath of Archangel Michael and Jesus Christ, the one and only Son of God. It was Michael who once cast you out. It is Michael who will cast you out now."

The demon sat up and expelled a long, steady stream of yellow mucus all over the blankets. Finally it gurgled, "I spit on thee in the name of Satan."

"Jesus, dear Jesus, bind the tongue of this serpent!" The Bishop inserted a St. Benedict Jubilee Medal into its mouth and onto its tongue, now forked and writhing. "Silence it forever more!"

The demon growled and spat the relic out. It landed at Vincent's feet. It flicked its tongue at them all. It flailed like the tail of a lizard and then transformed right before their eyes into the tail of a rat. It looked at each one of the spectators, obviously attempting to lock eyes with them, but everyone was instantly aghast, and recoiled at the revolting display the inhuman beast made.

"Jesus Christ, Son of God, Savior of humanity, bind the tongue of this devil."

The demon covered its ears, roared in defiance and said, "Stop! Stop! No more words!"

"Then leave this man now in the name of Jesus Christ! It is through Jesus' blood that we are saved, and we give this man to the blood and heart of Jesus Christ now and forever more."

"No..."

The Bishop and the priests continued, relentless in their recitation. "Pater noster, qui es in caelis, sanctificetur nomen tuum..." The moans and deafening screams that the demon made became louder, more pronounced, and nearly intolerable. But the priests continued. "Adveniat regnum tuum. Fiat voluntas tua, sicut in caelo et in terra. Panem nostrum quotidianum da nobis hodie, et dimitte nobis debita nostra sicut..."

Suddenly a thunderous boom came from the entrance of the chapel and bright white light shone in from the doors.

Vincent shielded his eyes. Two silhouettes stood in the doorway. Vincent rushed over, determined to send them away.

"Vincent?" the familiar voice called out. "Mr. Decker?"

When he came closer he asked, "Yes. Who is it? Who's there?"

A pair of teenage boys stepped forward. "It's Jimmy and Kyle. Jason says you'd better come back to the house quick!"

Vincent felt his heart drop into the pit of his stomach. "Of course," he said. "If we don't have enough supplies at the house and if we aren't actively performing suffumigation, the demon will go right back there when the exorcism is successful here."

The demon's nostrils flared. It inhaled deeply as if sensing something. Its eyes darted back and forth. It turned its head and growled. "I know your sins, Kyle Foster!"

Vincent grabbed the guys by the arms, spun them around and said, "Don't listen to it. Leave this building at once. Get out now!"

Deep resonating laughter echoed throughout the chapel. Jimmy and Kyle became suddenly and completely overwhelmed with fear. They ran outside, leaped down the front steps and waited by the cars, panting.

Vincent shot his head in the demon's direction. He stormed over to it, jabbed it in the forehead with his index finger and said, "Your suffering will continue in this chapel or in the house. It makes no difference to me. It will continue here or there, anywhere and everywhere until I am satisfied that you have been forced to leave, and will certainly not stop until I send you back to the black pits of hell from which you came and where you most certainly and rightfully belong!" He held the vial of holy water over its face. The demon's eyes opened wide as it gazed upon it. It sneered. Vincent poured the holy water onto its forehead and it flowed down into its eyes and into its mouth. The demon roared in sheer agony. It gasped and choked and spat.

Vincent looked back and waved Tyler over. Tyler rushed to Vincent's side. Tyler asked, "What is it?"

"We need to get back to your house and perform another suffumigation! And...I need your help!"

Tyler nodded, took Vincent by the arm and led him out the door and down the front steps to the cars. When they got to the car, he said, "I know a short cut. Follow me!" He hopped into the driver's seat and Vincent, Kyle and Jimmy piled inside. The tires kicked up fallen leaves as they turned onto the road and sped away.

Chapter 34 – Dousing Flies

VINCENT OPENED THE McLaughlins' front door and rushed inside with his Bible in one hand and his black leather bag in the other. The others followed. Time was of the essence. Jason was reciting the Our Father in the living room. Vincent nodded, yanked out bags of charcoal and frankincense, tore holes in the bags with his teeth, spat out the torn piece of plastic, and replenished the bowls. He flung a pack of matches at Tyler, who hurriedly lit the incense and followed him into the dining room.

Tyler snatched the bag from Vincent's hands and said, "I'm much faster, Mr. Decker. No offense." Tyler dropped to his knees and poured some of the materials into the ceramic bowl. Jimmy dove down and lit it before Tyler even had to ask him to. Purifying perfumed smoke rose up into the air and quickly spread throughout the room. They worked very quickly together and completed refilling and lighting every bowl in the lower level of the house within minutes.

When they started upstairs, they ran into an invisible mass that became thick and impassable. Vincent closed his eyes and prayed silently. He held the bag under his arm and pulled out a vial of holy water. A growl came from upstairs and a black mass appeared on the landing above them. Vincent shouted out to it, "In the name of Jesus Christ, I command you to leave this house!" He felt the pressure let up and he climbed one stair. "The Lord is my shepherd, I shall not want." He climbed another slowly. The mass swirled around itself and shrunk in size. Vincent ascended further. He gritted his teeth and pushed against the invisible barrier that was blocking his path. "He maketh me to lie down in green pastures..." He shot an arc of holy water across it. When he felt it let up, he grasped the banister and charged up the stairs. The black form fled out of sight. Tyler gulped, holding onto Vincent's sweater.

When they rose to the upstairs level and turned the corner, they saw a squat, pulsating black specter standing at the end of the hall. Vincent made the sign of the cross before him with the holy water and said, "He leadeth me beside the still waters. He restoreth my soul." The thing with cloven hooves, black furry legs and a bull snout just stood there defiantly. "He leadeth me in the paths of righteousness for His name's sake," Vincent shouted as he walked forward with determination. "Though I walk through the valley of the shadow of death, I shall fear no evil..." The thing quietly disappeared.

They went into the Kelly's room and lit the incense there. When they were finished, they checked the hallway again.

Vincent looked up at the attic door and nodded at Tyler. Tyler grabbed the cord, pulled down the steps and extended the ladder. Vincent climbed them. He handed the spent, charred bowl down to Tyler who filled it, lit it and handed it back. Vincent set it into place and continued, "...for the Lord is with me."

Vincent continued with the recitation of the twenty-third psalm as they completed the task inside Sarah's room, then Tyler's room, the hall bathroom, and finally in the master bedroom and master bathroom. The smoke rose up unhindered, and it totally and completely fumigated the entire house.

Meanwhile in the chapel, the demon's wails and groans continued unabated. When Linda thought that she could bear no more, the demon suddenly went silent. The bishop and priests whispered to each other. Linda looked up and took her hands away from her face. She examined the holy men from afar. She rubbed her temples in small tight, circular movements, trying to relieve her terrible headache. Still, solemn silence prevailed, and then came an encouraging smile from Bishop Phelan.

Linda and Sarah exchanged hopeful glances. They stood and walked closer to the gurney, unsure what they would find. Linda's heart raced when she thought she heard Matthew's own voice cry out for help.

The bishop and the priests closed their Bibles, made the sign of the cross over their chests and backed away, exhausted. "It is done. The demon is gone. Praise be to God."

Linda and Sarah reached out to hug each other.

Then, the faint, terrible laughter caused their hearts to sink. It began as a slow, terrible hiss. Then it grew in power and ferocity until it echoed and boomed throughout the entire chapel. It sounded like eight distinct voices all in one terrible dark symphony.

The bishop and the priests wheeled around in horror. They leaped back and cringed as the gurney levitated straight up into the air until it was hovering vertically, three feet off the floor. Then it spun completely upside down. The demon's eyes rolled back in its head.

The bishop shot his aspergillum up and before him in an effort to shower the gurney with holy water, but the water inside it had been expended. The bishop held the silver device before his eyes in shock. Suddenly, the restraints that were binding Matthew's wrists, legs, and ankles all unwound by themselves, as if they were being untied by several pairs of invisible hands. In a horrific display of preternatural power, the beast floated off and away from the gurney. Matthew's arms fell to his sides and were held out at ninety-degree angles. Then, as if a switch went off that was holding the gurney in suspended animation, it fell and smashed onto the floor creating a huge, thunderous crash.

Bishop Phelan lunged to the side and fought to make his way around the demon and into the aisle between the pews, but some invisible force had slowed his advance to a crawl. He watched spellbound as the demon maneuvered its feet so that one was in front of the other. The sound of a hammer striking a metal spike echoed throughout the chapel. A gaping bloody wound appeared in the center of its foot, and blood trickled down its legs, to its knees

Linda screamed in terror. She fought herself against rushing forward to help her husband. But she knew that it was not her husband at all. It was trying to destroy his body. She roared in opposition.

Then the sounds of a hammer striking a metal spike came again, shrill and awful sounding. The wounds appeared in the center of its wrists. Blood flowed from its wrists onto the floor. It collected in pools that spread out began to sizzle and burn away completely. It was plainly obvious. The beast was mimicking a crucified Christ on an inverted cross.

The bishop roared in defiance as he used every ounce of his strength to move closer to the chapel entrance. Then tiny holes appeared on the demon's head from the invisible mockery of the crown of thorns. Tiny trickles of blood ran down its forehead and face. The bishop prayed silently as he continued.

Then it spoke. "And now you shall all suffer, for I am pain! I am fear! I will tear out your hearts until you bleed and collapse dead and rotting on the floor! And then I shall deliver your souls to Satan himself and you shall be his forever!" Its chapped, bleeding lips parted and its mouth opened impossibly wide. Its throat began to bulge and collapse, rising and falling as an incredible buzzing sound became clearly distinguishable deep within it.

Suddenly, tens of thousands of black flies screamed out from its mouth and flew out from its nostrils, completely filling the chapel in an obsidian swarm like none of them had ever seen before.

Vincent returned to the kitchen when they heard the loud crash below them in the basement. Tyler felt fear completely envelop him. The basement was the one last place for them to go and somehow he instinctively knew that it was positively the worst.

Undaunted and unafraid, Vincent reached out for the doorknob and recoiled. The flesh on his hand sizzled. He recoiled and winced in pain. He examined his palm. Blisters rose up around the reddened skin. Then, they popped before his eyes and the water inside them ran down his hand. It smelled like rotten fruit.

Jimmy ran to the sink and wet a dishtowel. Vincent gladly took it, wrapped it around his hand, grabbed the doorknob and tried it again.

Tyler shot his hand before his nose and mouth. The basement reeked of excrement and sulfur.

"Jesus, protect us," Vincent said. "Stand by our side and expel these evil spirits from this house, for this is your divine work." Vincent looked back at the guys, turned around, flipped on the light switch and took two steps downwards. Then the door vibrated and slammed shut behind him.

"No!" Jason tried the doorknob, but he too burned his hand. "Vincent?" he called out. "Are you alright?" They paused.

Jason looked at Tyler who lunged forward and kicked at the door. Jason joined him so that they kicked it unison. "Stand back," Jason said. Tyler pulled his friends gently away by the arms and ran into the garage. Jason walked back, and then rammed the door with his shoulder. Jimmy rammed it also. Jason struck the door like a truck and then kicked it four times. The door began to give way. "Vincent! Are you all right?" Jason pleaded.

Kyle ran into the garage and came back with a crowbar. He handed it to Jason who drove it in between the door and the frame. They heard Vincent cry out and then heard the sounds of a monumental struggle below.

Fire emanated from Jason's eyes. He gritted his teeth, roared and tugged at the crowbar with all of his might. The door began to break loose. He tugged again and a third time until it broke off its hinges. He tossed it into the garage. It made a tremendous crashing sound that echoed throughout.

Tyler ran down the steps first, then Jason, and then the others. A high-pitched, squealing, animalistic whine sent Tyler into the deepest recesses of fear and despair.

"Jesus, help me!" Vincent screamed.

Meanwhile, back at the chapel, the black flies swarmed over toward the bishop and the priests who were attempting to follow him. They attacked the orderlies and Dr. Kent next, and then attacked the women. They all cried out for help, but none came.

An endless stream of black filth cascaded out of the demon's mouth and attacked everyone and everything. There were so many of them that the entire chapel interior went pitch black. They tried to wipe them away, but more and more kept landing on them and crawling on them, buzzing and biting their bodies.

The demon turned its head toward the great stained glass windows. The swarm of flies streaked toward them and began to completely obscure the light coming in from outside.

The bishop and the priests made it to the aspersorium and the bishop drove his aspergillum into the vast pool of holy water within it. He cupped his hands, filled them, and splashed his face. Every single fly that was attacking him suddenly and completely disappeared into curling wisps of black smoke that faded away completely. He cupped more into his hands and threw it onto the priests beside him until the flies were totally dispelled. Bishop Phelan took off his stole and soaked it in the holy water. He said, "O God, who for man's welfare established the most wonderful mysteries in the substance of water, hearken to this prayer, and pour forth Your blessing on this element. May this creature of Yours, when used in your mysteries and endowed with Your grace, serve to cast out demons and to banish disease. May everything that this water touches be delivered from all that is unclean and hurtful; through Your holy name. Amen."

When his aspergillum was full, he yanked it out of the water and sprayed the priests. When they recovered from the diabolical attack, they dipped their own aspergillums into the water and refilled them. He tore off the priests' stoles and soaked them in the holy water. Then he wrapped them around their necks. Each of the priests sprayed the bishop with their aspergillums. They all made the sign of the cross and nodded. Bishop Phelan took his soaked stole out of the water, draped it around his neck, shot his aspergillum before him in the aisle and hurried off toward the women.

Sarah had fallen to her knees and had buried her face inside her shirt. Linda and Yvonne were curled over and screaming, spitting flies out of their mouths as best they could as they desperately tried to wipe the flies off them. Bishop Phelan doused Sarah first. Then he doused Linda and finally Yvonne. The priests had reached Dr. Kent, Daniel and the orderlies and relieved them of the repulsive, revolting attack in the exact same manner. The priests doused the altar and the flies gathered there and shot their hands up toward the stained glass window. Every swipe of the aspergillum dispelled a whole group of flies. One of the priests ran into the back and up the stairs until he reached the choir balcony. He splattered the stained glass windows three times and each time more and more of the flies disappeared.

The demon must have seen that the priest was all alone and vulnerable. It uttered the word, "Fool." The flies descended upon him in a thick, black cloud. The priest was being smothered. He dropped his aspergillum and crouched to retrieve it. He lost his balance and fell off the stair that he was on and he rolled fell down and into the railing. They all heard the sound of cracking, splintering wood and gazed in horror as his legs dangled from the damaged balcony. Two of the orderlies stood underneath him to catch him if he fell. The third raced up the steps.

The demon chanted in some strange, muted, undecipherable language. The bishop and the two remaining priests reacted quickly and splattered the demon with holy water. The flies that the water hit vanished. Others crawled back into its mouth and nostrils. They continued spraying the demon until all of the flies had completely disappeared. Bishop Phelan showered the wounds on the demon's wrists. As soon as the holy water struck them, the bleeding instantly stopped and the wounds closed.

Bishop Phelan shouted at the demon, "The power of Christ overwhelms you and commands you to release your diabolical hold on our brother Matthew. You will submit to the angelic host here now assembled. The power and the blood of Jesus Christ is impossible to resist. It vanquishes you completely. It disrupts you utterly."

The bishop and priests shot their hands forward and completely soaked the demon. They heard a great clamor and looked up to see the one orderly who had raced upstairs grab the priest's arm and haul him up to safety. Dr. Kent called out to the two other orderlies and urged them to gather underneath Matthew. They tore a sheet from the gurney and each took a corner essentially creating a safety net beneath him. "Release him now, vile and dark spirit!" Matthew's body arched back and the demon roared in opposition. A long and terrible scream issued forth and then the demon released him. He fell suddenly.

"Hold tight! Don't let him fall," Dr. Kent roared.

They pulled the sheet taut and it took every ounce of their strength to catch Matthew's body as it fell. They gently lowered him down onto his back.

The demon stirred and began whispering. Bishop Phelan wedged his aspergillum into its mouth. The holy water dribbled out of the small holes, ran down the sides of its mouth, down its neck and soaked its shoulders in a pool of holy water beneath them. The flies covering the stained glass windows and every last fly inside the chapel suddenly vanished into tiny wisps of black smoke.

Bishop Phelan peeled the purple stole off his neck and knelt before Matthew. He cleared his throat and began chanting, "Psalmus David Dominus reget me et nihil mihi deerit, In loco pascuae ibi me conlocavit, super aquam refectionis educavit me." The powerful chanting echoed throughout the chapel and renewed their conviction. The three priests joined the bishop and recited the psalms with him in unison, "Animam meam convertit deduxit me super semitas iustitiae propter nomen suum."

Linda screamed and screamed at the varied disfigured faces that began appearing over Matthew's face as they continued the recitation.

"Nam et si ambulavero in medio umbrae mortis non timebo mala quoniam tu mecum es virga tua et baculus tuus ipsa me consolata sunt, Parasti in conspectu meo mensam adversus eos qui tribulant me inpinguasti in oleo caput meum et calix meus inebrians quam praeclarus est, Et misericordia tua subsequitur me omnibus diebus vitae meae et ut inhabitem in domo Domini in longitudinem dierum."

Bishop Phelan looked down at his feet. He retrieved the St. Benedict Jubilee Medal from the floor and slid it under the demon's tongue. The demon choked and moaned. The bishop held the demon's chin firmly in his hand, slid his thumb inside its mouth and held its tongue down over the medal. He could feel the cold, clammy tongue writhing to break free and sizzling against the blessed, holy relic beneath his thumb. Then he shoved half of his stole into the demon's mouth, bit by bit, until its mouth was completely full. The other end lay draped over its chin and jaw and down over the front of its neck. The demon went berserk.

Bishop Phelan held out his hand and flipped his wrist, beckoning a priest to his side. He commanded, "Your stole, Father!" The priest handed the bishop the holy water-soaked stole and he secured it around Matthew's mouth and tied it around at the back of his neck so that there would be no way for the demon to spit out the medal. When he was confident that it was secure, he turned toward the orderlies and said, "Bring him to the altar."

The orderlies grabbed him under the armpits but the demon had far too much power and far too much fight left in it. It struck one of them and blasted him into an adjacent pew with such force that the pew cracked along its entire length. The orderly's limp body fell to the floor with a horrific thud. Three hymnals fell to the floor in unison from the shattered remains of the small shelf behind the pew. A priest pressed his crucifix against the demon's forehead and the beast made repulsive gurgling sounds. Dr. Kent stuck the demon in the neck with a syringe and stepped back to watch it take effect. The bishop ran behind the altar and turned the black iron hand crank that secured the massive crucifix above the altar by thick black chains. As he continued turning the crank, the chains rattled and the crucifix descended slowly.

Finally, the bishop let go of the crank and leaped back out of the way. The wheel spun around unhindered and the crucifix struck the wooden floor with an incredible, thunderous 'boom.' Linda thought of the terrible booming noises that she and her family had to endure over the past several days and smiled when she thought about how the vile thing inside her husband must have just felt when it heard the holy relic strike the ground with its own unique, powerful and profound spiritual impact.

An altar boy opened an adjoining door and peeked outside at the commotion. He cautiously approached and observed. The bishop shouted to the orderlies, "Quickly, help me lower it to the ground before the altar!" They rushed over and lay the crucifix down on its backside, flush against the floor. The august image of Jesus Christ's likeness was intricately captured and cast in colored plaster. It was breathtaking to behold.

"Lay Matthew's body upon it, face first, so the demon can stare into the face of the Son of God—the Redeemer of All of Life, The Savior of all mankind!"

The demon's eyes bulged out of their sockets as the priests subdued it with holy water and the orderlies hauled Matthew's body closer to the massive crucifix. They turned it around.

"Bind his arms," the bishop demanded. The curious altar boy came closer and finally gathered enough courage to stand at the bishop's side.

One of the priests removed his wet stole, kissed it, and tied Matthew's hands behind his back as securely as he could.

The orderlies lowered the beast onto the likeness of Christ until their faces were mere millimeters apart. Bishop Phelan looked down at the demon with utter contempt. "You like to play games with crucifixes?" The bishop nodded. "Let's play this game, shall we?" The beast rocked, wailed, shook, convulsed and arched up and away as far as it could to get away from the likeness of Jesus Christ.

The bishop grabbed the golden chalice in the center of the altar and handed it to the altar boy beside him. He wrapped the boy's hands around it and squeezed until the boy's knuckles were white. When he was sure the boy had it firmly in his grasp, and that he wouldn't let go, he placed his palm against his cheek, smiled, walked up to the altar, and pulled off the blessed white cassock that had once belonged to Padre Pio. The bishop draped it across the demon's back so that the violet cross that had been sewn upon it was perfectly situated on his back. The beast convulsed, bucked, and shook wildly like a horse protesting the imminent application of its saddle.

Bishop Phelan nodded at the trembling altar boy who held the chalice, unwound his ice-cold fingers and eased the boy away. He raised the chalice above his head and said, "Now stare into the eyes of the Son of God, you vile and foul, traitorous spirit! Bask in the glory of the Lord as you are cloaked in the holy vestments of His most faithful servants. Feel the love and purity of God's one and only Son, Jesus the Christ, Our Savior—who has poured out His blood and thus granted all of His children eternal life in the Kingdom of Heaven. The majesty and the power of the Lord Our God commands you to vacate the body of Matthew McLaughlin now and forever more."

The demon moaned and bucked.

"You are commanded never to return as we now baptize Matthew in the blood of Jesus Christ!" He poured the contents of the holy chalice onto the back of the demon's head and down across its neck, back, torso, legs, and feet. The beast wailed in agony. "Turn him over!" The orderlies lifted and turned the demon over. The agony in its eyes was unmistakable. Linda cried uncontrollably.

Bishop Phelan smiled at the demon. He held the chalice above its face. It glistened in the light streaking from the stained glass window above.

"Azandrathu, disfavored and rebellious, traitorous spirit, the Lord Thy God commands you to leave the body of our Brother, Matthew, now and forever more." The demon shook its head from side to side so violently it seemed as if it would break Matthew's neck. It growled fiercely.

Bishop Phelan tilted the chalice down toward him and the blood red wine dripped down onto its forehead, then into its eyes, down its nose and into its flared nostrils. The demon hacked and coughed and gagged and choked. The wine poured down the contours of its face and down into its lips. It writhed and convulsed. The orderlies held it in place and the priests doused its hands and arms with holy water.

The bishop pulled back the stole around the demon's mouth, so that it draped across its chin. He reached his trembling fingers into its mouth and pulled out his own holy water-soaked stole. A river of yellow pus flowed out behind it. He grabbed his crucifix in one hand, reached under and held it against the back of the demon's head. He curled his fingers into its hair and held on tight. Then, he poured the blessed wine, the physical representation of the manifestation of the blood of Jesus Christ into the demon's mouth. The pus around its lips sizzled and boiled away into nothing the instant the wine came into contact with it. The beast hacked and choked.

The bishop said, "The Lord Jesus Christ commands you to leave...now and forever." The demon wailed and wailed in a cacophony of vile vociferous voices. The bishop sneered at the demon, his arch-nemesis, and shouted, "Drink...the blood of Jesus Christ and find salvation and redemption." The demon growled in protest. The bishop screamed as loud as he could, "Then leave now and forever more." He poured the remainder of the wine down Matthew's throat. The beast kicked out its legs and arms in one last wild protest. "The blood of Jesus Christ casts you out!"

Then, finally, its eyes fluttered. Its chest shot up into the air as it arched its back. The demon shook in defiance and then fell back down onto the crucifix with one continuous gurgling exhalation. It became completely still, and the entire chapel went quiet. They waited for several minutes watching and waiting for a sign that the demon had hung on, but it never came.

Finally, Bishop Phelan raised the chalice toward the ceiling and said, "Victory in the blood of Jesus Christ!"

Back in the basement of the McLaughlin house, Tyler watched spellbound as saliva-muted growls echoed throughout the basement, and invisible claws dug into Vincent's shoulders and hips, fighting to control him, to overpower him, and to ultimately drive him into submission.

For some strange reason, Tyler knew that if Vincent gave in, he would be the next to become possessed. "Get off me!" Vincent demanded.

The invisible beast stunk of old, wet fur. Vincent had collapsed onto his hands and knees and gagged. He held his breath, trying to avoid the noisome stench that sat over him like a noxious cloud. An ear-splitting screech came from thin air, long and potent, like the combined calls of a lion, a pig, and a crow.

Tyler thought Vincent was going to die.

Vincent moaned. Deep gouges appeared down his back as if he were being raked by impossibly sharp, invisible claws. "Jesus help me!" He found the strength to stand. He spun around, trying to shake the thing from his back. Then he gagged and grabbed his throat. The life was being squeezed from him.

"Vincent!" Jason screamed. He reached for a shape on Vincent's back. He grabbed hold of something gelatinous, hot and bumpy. Its four limbs ended in clawed hooks that dug into Vincent's sides like pincers.

"Jesus Christ," Vincent shouted, gagging and vomiting. "In the name..."

Jason caught on and they both continued in unison. "... of Jesus Christ, we command you to leave!"

Savage licking sounds came from thin air as if the demon was fighting for control of him.

Jason patted his pocket, pulled out his vial of holy water and uncorked it. He saw Vincent collapse, drained and in terrible pain.

"The power of Christ compels you," Jason said. He shook the bottle and held it before his face. It was empty. He panicked. He made the sign of the cross over Vincent's back and over the beast riding it. High-pitched whines followed and then Vincent's face lost all of its color. He gasped for breath and reached out.

Jason said, "In the name of Jesus Christ, I command you to leave!"

"Jason," Vincent gagged. Jason looked down on him. "The incense," Vincent continued. "Light the incense and candles." Vincent's body was thrown forward over the workbench.

Jason nodded, tore open the bag and dumped it into the bowl. He searched around for a light, then lunged for a pack of matches lying along the edge of the steps. The matches slid away on the cement floor, as if by some invisible wind.

Tyler dove after them and snatched them up. He fumbled with the pack, tore off a match, and went to strike it when it was batted out of his hand. He tore off a second match and swiped it across the package. Time seemed to slow to a standstill. He noticed the first miniscule plume of smoke rise off the match. Then, a tiny spark came to life and ignited into a roaring, bright flame. He held it against the charcoal. The incense crackled and sizzled. He fanned the smoke so that it would rise and spread faster. Then he blew it onto Vincent and onto the beast riding him.

A great wail erupted, shaking the entire foundation of the house. Dreadful sounds like those of some wild beast savagely devouring its prey boomed throughout the basement. Vincent fell to his knees screaming, grabbing at his head. Horrible, vicious snarls and growls filled the basement. Vincent recovered his breath. He reached up to touch his head and recoiled due to the sharp pain he felt when he touched the dozens of small sharp points embedded into his skull in two even arches from close to his forehead, all the way around to the base of his neck.

The beast had been forced to flee, but not without one last display of power, one dire, vile, desperate strike, so that it would never be forgotten.

Jason fished through Vincent's hair and winced. He wiggled one of the objects and tried to pry it loose as Vincent cried out in pain. When he finally pulled it out, he saw that it was a yellowed, half-inch-long, bloody, flesh-tipped fang.

Vincent winced and stood up. He shook the dust off his sweater and pants. "We've done it. We've won." Then he raised his hand and reached to the back of his injured head again. "What in the name of God is stuck into my head, Jason?"

"Vincent, so help me...they...they look like...teeth!"

"It's no matter," Vincent said. "We've done it, Jason. We've been victorious."

"Thank God," Jason said. He helped him to the stairs and said, "Let's get the hell out of here."

They ascended the basement stairs into the kitchen. The high-church incense filled the entire house with plumes of beautiful, holy smoke. The faint but clearly distinguishable scent of fresh roses filled the entire house.

"It's clear," Vincent said ecstatically.

Jimmy and Kyle walked downstairs and met them in the foyer.

"We made sure that all the bowls were smoking," Jimmy said.

Jason shook his head and said, "Good work, guys!"

Vincent laughed. "It's done!"

Tyler opened the front door and said, "Hurry. I've got to see if my Dad's okay."

"Right," Vincent said. "We've got to get back to the chapel!"

Jason opened the car door for Vincent. He got in stiffly and moaned as he sat down. He put on his seat belt and closed the door as Tyler started the car and Jason, Jimmy and Kyle crawled into the back seat.

As they raced off to the chapel, Vincent gently pulled the teeth from his skull one by one, wincing at the sting they created as he freed them. When he had collected all forty-four of them he shook them in his palm. Loose bits of flesh dangled from the parts of the teeth that must have been attached to the beast's gums. He reached into the glove compartment and retrieved a napkin, wrapped the teeth inside it and put them into his shirt pocket. He then pulled out a handkerchief from his pants pocket and dabbed his wounds.

As they approached, the chapel, the doors swung open. Yvonne walked out and stood triumphantly on the landing. Linda and Sarah came after Yvonne and behind them, Dr. Kent and the orderlies rolled Matthew out on the gurney.

Tyler ran up the steps to his father's side. 'Has he endured too much?' he wondered. His face looked better, but he still looked entirely awful and nothing like the man that he knew and loved. 'Could my father ever recover from this?' he wondered. 'Will any of us recover from this terrible ordeal?'

Linda reached over and hugged Tyler. She said, "It worked! God bless us all! He's free! Your father is free." Linda sobbed. She looked down at the vehicles and saw Jason helping Vincent toward them. She rushed down the steps, ran across the lawn and hugged him. Tears of joy rolled down her cheeks. "Thank you, Vincent. Thank you, Jason. Thank you, all."

Vincent nodded and said, "It's over, Linda. It's what I do. It's what we all do." Linda wrapped her arm around his waist and held his chest. She hugged him again.

"Matthew will be ignorant of the fact that there was ever a demon inside of him. He, like so many others who have undergone possession, will have to see the video with his own eyes to believe it."

Dr. Kent escorted the orderlies and the gurney across the lawn. He nodded at Vincent and said, "We've got to get him back to the hospital immediately. This man has been through the wringer. If he makes it out of this, it will be a miracle as far as I'm concerned." He directed the orderlies to load him into the ambulance.

Vincent held up his hand and stopped them cold. "Wait a moment, please." The orderlies stopped in their tracks. They all watched as Vincent walked around the gurney and stared down at Matthew. He examined him carefully. Then he reached around his neck and unclasped his crucifix. They all waited anxiously as he held it dangling above Matthew's forehead. He held it there for over a minute. Finally, Vincent smiled, pulled it away, and clasped it around his neck. "He'll be just fine, Doctor." Everyone sighed in relief. They loaded Matthew into the ambulance. Dr. Kent helped Linda up into the seat beside her husband.

"Vincent, thank you," Dr. Kent said. He closed the doors from inside and the ambulance drove away seconds later.

Vincent smiled. He turned toward the chapel and saw Bishop Phelan, who was standing with his eyes closed just outside the doors, basking in the sunlight. Vincent and Jason walked up to him and shook his hand. The three men looked toward the brilliant sun shining above and smiled together.

Tyler watched them. Those smiles brought the greatest sense of relief he could imagine.

Then the priests and altar boys filed outside, nodded at Bishop Phelan, and started down the steps toward their cars.

Daniel came out last with all of his recording equipment, exhaled heavily and conversed with the others.

Bishop Phelan smiled warmly and shouted, "Victory in Christ, my friends."

Vincent nodded. "Praise be to God!" He took the napkin from his pocket, unfolded it and slid the fleshy, bloody teeth into his palm.

The bishop looked confused and enthralled. "What's this?"

Vincent said, "In the house, in the demon's last ditch attack while performing the second suffumigation, I was bitten in the head, and I pulled *these* out of my skull."

Bishop Phelan leaned over and examined them for several long seconds. His eyes grew wider with each passing second. He whispered, "Physical manifestation of the preternatural." He patted Vincent on the back as they walked down the stairs. He shook his head and said, "And to think there are still people out there who don't believe." They turned and walked together across the lawn.

"I'll have my friend at Yale analyze the teeth," Vincent said.

"That's a good idea," Bishop Phelan said.

Vincent asked, "Would you like to keep one?"

Bishop Phelan held up his hand and replied, "No, thank you. They belong in your collection. I have no need for cursed artifacts, and neither do you. I've warned you about keeping things like these in your office." He waved at the priests as they drove out.

The exorcism was successful, and the doorway that Tyler and his friends had inadvertently opened had been sealed. The demons had been forced to leave. The McLaughlins could now return to their normal lives at last, but only time would tell if the suffering that they had endured would allow them to ever again find peace.

Chapter 35 – Manifesting the Preternatural

VINCENT SAT IN an old studded-leather chair in his home office, flipping through the messages that his assistant had left for him. He pulled a brand new cassette tape off a shelf behind him, opened it, slid it into his tape recorder, picked up the hand-held microphone, and switched it on. He leaned back in his chair, closed his eyes and said, "The date is October 31, 1993. Bishop Phelan and I have just completed the exorcism of Matthew McLaughlin and the second and final suffumigation of the McLaughlin home. Both were successful.

"I first became aware of the case when I received an urgent telephone call in the late evening hours..."

Fifty minutes later, when he'd finished, he put the tape in a plastic case, labeled it, spun around in his chair and put the cassette on a shelf with hundreds of others just like it. He sighed in relief. All was quiet. All was as it should be.

Then the telephone rang and the silence was shattered.

Vincent hesitated. The telephone rang again. Vincent slowly spun around in his chair, back toward his desk, and studied the telephone very carefully. It rang a third time. He closed his eyes. 'Is this yet another case of demoniacal infestation and oppression,' he wondered. 'Did the demons find a way to return to the McLaughlin home? Is it something new and something so terrible that I would be totally unsuccessful at stopping it?' The telephone continued to ring. He knew that no matter what the reason was for the call, he'd have to answer it. Someone could need his help. Finally, with his eyes still closed, he reached over, picked up the receiver and answered. "Hello?"

"Vincent?"

The voice was familiar but he could not place it. "Yes? Who's calling, please?"

"This is Dan Pfeifer at Yale Medical Hospital."

Vincent sighed, opened his eyes and chuckled. "Yes, Dan. How are you?"

"Well, to be honest, I'm quite disturbed about something, thus the reason for my call."

"Oh?" Vincent replied. "What's the matter, Dan?"

"It's about the tooth that you sent us for analysis."

Vincent suddenly became very serious and asked, "Yes? What about the tooth?"

"It's a fetal boar's tooth from a genetic strain that is unlike anything that I've ever seen."

"Well, that's interesting," Vincent admitted.

"Yes, it is, but that's not all."

"What is it?"

"I have to ask where you got a hold of it."

"You wouldn't believe me if I told you, Dan," Vincent chuckled.

"You're probably right," he replied.

There was a long pause.

"Vincent?"

"Yes?"

"It's over eight hundred thousand years old."

Vincent frowned, cradled the telephone receiver in the crook of his neck, fished the remaining teeth out of his pocket, rolled them around in his palm, and examined them carefully. "No kidding," he said. He spun around in his chair, reached up onto a shelf, grabbed a small empty hexagonal glass jewelry box with brass framework, pulled it down, opened the lid, and slid the teeth inside. They clattered against the glass. "I'd like you to authenticate these findings with a notarized affidavit for my records, Dan. Can you do that for me?" He snapped the lid shut.

"Sure, Vincent, that's not a problem."

"Thank you, Dan. When can I expect that in the mail?"

"I'll send it out tomorrow," he replied.

"Thank you, and great work." Vincent hung up the phone. He opened his desk drawer, pulled out a pen, filled out a small label, and stuck it on the underside of the jewelry box.

He shook the ancient boar's teeth around inside and studied them one more time. After a few moments of silent contemplation, he stood up and looked around at his unique collection of dozens of negatively-charged arcane objects that he had collected over his lengthy career as a paranormal investigator. After searching around for the perfect spot, he slid the jewelry box onto a shelf in next to a gargoyle statue, a set of half-melted Black Mass candles, a spell book written in blood and bound with human flesh, and a bloodstained sacrificial dagger.

He inhaled deeply and said, "Sooner or later, I'm going to need a larger office." He exhaled heavily, chuckled to himself, walked down a long candle-lit hallway, grabbed hold of the railing and started walking up the old, creaking staircase. The McLaughlin case was closed, but there was one last thing yet to do.

Chapter 36 – Resting in Peace

TYLER, JIMMY AND KYLE walked together solemnly through Union Cemetery. They marveled at the last few colored leaves that broke away at their stems and drifted away down past the memorials throughout it. Tyler said, "It's so peaceful here now. I can't believe that after all we've been through, it's finally, really over."

"Thank God," Kyle said.

"Literally," Jimmy added. "Amen to that, guys."

Tyler said, "Yeah, what a difference it makes, with the sun shining and all. It's a far cry from that stormy night, isn't it?" He wedged himself between his friends as they walked. He wrapped his arms around their shoulders and said, "Guys, thanks so much for sticking by me through all of this. You're real, true friends."

"This has been one hell of an experience, no doubt about it," Kyle replied.

"I'm really sorry that your dad couldn't make it," Jimmy said.

Kyle added, "Yeah, I mean really after all he's been through. What did the doctor finally say?"

Tyler sighed. "Dr. Kent said that it was just all too much for his system to cope with. He just didn't have the strength." Tyler looked up at the clouds. Tears welled up in his eyes.

They walked down toward the rest of the group, just as they were getting ready to begin the funeral service.

Vincent and Yvonne pulled in next to the rusting gate

along the edge of the cemetery and got out of their minivan. Vincent closed the door, adjusted his jacket collar, and waved at the others. He took Yvonne's arm, stuck the other hand inside his pocket, and they wound their way through the gravestones toward the grave site.

Linda, Sarah, Bill, Julie, and Kelly stood side by side before the grave, each holding a single rose. Jason, Daniel, and Aaron were conversing with them. When Vincent and Yvonne arrived, Linda handed them each a rose. Yvonne hugged Linda tenderly. Vincent squeezed Kelly's chin gently and smiled at everyone. Kelly looked up and admired him. She then walked over to Tyler and held his hand.

Once everyone had assembled, Bishop Phelan cleared his throat and opened his Bible. Tyler noticed that it was the same Bible that he had used during his father's exorcism. Vincent told the family that the bishop had decided to stay in town to preside over the funeral service personally to bring total and complete closure to terrible events that had changed all of their lives completely.

"Let us begin," the bishop said. Everyone stilled themselves and bowed their heads in prayer. "Heavenly Father, we are gathered here in this place of eternal rest to pray for the soul of our lost brother. We find comfort in and trust in your perfect, divine plan for all of mankind." The bishop gazed up at the sky, turned the page in his Bible, and continued. "A reading from the Letter of Saint Paul to the Romans: No one lives for oneself, and no one dies for oneself. For if we live, we live for the Lord, and if we die, we die for the Lord; so then, whether we live or die, we are the Lord's. For this is why Christ died and came to life, that he might be Lord of both the dead and the living. Why, then, do you judge your brother?"

Intrigued, Kelly looked up at Tyler and smiled. He looked down at her, squeezed her hand gently and winked.

Bishop Phelan continued, "Or you, why do you look down on your brother? For we shall all stand before the judgment seat of God; for it is written: As I live, says the Lord, every knee shall bend before me, and every tongue shall give praise to God. So then, each of us shall give an accounting of himself to God. The word of the Lord."

Linda wrapped her arm around Julie and leaned her head on her shoulder.

"The souls of the righteous are in the hands of God, and no torment shall touch them. They seemed, in the view of the foolish, to be dead; and their passing away was thought an affliction, and their going forth from us, utter destruction. But they are in peace." The bishop raised his arms before the others and said, "Brothers and Sisters, if God is for us, then who can be against us?"

Linda walked over and hugged Sarah. They all shared heart-felt glances with Vincent, Yvonne, Jason, Daniel, and Aaron.

"Who will separate us from the love of Christ? Will anguish, or oppression, or persecution or peril, or the demon, or the sword?" They all looked at each other. "No, all of these things we conquer overwhelmingly, through Our Lord Jesus Christ and his unconditional love for us all." They all smiled and nodded their heads as Bishop Phelan sprinkled holy water onto the grave.

Yvonne leaned toward Linda and said, "He's at peace now."

Linda asked, "Can you see him?"

"I can hear him," she replied. "He's on the other side, in the realm of spirit, watching the funeral service. He's very happy now. You see, he had led an extremely lonely and unfulfilled life. He had no one who cared for him. No one except his sister came to remember him at the funeral. No one else came or had anything positive to say about his life. That was why he was so angry, so bitter, and so full of rage. That's why he was so anxious to make contact with Kelly when the two of you drove by the cemetery." Yvonne knelt before Kelly. "He never meant you any harm, honey." Kelly smiled. "All he wanted to do was to tell his story."

She looked up and suddenly became very serious. "Then the others came in." She nodded. "He actually tried very hard to fight against them, but they were simply too powerful." Yvonne giggled and said, "He says that he prevented Julie's van from flipping over when one of the demons took the form of the black dog in the road." She stood and looked at Linda. "He also says that he never meant to frighten you when he came through the wall in the laundry area, and he didn't mean to cause you to get burned. He was simply trying to make contact with you. It was the others who attacked you and who caused all of the terror."

"That makes sense now," Linda nodded.

Bishop Phelan stood before the head stone and said, "Ashes to ashes, and dust to dust." He nodded toward the others and smiled as they smelled their roses and waited for their turn to offer their peaceful blessings to the spirit of the man who started it all. "You may now consecrate the grave," he said.

Linda urged Kelly forward with a pat on the behind. "Go ahead, honey. You should be first." Kelly stepped forward and placed the rose in front of the headstone. She paused, turned back toward the others, and smiled brightly.

Linda and Julie went next. "Rest in peace," they said in unison. The rose petals rustled gently in the wind.

Sarah, Bill, Jimmy, Kyle, and Tyler went next as a group and laid their flowers on top of the others. "Rest in peace, Brock," Tyler said.

They all bowed their heads in silent recognition of all that they had been through. After several moments, Bishop Phelan closed his Bible and said, "Go now in peace."

Tyler patted his friends on the shoulders. Then they turned around and walked away back toward the cars.

Linda reached down for Kelly's hand and said, "Let's go to the hospital and see Daddy."

Kelly smiled brightly and said, "Okay." They walked away together. Kelly paused, looked back at the graves and smiled. A light breeze blew past them. She tugged on her mother's hand several times and said, "See, Mom?"

"What is it, honey?" Linda asked, leaning down before her daughter. She touched Kelly's nose with the tip of her index finger.

Kelly smiled and said, "There are ghosts." She giggled. "Really, there are."

Linda sighed, knelt down and said, "I know, honey." She hugged her daughter warmly. "I know that now." She kissed her on the cheek. When she stood, Kelly was looking up at her and smiling brightly, reaching out for her hand. Linda took her daughter's hand, and they walked through the cemetery one last time toward the cars, toward their family and toward their friends.

That afternoon, they had finally laid the terrible haunting that they had all endured to rest. They also said goodbye to the autumn, hoping that the quiet stillness of winter would soon silence their pain.

Part 4

Chapter 1 – Analysis

Late October is a magical time of year, especially in New England, when the leaves turn into beautiful shades of red, orange, and yellow. It's the picture-perfect time of Halloween, spirits, witches, and warlocks. Everyone is in tune, because every place they go, they see the decorated store windows, the scarecrows, the pumpkins, the plastic skeletons, the witches, and of course, the monsters. And here, we have this child traveling with her mother along the edge of one of the most haunted cemeteries in the country on a dark, stormy afternoon.

What most adults don't realize or remember from their own early childhood is that children are often very sensitive, meaning they can see and hear what most adults cannot. Sadly, they lose that sensitivity as they grow older, because they are told that what they are able to see is only fantasy, or child's play. They are told that it is time to 'grow up,' and so in what is sometimes called 'pulling down the veil,' the subconscious mind closes off those special innate abilities which connect them to a vastly greater range of frequencies and vibrations that exist all around us. Whether or not we have full waking conscious access to them, these vibrations, dimensions, and densities are very real and they interpenetrate us and connect us all to each other, to the rest of the universe, and ultimately, to all of creation.

Sensitive children view their psychic abilities as if they are completely normal, because, of course, they are.

Children who use their psychic awareness have a very special, close and lasting bond with animals, especially their feline, equine, and canine companions. Some lucky children are raised by parents who nurture their beautiful abilities and encourage their growth, expansion, and development. Other children simply refuse to shut them off or find it impossible to shut them off, and those people are called 'mediums' or 'clairvoyants'. Everyone has the potential to be a medium or clairvoyant. Everyone is psychic. Some are beginners, intermediates, and others masters, just as is the case with any other ability or skill that we use. It all depends on how much time and energy we spend on developing them. Unfortunately, rather than honor our psychic abilities, we are taught to shun them, or to shut them off, because they are not considered normal.

Artists of all kinds use their natural sensitivity to find inspiration and most don't even know that they are doing it. It is this sensitivity that allows them to connect a series of vast dimensions just outside of the range of frequencies that our limited five senses can properly decode. Some people spend their entire lives accessing these frequencies; others only dabble in them; and sadly, for the majority of the population, most never even try to utilize them at all, nor do they even believe that they exist.

A major storm was coming, and it was getting dark. Linda and Kelly were marveling about the beautiful fall leaves coming down. The atmosphere was being filled with electricity due to the developing thunderstorm. This natural energy is often used by discarnate human spirits to manifest into the physical likeness that most often resembled their own body during their most recent lifetime or incarnation. They do this to become visible to the human that they wish to appear to.

How is this accomplished? It's simple. An unlimited field of electromagnetic energy exists all around us. It is everywhere. Every living thing is surrounded by its own electromagnetic field. Spirits find it very easy to take and use this energy from the plant life, the trees, and the atmosphere. A lot of electromagnetism was in the air due to the approaching electrical storm. So, things were just perfect for a manifestation.

How does someone passing by a graveyard attract spirits when others do not? It happens through the Universal Law of Attraction. Spirits can be attracted to someone for many reasons, including natural human charisma, their personality, the sound of their voice, their mood, their energy level, or the size, shape and color of their energy field or aura. The spirits that are lurking inside old cemeteries are not usually the spirits that once inhabited and animated the bodies that are buried there, though sometimes, on rare occasions that is indeed the case. Most human spirits cross over correctly and have no need for their physical bodies when they are done with their life here on earth. Many other human spirits however remain earthbound, but they usually are more attached to their former surroundings than the physical remains of their bodies.

Most spirits lurking inside old graveyards are not human spirits at all, but are those *other* spirits that were summoned there by thrill-seeking kids who used occult paraphernalia like Ouija boards or who had conducted séances there through the years, because graveyards are very spooky, morbid places. Unfortunately, there are other negative people who are very serious about summoning inhuman diabolical spirits into the world *on purpose* through witchcraft, black magic, sorcery, or necromancy.

These are the spirits that are usually attracted to or interested in living people with the intention of doing them harm, and they are just waiting for the opportunity for a sensitive person like Kelly to pass by, so that they can invade her world. It just so happens that the first spirit that Kelly encountered was actually the discarnate spirit of a human being—albeit a very negative human being, who was quite unhappy about an unfulfilled life, and also enraged about the death of his physical body.

What happens when someone leaves their physical body at death? When I was in my freshman year of college, I learned more about what happens to the human spirit when I read a book, called *Life After Life* by Dr. Raymond Moody, which, synchronistically, was required reading for my English class. In his book, Dr. Moody detailed the cases of many people who were clinically dead who came back to life to discuss their experiences in the realms beyond.

One of the most interesting accounts of a near-death experience (NDE) was the story of a young man who got caught underneath a powerful waterfall current while white-water rafting. When he finally succumbed to the death of his physical body, he felt no pain or suffering of any kind. Instead, he felt his arms and legs contract until he was a ball of energy. He willed himself to rise out of the water. Everything around him was crystal clear. He could see, or he was completely aware of, everything all around him. His hearing was also crystal clear, even though he had damaged one of his ears in a firecracker explosion when he was younger. Naturally, because his body was pinned beneath the water, and because he left it behind, he no longer had any physical eyes or ears, or physical body of any kind, or a brain for that matter, yet he maintained full conscious awareness. *Life After Life* is full of beautiful stories like that. I encourage anyone interested in what happens when we leave our bodies during a near-death experience (NDE) or when the body actually dies to read it.

Then I was led to the book, *Life Between Life*, which detailed the fascinating accounts of people who were hypnotized and brought back into the time just before birth, just after death, or to the time between incarnations or between lifetimes.

One instance was a woman who was hovering over her

mother's pregnant body as her mother was pumping water out of a well. During hypnosis, she said that she had not yet entered her mother's body, because it wasn't time to be born. The general theme here was that the infinite, immortal soul enters the body mere minutes before, during, or after birth. It is an excellent way to understand just what happens when the soul leaves the body.

No one really ever dies. The earthly, physical, three-dimensional body is simply the vehicle we use to interact with the third dimension. When we are done using it and when we are ready to move on to other adventures, lessons, or experiences for our soul's evolution, we simply leave the body behind. If the body takes a fall, or grows old, malfunctions, becomes ill, or if it is damaged beyond repair, we simply discard it.

Our soul is never harmed in any way, shape, or form, because it is eternal. It has no form. Nor does it have a gender. We experience many lifetimes in both sexes. We also have both masculine and feminine energy. Some people have more of one than the other. Other people are balanced equally. That is why we have such remarkable diversity among the population. When we leave our physical bodies, we retain all of our experiences and memories. Many people die a peaceful death and are glad to be free of their aging or failing bodies. Many people who are killed suddenly in a car accident, or in a tragic way, or in battle often find it very traumatic or shocking, depending on their state of mind when they had experienced the sudden death of the body.

One such example details the account of an adult woman and her elderly mother traveling in the car on their way home during a snow storm. The elderly woman was at peace, admiring the beautiful landscape. She had not a care in the world. The daughter was anxious to get home to her children, and she was frightened about the driving conditions. Sadly, moments later, their lives were cut short instantly in a car accident.

Because the elderly woman was at peace when they crashed, she entered the tunnel of light that opens for us all and therefore completed her death transition naturally and correctly. Because her last thoughts before the crash were focused on being home with her children, the woman who was driving ignored the tunnel of light completely and went immediately to her home and to her children.

Over the course of the next several months, the family would smell her perfume, feel or sense her watching them, and even find that blankets were moved over the sleeping children to keep them warm at night, and in the morning, they would discover that someone had made the beds. When paranormal researchers investigated, it was determined that the spirit of the woman was indeed in the house, watching over and taking care of her children. Eventually, she was assisted into coping with her situation and to cross over correctly, thus completing her death passage properly.

One of the most comforting lessons learned in Life After Life was the fact, based on over one hundred cases of past life regression, that no one ever leaves behind their lifetime, or body, or family unless they *choose* to do so. When they come to understand that the afterlife will always be there for them and that it is a place of beauty and peace beyond their wildest dreams, and when they choose to go back and complete their original lessons in the life they were just experiencing, they find themselves immediately back inside their bodies.

How does this happen? It happens because outside of the third dimension there is no time. The human soul can go back and avoid a tragic death scenario, in which case onlookers couldn't believe that they had survived, or couldn't fathom how lucky they were to have narrowly escaped certain death, or how they made such a remarkable recovery through an illness or life-threatening situation that should have, according to medical professionals—killed them. In reality, they did die, but because they chose to come back to learn what they initially came here to learn, or accomplish what they had originally planned to accomplish in the lifetime that they had planned, they came back in a spectacular display of luck, somehow just making it out of an event that could have, should have, and would have ended their life.

You see, when the soul is finished with its current incarnation, it has no qualms about leaving behind friends, or family, or the mind's unfinished business. We think that the mind has control of us on the highest levels, but its needs, wants, and desires come secondary to the needs of the soul, which is the true essence and totality of who we are. We are not the brain, or the mind, nor are we the body, nor are we the story of our current lives. We are fields of infinite consciousness awareness experiencing our current lives, in our current situations, with our current families and our many friends and life partners, to learn and evolve.

Souls coming in and souls going out are always interacting with their families and loved ones. Spirits are around us all the time, sometimes throughout our entire lives. They come and go, just as friends come and go. Often times, people sense departed loved ones in their presence and smell their perfume or scents that were associated with their body. Just because we don't see them doesn't mean they aren't there. Sometimes we hear them whispering, or think that we catch a glimpse of them out of the corner of our eyes, or pick up or sense their wisdom or counsel when we are perplexed and especially when we are thinking about them. It's nothing unnatural. We are all connected—always.

Sometimes even our pets remain earthbound once their bodies die. I had a beautiful, pure white Persian cat named Frost who passed away in an animal hospital near my home in Austin, Texas. Guests in my home who had never seen my cat previously, and who never knew that I ever had one, asked me if I had a white cat, because they saw him here and there out of the corners of their eyes. The consciousness that was Frost returned to our home, the place where he felt at peace during his past incarnation.

All living beings with intelligence survive the death of the physical body. It's just the natural way of things. All that they are doing is shifting from the third dimension into the next, which is just outside of the narrow range of frequencies visible to our physical eyes. Frost was and is very much alive in his spirit body. I talk to him all the time as if he is still around me, because he is. I don't hear him talking back to me, but I do often feel and sense his presence. Because we had a close, lasting, special, loving bond, he was then, and still is with me now, even though my conscious mind cannot detect him.

Spirits find it easy to reflect their image onto glass or onto any shiny surface—much like The Ghosts of Flight 401, one of the most well-documented and credible cases of ghost phenomena ever recorded. In this case, in late 1972, Eastern Airlines Tri-Star jetliner 401 crashed into the Florida Everglades, killing the pilot, Bob Loft, and the flight engineer, Don Repo, along with close to one hundred passengers—a horrible tragedy to be sure.

What makes this case so interesting, however, is that the ghosts of the pilot and the flight engineer were seen on over twenty different occasions on multiple Tri-Star jetliners—especially on those airplanes where salvaged parts from Flight 401 were installed. In one case, on Tri-Star jetliner number 318, a flight attendant saw the clear likeness of the face of Don Repo in the shiny surface in and on an oven in the galley of the airplane during flight. Alarmed, and intrigued, she called out to her colleagues. One of them, who had known Don Repo personally, immediately identified his image. The ghost even talked to the crew and forewarned them about the possibility of a fire breaking out on the aircraft during that very flight. His warning was well founded, as the pilot had to make an emergency landing due to equipment malfunction. Interestingly enough, several parts used in the galley on Flight 318 came from the wreckage of Flight 401. In another case, a concerned passenger sought help from one of the crew members when the passenger noticed an unresponsive man in a pilot's uniform sitting in one of the seats. Screams were heard throughout the plane when several people saw the mysterious pilot slowly vanish into thin air.

How did the spirit of a man keep up with a passenger plane traveling at hundreds of miles per hour? He did it simply by *thinking* about being on board that aircraft. Our perception of space and time while inside these physical three-dimensional bodies is severely limited or handicapped, if you will, perhaps to the point of totally malfunctioning when you really think about it. Ghost stories should not be dismissed as fantasy simply because they cannot be explained by the limited ability of our human body to decode anything outside of what we believe to be our five-sense reality. Only when we come to the realization that we are vast fields of conscious awareness temporarily animating a physical body to interact within the third dimension, while immersed in, resonating with, and interacting within a vast, limitless sea of frequencies, vibrations, and dimensions and with the intelligences within, will we have a clearer understanding of who we truly are. Only then will we clearly understand that we are all connected, and in essence, how we are all One.

When Kelly was looking out of the window, she could have seen the ghost very easily, *if* the ghost had wanted to project its image onto the window of the moving station wagon. He could have done it simply by *thinking* about it—the same way that the spirit of Don Repo could be aboard an airplane traveling at hundreds of miles per hour projecting his image onto a shiny surface for the flight attendant to see.

Here we had an in-tune, attractive little girl who was

open to suggestion and actively looking for ghosts; we had an intelligent earth-bound, discarnate spirit with a soul mind actively looking for an opportunity to interact with someone; we had an electrical storm lending the spirit all of the energy that it needed to manifest a physical form or likeness that Kelly could identify with; and finally, the car was just about to pass by him, so things were just right for the haunting that was about to take place.

And so, the spirit appeared. How could it have suddenly been closer to the car when the car had been speeding away? It could have done it simply by *thinking* of being there. There is no space or time outside of the third dimension where these spirits find themselves after they have left the remains of the physical body. The spirit could have been in Germany, or deep under the ocean, or on the Moon for that matter, simply by *thinking* of it, and snap, it'd be there. That's how fast a spirit can travel. They don't have to get on a train, a plane, a boat, or a spaceship. What would an immaterial spirit need with a material convey-ance? Wherever and whenever they *will* themselves to be, there they will be—instantly.

We are all connected to a vast field that some scientists now call the Quantum Field. Whatever the name for it, it has always existed, and it is nothing new at all. I had discovered on my own, well before we had the advent of the world-wide web, that we were all connected to a vast, invisible web-like construct, and that everyone that we had ever made a connection with in our lifetime had a strand that was intricately connected to our web. When we think of someone, it's like jingling that person's strand, like a spider senses a fly caught in its web. There are hundreds or even thousands of strands in its web, but even though the fly is caught on a very specific strand, the spider immedi-ately knows which strand that the fly is attached to. It's as simple as that. Some call it Quantum Entanglement or

String Theory. Regardless of its title, or its explanation, we are all connected—in all ways, always.

Let me give you an example that you can use to test this theory for your own benefit. Think about someone you haven't thought of in a while, whether you visualize their face, or think about their mannerisms or personality, or reflect upon a particular circumstance in which you interacted with them. Whether you call them or they contact you, they will often tell you that 'they were just thinking about you.' You may think of it as a strange coincidence, but it is not. Of course, they were just thinking about you. Why? The reason is because you thought about them, and they had no choice but to think about you because you were jingling their end of the strand. It's that simple. It happens that fast.

While I was attending Sacred Heart University, I was writing about a case that I had just investigated in Vermont for my column, "Hauntings," in The Spectrum Newspaper. I thought very specifically about the ghost of a woman there that I had made a very special empathic connection with. By simply *thinking* about her, I instantly attracted her consciousness right into my home in Connecticut. I instantly picked up the immense sadness that she felt due to her unquenchable desire to find the baby that she had lost in a tragic horse and carriage accident as she was being rushed to the midwife to give birth.

Recall the case where the woman and her elderly mother were traveling in the snow storm and died tragically in much the same way, and recall how the mother went immediately home rather than completing her proper death passage. In this case, over one hundred years ago, since the moment of this pregnant woman's death, her consciousness went immediately to the house she was intent on reaching to give birth, and she remained in and around the house searching for her baby in immense, overwhelming sadness. She could not find her baby because that soul or consciousness had never entered its body. The life experience the baby's soul had planned was not going to be possible, because its body was damaged beyond repair in the accident, or if it was attached to the body, it crossed over immediately and properly. In either case, the baby was nowhere to be found. Because I had thought of this woman who believed that I could help resolve her plight, she immediately projected upon me the urgent desire to return to Vermont and help her find peace.

Naturally, I called my mentor, Lorraine Warren, with an urgent appeal that we return to Vermont as soon as we were able to. I was told that the family could not be contacted because they had fled the house due to the activity going on inside the house and on the property. After I accepted the explanation, I politely explained that I understood, said goodbye and ended the telephone call. No less than one minute later, I called back, again suggesting and requesting an urgent return trip to Vermont. It was again explained to me that it was not possible to return because we did not have permission to return, nor were we able to make contact with the owners to gain that permission. Of course, that made perfect sense, and again I acknowledged it and ended the call. Only after I called back the third time, one minute later, did we both realize that I was being influenced by the spirit in that house in Vermont. Lorraine knew that I was a journalist, and she asked if I was writing about the case for my column. I admitted that I was.

Do it yourself. Think of someone you haven't spoken to, or someone that you miss. Visualize their face, and think about them. If you love them, feel the love that you have for them, and I mean 'feel' that love. Think about how you feel when you are with them, or what they mean to you. Love them like you are hugging them as tenderly as you ever have before. Unless they are incapable of contacting you, or unwilling to for some reason, they should contact you very quickly. They will absolutely think about you as you send them that love, there is no escaping that.

Naturally, you have to respect their free will to choose to contact you in return, but rest assured, by your thinking of them, you have contacted them, and they are definitely picking up your thoughts subconsciously. At that time, their subconscious mind convinces the conscious mind that they should contact you back. Sometimes we act upon that impulse and take notice of the apparent coincidence, but it is nothing of the sort.

Think for a moment how powerful that is. Think about how you can send someone love from a distance, any distance, no matter how great or how far—whether they are in a third-dimensional body or if they are in their true non-corporeal form or spirit. By consciously sending that person love, you are doing a wonderful thing. We are all infinite fields of awareness, consciousness, and love—it is our true nature. It is why we nurture a baby, or why we pet a dog, or rub the ears on a cat to bring them pleasure. It is why we help a stranger who is desperate, or intervene on someone's behalf if their life is in danger. That is why energy healing is so wonderful, and why long-distance healing not only works, but is very powerful. Why? Because if you use your 'free will' to send someone your life force energy to help heal an affliction, or cope with a disease, or help mend a broken heart, you are performing a miracle, and you are absolutely helping their body, mind, and spirit with your intention to assist them. In reality, there is no distance between us. Our energy fields are all entangled and intermingled.

The very same can be said about sending someone negative energy, or hatred, or hurling curses toward someone. So, please always pay close attention to what you are thinking, because our thoughts are very powerful, and they do affect other people. We affect and interact with other people or beings simply by thinking about them. Sending loving energy heals the recipient. Sending negative energy harms its target. I use the term "target" here for good reason, because no one wants to be the willing recipient of negative energy.

I can share something that happened to me recently along these same lines. I was in my car, turning out onto a busy road and did not see a car racing up in the lane that I was turning into. I heard the car's wheels squealing and the horn blaring. I looked into my rear-view mirror to see a man screaming at me. He was bombarding me with all kinds of rage and hatred. I decided that I could become enraged myself and fire all kinds of negative energy right back at him, or I could do something completely different. So, I centered myself, surrounded myself with love, and spread that field out, so that it encapsulated both of our cars. Because I used my free will to deflect or transform the negative energy being directed at me, I transformed or dispelled it. The man simply stopped screaming and let the situation go.

We all get angry. We all get upset, especially when driving. If we imagined the person cutting us off to be our sweet old grandmother rather than some reckless man inconveniencing us or putting us in danger, our reaction would be much less intense, wouldn't it? Whenever I catch myself thinking negative thoughts, I quickly cease thinking them and transform them into positive thoughts.

Union Cemetery in Easton, Connecticut is over four hundred years old with a broad history of haunting phenomena. This is where many specters have been seen for over sixty years, not just this man in dark clothing but "The White Lady" who has been captured on film by Ed Warren and many others. The mysterious specter nicknamed "Red Eyes" has also developed quite a reputation there because while in the cemetery, many investigators have often photographed a pair of red glowing orbs that looked like eyes. If there were a cemetery where haunting phenomena would manifest, this has been and would long be such a place.

The reason Kelly saw the spirit and Linda did not is because Linda wasn't open or sensitive at the time that Kelly was open *and actively searching* for ghosts. Linda planted the idea in Kelly's mind which is where all hauntings start. Spirits project themselves directly into the pineal gland, aptly called the 'mind's eye' or 'third eye,' while bypassing the physical eyes. The pineal gland is photosensitive and responsible for 'psychic sight.' Just as our eyes receive information about our third dimensional world, the pineal gland receives information from other vibrations or frequencies outside of the third dimension. As I have said earlier, we are all multi-dimensional beings interacting with a much wider range of frequencies and vibrations than are registered by our limited five senses.

Chapter 2 – Analysis

Being the typical rational adult that she was, Linda dismissed the very notion of ghosts even though Kelly kept insisting that they were real. During the ride home after the scary haunting had passed, Kelly tried to force the image of the spirit out of her mind with just about anything that she could think of.

What they both didn't realize was that just because Kelly wasn't actively thinking about the spirit, she had already made the necessary connection. The spirit didn't need to prove its existence by making itself visible when it followed the car home. Because Kelly and the spirit were already connected, the spirit could have followed Kelly home immediately, or any time it wished.

When they got home, the spirit knocked the telephone off the wall and into the bowl filled with the cake batter. Kelly saw the phone fall off, but she didn't realize that the spirit had caused it. The spirit had already invaded the house, and it was immediately attempting to make contact with the family.

Everyone likes a good ghost story, especially when the activity is real and when it happens to people that we know. So while the family was eating dinner, Tyler instantly poked fun at the situation and quite naturally wanted to learn more. Unbeknownst to them, this was already giving the spirit recognition and lending it energy with that very recognition. Matthew did the right thing by insisting that there would be no more discussion about ghosts, but it was far from over.

When Tyler pretended that he was the ghost to scare his little sister later in the evening, it was the spirit who had influenced him to cause Kelly to cast off as much fear energy as possible, so that it could energize itself and use that energy later.

Chapter 3 – Analysis

When Linda saw the gray shadow, she was seeing the essence or the vibrational frequency of the spirit itself. Color is vibrational frequency. Gray shadows suggest a negative human spirit or a less powerful demonic spirit. Black shadows suggest a very powerful negative human spirit or an inhuman spirit. Negative black shadows, meaning that they stand out even in the deepest midnight blackness, are extremely powerful inhuman diabolical spirits. In this case, what Linda saw was the spirit of a man with a lot of negativity, but he was not necessarily someone of an evil nature. When the spirit materialized before Linda, it frightened her, so she cast off a lot of fear energy. Even though that was not its intention, the spirit was able to take advantage of that free-flowing energy and utilize that energy moments later.

Because the majority of people cannot see the spirits themselves, the spirits manipulate nearby physical objects that the people *can* see. They obviously have no physical limbs of any kind to manipulate physical objects, so they use their soul mind, their consciousness, or intention to do so. By concentrating on the temperature dial of the iron for instance, the spirit caused it to turn to the highest setting to generate enough heat to cause steam to erupt. The human spirit can only affect lightweight physical objects, up to a few pounds in weight at most, so when they get the hang of it, they find it fairly easy to rotate a dial on a stove or on an iron.

When Linda experienced the dials turning, it appeared as if the dials were turning by themselves, because she was incapable of seeing the energy that the spirit was projecting onto them. In this case, the spirit was making contact with Linda by turning the dials. It did not intend to cause steam to erupt from the iron and burn Linda's arm. It was merely a consequence of moving the dials.

In infested homes, spirits can suddenly shift the focus of their attention or their attacks from one family member to the next in rapid succession whenever they see fit to do so. In the beginning of the story, Kelly was the obvious target. As we saw later, Linda was next.

In general, negative spirits causing disturbances in homes always have the same primary goal in mind and that is to cause as much fear and panic as possible, whenever and wherever they can.

In this particular case, the spirit was merely attempting to make contact with Linda by manifesting itself in the exhaust behind Kelly's school bus where Linda's attention was already narrowly focused to maximize its chances of being seen. It most likely did not intend for Linda to become frightened, but unfortunately for Linda, that is exactly what happened.

Linda was wise to get out of the house when she did to avoid any further trouble. This prevented the siphoning of even more of her energy. But could Linda escape simply by leaving the house? The answer is no. By ignoring it, Linda simply hoped that it would just go away. Unfortunately, for the family, the spirit had no intention of leaving. The spirit could have followed Linda simply by thinking of her. It could have gone immediately to be with Kelly in an instant if it intended to do so, because all it had to do was *think* of Kelly at any point and it would appear wherever she was. Remember how easy it is to interact with someone, once you have made a connection. Remember the speed at which a spirit can travel. In reality, there is no distance, time, or space—everything simply is.

Chapter 4 – Analysis

When it comes to energy, teenage boys usually have more than they know what to do with. In the many cases that I have researched or have studied, having young teenagers in a house almost always causes a sharp increase in the activity going on. That is because the energy that they don't use is cast off. When Tyler and his friends came home after school, the spirit in the house was ready, willing, and able to use that excess energy for its own needs. The spirit used some of that energy to cause a 'thump' to occur on the sliding glass door. How did this happen? How can an immaterial spirit cause a sound on a material object?

When people hear footsteps, or weeping, or moaning or any number of other strange sounds in haunted homes, the sounds are coming from what is called telekinesis—sound telepathically projected to the person who is the receiver of that sound. For instance, if the spirit wanted you to hear a door slamming, all it would need to do is to *think* about what that would sound like, project it directly into your mind and you would pick that sound up telepathically. Often times when investigators use video cameras or audio recording devices inside houses that they are investigating, there will be no evidence left on the recorder even when multiple people hear or see spirit phenomena that it should have recorded.

The same can be true when only one person in a group hears a sound or sees certain energies, or lights, or apparitions and the others do not. The sight or sound was projected to them and them alone. I had personally experienced just such activity on the very first case that my friend and I had investigated together on the Warrens' behalf. The man and woman whom we were interviewing claimed to see a ghost walk through a wall in their bedroom each night, walk down the hall into the baby's bedroom, approach the crib, scare the baby out of its wits, walk through the crib and the wall, and vanish completely. After we had conducted our interview, we had closed the blinds and set up my camcorder in the master bedroom and left a burning candle in there as the sole source of illumination. While the four of us waited in the baby's room staring down the hallway with a clear view of the other bedroom, we saw a huge, bright blue flash of light that lit the entire room like a flash of lightning had gone off inside. We didn't see an apparition, but when we entered the master bedroom, my friend and fellow investigator detected a powerful almond smell that he described as being almost sickly sweet. Naturally, we were very excited, because we were all sure that we had recorded that bright blue flash of light on our very first case.

About thirty minutes later, we witnessed an identical flash of light in the same room, but it was only half as intense, as was the smell. When we were finally wrapping up our investigation for the evening, we all wanted to see the video evidence that the camera had recorded, so we put the videocassette into the VCR. Our expectations were quickly dashed, because the only light we ever saw on tape was from the flickering candle. When we finally heard my voice, it said: "We've just experienced the second flash of light." We were all deeply disappointed. How in the world could the camera have missed such a bright display of supernatural activity, especially when we all saw it as a group with our very own eyes?

What we all saw was a mass projection of psychic energy. As I mentioned before, our pineal gland is photosensitive. We saw the light only in our minds eye, or third eye. It was a message to all of us from the spirit, that it was definitely there, but for some reason, it wasn't going to give us any video evidence. Why that was the case, was and still is a mystery. We all would have missed an obscure sound on the tape if my friend and cohort weren't there to identify it. Ed Warren would have identified it upon viewing the tape himself, but my friend zeroed in on it instantly because he was a paramedic, and he easily identified the sound as a specific heart rhythm. Then, he identified and pointed out a second and third distinct rhythm that only he could recognize, much like the almond smell was a message directed specifically at him. Obviously, because there was no physical body in the room with a beating heart when the activity was recorded, and because the camera was not sensitive enough to detect one, even if there were a body standing right next to it, the pheno-menon was clearly the result of the spirit imprinting the sound onto the nearby camcorder. The spirit projected what it 'thought' to be a series of heartbeats and projected them at the camera as it was recording. Our physical ears did not hear it at all while it was happening in the other room, nor did the ghost project the sound of what a heartbeat would sound like to anyone in the other room where we were all gathered.

Whether you hear a voice, you hear a door opening or closing, or footsteps walking on a floor above you when you know that no one else is home, and you do not capture any of those sounds on a recorder, those sounds are coming to you via telekinesis.

When objects move by themselves, or when doors open and close on their own accord, we are dealing with a powerful soul mind that is using a process called psycho-kinesis—the movement of objects purely by projecting their intention to move the object.

When Kyle saw the shadowy man walking outside on

the wall, the spirit projected its image into his mind, and his mind alone. After it had succeeded in luring them all outside, it simply ceased projecting its image into Kyle's mind. Of course there were no footprints in the snow, because there was never any physical body out there to create them. When the spirit wanted to be inside the house again, it simply thought about being inside the living room and there it was. It projected its energy onto the door, slid it shut and locked it. It toyed with them shortly afterwards by locking and then unlocking the door.

The natural reaction was for Tyler to accuse Jimmy of playing games with the sliding glass door. Then, of course, they blamed Sarah for the strange activity going on. When they scoured the house and found no trace of Sarah and when they ran into the garage and the spirit slammed the door behind them, Tyler and his friends realized that they were dealing with something out of the ordinary.

Chapter 5 – Analysis

When people experience haunting phenomena for the first time, they almost always have a very hard time coping with it. While Tyler and his friends knew that something was dreadfully wrong inside the house, they clung onto the false hope that everything was explainable and that everything would be okay. As soon as the whispering and laughter started, their hopes were instantly shattered.

In many cases, immediately before physical objects are manipulated, there is most often an ozone smell in the same general area. This is the same smell we sometimes detect outside when an electrical storm is on its way. This is because the spirit is building up a great deal of electro-magnetism in the room that it intends to use. We know how easily glass bottles can crack or break, and how easy it would to tip over an aluminum cup with plastic stirrer sticks inside, so it was an easy feat to cause the stirrer cup to move and tip over and to do some damage to the liquor bottles behind the bar.

Of course, the boys were afraid. Who wouldn't be? I challenge any man, woman or brave teenager to go into a home and witness the kinds of activity that these young men were experiencing, and see if they don't run away with the hair standing on end, as Tyler and his friends did. But by asking the spirit to identify itself and therefore challenging it, they were asking for serious trouble.

Chapter 6-7 – Analysis

A Ouija board is the single most dangerous piece of occult paraphernalia in history and its sole purpose is to enable contact with and to invite negative, inhuman diabolical spirits of all kinds into this world. It is an instrument with which to open a channel of communication to the spirit world, and if we are not extremely careful, a key that can unlock a doorway into our own. Nothing good ever comes through them to communicate with us, and immeasurable harm often comes about as a consequence of their use.

Luckily for them, as the young men were fooling around with the Ouija board in the store, a messenger of the light appeared, as if by divine intervention, to dissuade them from purchasing the board and to prevent them from opening a doorway that would cause unimaginable harm. Unfortunately, the guys didn't heed the warning and they laughed it off. They were given their chance to exercise their free will and when they made fun of the situation and of her, the woman vanished without trace. That alone should have been enough to influence them put the game back and wash their hands of it completely. Who was she? What was she? Because we are multidimensional beings, immersed in a vast universe, it could have been any number of things. The identity of the messenger was not significant. The *intention* of the intelligence interacting with them and *the message* it was attempting to convey is what was important. We are often given a chance to re-think our actions by divine intervention—by the august hand of God or one of his messengers, by one of our own spirit guides, or even by a higher dimensional aspect of our self. Regardless of who or what it was exactly, it was a positive intelligence trying to convince the guys to put the game back to avoid opening a doorway to inconvenience, harm, ruin, or even death. Going ahead with the purchase of the Ouija board was *the single worst mistake* that Jimmy and Kyle could have made.

When the guys returned home, they had no idea of the suffocating terror that would be unleashed upon them when they reached out with their psychic senses and attempted contact with the spirit in the house, because using a Ouija board is like using a two-way radio, or like using an online service on the Internet. You never actually know just who is on the other end of the line. Given today's surveillance society, it's easy to understand that even though they were attempting to *and may have been* communicating with *one* entity in particular, *many more* could have and probably were listening or paying attention and were taking a great interest in the conversation going on so that they could get in on the action.

When we use a Ouija board, we are essentially invoking the spirits we are attempting to communicate with. By that, I mean we are asking them, whether we know it or not, to enter our bodies and to use or manipulate our hands to move the planchette around on the board. To invoke something, we are inviting that thing inside us. This is incredibly dangerous.

When the ghost spelled out Kelly's name and informed the guys in a startling message that it was there for her, it of course enraged Tyler. This was a being with a soul mind, with a set goal and determination to accomplish its mission. It started to spell out the word 'others,' but the message it was trying to convey was not very well translated. It was actually not understood correctly at all. The mere fact that it was misspelled tells us that this may not have been a human spirit. I know this because I have learned from experience that spelling on a Ouija board is always bad—an English teacher's nightmare if you will. It is important to realize that at first, the guys were communicating in all likelihood with the earthbound spirit that had followed Kelly home from Union Cemetery, but shortly thereafter, other vastly more powerful diabolical intelligences took over the communication.

Tyler committed the ultimate mistake where haunting phenomenon occurs when he challenged the spirits. But, like most people in the world, who discard superstition, legends and myths, which had to be created based on some historical fact, Tyler didn't know what he was doing. And in his protective mode to protect his little sister Kelly, he not only opened the door to infestation, but swung it wide open. What most people don't understand when using a Ouija board is that, not only are they initiating contact, but they are also opening a doorway, a portal, or a vortex from the third dimension into other dimensions and realities through which anything and everything who notices it can come through—and worse still—it is left wide open unless someone who knows how to close it does just that, and seals it for good.

Not only did Tyler challenge the spirit speaking to them, but any *other* spirit in the house and or any other spirit on the other side of the doorway. Jimmy was right in warning Tyler against challenging it. Unfortunately, it was too late to stop Tyler from issuing that challenge. When Tyler demanded that the spirit show itself, the activity suddenly stopped. Why? It's like talking on the phone with someone and asking them to come over to your house. The intelligence on the other end of the line agrees, hangs up the phone, and heads out. The invitation was all that the spirit or spirits needed to fully intervene in the lives of those three young men, and after that happened, unfortunately for them, the lives of everyone else in the house where the Ouija board was used as well.

The guys decided to leave the room where they used the Ouija board, so they retired up to Tyler's room, so they could simply forget about it. That's like inviting people over to a party and leaving the door open while you're out at the pool. They're still going to come over and roam through the house until they come and find you.

Alcohol, drugs, stress, fear, and the health of the physical, spiritual, emotional, and mental bodies all affect the strength of the aura—the energy defense shield that surrounds us all and protects us from negative entities and evil. Who or what gave the young men the suggestion to drink the remaining alcohol in broken bottles in the bar in the living room? Maybe it was nothing but teenage antics. It could also have been the spirits' desire to influence the guys to consume that alcohol to break them down and make them more vulnerable to attack than they would be in their natural state if they hadn't consumed it. The reason this happens is because whenever someone does drugs or drinks alcohol, small holes open up in their auric fields which result in energy leaks and breaches in their defenses for other energies and entities to slip through. This does not lead to possession, but it does allow the spirits to use the power of suggestion to influence behaviors, by putting thoughts inside the heads of their targets that are indistinguishable from their own.

When Tyler got the impression that he was being watched shortly thereafter, he was right. He felt something was amiss outside and so he opened the window and stuck his head out to see what was going on. He couldn't see the spirits, but they signaled their presence with turning off and on the light downstairs. This was like a flashing lighthouse signaling the ships to come in. The spirits had been properly invited and they wanted to give the teenagers a symbolic gesture that they had finally arrived, so the doorbell rang seemingly by itself—eight times. It rang eight times because eight different demonic intelligences had come through the doorway or portal. Imagine if you will, black-colored, misshapen, ghastly-looking Halloween monsters ringing the doorbell as they walked through the front door and paraded through the house. It's almost comical when you think about the symbolism.

Once they were inside, they caused the planchette to spin around in circles and hover over the word 'Hello' to signal their arrival. Then it swung over to the word 'Goodbye,' which obviously meant that the teens were in for some serious trouble. Smashing the planchette into pieces signaled that the spirits had no further need for it or for the Ouija board. Tyler's attempt to throw the Ouija board away was futile and came much too late. That's like changing your screen name on the Internet when you've already given out your home address. The pathway was there and all anyone or anything had to do at that point forward was use it. The invitation was out, the door was wide open, and the party was just getting started.

Chapter 8 – Analysis

The guys awoke to a terrible rotting smell, and based solely on instinct, they quickly tried to associate it with a natural, unpleasant human smell. Bad smells, rotting flesh, excrement, urine, and sulfur are quite common smells associated with evil spirits. They sometimes go away as quickly as they come, but never without succeeding in their original purpose which is to frighten, disgust, and *weaken* those who are within their range. Remember, they are not real smells originating from physical sources, but merely the *impression* of the smells *projected* onto the recipients. We all know how we recoil when we smell a dead skunk on the side of the road or the smell of a rotting animal. It's repulsive, and we can't wait to travel outside the range of the smell that is repelling us. Pools of urine, excrement, blood, bodily fluids, insects, worms, and black flies tend to repel most people—and for good reason. The demons know this, so they project the images, or smells associated with these things to cause us pain, to induce fear, and to make us physically sick. All of these things cause us to broadcast *fear* and a whole host of other negative emotions. The negative spirits crave this cast off negative energy and feed themselves with it. I call it the "fear buffet."

Inhuman diabolical spirits can manipulate physical matter in ways that would seem simply unbelievable or superhuman to the casual observer. They appear that way because they are indeed superhuman, or in other words, beyond the capabilities of humans and human spirits.

Inhuman, diabolical entities, or demons or devils, as they have been called through history, are preternatural in origin —meaning they are not of this world, or of this dimension, for that matter. They never inhabited or animated a human body on the third-dimensional plane of existence. They are beings of vast power.

One of the most incredible tales I have ever heard was when a refrigerator allegedly dematerialized or disappeared in the kitchen of a demonically infested home and reappeared or rematerialized on the steps of the basement right next to Lorraine Warren. I have also heard tales of pets being teleported from one location to another, sometimes yards away, and sometimes never to be seen again. I have also heard of people being teleported from inside a house into the woods nearby. While investigating a demonically infested house with other investigators working with the Warrens, I learned that a good deal of activity was occurring inside the bathrooms. When I felt the need to use the bathroom, I elected to leave the house and walk down the street to use the bathroom at a restaurant. Because I hadn't told anyone that was what I intended to do, and since I had literally disappeared for over twenty minutes, the other investigators were deeply concerned because they feared that I was teleported out of the house by a demonic spirit.

I have never witnessed something being teleported. I have seen objects move by psychokinesis, objects as large as a wooden firewood box loaded with firewood that must have weighed over one hundred pounds, and of course, smaller objects. As Dr. Steven Greer, Director of The Disclosure Project, says about evidence of UFO's: "Absence of evidence is not evidence of absence." Just because I have never witnessed teleportation doesn't mean that I don't believe in it. I do, in fact, believe in it.

Chapter 9-11 – Analysis

When things get too intense in cases like these, the people involved always feel as if the location in which the activity is happening has been infested and taken over by entities that they find repulsive. Just like the positive end of a magnet is repelled by negative polarity, good people and their positive energy fields are naturally repelled by evil entities and their negative energies. It's the natural order of the Universe. It is the Law of Attraction at work. What happens then, when the infestation occurs in your own home and there is nowhere else to go?

The pool of urine and the black goo were the psychic manifestations of inhuman, diabolical spirits. They never existed anywhere else and were created by manipulating molecular structure out of space. Things of this nature never last long in the physical plane and often vanish without trace soon after. The swarms of black flies were created and projected en masse to the entire group inside the house via telepathy to instill the maximum amount of terror possible. It certainly worked.

After they had the wits to flee the house, the guys had to take their minds off the recent events, so they went to the movie theater and lost themselves in two films. This was also a smart idea, because it allowed them to vacate the house entirely, thereby not shedding off any more negative psychic energy that the spirits would be using against them later. It shifted their attention away from the situation at hand, which would also energize the spirits in the house, simply by thinking of the phenomena and about the spirits causing it. The best kind of movie that they could have seen would have been a comedy, because laughter is positive energy, and it repels negative energy. Of course, the worst type they could have seen would have been a supernatural horror movie.

When Tyler sat in the McDonald's restaurant and evaluated his situation compared to all of the other people who were seemingly going about their normal lives, he was at great risk of falling into depression. Do you know what depression does to your energy field? Think about when you see someone who is depressed. They tend to slouch, they have very little energy, they are lethargic and hang their heads low, and they isolate themselves from others. These people are suffering mentally, emotionally, and most often spiritually. Therefore, they are suffering physically, which almost always sends them plummeting into a sense of hopelessness and despair. They are generating negative energy rather than positive energy. As a result, their auras are full of breaks or holes or leaks and they are at great risk for supernatural and especially preternatural or diabolical attacks. In fact, what little positive energy they have left for themselves is often siphoned away from other earthbound, negative human spirits who come into their energy fields to recharge themselves.

The negative energy attracts more negativity into their lives and that creates a downward spiral into ruin unless and until they find help. People like this fall into the 'victim mentality.' They fall into separation consciousness, believing that God, or their family, friends, partners and finally the whole of humanity has abandoned them, doesn't care about them and would rather that they were dead. What kind of people do you think are then attracted into their lives? They attract more people just like themselves, of course. What does surrounding themselves with other negative people do for them or their energy fields? Nothing good, I can tell you that, other than reinforce the victim mentality within a group. Negative energy fields repel positive energy fields and attract only more negativity.

Now, compare and contrast depressed people with happy people. Happy people are vibrant, if not glowing. They stand erect, proud, confident, and they are full of peace and joy. Their energy fields or auras are bright, expanded, intact and very powerful. They interact with others easily and are protected from anything siphoning their energy, because they have a powerful shield around them. They are also much more centered and aware of their surroundings and can react more effectively, whether subconsciously or intuitively, to any strange situations, circumstances, people or energies that come into their lives. They are able to better discern if people that they meet or circumstances that they encounter are for their highest good, or if they would be better off going to do other things or to be in the company of other people instead. Positive magnetic fields repel negative magnetic fields and attract more positivity.

Tyler and Sarah elected to keep the fact that they had used the Ouija board in the house a secret. Even though their intention was good, this was a *major mistake*, because everyone should have and could have compared notes. Instead, everyone was fending for themselves rather than as a strong family unit which was exactly what the spirits wanted.

The spirits obviously desired to warn and frighten Jimmy by teleporting the Ouija board into his book bag. He didn't witness it disappearing from Tyler's garbage can into his book bag. That would have been really scary. It was definitely put there by the spirits to entice Jimmy to use it, to have him open a doorway or portal into his own house, so that they could gain entry there. Jimmy was wise when he said: "Of course, I'm not going to use it!" When the spirits heard him say that, and realized that Jimmy was not going to play along with their game, they teleported it right back to the McLaughlin's house and into the garbage can to instill even more fear in Tyler, but they had to get Tyler to go back to the garbage can to see it, didn't they? If their attempts to do so wouldn't work, they could have simply teleported it into Tyler's bag or onto his bed, or anywhere else they saw fit to send it.

Later in the evening, when Matthew walked through the kitchen, he suddenly became aware of a bad smell coming from what he assumed to be the garbage can in the kitchen. The demonic spirits projected the smell directly into Matthew's mind. He could have walked over and checked it himself, and if he found it to be the source of the bad smell, he could have personally taken it out of the kitchen and into the garage. Instead, the spirits influenced him to ask Tyler to take it out into the garage. Tyler had already experienced bad smells, especially in the kitchen. He agreed to take it out himself, but when he looked inside, the only garbage inside were the Chinese food cartons from dinner that he and Sarah had just a short time earlier. It did not smell bad at all. Tyler's psychic sense was right on the money when he felt like something was odd. When he went to put the kitchen garbage bag into the large metal garbage can in the garage, he was in for a real shock, because that was when he noticed that the Ouija board had returned.

At first, we were dealing with a human spirit. In addition to that human spirit, The McLaughlin's and their friends were dealing with something vastly more powerful. What they were dealing with now was pure evil.

The spirits brought the Ouija board back simply as a display of their power and to frighten Tyler. How exactly does a human spirit cause an object to move from one location to another, miles away? The answer is that they can't. No human spirit can lift over a couple of pounds in weight. They also cannot cause items to dematerialize into thin air, or change from physical matter into etheric energy, and then switch back and re-materialize in another location. How then does an inhuman, diabolical spirit perform such a feat? A great deal of scientific study suggests that everything we see, touch, taste, smell, and feel in the third dimension is nothing but a holographic illusion, and that everything is simply energetic patterns and subatomic particles swirling around that appear to us to be solid, when in reality they are nothing of the sort. It was said that the entire Kingdom of Heaven could be contained within a mustard seed, because that is how little actual physical matter there is in the universe. Everything is really simply vibration. Everything is a vibration frequency.

I liken this reality which we are experiencing right now on this planet to a massive online multiplayer role-playing game connected to the infinite web of consciousness. At some point we decided that earth looked like an interesting place to experience. To experience earth, we needed to incarnate there, so we selected what kind of avatar we wished to create that would allow us to experience it. In the earth game we are able to choose from a vast assortment of pure or mixed races. Because the soul is genderless, because it is pure energy, we then need to choose from the two genders that we have available to us.

Next, we can design our avatar, vehicle, soul container, body or whatever else we wish to call it from a whole host of interesting combinations and customizations. When we are finished spending a good amount of time selecting our perfect physical representation, we then get to select which classes or professions we wish to experience during our adventure. We have only a finite amount of skill points with which to spend at the outset of the game, prior to entering the game world, and we have a massive list of available professions, talents, trades, or crafts to choose from, so we need to choose them wisely with a great deal of consideration for what we ultimately want to achieve, because when we enter this world, we are stuck with what we have selected. When we are satisfied with our avatar and the life we had planned out, we then disembark from our own world into the game world, onto the planet, continent or region that we selected to spawn into.

Once we are born or spawn into the game world, we interact with hundreds and sometimes thousands of other characters, who, for their own reasons and with their own goals in mind, have chosen the same general locale that we did. Once we are there, we make friends with some of the other players and choose to adventure together. Thus, our story begins.

The interesting and most important thing we need to remember is that we are infinite consciousness that *chose* to experience earth by animating or controlling the avatar, therefore we are not the avatar, or its story. We are simply here to experience what being that avatar, with its own specific traits and skills, is like. We are unlimited, immortal awareness experiencing a limited, mortal adventure in a game world.

These game worlds that are available for us now here on earth in 2014 are so advanced, it boggles the mind. We see stunningly beautiful, sometimes breathtaking landscapes and scenery, such as in The Lord of the Rings Online. Everything looks and feels solid. In reality it is all just codes and digits in a massive software program, but it looks and feels absolutely real. Some games feel so real that they have captivated the hearts and minds of millions and millions of people who would rather live in the game world rather than in the world where you are sitting in right now, reading this book. Imagine that. Now imagine that our entire earth is nothing more than a highly advanced massive online multiplayer role-playing computer game. Imagine that somewhere in a higher dimension your higher self is interacting with some kind of incredibly advanced computer system playing an online game with you as its avatar. Imagine the incredible process involved designing the body that you are now using, its traits and capabilities and that this higher self is controlling or guiding your life and circumstances simply for its own pleasure and experience.

Imagine that your soul is the force behind the decisions about where you were born, what your body is like, and what adventures you are experiencing. If this is indeed true, and it makes perfect sense to me that it is, then it was my soul that had selected to incarnate or spawn on the planet Earth, on the North American continent, in the region of New England, in the State of Connecticut, in the county and city of Bridgeport, in the precise year, month, date, hour, minute, and second that would enable it to get the most out of the adventure that it decided it wanted to experience. It was *my soul* that designed this six-foot-six body and all of its traits and abilities that it has. What about everyone else? Why did they choose to come here to experience this world? Why did they choose to meet you and interact with you and to share in the adventure with you?

Several of my closest friends that I grew up with are close friends to this day, because I honor and cherish my friendships. I have friends who I play multiplayer games with online. We all usually decide to play the same game when it is released. Not only do we select the same world, but we also select the same planet or continent or region, so we can all adventure together. Sometimes, we want to experience something a little bit different that is only offered in other regions of the game world, so we agree to unite at a certain place in a specific time and circumstance, much like we meet people at different times in our lives who we instantly have an affinity towards or a friendship that is instantaneous as well as deep and meaningful.

My friends and I all tend to design our main characters or likenesses of ourselves with the same general characteristics, no matter which game world or software program we elect to play. We also tend to use the same names, no matter which game we play.

Considering this tendency, is Jason—my current physical avatar that I am experiencing now, in this game, here on earth—my overall general template that I choose to create over and over, with which to experience whatever adventures I embark on? If so, then because we don't just materialize out of thin air, and because we need actual genetics from our parents, in my case, to be six foot six, I'd need to select a father with strong traits and specific DNA that would allow me to reach my pre-planned, desired height. I did just that. My father Bill is a strong, hardy man who stands six foot two. Because my soul elected to be a writer, a singer, and a board game designer, it would also need to find a creative, artistic mother so that it could have access to her creative talents. My mother, Shirley, is a very creative person and a talented painter. My brother, David, has many talents and one of them is the ability to work with wood and stone to build amazing houses and create phenomenal stone walls and landscapes. Our grandfather, Floyd, had those skills in abundance, so not only do I believe that my brother had preplanned his incarnation with special regard to our parents' DNA, but also to our grandparents'. My sister, Laurie, who is also a talented artist, received her talent from our mother as well. I think our DNA is nothing more than an incredibly advanced software code. When you think of the billions of people living here, or experiencing this world, and the infinite combinations of genetics, characteristics, traits, skills, histories, potentialities, and possibilities involved, it becomes clear that something very profound is going on behind the scenes. Even though these complexities can and often do boggle the mind, we might be more in control of our lives and of our situations than we believe that we are, or at least our souls are.

What is so interesting about these games is they never

really end, until we choose to stop playing the game. Though our avatar might become overwhelmed in a fight, or fall off a cliff, or succumb to a disease and essentially die, we have the conscious choice whether to spawn right back into the game world, choose a completely new avatar, chose to focus elsewhere and come back to play later, or to ultimately play a new game altogether. When we play a game on the computer here on earth for hours and simply grow weary of it, or when we need to take a break, we "log out" of the game world and go about our lives. What if when our bodies suddenly feel the urgent need to sleep, our soul is simply wanting to take a break to do something else with a clear understanding that it can come back and pick up this game where it left off? What if our soul decides that it doesn't want to play this game at all anymore? Does that mean it severs the connection and the avatar dies? It certainly would explain sudden unexplainable deaths, wouldn't it? When our bodies die, are we "logging out" of the game world? It's truly incredible, when you think about it.

For example, after a game of paintball, my friends and I would discuss our experiences when we were safely back at base camp. We'd boast about our triumphs, laugh about our mistakes, rub our bruises, drink some water, have some lunch, and join another game when we all agreed that we were ready to play again. When our bodies die, do we wait for our friends and loved ones back at base camp until we are all gathered, healed and ready to start another game? Could it all really be that simple? I believe so.

Interestingly enough, before we are allowed to enter any game world to play a specific massive multiplayer game, we have to accept the Terms of Service Agreement that binds us to a specific set of laws and rules designed by the software engineers and game developers. Here on earth, we are all bound by the same rules and regulations. When it comes to earthbound spirits, they are the discarnate aspects of their former selves, no longer able to directly influence the physical world in the manner that they used to be able to. Inhuman diabolical entities, however, are beings that gain access into the world through deception, but were never of it. They *never accepted* the Terms of Service Agreement, and they are *not* bound by the laws and rules of the world that the rest of us are operating under. Therefore, they have immense power compared to the rest of us. Sometimes in a game we have to summon a developer to handle unruly players or people who somehow cheat or hack into the program to wreak havoc on the general population. Is this not the 'God' of the program or the 'Game Designer' that we are summoning for assistance? When demons that are operating outside of the laws and rules interfere with the experiences of those in the world and we call upon God, are we not then summoning the Creator of His program, and therefore are we not asking for His divine intervention?

Chapter 12-13 – Analysis

After watching the garbage truck drive away from the house, Tyler fell into a false sense of security by believing that his troubles were over. Then, when the Ouija board fell out of Tyler's locker, the young men knew that the spirits in the house were not through with them at all. At that point, they were pretty much convinced that the spirits in the house wouldn't rest until they used the Ouija board to communicate with them again. They were right.

The Ouija board is sold as a game. It's manufactured commercially and sold by the thousands, but it most certainly is not a game. Do you know where the company that produces it is located? Are you ready for this? Salem, Massachusetts. Are you familiar with Salem? If you're reading this book, I'd bet that you are at least somewhat familiar with it. Salem, Massachusetts is where the witch trials were held in 1692. They were a series of hearings and prosecutions of people accused of witchcraft. The amount of suffering, misery, injustice, and death that occurred there is staggering. As a result, the entire area around that province, including Salem Village (now Danvers), Ipswich, Andover, and Salem town is a supernatural and preternatural epi-center.

The most dangerous aspect of using a Ouija board is the gradual unquenchable desire to use it more frequently and for longer periods of time, until the point when the user can't seem to put it away, no matter how badly they want to and how many times they try. This is called obsession, and as with any addiction, it is *extremely destructive and dangerous.*

Obsessed users feel more and more unsatisfied with the answers that they might receive or with the quality of the communication in general, even though they spend more and more time using the board. They might make a connection with a particular spirit and never really know who they are communicating with on the other side. If they seem to have lost contact with their special spirit friend, they can't seem to rest until they are able to talk with them again. The user becomes a recluse in most cases, ignoring friends, family, and even foregoing food and sustenance.

This is all by design to wear the user down, lower their defenses, and quickly gain the upper hand, then offer—or in reality, demand—something of the user in exchange for more time and more information. This always comes at great cost in the long run, despite how attractive the offer seems to be at first.

Above all else, the spirits are attempting to gain the user's trust. They will try to imitate or claim to associate with or be connected to a pleasant personality that the user knew—or most especially, and most effectively—a recently deceased relative, loved one or friend.

The spirit will claim to be your grandfather, for instance. It'll tell you what your real grandfather bought you for your birthday, it will tell you about names, dates, and places that are absolutely accurate and therefore earn your complete trust.

If the spirit knew what present your grandfather bought you for your birthday, and it knows your actual birth date, and knows the unique term of endearment that your grandfather called your grandmother—that only he and he alone would know—then the spirit you are communicating with must be the spirit of your grandfather, right?

Wrong!

The spirits that you are communicating with are no

longer bound by the human body and are no longer shut off from their psychic abilities like the majority of the living are. They're energy, and they can read and influence your energy without you even knowing it.

When the user asks a question that he or she already knows the answer to, or when the user has a specific answer in mind when asking the question, all the spirit has to do is read the user's mind, get the answer he or she is looking for, and use it to satisfy and fool the user.

Then what? When the spirit has succeeded in gaining the user's trust, it's in. What wouldn't you do for your dear, departed grandfather who was trying to make contact with you from the great beyond?

One of the most infamous cases involving a Ouija board was the case of Annabelle in which an inhuman spirit fooled two women into believing that it was the spirit of a little girl. The women became so obsessed with the board and so concerned with the spirit of the girl that they were communicating with that they quickly agreed to try to help her. The only trouble was, it was definitely not the spirit of a little girl.

When the spirit asked for permission to live inside one of the two women, the woman knew that something was wrong, so she refused. Good choice. But she did give it permission to live inside the life-sized Raggedy Ann doll that they had in their apartment. The second that they gave the alleged spirit of the girl permission to live inside the doll, all of the contact on the Ouija board suddenly stopped. The chaos that broke loose in the following days produced some of the most frightening activity on record.

If you'd like to read the entire story about Annabelle, you can find it in the book *The Demonologist*, by Gerald Brittle. It is full of some of the most horrifyingly real cases of preternatural, diabolical infestation and oppression I have ever studied.

Tyler and his friends had no interest at all in using the

Ouija board again. The spirits knew that. So they used their awesome power to teleport the board back and forth, saying "Hey, it's me. Come and use me again. I'm not through with you guys, yet."

Not only did the spirits succeed in getting the guys to discuss and agree that they had to use it again, but they lured them into the darkest, most dangerous location possible. Why? To what end? Can you imagine any fate worse than falling into a dark hole and dying slowly? Inhuman spirits love it when human beings suffer, because we're made in the image of God. When a human suffers, the demonic spirits see God suffering. They can't harm God, but they can harm humans, so it's the next best thing.

When it comes to Ouija boards, you can't be sure who or what you are communicating with, nor can you can ever trust the messages being conveyed. Broken sentences or one-word messages are not very clear forms of communication.

Brock was a human spirit, and he was most definitely not from hell, as suggested by the message that was conveyed. Was he in a mental state of hell? Were the other spirits from hell? Were they evil? What did it mean when the message was interpreted that the spirits were there for all of them?

The only objective the spirits had was to frighten the guys and to make them cast off as much negative fear energy as possible. They were successful, because fear ran rampant—especially when they feared falling into the bottomless sinkhole underneath the school.

There was never a real sink hole under the high school in Monroe, and its name has been changed for legal reasons. I added the sink hole to make the story more interesting.

When Linda was attacked in her art studio, she experienced what is called 'psychic cold' or 'psychic heat," which is a localized designated area under the direct influence of a demonic spirit's power. Demons can cause spontaneous fires, areas of extreme heat or cold, freezing rain, and even solid ice. Demonic spirits can cause anything they desire, because they operate outside of the laws of physics that govern us here on Earth.

How would you feel if your name were called out of thin air several times from all angles around you and from above? As if that weren't bad enough, Linda watched in horror as the heat was sucked out of the room in an instant. When the sphere of cold air began to envelop Linda and she tried to run away, but found that the door was locked, it was because the spirits had locked the door. This was a very dangerous situation. Linda instinctively knew to call on Jesus to help her. The demon wanted no part of that, and released its hold on the door handle, allowing Linda to escape. She was very lucky.

Chapter 14-15 – Analysis

So many interesting books exist on the market about the subject of ghosts and paranormal phenomena that it should be common knowledge by now that the spirit world is a very real. Yet most people choose simply not to believe in it —until they experience a very real haunting of their own.

When Linda returned home with the books, it was considered a direct challenge to the spirits that were infesting the house. Why? Because she was armed to the teeth with information and knowledge that could inform her about what was going on, how to deal with it, or confront it, and ultimately—how to make contact with someone who could help the family force them to leave.

The spirits in the house were intelligent. They knew what the family was thinking. The inhuman, diabolical entities in the house had a genius level intelligence, perhaps super-human or even omnipotent—meaning they knew what the humans were thinking of doing even before they thought about it themselves. Imagine what an advantage that was. If that were the case—and it was a strong possibility, if not a high probability—then, the spirits knew that it was time to escalate their attack plans to wear down the entire family as quickly and as powerfully as possible, so they could accomplish their ultimate goal.

One of the most effective methods of attack used by demonic spirits is to divide and conquer families by creating as much internal strife as possible, and to turn loved ones against each other. In the beginning stages of infestation, they always go after the weakest members of the family first, and leave the most powerful member alone totally. Activity will be directed especially at the most vulnerable family member, the rebellious teenager, the trouble-maker, the addict, or the black sheep of the family—if there are any such characters in that family unit. They will not allow the most powerful member of the family to witness any activity whatsoever that could or would corroborate anything else that any other family member had witnessed, even if everyone else did. They know that most humans are shut off psychically and cannot make sense of what is going on. They also know that as a society, especially in western civilization, the subject of ghosts and supernatural activity, or spirits and demons, is ridiculed and dismissed as fantasy.

Intelligent negative spirits use all of these things to their advantage. They strike who they want to strike, when and however they please. They also lie dormant or hide when they want to. They did not allow Matthew to witness anything until this point of the infestation, because they wanted to sow the seed of distrust and discord within the family to split them up and turn them on each other. At this point, Linda was about to find help, so it was time for them to attack the alpha, the man of the house, their greatest obstacle to domination of the entire family.

They knew that Matthew had great pride in the home that he designed and built, so they attacked his pride. They made it sound like the walls were about to be blasted down by an invisible force that he could not believe in, understand, or explain. Then, as he was attempting to re-enter the house, they burned his palm so badly on the doorknob that it caused blisters to erupt. They knew that he would find it all impossible to believe.

It is one thing to know and understand that spirits and the phenomena that they can cause are a reality. It is dreadful to experience burning your hand on a doorknob, or to feel an icy cold hand seizing control of yours, or hearing a growl come from nowhere, even if and when you have a thorough understanding about the reality of spirits and the phenomena that they can cause. It is another thing entirely when you do not believe in ghosts at all and are then suddenly, viciously attacked by them. When this happens, people often snap, because they suffer the combined weight of the mental, emotional, physical, and spiritual effects of the attack. Matthew was being assailed from all angles and in full force—on purpose.

How would you react if you heard what sounded like a gigantic fist smashing against the floors, the walls, and the ceiling of your house, and it was so powerful that it cracked the walls and shook the entire place? This is undeniably some of the most frightening activity anyone could ever experience. No human spirit could do things of that nature. Only a tremendous diabolical force could do it. They could also solidify the atmosphere preventing passage from one area to the next. Imagine being trapped on a staircase with banging going on all around you, yet you are unable to move up or down the stairs, because there is an invisible barrier blocking you from moving.

Inhuman or diabolical spirits have so much energy and power they can cause a burn without affecting any material object that is capable of generating enough heat to cause a burn in the first place. They can also do it without any physical object nearby at all, and they can, for instance, as we saw later in the story, cause an unsuspecting person to burn their hand, simply by touching a doorknob. A doorknob can't generate any heat, nor can it generate frost. A doorknob is a doorknob.

Another example of this very activity occurred in a case I had investigated personally in Rathdrum, Idaho. In that case, the owner of the home that was infested by inhuman, diabolical spirits went into his basement, was shoved by an invisible force against an old, unused, cold, wood burning stove and burned his hand so badly that it instantly generated blisters. The stove was not generating any heat, because it was neither connected to an electrical outlet, nor was there any wood burning inside. This type of phenomenon occurs when preternatural or diabolical entities are at work. They can cause harm simply by using their soul minds to inflict it.

In haunted houses it is quite common for people to hear strange mumbling or whispering, or sometimes even multiple-person arguments, and even strange undecipherable music playing with no identifiable source.

The spirits in the house took advantage of the fact that Kelly was a sensitive by appearing as a fluffy black cat. It was so completely non-threatening to interact with a cat, even a spirit cat, that Kelly never even mentioned it to her family because the spirits pretended that they were nice and that they simply wanted to have fun. Nothing could have been further from the truth.

While Brock at this point in the story had a change of heart and sincerely wanted to help Kelly and her family and to protect them from the inhuman spirits who had gained entry into the house, he was essentially powerless to stop them.

This was a very dangerous time for Kelly because the spirits were trying to turn Kelly against her own family and to wear her down enough that they could begin to influence her more and more. This was a pivotal moment for Matthew, who suddenly came to understand the very dire situation that he and his family were in.

Chapter 16 – Analysis

There were definite sexual overtones when Linda was attacked in her bedroom. A spirit has no physical body, and therefore it has no gender. A human spirit incarnates innumerable times in innumerable shapes, sizes, and of course, in both sexes. An angel, an archangel, or a fallen archangel or devil has never had a gender, because it has never been inside a physical third-dimensional body. But, when it manifests itself and attacks a living human being, it takes on or assumes one of the only two genders that it has available to it. A succubus is believed to be a female devil that initiates sexual intercourse with sleeping men. It appears as a woman with breasts and female genitalia. An incubus is believed to be a devil that attacks sleeping women and takes the form of a male with male genitalia. Interestingly enough, the demonic spirit manifests in whatever form or gender that the target human prefers. First, to make it easier to succeed with the initial sexual advances and proceed to the sexual attack, the spirit appears in the most charismatic form that it can manifest. Then, later, once the spirit has engaged in the sexual acts, it shifts its appearance to something completely hideous—right before the eyes of the horrified human that it had seduced. One of most interesting aspects of this attack is the sticky, slimy, stinking residue from bodily fluids that remain with, inside and on the body of the human target—long after the spirit had dematerialized and disappeared.

Sexual energy is very powerful. It is cast off in incredible amounts when someone is being sexually assaulted. The fear of being violated is strong enough. Multiply that by a factor of ten when you can't see the invisible attacker that originates from another dimension or plane of existence entirely. Multiply that by another factor of ten when you know that the thing attacking you is a demon or a devil who hates you with every fiber of its being. The deliberate tingling and rubbing sensations on Linda's inner thigh were intended to cause Linda to experience as much fear and panic as possible to siphon off more of that precious energy. If she had remained in the room, Linda could very well have been paralyzed with psychic paralysis and sexually violated.

In some rare circumstances, if an incubus attack goes on long enough, women have actually been impregnated by the Incubus. Diabolical impregnation is the ultimate form of blasphemy. It is the reverse of the Immaculate Conception. Can you imagine what kind of child would come into this world as the result of the union of a demonic entity and a human being? These children are called 'killcrops.' These are the indescribably foul, mass-murderers, and despicable personalities throughout history. With regard to the vile things that these personalities do, we often ask how a human being could be so cruel. They are not human beings at all, but the offspring of inhuman, diabolical spirits. Fortunately for Linda, she got out of there just in time.

The spirits inside the house did not want Julie to interfere with their attacks so they prevented Linda from hearing the doorbell and the knocking on the door. Linda was elated when her friend Julie had witnessed enough activity to admit that they had a very serious problem on their hands. You can imagine how much that means to someone who had been experiencing supernatural phenomena by themselves.

When Linda and Julie decided to leave the house to find information on the psychic fairs and the people who run them, they were once again closer to attaining the professional help that they so desperately needed. The spirits knew this, so they locked the door on Julie and prevented her from opening it. Then they unlocked the door for Linda to turn Linda against Julie.

Do you understand how simple the process is? The spirits knew that Julie had come to the realization that the activity that was going on was real, so they tried to cause the two close friends to fight amongst each other. The strange black dog that walked into the road, frightened them, and caused them to swerve out of the way, was an inhuman diabolical spirit trying to prevent Linda and Julie from obtaining the vital information that would allow them to find the help that would force the spirits to leave the house.

When Julie swerved out of the way, the wheels almost left the pavement, which meant that the van was dangerously close to rolling over, in which case, the two women could have been severely harmed—or worse. Fortunately for them, Brock intervened and prevented the van from flipping.

After they had retrieved the phone number for the psychic fair at the library, and they were enjoying their ice cream at Friendly's, and Linda had informed Kelly that they were seeking help to make the ghosts go away, Kelly's personality changed from a sweet, smiling, adorable little girl, into a snarling, growling, violent beast.

The last thing Linda or Julie would have ever expected was Kelly's sudden, vicious attack and her incredible strength when Julie attempted to fight her off. It took a violent tug of Kelly's hair to cause the shock needed to bring Kelly back to full waking consciousness. When Kelly finally came to, she had no idea what had just happened.

But what exactly happened to cause Kelly to change personalities so drastically when Kelly is such a vibrant, happy child with a strong magnetic field or aura? Remember, she had been interacting with the spirits for several days, and in constant communication with them. They knew that they would never be able to take control of her unless they had worn her down, earned her trust, and tricked her into lowering her defenses enough so that they could penetrate them and take control of her. They succeeded for the first time, and turned her against Julie, because Kelly and Julie had a very close, special, loving bond. When you come to understand how this works, you will realize just what kind of personalities are behind the so-called friendly contact that Kelly was experiencing.

With regard to the phone call that Tyler made from the restaurant, there have been many interesting cases involving telephone calls from the dead. In most every case, the phone never actually rang at all. But, the voice came over the phone with crystal clear clarity, and when they checked with the telephone company, it had no record of the incoming phone call, nor could they identify from where it had originated. The purpose of the telepathic phone call was to confuse and frighten Tyler and his friends even more so than they already were. It's all always about escalation.

Chapter 17-18 – Analysis

Think for a moment about the powerful electromagnetism that must have been present to cause the kinds of activity going on inside the house when Tyler and his friends arrived after the bizarre phone call. It looked to them as if the grand finale of the Fourth of July fireworks for the entire town were going off inside the house in just a few moments. That power is being used and manipulated by the spirits inside the house. This energy is what caused all of the incredible activity with the silverware which streaked across the room like magic. This is possible because inhuman spirits can bypass the natural laws that govern us here on earth. Levitating objects are seriously scary things to witness inside haunted homes.

When Matthew gathered his courage and challenged the spirits in the house, it was the worst possible thing that he could have done, because it was exactly what the inhuman spirits wanted him to do—so they could take him up on his challenge.

When an inhuman spirit envelops someone in an invisible sphere of horrid-smelling rotting flesh, it sickens the human and forces him to flee out of its range. The exact opposite is true when a human burns high church incense or sage or sandalwood where an inhuman spirit is present. It is awful and debilitating for the negative or inhuman spirit.

Inhuman, diabolical spirits find great pleasure in harming human beings in any way that they can. They do this because they are furious at God for casting them out and for transfiguring them into vile creatures. Instead of dealing with their own mistakes and suffering for them in silent contemplation, as a general rule, they leap at any chance they have to cause mankind to suffer. In fact, it would seem that the only pleasure and fulfillment they seem to get is by causing mankind to suffer as they have suffered. They really haven't learned their lesson, have they?

Diabolical spirits can bring on incredible sickness and pain in a split second, and their goal is always the same—to weaken their targets, to punish them for resisting and to ultimately possess them and seize control of their bodies.

Prayers or expressions of faith, and earnestly asking for the aid of Jesus, God, or any of the angels or archangels, is very harmful to truly negative spirits, and is especially painful to demonic and diabolical spirits. When the family prayed together, it was the first time that they were calling on the forces of light for their own personal protection. They should have requested it with faith, rather than out of desperation and fear. Matthew provoked the evil spirits and threatened them. Challenging demonic spirits *is always a foolish thing to do*, because they are all too eager to accept those challenges and show the challenger what's what.

I have plenty of examples where the powerful name of Jesus Christ wreaks havoc in homes where demonic infestation is taking place. It's very strong and very real. Remember the Law of Attraction and the Law of Intention. When you think of, pray to, call out to, or beg for assistance from angels, archangels, Jesus, or God—you are instantly drawing those beings to you. When you do, they are with you *immediately*. There is no time and space where things of this nature occur. There is no delay.

That is why negative activity usually stops so suddenly when people pray or call out for divine assistance. The negative entities absolutely do not want anyone to invite or summon the forces of love and light into homes that they are infesting, because they are mortal enemies, or polar opposites. They will try and interrupt the prayers or calls for assistance as soon as anyone attempts them. They will try to do this by intensifying their own attacks, forcing people into a state of dread and panic, or by making them fear a vicious, relentless retaliation from the spirits.

When it comes to summoning angels or praying for divine intervention, I think that it is also very important to make sure that you know what your exact intentions are while you are calling out for help. The Law of Free Will is always in effect, and unless you ask specifically for help with a certain aspect of a problem, and for a specific response, the assistance you receive will be much less potent.

With respect to Linda being attacked in the living room, an example of a less potent request for help would be: "Jesus, help me!" A more powerful and specific request would be: "Jesus, help me now. Defend me from these psychic attacks. Protect my children with your divine power. Force these demons to leave my house now and forever more. Sound the trumpets to summon your legions of angels and post watch over this house. Defeat these dark spirits and remove them completely, in your name."

I believe that whatever you ask for in faith, you shall receive. I also believe that praying from a position of lacking something is not as effective as praying from a position of already having attained that thing. I absolutely believe that my prayer has already been granted, and the object of my prayer has already been manifested.

I believe that the most powerful prayer or method for enlisting the aid of the angels, Jesus Christ, God, Prime Creator, or Source would be to acknowledge that whatever you are praying for is already so, such as: "Thank you Jesus, for your divine intervention and protection. Thank you for gracing us with your presence here and now. Thank you for surrounding this house in your divine power and in your perfect, unconditional love. Archangels Michael, Raphael, Uriel, and Gabriel—thank you for being here now and for coming to our aid. Thank you for drawing your swords and closing any portals that may be open here in this house that are allowing these spirits of darkness entry. Thank you for protecting us from anyone, anything, and most importantly from any spirits who seek to do us harm. Thank you for defending us against all of the forces of darkness and for removing them from this, the Lord's house. Thank you for restoring peace and tranquility here in our home. Thank you for guarding us and for protecting us all, always and in all ways. Jesus Christ, thank you for sealing us in a field of brilliant, blinding, violet white light that will dispel all darkness and drive it away from us fully, completely, and forever. I know this. I *now* this. So be it. Amen."

In the above example, are we not therefore asking for exactly what we want, in full faith that is has already been received, before it has even been requested? I think this is the most important message about prayer that has been lost through the centuries.

When Linda was bitten after she read the Psalms, she was the victim of what are called 'psychic wounds.' Imagine being bitten, scratched, strangled, thrown around, and mauled by an invisible spirit. I can't imagine anything more terrifying.

One of the most well-documented examples of psychic wounds is the phenomenon called 'stigmata.' It happened to Padre Pio, who suffered the wounds of Jesus Christ for over fifty years on his hands, feet, and on his head from the crown of thorns. Critics said that he induced it himself, with acid, but after he died, the wounds finally healed by themselves and never bled again.. I don't know of any corpse that has ever healed itself, have you?

When Sarah was clubbed, when Linda was bitten, and when Matthew was batted away across the room and into the wall, we were witnessing the determination of the inhuman spirits to wear the family down, weaken them, and brutalize them. We were also seeing the raw power and strength that they possess. It's not muscle mass that makes them so strong; it is *their will* to accomplish a thing. They are beings of vast power.

Chapter 19-21 – Analysis

One of the most traumatic things that can happen to any family is being forced to leave their own home. It is especially traumatic for young children, because this is and was the only place of solitude that they have ever known and everything that they can identify with is suddenly taken over or lost, either temporarily or sometimes permanently, because many families flee their homes when preternatural activity is occurring, never to return. The families are permanently changed and their lives are never the same. How do you return to a demoniacally infested home after you have witnessed a million black flies pouring out of the sink drain, or pools of urine manifesting out of thin air to stain your carpets? How do you cope with horrendous banging and scratching noises that emanate from the very fabric of space with no identifiable origin? How can anyone cope with vicious assaults on their physical bodies by invisible invaders who seem to have powers beyond comprehension—especially when the victims can't even strike back in self-defense? All of these things are enough to drive an average person completely mad and sadly, sometimes they do. Most lives are never the same after things like this happen. It takes a great deal of will-power and resolve to overcome diabolical infestation and oppression.

When people are desperate and under heavy oppression, a great deal of animosity erupts. The spirits try to turn the people in the house against each other to weaken them and at the same time to energize themselves. While staying overnight in the Curtis House, Tyler didn't steal the money in his father's wallet—of course, he didn't. Instead, the spirits teleported the money from Matthew's wallet directly into Tyler's book bag. This caused Matthew to become extremely worried and agitated. At that point, Matthew wasn't necessarily possessed, but the spirits gave him the suggestion that maybe Tyler had stolen the money, something totally unlike Tyler, yet he somehow 'knew' that the money was in the book bag. When he had found it in there, of course everyone else was shocked and confused, especially Tyler.

The spirits however knew exactly what was going on, and orchestrated it all by essentially whispering in Matthew's ear: "Don't let him get away with that!" Those were the thoughts he had received, but he didn't realize that they weren't his thoughts. Only after he had struck his son several times and yelled and threatened Linda and Sarah did Matthew understand the severity of the situation. He knew that it was totally unlike him to strike out the way he did. Of course, it was unlike him, but the damage had been done. We know who the culprits really are, don't we?

This is the kind of trouble the spirits will try to create. If they can turn a family against each other—divide and conquer if you will—then they have already won. Strong families have the best chances of fighting away evil spirits.

We have all experienced the power of suggestion at work in our lives. It's easy to fall under the spell of the power of suggestion when you see someone eating something that you would find enjoyable. Well, what about when you have invisible spirits in the house suggesting that you commit a certain evil act that you would never do, yet you do it anyway? In the many cases that I have investigated and researched, I have learned that when spirits are present around people, they can influence them to say and do things that are entirely out of character for them, and it can cause all kinds of problems.

'Psychic paralysis' is when someone feels an intense pressure on their body. In effect, they are being immobilized and being prevented from being able to speak, so they can't call out for help. It is also used to immobilize people near the victim to prevent them from interfering. When the victims realize that the people they had been counting on for help are intentionally being prevented from doing so, they reach a state of hopelessness, helplessness, and an incredible state of panic. The more they panic, the stronger the paralysis becomes. At that time, the target is in incredible danger, because their defenses are worn down enough that the attacking spirits could actually enter them and seize control of their body.

The first stage in haunting phenomena is infestation, and the second stage is oppression. Possession is the third and most devastating stage in haunting phenomena where diabolical or demonic spirits are concerned. In this case, Matthew was already so terribly weakened due to his sudden unexplained illness that the spirits paralyzed Linda, entered Matthew's body, moved his consciousness aside, and possessed him almost effortlessly. When Linda was again able to move and when she protested, the demons simply laughed at her, because it was far too late.

Chapter 22-23 – Analysis

When people undergoing severe demonic oppression try to contact someone who can truly help them, they often have considerable difficulty making contact with those individuals, groups, or organizations. Compare it to an intruder in a home grabbing the phone away from someone who is trying to call the police because they are being robbed.

The very last thing evil spirits want for the family they're trying to ruin is for the family to contact anyone who can help them. They know in advance who are the investigators, mediums, psychics, clairvoyants, priests, and exorcists that their victims are trying to connect with. They know that those special people have the ability to identify what is going on inside these houses, how to find them and force them out of hiding, and ultimately, how to expel them from the house completely and permanently.

I have studied many cases of blocked phone lines, busy signals, garbled messages, and strange voices on the other end of a telephone line. There are even cases where one party may hear the phone or the doorbell ringing, but it never actually rings on the other end—much like Julie when she said that she rang the doorbell for several minutes even though Linda heard nothing inside the house.

Animals are very psychic. Cats, dogs, and horses can hear and see into the non-physical dimensions. They detect spirits easily. Unlike humans, they don't dismiss spiritual beings because they've been told that ghosts are figments of the imagination, or because they've been told that they should stop believing in foolish fantasies. Is it possible that Sarah's horse, Montero, was spooked by an inhuman spirit? Was Cinnamon barking at spiritual invaders, because he could sense them and perhaps even see them? The answer in both cases is yes. There are multitudes of stories about cats and dogs looking at something that clearly isn't there, according to the perceptions of their human companions, but the animals sense or see them just fine.

Babies and young children see them as well. As I sat in church one time, I had a child swing around, look at me, point, and say, "Jesus!" Naturally, I don't look like Jesus in any way physically, and I wouldn't want to compare myself to him, but perhaps the child was accessing his natural psychic awareness, and he was able to see the field of loving Christ Consciousness energy that I was meditating on. Perhaps the child was seeing the divine entities that I was calling to myself for the purposes of protection through prayer and recognition. Perhaps, I had nothing to do with it all, and the child was seeing divine energies or entities, angels, or Jesus, because we were in a place of worship where these energies were recognized, adored, prayed to, evoked and invoked throughout the day and night for years, if not decades or centuries.

When Linda was violently attacked in her studio, it was a classic example of demoniacal retribution. After someone who lives in an infested home makes contact with someone who has the capability to help, they are almost always punished for it—and almost immediately. Instances of post-contact retribution are some of the most violent activities on record.

One instance happened to me personally happened when I was working with Ed and Lorraine Warren as an investigator and journalist. We had planned to travel to Vermont to investigate a case up there. I had offered to drive, because I had access to my mother's brand new, seven-passenger minivan. One sunny November morning, on my mother's birthday in fact, I got into the van, evoked the protection of the angels and declared my intention to wash the van in the blood of Jesus Christ to ensure the protection of the van itself and all of the passengers inside in preparation for our journey to Vermont. Ten minutes later, while traveling along the Merritt Parkway in Fairfield, Connecticut, on my way to pick everyone up at the Warren's home, I noticed a car passing me on the right side. When it was about a car length ahead of me, it suddenly started swerving out of control, and it then crossed over into my lane. I slammed on the brakes and the van collided with the other car, striking it in the drivers' door, smashing the driver's window into tiny pieces. We were both completely unharmed. The driver of the car said it felt like his car hit a patch of solid ice, and despite his every attempt to counter-steer, he just lost control and the car was whisked into my lane like it was propelled by some unknown force. Too bad for the poor man, that his insurance policy did not have coverage for accidents caused by inhuman, diabolical spirits.

One hour later, when I was able to call Ed and Lorraine Warren from a payphone, I explained what had happened. We almost called the entire trip off due to the obvious diabolical attempt to disable the vehicle we were using for the trip. Lorraine Warren interpreted this as a desperate attempt by the spirits inside the house in Vermont to prevent us from reaching the house and from helping the family who lived there. This was a deliberate attack to protect themselves from discovery and eviction.

Think about the omnipotence we are dealing with here for a moment. Consider the fact that the entities in the house were not only aware that the family had made contact with a team of investigators, but they knew exactly who the investigators were, and they knew who the driver was going to be, me.

I firmly believe that because I prayed before I ever

started the engine that morning, everyone, including my-self, who got inside the minivan would be totally protected. The demonic spirits could not affect my vehicle or me personally, so they seized control of a nearby car *that was not protected* and caused it to collide with my vehicle.

When contact is established, and help is on the way, all of the phenomena are put into sudden overdrive, because the spirits know they are losing control. One of the things I have always admired about my friends and mentors, Ed and Lorraine Warren is that they always continue on undaunt-ed, no matter what the risks.

With regard the Vermont case, we all knew the risks, but we had to help the family involved. We made it to Vermont a little late, but we made it nonetheless.

Chapter 24-28 – Analysis

When inhuman diabolical spirits enter a location occupied by a human being, they almost always cause a drastic decrease in the local temperature. This is often instant and quite dramatic. The effect is often so drastic that ice crystals can manifest on the windows. The opposite is also true. In many cases, a sharp increase in the temperature of a room can be felt immediately. In either case, there is never an identifiable cause. When demonic spirits manifest into a physical form, there is always a feeling of dread accompanying their arrival, and they almost always appear as a mass of negative blackness. First, they appear as a small sphere in most cases, or if they have accumulated enough energy, they instantly appear as a large spheroid or even some variation of a humanoid, complete with arms, legs, a head, and a face—sometimes even with glowing, pulsating eyes. Sometimes, they will complete their manifestation right before terrified spectators. There is always something off about the manifestation. It just doesn't look or feel right. When there is a face, often the eyes are missing, or the face is obscured in some way. A powerful sulfur smell almost always accompanies the manifestation.

Perhaps, it goes back to the first accounts of diabolical manifestation where fire, brimstone, and sulfur were used to describe the encounters between people and demons. There certainly is validity to the old stories, if activity identical to the ancient stories takes place in the twenty-first century. On rare cases, fallen archangels or devils have been reported to have materialized complete with horns, cloven hooves, and all of the classical attributes of Satan or the Devil. Again, this image has been in the psyche of mankind since the beginning of recorded history, so there must be some reason why they continue to manifest like that to this day.

When an inhuman, diabolical spirit gains entry into the body of a beautiful human being, what do you think that it would want to do to it, once it had seized control? When a body is possessed, all kinds of horrible, debilitating, disgusting things manifest in, on, and all around it, such as the dry, raised patches of skin, the pneumonia, the thick yellow mucus, the cough, the guttural voice, the sickening smells, and so on.

When I first received Linda's desperate phone call and became aware that she had unsuccessfully tried several attempts to get through to me, I knew there was a great deal to be concerned about. When she told me that her family had been physically attacked, I knew that the spirits involved were not human spirits, but demonic spirits. I immediately called some of my fellow investigators and informed them of the urgency of the situation.

The goal all along had been to weaken Matthew's defenses enough to gain entry and seize control. Now that they had him, the plan was to maintain control as long as possible by keeping him barely alive, yet still be able to disfigure and dominate him until they no longer wanted to, at which point they could attempt to kill him—the ultimate pleasure, and the ultimate blasphemy against God. Can you imagine the kinds of horror that could happen if the spirits in the house were able to possess the entire family one by one until they were all seized?

Because Matthew was in the hospital and was essentially theirs, the spirits' next most prized target was Linda, so the spirits that remained in the house went right after her and attacked her in her art studio as she was painting. When they seized control of her hand and ruined her painting by forcing her to deface it, it was especially upsetting to Linda, and they of course knew that it would be.

When we arrived, we had planned on conducting the standard Warren investigation protocol by filming the entire property and the exterior of the house first. But when Linda crawled out of the front door on all fours after a diabolical attack, we quickly altered our plan. When most families finally get help after enduring brutal demonic attacks, the activity almost always stops completely. This is intentional, because the demonic spirits want the investigators to witness nothing out of the ordinary to corroborate the family's story.

I knew instinctively that the family's claims were genuine, but we conducted the same tried and tested protocol throughout the case. Once we had all family members and their friends gathered together for the interview, we began to put the pieces of the puzzle together. It is always very interesting to hear the varying perspectives when all of the participants share their versions of their experiences. The most important questions we ask when dealing with potential demoniacal infestation and oppression concern the use of Ouija boards and the practice of séances. *They are always at the root cause of over 95% of these types of cases because these demonic spirits need to be invited in.* When the family denied the use of Ouija boards and the practice of séances, my investigators and I knew that something just did not add up. We can learn a great deal by simply observing the people involved and by watching how they react and reply to certain questions, how they behave, and how they interact with each other.

Chapter 29 – Analysis

When Tyler asked if Ouija boards worked, I knew in my gut that he had withheld the truth when he denied using the Ouija board earlier during the group interview. Of course the teens didn't mean any harm. These were all fine young men. Fortunately, this information was revealed in the same evening, rather than weeks later, which saved us an immense amount of time should we have needed to delve deeper into the mystery about how and why demonic spirits gained access to the family. When I went upstairs and told my investigators that our suspicions were correct, both Aaron and Daniel knew who the culprits were. Rather than give the dishonesty any attention or energy whatsoever, we simply set up the equipment in the living room again and got the confession on tape so the vital information about the case would be captured correctly.

Once the spirits knew that their method and point of entry was revealed, things escalated as they always do, because the spirits knew that their reign of terror was about to come to an end.

One of the most fascinating aspects to the case was when we came upon all of the food that had been teleported from the containers in the refrigerator into a heaping pile on the kitchen floor. I had never seen anything like that—especially with regard to the spotless containers left in the refrigerator. The food should have still been relatively fresh when we encountered it, but it appeared and smelled as if it had all been sitting there rotting for over a month.

Aaron's injury concerned me, because it meant that the spirits would seek retribution at any time they could, if they had an opportunity to do so.

Many families flee their homes when the activity becomes too much to deal with. But how do you flee something that can *will itself* to be wherever you are, whenever it pleases? Fortunately, in many cases the activity involved is limited to the physical location where a doorway was opened and where the activity is taking place. But for those few people who are relentlessly pursued, things can quickly become overwhelming.

These unfortunate people found themselves victim to the same vicious attacks no matter where they fled to. The McLaughlins were lucky that nothing followed them to Julie's house and that no diabolical activity erupted over there, especially because Julie lived alone and was quite vulnerable.

In serious cases, investigators put themselves at considerable risk. Such was the case in the house we were investigating in Vermont that I had mentioned earlier. Several people had experienced feeling invisible hands on their backs pushing them forward as they walked down the stairs. No one was shoved so violently that they fell and injured themselves, thankfully, but the activity was escalating to such an extent that Ed and Lorraine Warren felt it would be best to leave the house and return to Connecticut before someone actually got hurt like Aaron did when he was shoved down the cellar steps in the McLaughlin house.

Inhuman spirits want to torment the people who live in the houses they infest as often as they can and for as long as possible. If they can, they injure or frighten the investigators themselves, because they are there to help the family out of the goodness of their own hearts and free will and accord. They are also there to attempt to ruin the spirits' plans. While injuries are common, it is a rarity that the spirits succeed in killing any investigators.

I have never been attacked in any way, shape, or form. I have always felt that I was very well protected, so nothing could affect me personally. I also believe that I am very knowledgeable about how to protect myself if the need arises, how to identify a dangerous situation, how to avoid injury, and how to summon aid in the event that I am unable to fight them off and make them stop. I have, however, witnessed other people being attacked and I know how to stop those attacks dead in their tracks.

Linda was attacked before she even was able to hang up the telephone. She was choked and inflicted with psychic wounds as her punishment. Sometimes however, the person attacked is one of the very psychics or investigators who will eventually become involved in the case. Sometimes it occurs hours, days, or weeks before they even become aware of the case that they will eventually elect to become personally involved in.

Think about the omnipotence involved when an investigator hasn't even become consciously aware of a case that will arise due to a phone call received from a chance passing by of a Psychic Fair advertisement and he or she is attacked *before* they even become a participant. It's truly incredible to comprehend, but we have to remember that we are dealing with inter-dimensional beings who are not bound by the rules and laws that bind us here in the third dimension. The deck is totally stacked against us, unless and until we call upon divine intervention. Then, the cavalry comes.

After Linda was attacked, she felt violated and her first impulse was to run upstairs, lock the door, turn on the shower, and scrub the remnants of the filthy encounter off her body. What gave her the impulse to run away from the men who were essentially her only protectors, and to lock the door where they couldn't get to her should she be attacked again? Perhaps nothing, but in all likelihood, it was the negative spirits who gave her the very suggestion. Any decision made by anyone involved in a demonically infested home needs to be evaluated carefully by everyone else.

The words 'No peace' on the bathroom mirror meant exactly that—the spirits would never allow them a moment's peace until their evil objectives had been met. They had already succeeded in making Matthew succumb to their power. Now they were after everyone else, one by one, or maybe even all at once.

Holy water is water that has been purified, prayed over, and blessed by a priest or holy man. The strength of the blessing is based on the strength of the faith of the one who has blessed it, and most importantly—his *intention* while he is interacting with it.

Japanese scientist, Dr. Masaru Emoto, discovered that thought and intention introduced into water changes and re-arranges the molecular structure of the water—depending on the thoughts, emotions, and intentions projected onto the water while doing so. After he had held a glass of water and focused his intention on a particular emotion, he froze the water, and upon examining the frozen water crystals, he noticed that they were all different, depending on which emotion was projected onto the water. This is explained as Sympathetic Vibratory Physics. The work is fascinating and I encourage everyone to read more about Dr. Emoto's incredibly profound work.

I believe that holy water is blessed and infused with the Ultimate Power in the Universe—the power of God. Think about how powerful water becomes when the intention is to supercharge it with the incredible power and positive energy of the Creator of all that is. What do you think that holy water would do when cast upon a negative spirit or a demonic spirit? It would be the equivalent of pouring sulfuric acid onto our human flesh. When we use holy water on the demonic, we often hear and record blood-curdling wails of agony, because obviously it works.

When a Ouija board is used with focused intention to open up a channel of communication between the third dimension and others—that is exactly what happens. The strength of the portal, doorway, vortex, star gate, wormhole —or whatever name you wish to use—depends on the strength and conviction of the users and again, as with all things, the *intention* used to open it in the first place. It is one thing to be a curious teenager who uses a Ouija board with the intention to 'test the waters' and see if contact with a spirit is even possible. It is another thing entirely to use the Ouija board with the intention of opening a permanent gateway into dimensions inhabited by diabolical entities, so that those denizens of the dark can use it to invade our dimension.

Naturally, Tyler and his friends didn't use the board with any desire to cause that to happen, but unfortunately, that is exactly what happened. Once they had used it, it created an invisible vortex of energy which allowed the transit of inhuman, diabolical entities of all kinds into the house. That doorway is what Yvonne sensed when she first entered the living room. When she zeroed in on it, she clearly identified it, and warned the others about its presence.

When things of this nature happen to the average family we find that many members of the household keep certain experiences to themselves. Why? Naturally, kids don't want to upset their parents or to get into trouble. Parents also don't want to upset and frighten their children or risk ridicule from their spouse or friends. It is also possible that they were being influenced by the spirits to keep their secrets to themselves. While it is important not to give activity of this nature, or the spirits in the house recognition, it is important to keep everyone informed that there are strange things going on.

Chapter 30 – Analysis

Religious provocation entails provoking the demonic spirits through the recitation of prayer, displaying religious artifacts, relics and holy symbols, and directly challenging and commanding the spirits to reveal or manifest themselves in the name of Jesus Christ and God. *It is extremely dangerous to do this in demonically infested houses.* Unless the person conducting religious provocation is intimately aware of his or her permanent and powerful connection to God; knows how to properly protect themselves spiritually before attempting it, and knows how to deal with the consequences of challenging demonic spirits—*it should never be attempted.*

You can be sure your house is infested by inhuman spirits when all hell breaks loose after reciting prayers or when verbally evoking the protection of the angels.

While investigating one of my first demonically infested homes with several of the investigators who also worked with the Warrens, I pulled blessed rosary beads out of my pocket for additional protection. According to the psychics who could see the demonic spirit standing on the stairs, the second I displayed the religious artifact, it streaked right off the stairs and came right up to me. I saw and felt nothing out of the ordinary, but one of the panicked investigators asked what I had done. Another told him that I had rosary beads. The panicked investigator urged me to put them away immediately. I wasn't frightened, but it took close to thirty seconds to get them all into my palm and to successfully put them back into my pocket. As soon as I put them away, the psychics said that the black form moved away from me and went right back onto the stairs. Later, I had asked Ed Warren what could have happened had I not put them back into my pocket as I was instructed to. He said that I could have been burned, mauled, choked, teleported, beaten, or worse. It was explained that since it was not my intention to challenge or provoke the demonic spirit, it left me alone.

I firmly believe that it left me alone because I know who I am, and that I protected myself with the innate power of God within me because I know that I and the Father are One.

Chapter 31 – Analysis

If undiscovered and left to their own devices, demonic spirits can take an otherwise healthy individual and completely incapacitate their body in a matter of days, leading to the total destruction of their immune system, severe pneumonia, sudden unexplainable medical conditions, organ failure, and even death. In all cases, the medical professionals who become involved are totally incapable of explaining or stopping it.

While it is silently destroying the body, the demonic spirit will go dormant and appear to the average person that it is not even there, and certainly won't offer any evidence to the contrary, unless it is intentionally forced to through religious provocation.

The only way to cast a demon out of the living is to force it out by calling upon the power of God. One way is through the ancient religious rite of exorcism, as described in the Rituale Romanum.

Vincent knew exactly what was happening to Matthew. He knew the demon would lie dormant and would do everything in its power to hide its presence. So, to gain Dr. Kent's cooperation, Vincent knew that he would have to provoke it, so there could be no denying that Matthew was possessed. Vincent also knew that the demon possessing Matthew wielded incredible strength and resolve, so he had Matthew's hands and arms tied down before pressing the crucifix onto his forehead. When the beads of sweat began to form on Matthew's forehead, it was because the demon was essentially being tortured every minute that it tried to resist. As expected, the holy symbol eventually became too much and the demon revealed itself. That was all it took to convince Dr. Kent that there was nothing that he could do to heal his patient and that something darker and more sinister than he could possibly imagine was the culprit behind the inexplicable illness.

Interestingly enough, just as demonic spirits possess the living, discarnate human spirits also possess or cohabitate the living. An amazing book about the subject is The Unquiet Dead, by Dr. Edith Fiore, which details the accounts of human spirit possession and the ramifications of having two or more spirits inhabiting the same body, competing for control of the same mind and causing all kinds of problems from addictions, to sudden mood swings, multiple or split personalities, gender identity issues and a whole host of mental illnesses. For the discarnate spirit, it is especially satisfying when they can possess or cohabitate another living human body to feel alive again. I highly recommend Dr. Fiore's book. It is fascinating.

One of the many ways in which to coax the earthbound spirit out of a living host in which it is cohabitating is to simply talk to it and convince it that it no longer has a body of its own, and that it is not only depriving itself of its own proper death transition through the tunnel of white light, but also its own evolutionary path by staying earthbound.

It is also important to let them come to the realization that they are doing immeasurable harm to the human body that they are cohabiting and to the soul of the original inhabitant by interfering with their own experience in its lifetime. It is important to invite them to call upon their loved ones, or Jesus, or the angels to come for them and take them across properly. Many spirits stay behind because they fear going to hell, or fear facing God, or facing a relative that they do not wish to interact with again. A vast majority stay behind due to some unfinished business or special relationship. I highly encourage everyone to mend all of their broken relationships while both people are still alive. It is much more difficult to deal with later.

One case of an unresolved relationship took place in Spokane, Washington, when the spirit of a man who had died was seen every evening inside of his home by his frightened family shortly after his funeral. When my psychic friend Valerie Crisp and I investigated the case, we had everyone sit in a circle and meditate. When we initiated contact, I intuited that because the spirit felt that he was a terrible father in life, he would not cross over until he heard his wife and every one of his children forgive him for whatever it is that he felt that he had done wrong. Everyone forgave him instantly, except for one of his sons. We told him that he had to forgive his father to allow him to go on in peace. He cried and cried, but he eventually said that he did indeed forgive his father and he meant it.

We visualized a pillar of white light emanating from the center of the circle where we had a huge quartz crystal. We all gave him our blessing and invited him to call upon God, Jesus, the angels or his own mother and father who had passed years earlier to come and get him. Immediately after, Valerie saw him leave up through the pillar of light and the family never saw him again.

Another huge reason people stay behind as earthbound spirits is due to the need to satisfy an addiction that they feel they can't fulfill if they cross over. They always find living human bodies that suffer from that very same addiction, and they hang around them to influence them or they cohabitate them so they can get their fix. It also explains the reason why it is so hard for someone who is cohabitated to quit smoking cigarettes despite their most earnest desire to quit. It is because there is *another* human spirit cohabitating their body who absolutely does not want to quit. There are two separate intelligences at work.

Chapter 32 – Analysis

Suffumigation is the blessing of places. It is essentially the process of fumigating the house with high-frequency, holy, high church incense, frankincense and myrrh, coupled with prayer to dispel negative energy and to make the location completely inhospitable to evil spirits. It is very effective if done properly by people who know what they're doing and by people who have the faith and conviction to see it through.

While attending Eastern Washington University in Cheney, Washington, I received a phone call from Lorraine Warren informing me of a case she became aware of in Rathdrum, Idaho. She asked if I would investigate the case on their behalf since I was one of their seasoned investigators and I was so much closer than they were—geographically. When we deemed it necessary, I performed suffumigation in the house one evening with one of my students. Every time I crossed the threshold into another room, the kitchen telephone would ring—three times. It rang three times to mock the Holy Trinity and it was intended solely as a distraction to break my concentration.

Fortunately, I was very familiar with the activity and distractions that can go on at times like these, and I continued on undaunted. To be successful with suffumigation, there must be nowhere for spirits to flee to while remaining inside the house. The smoke must completely billow through every square inch of the house in question.

Sage and sandalwood are also very potent where things of this nature are concerned.

Chapter 33-34 – Analysis

Exorcism is one of the fifteen sections of rites and blessings described in the Rituale Romanum, or Roman Ritual, as it is popularly titled. It is a very old and very serious ceremony used by trained Catholic exorcists. The Catholic exorcist is someone with intimate knowledge about the diabolical, and knowledge is power. Neither I nor or any of my fellow investigators are exorcists, nor would we profess to possess the willpower, commitment, and piety that these few special people do.

The spirits involved are either fallen angels or archangels. No mortal man has any power over them, nor could man contest that incredible power. Only as long as the exorcist is under divine protection—for he is doing the work of God—does he have any chance of success and to ward off possession of his own body. Because of this, before an exorcism takes place, an exorcist must obtain a state of grace with God. He does this by going into seclusion, by praying day and night for divine protection and assistance and by fasting for three days.

The exorcist will never warn the demon that he will personally cause it great harm or that he will personally force it out. That would be completely preposterous. It would be an open and direct challenge to the spirits possessing the possessed, and invite an attack on him. Instead, he uses the powerful names of God, Jesus Christ, and Michael, or words that the demon despises to make it vacate a human host. Some of the most violent activity ever recorded occurs during an exorcism. The distorted and screeching voices and screams and the foul language can be most disturbing indeed.

The last day or the last few hours before an exorcism is scheduled to take place is often the most critical when it comes to the safety, health, well-being, and even the life of the possessed. The entity or entities inside know that they are out of time and will either intensify their attacks on everyone else around them to break down their will in hopes of possessing them also, or they will try to cause as much damage as possible to the possessed before they are ultimately forced to vacate—including trying to kill their victim while the victim is still in their power. That is why Vincent sat in Matthew's hospital room dousing his body with holy water throughout the night prior to the exorcism and why Dr. Kent sedated the body whenever the demons began to stir. Bishop Phelan came personally to subdue the demons during transit to the chapel to ensure that nothing got out of control.

Driving a possessed individual to a chapel is a very frightening experience to behold. The spirits know they are being taken into a building filled with the smoke of frankincense and myrrh, of healing, holy, positive energy, of crucifixes, religious symbols, artifacts, and priests who have dedicated their lives to God and to good works.

To compare and contrast what that experience must be like to inhuman spirits, consider the horror a Catholic priest would experience if he were bound to a stretcher and escorted by a High Priestess of Satan in full black magic ceremonial garb into a Satanic cult compound where clouds of nauseating sulfur permeated everything causing him to hack and choke. Imagine the panic he would experience when he was hauled inside the compound and laid upon a black altar surrounded by impossibly sharp ritual daggers, chalices full of blood, and black mass candles, where three wicked-looking warlocks wielded their unholy, magical tomes bound in human flesh, and summoned diabolical entities into the room for the sole purpose of torturing him. Imagine that each time the priest attempted to pray, he would be immediately doused with burning tar sludge that was cursed day in and day out in black magic rituals. That is a very accurate comparison of the terror that is going on in the soul mind of these possessing spirits. They are in serious trouble and they know it.

So, when they arrived in the parking lot, the demons had one last chance to kill anyone they could before being hauled into the chapel. The doors closing and blasting open were all meant to injure as many people as possible. Of course, Vincent and Bishop Phelan were prepared for this, and even though it was frightening for a few minutes, it did not sway their determination to get Matthew into the chapel and free his body of the invading spirits.

Because the demonic spirits can read the minds of anyone they choose, they know and use people's sins against them, especially at critical moments during an exorcism when their concentration and focus is needed most. Interestingly, once a person confesses a sin to a priest or to God, the demon has no access to that personal information, as if it had never existed at all. It certainly would lend credibility to the claim that sins confessed before God are indeed forgiven.

Names are very powerful. When an exorcist succeeds in forcing the demon to reveal its name, the demon has given away a huge portion of its power. From that moment on, the exorcist can then direct his prayers and rites directly against the demon specifically by name. It is much more effective than a general prayer toward a nameless spirit or a group of them.

Time was of the essence. A second suffumigation had to be performed to prevent the spirits possessing Matthew from returning to the house. During the last stage of the suffumigation, in the last room of the house, the demons had little choice but to brutally attack Vincent in one last combined effort to prevent him from sealing off the house forever. It is a frightening, brutal, and terrible experience to be attacked by a single inhuman spirit acting alone, but to be singled out, and to face the combined efforts of a group of them, is debilitating, devastating and often deadly. The demons were furious at Vincent for interfering in their plans, so they raked and clawed, bludgeoned and battered him in every way that they could. Every second that they spent in the thick cement walls of the basement which prevented the wafting clouds of high-church incense from dissipating was agony for them. It sapped their power, drained their resolve, and withered away their will to fight. And so they forced him to undergo one last vicious attack—leaving their mark on him—the physical evidence of preternatural power for all to see as a permanent reminder of their resolve.

Chapter 35 – Analysis

Investigating terrible cases like the one that the McLaughlin family had experienced sometimes takes quite a toll on the investigator. Indeed, cases never come to a close without leaving some lasting scars and lingering memories, especially the fear that perhaps something was missed, or that the doorways weren't sealed properly, or the worst fear—that the spirits or demons would somehow find a way to return.

If the demons truly have omnipotence or precognition, and they can know who the investigators involved in the case will be before the investigators themselves do, one would think that they would have the foresight to know that many powerful, committed, pious religious men like Bishop Phelan would intervene and expel them from the house and ultimately free the possessed, so why would they even bother continuing the struggle when they are sure to be on the losing side? Perhaps it's blind ignorance or delusions of grandeur on their part. They did, obviously, rebel against God, which was sure to be a losing battle from the very beginning, so maybe they are so badly corrupted by their lust for power and their desire to dominate others that they just simply don't know any better or don't care about the consequences. Fortunately, there are many brave people in the world who are eager to do their part to help unfortunate people who are plagued by supernatural and preternatural infestation, oppression and possession.

Although this particular case used the profound and powerful exorcism ritual from the Rituale Romanum to expel the demons, and suffumigation to cleanse the house, it is not just Catholic exorcists using Catholic rites that are successful at driving away demons, and it is not just Catholic suffumigation that is successful at cleansing or purifying houses. I know of holy men, shamans, rabbis, Japanese Shinto priests, and very powerful spiritualists and light workers who have been equally successful at driving negative spirits and demons out of the possessed and at cleansing and purifying houses. Regardless of the modality or the particular religious faith, the primary, essential force that they all call upon is the power of our Divine Creator, Source, Father/Mother God. Whichever name you give to this consciousness, it is the same consciousness. Calling upon God is the one fail safe that all of creation can count on in our most desperate time of need.

We are all part of God. We can never be separate from God, because we are individualized aspects of the totality of God. A metaphor I love to use is: "We are all individual flares that were cast off from the Sun, but we are all still part of that glorious, radiant Sun." God created all of Creation. He also created the universal laws that govern his Creation, so that all of Creation functions in perfect, flawless harmony. Calling upon God for assistance in driving out rebellious, aggressive, evil-natured, diabolical spirits is all that needs to be done, as long as we have *absolute faith* that we have the *right* to call upon that aid, and that is for the *highest good of the possessed.*

We must also realize that God is the only real power behind expelling the demons. We could never expel them on our own. God is more powerful than any demon or devil, because God is the creator of all that is. God is life itself. How then can anyone or any individualized aspect of God rebel against the total sum of all of God's perfection?

Having absolute faith that it is God who is the ultimate power in all of Creation is the single most important thing for anyone to realize and remember when they embark upon the path of a paranormal investigator. One must have absolute faith and conviction that, because they are acting as a divine instrument of God, they are fully empowered and fully protected as long as they call upon God's power to expel negative entities, especially the demonic. This is especially essential when it comes to witnessing or performing an exorcism.

Witnessing an exorcism is undoubtedly one of the most horrific things one could ever imagine. It is one thing to go see a movie or read a book that does a very good job at making you feel isolated, alone, and vulnerable, or scaring you out of your mind. It's another thing entirely to witness the real thing in person.

It is always so interesting that demonic entities seem to know every last detail about the lives of the people interacting with them, especially their most intimate secrets and especially their sins—unless they are confessed before God prior to the exorcism. Once sins are confessed before a priest, the demons have no ammunition to use against us. It's as if they never knew of the sins at all.

If someone does not confess their sins before an exorcism, the demons will always use those sins to embarrass that individual by bringing those sins to the awareness of everyone else, often causing great shame and guilt. The intention is to sow distrust between those present during the exorcism to disrupt the flow, break the concentration of the exorcists and priests, and to ultimately bring the entire ritual to a screeching halt.

The devout holy men know this full well, so they will always make sure that everyone present confesses, whether they believe in Confession or not. Remember the Law of Intention. Regardless of your faith in any particular doctrine or religion, if your intention is to purge your sins and purify the body, mind and soul, and to prevent the diabolical from using your life experiences as a weapon against you and the mission at hand, then that is exactly what will happen.

Catholic confession, however, is not the only method with which one can purge themselves of their sins, mistakes, or bad choices. Everyone has the right and the innate capability to talk to God. God doesn't need an intermediary or priest to hear you. You are just as special as every other person on this planet. God created you, and therefore God will hear you, and if you quiet or still your mind, he will converse with you via telepathy. Remember, there is no space and time. There is no distance between you and God. You don't need to look up into the clouds or imagine God to be in some unreachable place where you are not permitted an audience with him. Merely think on God, and God will be with you, and you will be at peace.

I have always said that there is no difference between a Native American Indian climbing a mountain and and meditating on The Great Spirit in his own way, and someone who goes into a Catholic church and prays at the altar. It is the same God. The two methods are of equal importance and equally as effective based solely on their intention. Intention is everything in every circumstance, always. Earnest seeking will always be rewarded.

All beings, including all human souls, are immortal and timeless. We exist at all times, in all times simultaneously, in many concurrent lifetimes at once, as individuated aspects of the whole of Who We Are. I believe that is why we have an affinity for certain time periods and places and not others. It is quite possible, if not probable, that we are now or have recently experienced living in those locations and in those eras. Our fondness or affinity for them is directly related to our experiences that somehow spill over into the collective consciousness of Who We Are.

Inhuman, diabolical spirits are also timeless, but I believe that they are confined to certain distant realms, densities or dimensions, so that they cannot interfere with the free will of mankind unless mankind uses free will to open a gateway or portal with the intention to make contact with them, or in the cases of sorcerers and necromancers, to make alliances with them, and we all know how that turns out in the end.

When Vincent returned home, he brought with him pain, wounds, and the physical evidence of a preternatural demon that was close to a million years old. What did the fetal boar's teeth signify? Were they actual teeth from an actual living creature? Were they some hybrid monster that the demon elected to manifest when it attacked Vincent in one final last ditch effort to cause as much anguish and pain as possible? Did the teeth come from a physical manifestation that the demon took eight hundred thousand years ago when it preyed on some other unfortunate soul? Or was this its body after it was horribly transfigured as punishment by God for the great rebellion? Is the rebellion and transfiguration story the real truth about what happened to these beings of vast power in ages past? These are very intriguing questions, indeed.

When something materializes out of thin air that has never existed before, it is called an 'apport.' Often times the items that are manifested by inhuman, diabolical entities disappear and fade away as quickly as they came, such as the pool of urine on the living room carpet and the black ooze under the sink. Those were not illusions, like the swarms of black flies were, first in the house and then in the chapel. They never remain in physical form for more than a few hours, and that is why Vincent was jingling the teeth around inside the jewelry box and studying them intensely to see if they would remain or if they would disappear. It is different than the word 'teleport' which is what happens when an object that already existed on the third dimension suddenly dematerializes and re-materializes somewhere else.

Negatively-charged items such as the Ouija board used in a case, or the boar's teeth, or items that have been used in ceremonies involving black magic, black witchcraft, and the like are very dangerous. If they are not immediately removed from wherever the case took place and kept under close guard by someone who knows what to do with them, it is just asking for trouble.

One time at The Warren School of Paranormalology Museum, I accidentally bumped into a dragon-like sculpture that was suspended from the ceiling on fishing wire. Ed had signs everywhere warning people that if they touched anything by mistake to immediately inform him so he could deal with it personally. When I told him what had happened, Ed told me that I just happened to have touched 'the worst' item in the entire museum and that he had to immediately bless me and coach me to create the Christ Light around me to make sure that, even though this was accidental contact, the interaction didn't bring me any misfortune or make any connection possible between myself and the entity associated with it—in this case a very powerful demon.

To form a Christ Light around yourself as protection, bring your focused awareness to your body center, visualizing a brilliant white ball of light there. Imagine that this is your divine light, your intimate and permanent connection to God or Source. It is His immense power within you. Imagine it growing into a sphere that radiates out, pushing out all negativity or low frequencies, and continue until it completely encapsulates your entire body and expands out as far out as you intend to expand it. Imagine and intend that this is the Christ consciousness—an impenetrable field of such incredible, brilliant positive energy that nothing of a lower frequency or vibration could ever come near it, much less penetrate it. Visualize Jesus Christ or Archangel Michael or any other religious or spiritual master or adept standing inside of the field with you, even overlaying you. Through the Law of Attraction and the Law of Intention, you are summoning that incredible energy right to you, and it is absolutely doing exactly what you intend it to do. It's like donning the armor of God. Visualize a deep violet light around you as well and then a golden light.

Another very powerful defense is baptism, which adds an additional layer of protection in our energy fields or auric fields or auras. People who have recently taken communion or who have been blessed also have extra layers of protection. Praying is especially powerful.

When we recite the 23rd Psalm, our aura expands and becomes very powerful. No matter what the religious doctrine, or what the ritual, positive blessings offer positive protections. Wearing crucifixes, medals, relics and crystals also offer powerful levels of protection. The level of protection gained from wearing such an item is based upon the intention that the creator had for the item when it was originally crafted, the intention of the wearer, the faith that the wearer has in the object being worn, and the innate abilities of the material that it was crafted from. Crystals have incredibly beneficial, powerful natural abilities that we can take advantage of, should we take the time to learn about them and use them as they were intended to be used.

We are interacting with positive and negative energies all the time throughout our day in the places we go and through the people that we interact with. One valuable assortment of tools we can use is the vast and powerful natural crystal formations that have formed deep inside the earth that are capable of absorbing, conserving, storing, focusing, and emitting energy. Each type of crystal is unique, as are its abilities. They are living first-dimensional beings, each with their own memory, personality and capabilities. Each crystal has a color. Color is frequency or vibration.

If people want to protect themselves from negative energies, they should wear crystals that deflect or absorb those energies.

One of the many crystals that have an especially powerful effect on deflecting negative energy is the amethyst.

Amethysts are violet in color and violet frequencies found in lavender oil, meditating on a violet light, or wearing purple or violet clothing protect the wearer by deflecting negative energy. Catholic priests hearing confession wear purple stoles around their necks to deflect the negative energy that is projected on them when sins are released to God. Catholic exorcists wear purple stoles to protect themselves against evil spirits. Wearing an amethyst crystal around the neck for protection is an excellent way to deflect negative energy. The size of the crystal does not matter as long as the color is on the deeper side rather than on the clearer side.

Wearing black or green tourmaline or carrying a chunk in your pocket is a great defense against negative energy because it absorbs negative energy. It is very important to learn how to routinely cleanse and purify your crystals, however, so that they can release, clear, and transmute the negative energy that they have absorbed. For example, if a black tourmaline is full because it has absorbed all of the negative energy that it can, it could actually harm the wearer because it is so full of negative energy. Why? What does negative energy attract? It attracts more negative energy.

By smudging crystals with the smoke of sandalwood or sage, you are doing your crystals a great service by making them useful to you again. If that sounds fantastic, remember that many ancient cultures knew about, worked with, and adorned themselves with crystals of all shapes, colors and sizes.

There are multitudes of planes and dimensions that exist all around us simultaneously. It has been said that the first dimension is the mineral kingdom. It is the realm of the intelligent crystalline entities that live and grow and thrive in their own way. The second dimension is the plant kingdom. It is the realm of the intelligent plant life that lives, grows and thrives in its own way. We live in the third dimension. It is the realm of intelligent animal life. At least our conscious awareness here in this limited three-dimensional body is focused on the third dimension, so technically we say that we live in the third dimension, when in reality we live eternally and we exist in multiple dimensions simultaneously. The fourth dimension and those above it all have their own intelligences that live, grow, learn and thrive and so on.

Chapter 36 – Analysis

When the human spirit vacates the physical body upon death, at best it is usually a seamless, instantaneous, beautiful, peaceful experience. The soul rises up through the crown of the head and out of the body, realizes that it is still conscious and aware of its surroundings and that it has left its physical remains behind. Remember the tale of the young man who was trapped beneath the waterfall earlier.

In chaotic or tragic situations, the soul is often thrust out of the body in a sudden way leaving the soul very much aware and conscious, but also confused and in great distress. Eventually, all human souls come to the realization that they are just fine, in fact more so than when they were essentially stuck in the body, because even though the body ages and malfunctions, the soul, in its total perfection, does not. Though the body may be completely destroyed, the soul is never harmed at all.

I have heard many stories about people who were on their deathbed, slipping in and out of consciousness, in and out of their bodies, and came into direct contact with the conscious awareness of loved ones who had passed on before them. They communicated with them and often called out their names as they were inching closer to the death of their own physical bodies. One personal experience I witnessed was when my own grandmother, Rose, called out to her sister Yolanda several times for several days before she herself finally passed on.

According to the records of many hundreds of thousands of cases of near-death experiences and hypnotic regressions, the spirit slips into and out of the body many times before birth and during the cycle of death. Where do these spirits go? What do they do? Remember, as I have said, we exist on multiple dimensions at once. When we sleep, while our physical body is resting, rejuvenating and re-energizing, our consciousness goes off into those other dimensions and densities to experience those other aspects of self, other experiences and to communicate or commune with other entities. It is only through waking consciousness while inside the human body that we are so limited and separated from those many other aspects of ourselves so that we could experience the illusion of individuality or duality—separation from Source. Many people who are on their deathbed claim that everything is completely beautiful, perfect, and simple on the other side. They say that because the illusion is lifted and they are finally reconnected. They suddenly understand everything, and that there is nothing to fear. Indeed, there is nothing to fear. Everything is in perfect divine order, for it is God the Creator who made it so.

The death of the physical body is nothing to dread. The human spirit is immortal and nothing that happens to the body in life can affect it. The only reason we are here is so that our soul can experience whatever it came here to experience. When it has accomplished the tasks it had set out to complete, when it has learned the lessons it came here to learn, when this brief particular life is complete, the soul leaves the body behind, enters the great white tunnel of light into the spirit world and into the higher dimensions, evaluates its most recent life, rejoins all of the other aspects of the over soul or the total culmination of all of the aspects of the self that has existed since it was created, and moves on. Eventually, it will rejoin all of the other souls that it has loved and cherished in all of its many journeys and incarnations. Indeed, we will all see each other again. This life that we are living right now is but a blinking of an eye and but a single thread in the grand tapestry that is our conscious awareness.

We come into this world alone, and we leave this world alone. The only things that we take with us when we die are our thoughts, emotions and experiences of the life that we had just lived. Love is the highest frequency that there is. Love conquers all. Love repels all negativity. Therefore, my advice is to love everyone and everything that you encounter every waking moment of every day. By broadcasting love, we affect everyone in a positive way. By being love, we attract love.

We are all individualized fragments of the whole of God experiencing third dimension in the body to learn whatever the soul came here to learn and experience. Therefore, love others without conditions. Love yourself and everyone else unconditionally. Love them that they are.

I now close this book with a quote from one of my favorite researchers in the world, whose courage to stand tall before all adversity and ridicule, whose tenacity to continue, undaunted, bringing truth to the sleeping masses, and whose dedication to bringing the real history of the world to light has revealed the most incredible, mind-blowing, groundbreaking, consciousness-expanding information about the world in which we live and about 'Who We Really Are' to me and to all of mankind, should they simply read his astounding life's work:

"Infinite love is the only truth. Everything else is
an illusion."
—David Icke.

About the Author

Jason McLeod is a paranormal investigator, spiritualist and empath. He has spent the last 28 years helping individual families deal with both the human spirits who linger in their lives and the inhuman spirits who seek to ruin them. His training and experience began by following in the footsteps of his close personal friends and mentors—the late Ed Warren and his wife Lorraine, bestselling authors, movie consultants, and the original ghost busters who started the modern ghost hunting craze that thrives today. He conducts engaging presentations on the subjects of Spirituality, Consciousness, Quantum Physics, Meditation, Metaphysics, Paranormal Investigation and Demonology on Radio Broadcasts, and at Paranormal Conventions, Spirituality Expositions, in Churches and at New Age Events throughout the world.

If you've found this book interesting, the Author would sincerely appreciate it if you would please kindly take the time to write an honest review about it and post it on amazon.com.

Please visit the author's website: www.darksiege.com for information on his investigations, classes, upcoming releases, personal appearances at paranormal conventions, photographs, audio and video presentations, and more.

If you wish to contact the author directly, you are encouraged to do so by email at: darksiegebook@gmail.com

The Nightmare is *Far* From Over...

Don't Miss The Terrifying Sequel:

Available October, 2014,
in Paperback and Digitally
through Amazon and B&N